THE LINGUISTIC P/
TWELFTH-CENTURY

CW00918280

How was the complex history of Britain's languages understood by twelfth-century authors? This book argues that the social, political, and linguistic upheavals that occurred in the wake of the Norman Conquest intensified later interest in the historicity of languages. An atmosphere of enquiry fostered vernacular literature's prestige, and led to a newfound sense of how ancient languages could be used to convey historical claims. The vernacular hence became an important site for the construction and memorialisation of dynastic, institutional, and ethnic identities.

This study demonstrates the breadth of interest in the linguistic past across different social groups and the striking variety of genres used to depict it, including romance, legal texts, history, poetry, and hagiography. Through a series of detailed case studies, Sara Harris shows how specific works represent key aspects of the period's imaginative engagement with English, Latin, French, and the Brittonic languages.

SARA HARRIS is a Junior Research Fellow at Sidney Sussex College, Cambridge.

CAMBRIDGE STUDIES IN MEDIEVAL LITERATURE

General Editor
Alastair Minnis, *Yale University*

Editorial Board
Zygmunt G. Bara'nski, *University of Cambridge*
Christopher C. Baswell, *Barnard College and Columbia University*
John Burrow, *University of Bristol*
Mary Carruthers, *New York University*
Rita Copeland, *University of Pennsylvania*
Roberta Frank, *Yale University*
Simon Gaunt, *King's College, London*
Steven Kruger, *City University of New York*
Nigel Palmer, *University of Oxford*
Winthrop Wetherbee, *Cornell University*
Jocelyn Wogan-Browne, *Fordham University*

This series of critical books seeks to cover the whole area of literature written in the major medieval languages – the main European vernaculars, and medieval Latin and Greek – during the period *c.*1100–1500. Its chief aim is to publish and stimulate fresh scholarship and criticism on medieval literature, special emphasis being placed on understanding major works of poetry, prose, and drama in relation to the contemporary culture and learning which fostered them.

Recent Titles in the Series
Lee Manion *Narrating the Crusades: Loss and Recovery in Medieval and Early Modern English Literature*
Daniel Wakelin *Scribal Correction and Literary Craft: English Manuscripts 1375–1510*
Jon Whitman (ed.) *Romance and History: Imagining Time from the Medieval to the Early Modern Period*
Virginie Greene *Logical Fictions in Medieval Literature and Philosophy*
Michael Johnston and Michael Van Dussen (eds) *The Medieval Manuscript Book: Cultural Approaches*
Tim William Machan (ed.) *Imagining Medieval English: Language Structures and Theories, 500–1500*
Eric Weiskott *English Alliterative Verse: Poetic Tradition and Literary History*
Sarah Elliott Novacich *Shaping the Archive in Late Medieval England: History, Poetry, and Performance*
Geoffrey Russom *The Evolution of Verse Structure in Old and Middle English Poetry: From the Earliest Alliterative Poems to Iambic Pentameter*
Ian Cornelius *Reconstructing Alliterative Verse: The Pursuit of a Medieval Meter*
Sara Harris *The Linguistic Past in Twelfth-Century Britain*

A complete list of titles in the series can be found at the end of the volume.

THE LINGUISTIC PAST IN TWELFTH-CENTURY BRITAIN

SARA HARRIS

University of Cambridge

CAMBRIDGE
UNIVERSITY PRESS

CAMBRIDGE
UNIVERSITY PRESS

University Printing House, Cambridge CB2 8BS, United Kingdom

One Liberty Plaza, 20th Floor, New York, NY 10006, USA

477 Williamstown Road, Port Melbourne, VIC 3207, Australia

314-321, 3rd Floor, Plot 3, Splendor Forum, Jasola District Centre, New Delhi - 110025, India

79 Anson Road, #06-04/06, Singapore 079906

Cambridge University Press is part of the University of Cambridge.

It furthers the University's mission by disseminating knowledge in the pursuit of
education, learning and research at the highest international levels of excellence.

www.cambridge.org
Information on this title: www.cambridge.org/9781316631874
DOI: 10.1017/9781316841310

First published 2017
First paperback edition 2019

A catalogue record for this publication is available from the British Library

Library of Congress Cataloging in Publication data
Names: Harris, Sara, 1986– author.
Title: The linguistic past in twelfth-century Britain / Sara Harris.
Description: New York : Cambridge University Press, [2017] | Series: Cambridge studies
in medieval literature ; 100 | Includes bibliographical references and index.
Identifiers: LCCN 2017011177 | ISBN 9781107180055 (hardcover : acid-free paper)
Subjects: LCSH: English language – Middle English, 1100-1500. | English language – Middle English,
1100-1500 – Discourse analysis. | English language – Middle English, 1100-1500 –
Texts. | English language – Middle English, 1100-1500 – Variation. | Discourse analysis
(Linguistics) – History. | Discourse analysis, Literary – History. | Language and culture –
England – History – To 1500. | Historical linguistics.
Classification: LCC PE525 .H47 2017 | DDC 409.41–dc23 LC record
available at https://lccn.loc.gov/2017011177

ISBN 978-1-107-18005-5 Hardback
ISBN 978-1-316-63187-4 Paperback

Contents

Figures

Acknowledgements

I am particularly indebted to Helen Cooper, who has been the source of much measured and insightful guidance. Christopher Page nursed this project through its infancy and has since continued to offer appreciated support. Elisabeth van Houts and Ad Putter provided invaluable advice. Jane Hughes has encouraged me throughout my academic career, and Richard Beadle sent many kind opportunities my way. Jo Bellis, Venetia Bridges, Julia Crick, Lesley Coote, Jane Gilbert, Ben Guy, Tony Harris, Bruce O'Brien, and George Younge have all been extremely generous with their comments, time, and written work; Michael Curley, Richard Dance, Rosamond McKitterick, Philip Shaw, Carl Watkins, Teresa Webber, Judy Weiss, Laura Wright, and Neil Wright answered questions. Magdalene College, Sidney Sussex College, and the Arts and Humanities Research Council have funded my studies; Cambridge University Library provided an excellent research environment. Thanks to Cambridge University Press for publishing the project, and particularly to their anonymous readers for such constructive and detailed feedback. Finally, I could not have written this book without the inspiration and help of my family.

An earlier version of Chapter 4 has been published as 'Ancestral Neologisms in Richard fitz Nigel's *Dialogue of the Exchequer*', *Journal of Medieval History*, 39:4 (2013), 416–30.

Abbreviations

AND	*Anglo-Norman Dictionary*, ed. by William Rothwell et al., online edn (Aberystwyth: Aberystwyth University, 2012), www.anglo-norman.net
ANS	*Anglo-Norman Studies*
ASE	*Anglo-Saxon England*
Bosworth and Toller	Joseph Bosworth and T. Northcote Toller, *An Anglo-Saxon Dictionary* (London: Oxford University Press, 1898, repr. 1954)
CCCM	*Corpus Christianorum Continuatio Mediaevalis*
CCSL	*Corpus Christianorum Series Latina*
DMBLS	*Dictionary of Medieval Latin from British Sources*, prepared by R.E. Latham et al. (London: Oxford University Press, 1975–2012)
EH	*Bede's Ecclesiastical History of the English People*, ed. by Bertram Colgrave and R.A.B. Mynors (Oxford: Clarendon Press, 1969, repr. 1991)
GPC	*Geiriadur Prifysgol Cymru: A Dictionary of the Welsh Language*, ed. by R.J. Thomas, Gareth A. Bevan and P.J. Donovan, 1st edn (Cardiff: Gwasg Prifysgol Cymru, 1967–2002); 2nd edn (currently to *brig*) at http://welsh-dictionary.ac .uk/gpc/gpc.html
HRB	Geoffrey of Monmouth, *The History of the Kings of Britain: An Edition and Translation of* De gestis Britonum [*Historia Regum Britanniae*], ed. by Michael D. Reeve, trans. by Neil Wright (Woodbridge: Boydell, 2007)
Isidore	Isidore of Seville, *Etymologiarum sive originum*, ed. by W.M. Lindsay, 2 vols (Oxford:

	Clarendon, 1911); *The Etymologies of Isidore of Seville*, trans. by Stephen Barney et al. (Cambridge: Cambridge University Press, 2006)
Lewis and Short	Charlton T. Lewis and Charles Short, *A Latin Dictionary* (Oxford: Clarendon Press, 1879)
MED	*Middle English Dictionary*, ed. by Hans Kurath et al. (Ann Arbor: University of Michigan Press, *c*.1952–*c*.2001), http://quod.lib.umich.edu/m/med
OED	*Oxford English Dictionary*, 3rd edn (Oxford: Oxford University Press, 2011; online edn 2012), www.oed.com
ODNB	*Oxford Dictionary of National Biography* (Oxford: Oxford University Press, 2004; online edn 2007), www.oxforddnb.com
PL	*Patrologia Latina*
RS	*Rolls Series*
Toronto A-G	*Dictionary of Old English, A–G* (Toronto: University of Toronto, 2009), www.doe.utoronto.ca
TRHS	*Transactions of the Royal Historical Society*

When transcribing from manuscripts, abbreviations have been silently expanded and punctuation modernised. If no other source is indicated, translations from medieval languages are my own.

Introduction

The linguistic history of Britain often surfaces in unexpected contexts in twelfth-century literature. Discussions of the development and decline of languages facilitated the consideration of the political fortunes of speech communities, the historical interaction between peoples, and the nature of genealogical descent. Interpretations of language history ranged from those prompted by the demands of serious scholarship to those of a more whimsical character. At the height of Henry II's power in the early 1180s, one of his courtiers exasperatedly complained that there was only one other court which was as incessantly peripatetic: the supernatural band of followers of Herla, an ancient British king. The despairing courtier was the cleric and Latin satirist Walter Map (d.1209/10), who explained the paranormal compulsion behind Herla's enforced wanderings. A pygmy king had appeared to the surprised Herla, and suggested that they should be guests at each other's weddings. That very day, ambassadors arrived to propose a marriage to the daughter of the king of the Franks, and in due course, the pygmy attended the ceremony and catered for all the guests magnificently. In turn, Herla came to the pygmy's own wedding feast, held in an underground palace lit by innumerable lamps, but only approachable through a dark cave at the foot of a cliff. On his departure, the pygmy gave Herla a small bloodhound, and sternly enjoined him to not alight from his horse before the dog had jumped down. The party emerged into the light, and the king immediately asked an old shepherd (*ueteranus pastor*) for news of his queen. To his horror, the shepherd was barely able to comprehend his archaic language:

> Domine, linguam tuam uix intelligo, cum sim Saxo, tu Brito; nomen autem illius non audiui regine, nisi quod aiunt hoc nomine dudum dictam reginam antiquissimorum Britonum que fuit uxor Herle regis, qui fabulose dicitur cum pigmeo quodam ad hanc rupem disparuisse, nusquam autem postea super terram apparuisse. Saxones uero iam ducentis annis hoc regnum possederunt, expulsis incolis.

> Sir, I can hardly understand your speech, for you are a Briton and I a Saxon;
> but the name of that Queen I have never heard, save that they say that long
> ago there was a Queen of that name over the very ancient Britons, who was
> the wife of King Herla; and he, the old story says, disappeared in company
> with a pygmy at this very cliff, and was never seen on earth again, and it is
> now two hundred years since the Saxons took possession of this kingdom,
> and drove out the old inhabitants.[1]

In his distress on hearing this news, one of the courtiers dismounted from
his horse, and crumbled to dust as soon as his feet touched the ground.
Herla then understood that they were condemned to wander the earth forever, as the dog, it seemed, would never alight.

The story draws its inspiration from various folk tales circulating in the
Anglo-Norman realm of an eternally nomadic spectral host; Map's particular interpretation satirically emphasises the vacuity of the peregrinations of
Henry's court, perhaps implicitly contrasting it with divine stability.[2] Yet
if the pygmy's mansion is situated in an unspecified otherworld, Map is at
pains to locate Herla's later career in a Britain contiguous to the twelfth-
century Henrician realm. In making an imaginative leap into the mind of
a Saxon shepherd, he draws on the body of knowledge which forms the
central concern of this study: the history of Britain's vernacular languages.
For Map, the best way of indicating the passage of time is to dwell on the
difficulties of communication experienced by Herla, whose British is now
both lexically and politically outdated. It is made clear that the shepherd's
choice of language has been dictated by the Saxon invasion of Britain, but
other aspects of this linguistic conquest seem less complete. Ignoring the
fact that English and British were not mutually intelligible, Map depicts
the Saxon shepherd as still just (*uix*) able to understand Herla, who in turn
is able to assimilate the shepherd's information. This continuity of comprehension implies that more is at stake here than linguistic verisimilitude.
The shepherd, by inhabiting the same place as the king, seems to have
inherited some knowledge of his language: Saxon and British culture are
linked by their shared territory.

We might ask whether this depiction of a linguistic past which commu-
nicates across conquest also figures a different dialogue with insular history:
the engagement of Map's own contemporaries with the Anglo-Saxon era.
Twelfth-century history writing shows a desire to understand the motivations behind the events of 1066, and to uncover or to create connections to
earlier times. In part, this florescence of historiography was prompted by
practical concerns as monasteries sought to defend the rights and property
they had enjoyed before the Conquest. However, the variety, inventiveness,

and sheer scope of twelfth-century historical enquiry show that an interest in the past extended far beyond mere pragmatism: the grandchildren of the original invaders were fascinated, and haunted, by a previous age. Map's portrayal of Herla indicates a realisation that his generation was separated from the past by more than politics. When the king emerges from the cave as a figure from a former time, he presents the shepherd with a linguistic challenge which marks the temporal separation of the two men, even as it invites the discovery of their continued connection via a thread of shared linguistic tradition. Twelfth-century depictions and manipulations of Britain's vernacular language history allowed writers to position their work in relation to the insular past, and to explore how far that past could be retrieved through linguistic interpretation. The authorial strategies they employ range from comparatively subtle uses of archaic terminology to more direct considerations of language history in the form of etymologies and extended discussions. Most audaciously, some writers created new, ostensibly factual versions of the linguistic past through literary invention, portraying their works as translations from ancient source texts. Finally, Walter Map's anecdote is part of a small group of elaborate wonder stories which employ language to heighten a sense of the *unheimlich*. Responses to Britain's linguistic history were prompted as much by emotional and imaginative concerns as by analytical curiosity.

Whilst all the material discussed here can be considered as in some sense historical, it is situated at varying points on a continuum of fact and fictionality: explorations of language history are found throughout a diverse group of literary genres. The heterogeneity of medieval historiographical modes was made possible by drawing simultaneously on different standards of veracity. Instantiations of God's divine law provided a more important form of truth than empirically verifiable facts, rendering it acceptable to tailor any narrative in order to maximise its didactic potential. Ruth Morse has noted that 'it is this idea of the past as a *moral* example which constantly legitimated the embellishing or moulding of earlier accounts'.[3] Writers of history therefore did not hesitate to use all the rhetorical techniques at their disposal to convince their readers of their truthfulness: authority was as important as accuracy. Linguistic data could help to further these rhetorical aims. Alastair Minnis sees medieval assessments of textual authority as based on two criteria: conformity with Christian truth, and 'authenticity'.[4] Judgements concerning the authentic were highly subjective. It was desirable that a text be the product of a named, and preferably well-known, ancient author; its age was also a significant factor in appraising its worth. William of Malmesbury evaluated differing exemplars of his sources by

comparing their antiquity.[5] Bernard of Chartres's deprecating comment
that the writers of his age were merely the dwarfs sitting on the shoulders of
the giants of the classical era was widely accepted as correct.[6] To be old was
to be authoritative. Archaisms, etymologies, and depictions of crumbling
sources provided an obvious means of demonstrating the age of a work or
of constructing an impression of ancientness. They were able to heighten
the value of the text as a witness to what was, or should have been, true.

The beneficial effect of references to language history on a text's authority did not necessarily end here. The worth of any given historical work was
assessed on the basis of a hierarchy of sources. Eyewitness data were most
highly prized; the later accounts of other historians were only of secondary
importance.[7] Considerations of this hierarchy may have augmented the
appeal of recourse to language history: in particular, etymology worked by
extrapolating past events from contemporary linguistic data. As the relevant
words could be selected on the basis of their availability to the intended
audience, etymological exegesis could potentially transform every reader
into a kind of eyewitness, building on his or her knowledge to establish
the credibility of the author's narrative. Presentations of language history
were also extremely flexible, both in the variety of discursive approaches
that could be adopted, and in the many different impressions that could
conceivably be given by the same linguistic data. Part of the attraction of
archaic language lay in its ambiguity.

Moreover, despite a widely held belief in the allegorical nature of God's
creation, twelfth-century historians were aware that not all natural or supernatural phenomena (such as the tale of Herla) could easily yield a didactic
interpretation. Taking refuge in a modest view of the historian's role as a
compiler of historical record, William of Newburgh stressed that he was
a simple chronicler ('simplex [. . .] narrator'), rather than an expounder
of the hidden future ('praesagus interpres').[8] Orderic Vitalis was equally
subdued, protesting, 'I am not able to unravel the divine plan by which
all things are made and cannot explain the hidden causes of things; I am
merely engaged in writing historical annals' ('Diuinum examen quo cuncta
fiunt discutere nescio, latentes rerum causas propalare nequeo; sed [. . .]
annalem historiam simpliciter actito').[9] This acknowledgement that the
decipherment of the divine order was not always possible allowed historical accounts of language to be shaped by factors beyond those contingent
on divine truth. Yet whilst these accounts were not exclusively concerned
with moral exemplarity, neither did they concentrate only on the reconstruction and verification of historical detail. Monika Otter has argued that

the episodes of archaeological discovery in the historical writing of twelfth-century England provided a locus for displays of 'self-conscious textuality' which explored the action of creating historiography.[10] Discussions of the history of Britain's vernacular languages exhibited a similar self-awareness, functioning not only as rhetorical devices to validate authorial aims and agendas, but also as a nexus for speculations about the past which did not necessarily have to be correct to be 'true'. They thus became a space for literary explorations of history, style, and identity.

The Languages of Britain

Twelfth-century writers were particularly sensitive to the linguistic past because of the depth and variety of Britain's multilingual cultures. Medieval interpretations of the island's languages saw them as witnesses to successive European invasions and continental contacts ranging from the Trojans to the Normans. Pre-Conquest eleventh-century Britain was already highly multilingual. In addition to English, Norse, and Latin, there were communities of differing Goidelic and Brittonic language speakers in Scotland, Cumbria, the Isle of Man, Wales, Cornwall, and some adjacent areas in the South and West of England. The Norman Conquest merely increased the extent of this insular polyglossia. It also continued a trend for ever closer cross-Channel ties. Late Anglo-Saxon England had significant diplomatic, economic, and linguistic connections to Normandy and the Low Countries. Emma of Normandy was queen of both Æthelred II and Cnut, and mother to Harthacnut and Edward the Confessor. Edward himself spent much of his youth in exile in Normandy, before returning to claim the throne in 1043.[11] Links to the continent extended beyond the court. The Domesday Book testifies to the presence of seventy-nine pre-Conquest individuals whose names potentially reflect some form of French ethnicity; a small contingent of urban property owners may have been in England for business reasons.[12] To a limited extent, the French language was hence already known in Anglo-Saxon England, and its presence was reflected by rare borrowings into Old English, such as *prūt* ('arrogant').[13]

Before 1066, English was already marked extensively by language contact resulting from conquest.[14] During the second half of the ninth century, large parts of England had been subdued and settled by Scandinavian invaders, leaving only Wessex, a small part of western Mercia, and an area of land in northern Northumbria under insular control.[15] An alliance of West Saxon and Mercian kings in the tenth century was able to recapture, and to rule over, the whole of England, but from the 990s, Swein Fork-beard began to raid the kingdom once more: his son Cnut was crowned king of the entire country in 1017. Cnut's sons would only lose power in 1042, when Harthacnut died childless, leaving the throne to his maternal half-brother, Edward the Confessor. Eleventh-century England had thus already experienced one conquest, and a trilingual court which featured Norse, English, and Latin.[16] By 1066, communities of Norse speakers were receding northwards, but runic inscriptions survive which indicate the language's presence in North-West England as late as c.1100.[17] Scandinavian linguistic contact continued to exert an important influence on English well after the original settler communities had ceased to speak Norse. There seems to have been a degree of mutual comprehensibility between the two languages, although its exact extent remains highly debatable.[18] Scandinavian authors were aware that the languages had shared origins, even if their contemporary usage was divergent: the Icelandic author of the *First Grammatical Treatise* wrote of the English in the mid-twelfth century that 'we are of the same tongue, although there has been much change in one of them or some in both' ('vér erum einnar tungu, þó at gǫrzk hafi mjǫk ǫnnur tveggja eða nǫkkut báðar').[19] Comments like this suggest that there was a perceived similarity between Norse and English.[20] The large body of Old Norse loanwords in Middle English reveals that there was certainly extensive linguistic contact between the communities: these loanwords may originally have been adopted by the English as lexical variants to enlarge their native vocabulary.[21] The pervasive influence of Old Norse on English only becomes fully visible to us from the late twelfth century onwards, notably in the experiments with a language of regionally distinctive literary composition by the Lincolnshire priest Orrm, and in the South-West Midlands dialect of the Katherine Group and the *Ancrene Wisse*.[22] This lexical innovation is a reminder that if in some ways the Norman Conquest affected literary production in English, it also presented exciting opportunities for new vernacular borrowings, for literary experimentation, and for increased linguistic diversity.

When William I invaded, he brought with him a new set of linguistic practices which created a clear differentiation between his own reign and that of the previous Anglo-Saxon kings. Most strikingly, 1066 saw the widespread introduction of French to England. The leaders of William's army were mostly from a single area: nine of the eleven most powerful magnates recorded in the Domesday Book were all from the region of Lower Normandy, clustered around William's pre-Conquest ducal court in Caen.[23] Their influence ensured that the prevalent insular form of the language was based on a northern form of the *langue d'oïl*.[24] By the first third of the twelfth century, this had begun to develop the orthographical features that we now associate with the dialect of Anglo-Norman, the French commonly spoken in England (although closely connected to wider continental networks).[25] Many of the Normans soon became bilingual, with the result that monoglot French speakers were worthy of comment in England by the end of the twelfth century.[26] Anglo-Norman continued to be used as a written insular language until the end of the Middle Ages and beyond; recent research indicates that as a spoken language learned in infancy, developments in its syntax mirrored those of continental French until the late fourteenth century.[27] William's followers also included smaller groups of Bretons and Flemings, whose cultural influence is still sometimes discernible in late-twelfth-century literature.[28] Although 1066 represented the most visible influx of foreigners, immigration from the continent continued throughout the twelfth century. The Normans also connected England to a shifting collection of territories which momentarily stretched as far as Toulouse in 1159 at the height of Henry II's power (well into the *langue d'oc*). The linguistic and political contacts they facilitated extended even further into the multilingual Norman principalities of southern Italy (first invaded in the early eleventh century) and Sicily (conquered between 1060 and 1091). During the twelfth century, francophone communities were found in Ireland, Scotland, Wales, England, France, the Low Countries, Italy, North Africa (briefly), Sicily, Malta, Cyprus, and the crusader states; forms of French were also employed across the continent as *linguae francae*. The court of Edward the Confessor had already been marked by its internationalism; the Norman Conquest expanded English cultural horizons yet further.

The bureaucratic practice of the new leadership had consequences that were subtle, but equally significant. The late Anglo-Saxon administration had employed Standard Old English for its official documentation: this is an orthographically regularised form of late West Saxon dialect which occurs ubiquitously in eleventh-century manuscripts, regardless of their location.[29] The Normans had initially continued to compose royal writs in Old English, but around 1070, this was replaced by Latin as the primary language of written administration.[30] Without the incentive to make English writing conform to a unified royal standard, new orthographies once again began to emerge. Standard Old English is likely to owe its genesis to a desire to demonstrate the united state of England under

King Edgar in the 970s.[31] By the time its widespread use declined a
hundred years later, inevitably its written form did not reflect subsequent oral developments. Although some writers were able to demonstrate
their continued mastery of classical Old English, many others increasingly chose to compose works in more contemporary forms of the language, characterised by a wide variety of dialectal features, a significant
loss of inflectional endings, and a higher proportion of borrowings from
Norse and French.[32] It has often been posited that the existence of the Old
English vernacular corpus may have inspired the Normans to begin creating literature in their own language: late-eleventh- and twelfth-century
England provides the first surviving evidence for a widespread movement of French literary composition.[33] Another potential consequence of
engagement with Old English has been less discussed. The widespread circulation of material in an increasingly archaic form of the language heightened an awareness of linguistic change, drawing attention to the dispar-
ities between contemporary speech and the idiom of the pre-Conquest
past.

   Throughout the period, Latin remained the main language of the liturgy,
the Bible, and scholarship. Aspects of its relationship with the vernaculars
therefore recall the phenomenon known as extended diglossia, where different languages are assigned H(igh) and L(ow) prestige values, and are func-
tionally compartmentalised for use in separate situations.[34] But this relationship should not be seen as a straightforward opposition or dichotomy
between Latin (H) and vernaculars (L).[35] The perceived status of Britain's
languages varied according to context: separately or in combination, Latinity and vernacularity offered fluid stylistic practices. Given Latin's foundational role in literacy, all other written vernaculars in twelfth-century
Britain drew on its traditions of reading, writing, and interpretation to
some extent. But whilst authors periodically stressed the internationalism
and classical heritage of their writing, at other times, orality, localism and
historical specificity were of greater interest: different stylistic practices in
both Latin and the vernaculars could emphasise these characteristics to
varying extents.[36] Whilst liturgical and classical Latin remained conceptually distinct from the vernacular languages of Britain in some areas, significant functional overlaps remained elsewhere. In some contexts, Latin
authors made extensive use of lexis derived from the vernacular to accentuate the regional and temporal distinctiveness of their work. This was part
of the wider interest in vernacularity which informed appeals to linguistic history. Precisely because they bore very obvious traces of their historical and geographical origins, vernacular languages often had great literary

potential to authenticate authorial claims. Their wide range of possible variants meant that linguistic data could be precisely situated in time and space. The mutable nature of the vernacular paradoxically heightened its value as convincing evidence of a text's history.

Scope of Volume

This book focusses on responses to the history of Britain's vernaculars written in English, French, and Latin; all the authorial perspectives examined here were connected to the Norman establishment in some way, whether through the Church or the court, or through their use of French. These perspectives have influenced the work's geographical range. Anglo-Norman writers on language history predominantly had contacts with regal and ecclesiastical centres of power across Normandy and southern England (amongst others, those connected to London, Caen, Canterbury, Oxford, St Albans, and Exeter are examined here). For them, swift sea travel ensured closer links between the continent and the South Coast than with northern or western Britain. They also had much fuller opportunities to acquire linguistic expertise in areas under Norman control. Their view of Britain therefore lingered on certain regions in much more detail than others, notably England, Wales, and Cornwall. Sometimes, the parameters of individual countries were imagined to encompass the whole island: 'Britain' was often used as a synonym for England or Wales, depending on the territorial loyalties and ambitions of authors.[37] Shaped by their interests, this book is largely concerned with the southern half of the island: it explores depictions of French, of English, and of the Welsh and Cornish employed to provide evidence of the ancient British language. Direct attention is not devoted to twelfth-century insular views of classical Latin in this volume. However, as part of its focus on the history of Britain's vernaculars, two aspects of Latin's legacy are explored in depth. Firstly, the entire work engages with the grammatical and etymological frameworks developed to study the languages of the ancient world: these underpinned every twelfth-century engagement with language history by the literate. Secondly, one chapter explores Norman perceptions of Latin legal and administrative registers which heavily feature vernacular loanwords. Another work remains to be written on Scottish, Irish, and Welsh perceptions of their own linguistic history.[38]

My strategy of selecting material based on the interests of medieval authors could have been extended further. Twelfth-century Britain was a porous, expansive polity, whose cultural and conceptual boundaries were

profoundly fluid. Geographically and politically, Norman rule encompassed a much broader range of connected territories than England, Wales,
and Cornwall. By the late twelfth century, the Angevin realm stretched
from Ireland via Normandy and Brittany to southern France. Even after
John's military defeats (notably the loss of Normandy in 1204), the kingdom still retained significant territories amidst the *langue d'oc* communities in Gascony.[39] Linguistically, French and Latin linked the island to cosmopolitan intellectual and trading networks across Europe. Immigration to
Britain strengthened this internationalism: English, French, Norse, Gaelic,
Welsh, and Cornish were supplemented by smaller speech communities
such as Flemish, Breton, and Hebrew. The potential scope for linguistic investigation was therefore vast, and took many directions. For example, twelfth-century Anglo-Norman authors demonstrated some interest
in the languages of Scotland, part of Britain but never under Norman
rule,[40] and of Brittany, a client duchy of the Normans until 1166, when
it came under the direct control of Henry II.[41] The Bretons spoke a language very similar to Cornish, and Brittany was understood to have been
populated originally by settlers from South-West Britain.[42] From 1169
onwards, the Normans began to lay the foundations for rule in Ireland,
opening a further field of potential linguistic enquiry.[43] The perceptions of
England, Wales, and Cornwall discussed here therefore present only one
part of the sensitivity to linguistic history shown by twelfth-century
authors.

The socio-economic framework of the Anglo-Norman source material
has led this study to concentrate on the languages of those under Norman rule in Britain. However, the extant corpus of twelfth-century insular responses to language history has also influenced the parameters of the
enquiry in a second way: it primarily concerns the linguistic perceptions
of a very small, educated minority. Many aspects of linguistic history were
only visible to the fraction of the population that was Latin literate (roughly
6000 people in England at the time of the Domesday Survey in 1086,
or 0.27/0.55 per cent), because comparisons between archaic and modern
usage were mostly rendered possible through exposure to historical texts.[44]
This portion of the population formed a linguistic and educational elite:
in the Middle Ages, to be called *litteratus* implied not merely an ability
to read, but also a knowledge of Latin letters.[45] As practically all the conceptual tools for the academic study of language in medieval Britain had
arisen from the study of grammar and rhetoric in Latin, understandings
of language history were profoundly influenced by classical methods. At
the same time, the large amount of vernacular literature produced in the

twelfth century encouraged the expansion of scholarly horizons to include new languages.

Models of Understanding Language History in the Twelfth Century

Biblical Narratives of the Creation of Languages

In order to establish the indebtedness of twelfth-century linguistic scholarship to patristic thought, the rest of this introduction will be devoted to a discussion of the biblical and Latin models which laid the foundations for the study of vernacular language history. It will then examine the ways that these paradigms were themselves modified by their application to the vernaculars. The most widely referenced and authoritative view of language development in the Middle Ages was provided by the Bible. It offered different models of linguistic temporality: the eternity of God as Word; the Edenic language spoken by Adam as he named the animals; the speech that Adam and Eve bequeathed to their descendants after their expulsion from the garden; and the mutable, fragmented tongues spoken after the destruction of the Tower of Babel. These levels of language charted a clear decline from the unchanging Word to a confused multiplicity of speech, influencing medieval perceptions of multilingualism.[46] As an index of mankind's fallen state, the plurality of languages in twelfth-century Britain was not necessarily something to be celebrated. In the section of the *Glossa ordinaria* which forms a commentary on Genesis 11 (probably composed by Gilbertus Universalis, Bishop of London (d.1134)), multilingualism was interpreted as a divine punishment for mankind's presumptuous attempt to build the Tower of Babel, and hence a direct consequence of human sinfulness.[47] However, it was also possible to take a more optimistic view of linguistic diversity. The Tower of Babel was widely considered to be a typological prefiguration of Pentecost, when the Holy Spirit came down to the Apostles, rendering them miraculously able to preach in all the tongues of the world. This diversity could also be seen to foreshadow either the future languages of the Church on earth, or the variety of graces given to men through God's love.[48] Language in the Bible could hence be read as a simultaneous symbol of destruction and reconstruction, presenting a tension between loss and redemption. Engagement with linguistic history offered medieval readers both a reminder of the decay and corruption inherent in the mortal world, and an opportunity to arrest or reverse the corrosive effects of mutability.

The pursuit of language history was often framed as an enterprise of restoration. Drawing on different classical understandings of signification,

Augustine (d.430) understood the pattern of linguistic decline delineated
in the Bible as the result of a semiotic shift caused by the Fall. In Eden, God
had spoken to Adam via an 'inner word', communicating directly with his
soul ('loquens in intellectu eius').[49] The Fall compromised Adam's capacity
for spiritual apprehension. Now, meaning could only be adduced via verbal and visual signs. The necessity for language itself became an indication
of exile. In his later works, Augustine accepted that external language had
also existed in Eden alongside the 'inner word'. He suggested that God
appeared to Adam in the form of a man, as He had to some of the Old
Testament Patriarchs, and that He sometimes spoke to him in human language.[50] The expulsion from the garden prevented Adam and Eve from
hearing the 'inner word', restricting humans to a sole reliance on the inferior, secondary method of communication of external words. Even in its
current state of corruption, therefore, language originates in God: the Fall
did not alter the necessity for signs, but their method of reference. Whilst
in Eden, every word reflected the innate characteristics of its referent, after
Babel, humans were obliged to create new words which only signified their
meaning arbitrarily or by convention. This was the product of a fundamental semiotic shift: in paradise, God created man in His own image
and likeness ('ad imaginem et similitudinem nostram'), but after the Fall,
we now live a region of unlikeness ('in regione dissimilitudinis').[51] At first,
Augustine held that when Adam named the animals in Eden, the language
he used was the original tongue of humanity, and that elements of this language might perhaps still be found in contemporary names for animals.[52]
Later, he suggested that this tongue was Hebrew, which survived Babel to
become the language of Scripture.[53] The Fall hence did not hinder Adam
and Eve's ability to speak the Edenic language, Hebrew, but it did deprive
them of the guidance of God's 'inner word'.[54] Augustine's model allows
for language after Babel that can still in places preserve a primal, divine
unity between word and referent, even whilst marked by an ever-increasing
corruption. In one view, linguistic study was justified by the insights into
Edenic truth which etymology might yield.

Augustine believed that it was Eve's acceptance of temptation, rather
than the Tower of Babel, which constituted the main act of linguistic rupture. Babel, however, remained a very important focus for understandings
of language, and its connections with identity. God punishes the human
race for pridefully trying to build a tower that reaches heaven:

> Et dixit ecce unus est populus et unum labium omnibus coeperuntque hoc
> facere nec desistent a cogitationibus suis donec eas opere conpleant. Venite

igitur descendamus et confundamus ibi linguam eorum ut non audiat unusquisque vocem proximi sui. Atque ita divisit eos Dominus ex illo loco in universas terras et cessaverunt aedificare civitatem. Et idcirco vocatum est nomen eius Babel quia ibi confusum est labium universae terrae et inde dispersit eos Dominus super faciem cunctarum regionum.

And He said: 'Behold, it is one people, and all have one tongue: and they have begun to do this, neither will they leave off from their designs, till they accomplish them in deed. Come ye, therefore, let us go down, and there confound their tongue, that they may not understand one another's speech'. And so the Lord scattered them from that place into all lands, and they ceased to build the city. And therefore the name thereof was called Babel, because there the language of the whole earth was confounded: and from thence the Lord scattered them abroad upon the face of all countries.[55]

Although this provided a clear narrative for the origins of linguistic incomprehension, the exact method for creating the languages was left ambiguous: the account uses the terminology of confusion (*confundere, confusio*) and division (*dividere, dispergere*).

Not everyone was satisfied with the vagueness of Genesis 11. Peter Abelard (d.1142) argued that language originated with man when Adam named the animals, so God had not created languages at Babel, but merely confused or scrambled them.[56] He was troubled by the chronology of Adam's stay in paradise. Abelard wondered if it would have been possible for Adam to have developed an entire language in sufficient time to fulfil his onomastic duties. He concluded that perhaps, as elsewhere in the Bible, the temporal order of events had become jumbled: the passage describes a process which would have taken many years, and so the naming was probably completed later, outside Eden. Taking an optimistic view of human ingenuity, he thought it clear that God still wished Babel to be a continuing punishment for pride, because if words were created through human will or mutually agreed convention, then mankind should gradually have been able to reconstruct a universally comprehensible dialect over time. In contrast, John of Salisbury (d.1180) focussed on the perplexing differences between this passage of Genesis 11, which discussed human language as a singular entity (*lingua, labium*), and Genesis 10.20 and 31, which treated *linguae* as plural.[57] Confronted with this seeming inconsistency, he argued that there was, in fact, not one language before Babel, but many languages. Although Genesis 11 stated clearly that the earth was initially of *unum labium*, John reasoned that this was because all the pre-Babel tongues were mutually comprehensible. God punished mankind for their pride by rendering the languages opaque to each other, and it was this that led to ethnic division. Abelard and John responded to perceived inadequacies in the biblical account, attempting to accommodate other salient factors: they showed an awareness that languages were formed gradually over time and developed from close and continued contact amongst a group of people.

Their subtle redefinitions suggest discomfort with other interpretations of Babel which depicted a more static relationship between languages. Augustine had influentially suggested that the events of Babel in Genesis 11 had in fact preceded Genesis 10, which discussed the descendants of Noah. This implied that the division of mankind into linguistic groups had led to an eventual separation into ethnic groups. Augustine further calculated that there were seventy-two languages and peoples.[58] Whilst this rendered language an integral part of medieval ethnic identity, it also raised further questions. If God had created languages, and thence peoples, it was unclear whether more could be created, whether two languages or peoples could merge, or whether they could die out altogether. In many cases, twelfth-century authors simply noticed the occurrence of contemporary linguistic and ethnic changes without relating them explicitly to Babel; others were more troubled by tensions between the Bible and the reality of the twelfth-century linguistic situation. The biblical account of Babel underpinned all medieval engagements with language, but its depiction of multilingualism also contained obvious discrepancies.

Understanding the History of the Tres Linguae Sacrae

Beyond Babel, the most significant framework for the investigation of language history was provided by the principal languages of the Bible: Latin, Greek, and Hebrew. Patristic and medieval portrayals of the world's languages were strongly hierarchical, and this influenced the direction and intensity of academic endeavour. The languages of the Scriptures received the most sustained scrutiny, and for many commentators, they were the ones most suitable for the praise of God.[59] Extrapolating from John 19.20, where the Evangelist stated that Pilate placed an inscription on Christ's cross in Hebrew, Greek, and Latin, Isidore of Seville considered these three languages to be sacred.[60] Their supremacy was confirmed by their use in the Bible, and by their later uses in the liturgy.[61] However, they were also more obviously ancient than writings in the vernaculars of Western Europe: all of the tres linguae sacrae were linked to wider literary communities which had endured from antiquity into the twelfth century. Although Jerome had stressed that the original languages of the Old and New Testament should be examined in cases of textual doubt, a confident mastery of Greek and

Hebrew was relatively rare: only a few members of the twelfth-century Anglo-Norman scholarly elite possessed the necessary expertise to read the Bible and its associated commentary traditions in these languages.[62] However, a much wider audience consulted Greek and Hebrew glossaries, and copied alphabets. These reference tools attest to a high awareness of the sacred authority of these languages; in the case of Greek, this authority was augmented by a desire to emulate the stylistic display inherent in the grae-cisms employed in classical texts.[63] Although its biblical inheritance was the least prestigious, Latin was the most widely known of the *tres linguae sacrae*; its scholarly classical inheritance hence remained the most accessible to the medieval West. The sophisticated interpretative techniques developed for its study by ancient authors provided the underlying methodological struc-tures for the exploration of vernaculars in the Middle Ages.

Although, as we have seen with Augustine's earliest views, it was possible to be uncertain about whether Hebrew was the language spoken in the garden of Eden, most scholars agreed with Jerome that it was 'the mother of all languages' (*omnium linguarum matrix*).[64] A twelfth-century *Tractatus de philosophia* influenced by the school of Chartres even claims that out of the *tres linguae sacrae*:

> Est autem hebrea dignior, uel quia prima fuit, uel quia ipsa in confusione sola remansit, uel quia ea sola puer aliquis per se sine doctrina naturaliter loqueretur.

> Hebrew is the worthier, whether because it was the first, or because it alone remained in the confusion [of the Tower of Babel], or because it is the only one in which a child without instruction will naturally express himself.[65]

Although several experiments on child language acquisition were carried out over the Middle Ages, this quotation clearly does not reflect the fruits of empirical enquiry.[66] Rather, the author's opinion is the logical extension of a belief that Hebrew continued to preserve the original form of speech: humans seem to have retained a sub-conscious knowledge of the language, and return to it naturally when their environment has not induced them to adopt other tongues.[67] This belief that Hebrew formed the underlying structure of all speech also influenced medieval expectations of heaven. In southern England in the 1080s, the monk Goscelin of St Bertin wrote a long letter to his former pupil Eva, after her departure from the Benedic-tine convent of Wilton to an anchorhold at Angers. He was keenly aware of the pain of exile: Goscelin was originally Flemish, whilst Eva, now in France, was the daughter of a Lotharingian mother and a Danish father.[68]

This heightened his awareness of linguistic alienation: he emphasised Eva's good fortune to have avoided the fate of princesses sent to foreign lands and forced to learn strange languages.[69] In heaven, Goscelin imagined that things would be very different:

> Omnes scient omnes linguas, sed usitatius una loquentur matre linguarum Hebrea, ut sit una ciuitas omnium concordia.

> All will know all languages, but they will speak more commonly using one, the mother of tongues, Hebrew, so that there is one city by harmony of all.[70]

Whilst his portrayal of communication played on the typological connections between Babel and Pentecost, Goscelin transformed both events into a foreshadowing of the divine reunion that he would enjoy with Eva in Christ.

Although Hebrew was theoretically the most ancient of the *tres linguae sacrae*, all the methodological tools used for thinking about historic language in the Middle Ages were provided by Latin. In the early fourteenth century, Dante contrasted the fluctuations of vernacular language with the unchanging grammatical standards of Latinity, but a closer inspection shows this to be something of a rhetorical construct.[71] Ancient authors were aware that Latin had altered over time, and they made nuanced use of archaic language.[72] Caesar's librarian, Varro, had composed a twenty-five book treatise on the Latin language and its history, but only a portion of the work is now extant, and it was only known in the Middle Ages through a single late-eleventh-century manuscript at Montecassino.[73] However, other classical views on the use of old words were available in the medieval period. Horace's influential manual of composition, the *Ars Poetica*, included a section where he praised neologisms, on the grounds that an author cannot fight the mutability of nature and language:

> licuit semperque licebit
> signatum praesente nota producere nomen.
> ut silvae foliis pronos mutantur in annos,
> prima cadunt; ita verborum vetus interit aetas,
> et iuvenum ritu florent modo nata vigentque.

> It has ever been, and ever will be, permitted to issue words stamped with the mint-mark of the day. As forests change their leaves with each year's decline, and the earliest drop off: so with words, the old race dies, and, like the young of human kind, the new-born bloom and thrive.[74]

At the same time, he allowed for the eventual reinstatement of some of the most ancient terminology, predicting that even as today's neologisms lose their currency, 'many terms that have fallen out of use shall be born again' ('multa renascentur quae iam cecidere [. . .] vocabula').[75] Whilst Horace argued that all available vocabulary is permissible, others noted the potentially detrimental effects of over-using old words. Seneca and Quintilian spoke scornfully of those who employed archaisms, although, in some circumstances, Quintilian accepted that words taken from antiquity could lend style 'a certain grandeur not unmixed with charm' ('maiestatem aliquam non sine delectatione'), noting that 'they have both the authority of age and, because they have fallen into disuse, an attraction like that of novelty' ('nam et auctoritatem antiquitatis habent et, quia intermissa sunt, gratiam novitati similem parant').[76] Although these authors were aware of archaic language, they did not necessarily sanction its use.

Late antique sources were even more explicit about historical changes in the Latin language. Isidore of Seville made clear that it evolved over time, noting four varieties of Latin: Ancient, Latin, Roman, and Mixed ('Priscam, Latinam, Romanam, Mixtam'):

> Prisca est, quam vetustissimi Italiae sub Iano et Saturno sunt usi, incondita, ut se habent carmina Saliorum. Latina, quam sub Latino et regibus Tusci et ceteri in Latio sunt locuti, ex qua fuerunt duodecim tabulae scriptae. Romana, quae post reges exactos a populo Romano coepta est, qua Naevius, Plautus, Ennius, Vergilius poetae, et ex oratoribus Gracchus et Cato et Cicero vel ceteri effuderunt. Mixta, quae post imperium latius promotum simul cum moribus et hominibus in Romanam civitatem inrupit, integritatem verbi per soloecismos et barbarismos corrumpens.

> The Ancient is that uncouth language that the oldest people of Italy spoke in the age of Janus and Saturn, and it is preserved in the songs of the Salii. Then Latin, which the Etruscans and others in Latium spoke in the age of Latinus and the kings, and in this variety the Twelve Tables were written. Then Roman, which arose after the kings were driven out by the Roman people. In this variety the poets Naevius, Plautus and Vergil, and the orators Gracchus and Cato and Cicero, and others produced their work. Then Mixed, which emerged in the Roman state after the wide expansion of the Empire, along with new customs and peoples, corrupted the integrity of speech with solecisms and barbarisms. (IX.i.6–8)

Isidore's portrayal of Latin's history is not a biblically inspired narration of an inexorable decline from original purity. Rather, the language continues to improve until the Roman age; only after this does it become 'corrupted'. The lexical choice of *corrumpo* lends a note of moral condemnation to the changes which result from language contact. In his discussion of barbarisms, he depicted foreigners as bringing *vitia* ('mistakes' or 'vices') to Rome: these affected not only words, but also *mores* ('customs' or 'morals', I.xxxii.1). Mark Amsler points out that it is very rare for speakers to describe their own language in this negative way, given that geographical and temporal distance from a standard language such as English or Latin tends to lead to the acceptance of new standards of correctness based on local norms.[77] Isidore's treatment of 'mixed' Latin seems simultaneously to celebrate its existence as part of the history of Latinity, and to condemn its failure to maintain classical standards uninfluenced by later loanwords and other innovations.

The standard grammatical authorities, Donatus (Jerome's fourth-century teacher) and Priscian (active c.491–518), were similarly clear that the usage of the *antiqui* had differed from that of their contemporaries.[78] This information could be exploited by medieval readers: Gerald of Wales used the data on sound shifts found in Priscian to uncover the relationship between the words for 'salt' in seven languages, anticipating the later discovery of Indo-European in the eighteenth century.[79] Although undoubtedly aware that some usage was archaic, insular medieval authors were not able to exploit ancient Latin in any systematic way. Few texts which provided examples of early language were accessible, with the exception of Plautus and Terence: the principal source of archaic vocabulary was provided by the glossaries of unusual words handed down from late antiquity.[80] Although much of this lexis had been selected because of its ancientness, most glosses merely provided the word's meaning without further comment. The majority of vocabulary acquired in this manner was hence employed without a knowledge of its age.[81] Most authors confined their use of archaisms to one or two features, such as the passive infinitive ending in *-ier* before a following vowel.[82] Whilst medieval writers had various potential sources of information on the development of Latin, it required determination and curiosity to acquire a detailed understanding of the subject.

Besides direct discussions of linguistic evolution, and an awareness of the stylistic effects of archaisms, Latin culture also bequeathed to the Middle Ages a third way to explore language history: etymology. This is first visible as a Greek grammatical technique for the explanation of a word's meaning and development in a work attributed to Dionysius Thrax (probably dating from the second century B.C.), but was mostly fully explored in the highly influential *Etymologies* of Bishop Isidore of Seville (c.560–636), an encyclopaedic project which elucidated the formation of a huge range of Latin lexis.[83] Isidore's definition of etymology emphasised the importance of language history for an understanding of the object under discussion:

> Etymologia est origo vocabulorum, cum vis verbi vel nominis per interpretationem colligitur. [...] Cuius cognitio saepe usum necessarium habet in interpretatione sua. Nam dum videris unde ortum est nomen, citius vim

eius intellegis. Omnis enim rei inspectio etymologia cognita planior est.
Non autem omnia nomina a veteribus secundum naturam inposita sunt,
sed quaedam et secundum placitum, sicut et nos servis et possessionibus
interdum secundum quod placet nostrae voluntati nomina damus. Hinc est
quod omnium nominum etymologiae non reperiuntur, quia quaedam non
secundum qualitatem, qua genita sunt, sed iuxta arbitrium humanae voluntatis vocabula acceperunt.

Etymology is the origin of words, when the force of a verb or a noun is
inferred through interpretation. [. . .] The knowledge of a word's etymology
often has an indispensable usefulness for interpreting the word, for when
you have seen whence a word has originated, you understand its force more
quickly. Indeed, one's insight into anything is clearer when its etymology
is known. However, not all words were established by the ancients from
nature; some were established by whim, just as we sometimes give names to
our slaves and possessions according to what tickles our fancy. Hence it is the
case that etymologies are not to be found for all words, because some things
received names not according to their innate qualities, but by the caprice of
human will. (I.xxix.1–3)

To construct his definition, Isidore drew on two available understandings of the origin of language. Plato's *Cratylus* explored the idea that some
words were marked by the physical qualities of the objects they signify, a
position later adopted by the Stoics, who argued that language was originally natural: although now corrupted, at first words had figured the truth
of creation.[84] Aristotle's *De interpretatione* (available in Boethius's Latin
translation) took the opposite approach, arguing that a word expressed its
meaning 'by convention' ('secundum placitum'), and that 'no part of it
is significant on its own' ('nulla pars est significativa separata').[85] Isidore
adopted the middle ground, suggesting that language falls into two categories differentiated by their openness to etymological enquiry: some words
retain a connection to nature, but those which have been imposed arbitrarily have no inner rationale. His view of lexical signification as partly
natural and partly conventional was shared by many medieval authors.
However, the dismissal of the etymological study of words named from
caprice presented difficulties to those with an interest in the history of neologisms, new coinages created in response to specific modern circumstances.
Isidore's *Etymologies* remained central in the Middle Ages, but its vision of
the study of ancient Latin lexis was frequently reorientated by the extension
of its techniques to vernacular and contemporary vocabulary.

Isidore was profoundly influenced by Augustine's views on language:
etymology permitted a recovery of the linguistic integrity lost as a
consequence of the Fall. Following many patristic authors, Isidore believed

that Hebrew was the language spoken in the garden of Eden. However, for him it remained possible to recapture the divine truth embodied in the Hebrew through a careful study of Latin: its alphabet is derived from the Greek, which in turn is derived from the Hebrew (I.iii.4). This view of Latin's linguistic genealogy implies that the Edenic *Ursprache* may be recovered through diligent scholarly scrutiny. It transforms etymology into an enterprise which attempts to reconnect Augustine's post-Lapsarian 'region of unlikeness' to a lost pre-Lapsarian unity of sign and referent. Although twelfth-century readers of Isidore did not abandon his vision of linguistic recovery, they did enlarge its scope. Suzanne Reynolds has emphasised the rhetorical potential of medieval Latin etymology, arguing that it offered 'an almost playful way of reading the text and of generating or "inventing" verbal knowledge out of it'.[86] Not all medieval uses of etymology therefore reflected the demands of historical linguistics. Etymology's basic chronological framework could be complicated by its potential as space for imaginative excursus, and by its ability to reintegrate language with an eternal, divine Word, which operated outside human time. The technique continued to be fundamental to considerations of language history, but far from being a transparent medium for grammatical elucidation, it was frequently manipulated in order to substantiate the claims of the text.

The Bible and Latin scholarship offered a variety of narratives and methods which shaped understandings and investigations of language history, but these often received a certain amount of modification when applied to the linguistic circumstances of the Middle Ages. This introduction now turns to some new ways of understanding the vernacular in high medieval England, and its implications for the study of the linguistic past. It suggests that the sophisticated state of Old English grammatical culture made an important contribution to post-Conquest scholarship by initiating and authorising the detailed study of insular vernacular languages.

The Academic Study of the Vernacular

By the late tenth and eleventh centuries, Anglo-Saxon writers were innovatively extending Latin grammatical scrutiny to encompass written Old English.[87] During his time as a monk at Cerne Abbas between the late 980s and *c*.1005, the scholar and homilist Ælfric produced various teaching materials for use in the school there: the first extended Old English explanation of Latin grammar, a Latin-English glossary, and a Colloquy which provided a series of dialogues intended to enlarge vocabulary.[88] The *Grammar* was probably composed sometime between 993 and 995, and was addressed to 'tender little boys' ('puerulis tenellis'), enlarging the class-room methods and materials used in the Winchester school of Ælfric's own teacher, Æthelwold.[89] It elucidated the grammatical terminology employed by Priscian and Donatus, adhering to their view that the basic structure of the Latin language could be divided into eight parts of speech.[90] Ælfric presumably chose to expound Latin with reference to Old English because the text was intended to be elementary. However, his decision had revolutionary implications. He assumed that the grammar of the two languages was parallel, inventing equivalent Old English terms in order to explain the Latin parts of speech.[91] In practice, the two grammars did not always mesh, and Ælfric was sometimes obliged to make English artificially conform to Latin through extended explanations:

> FVTVRVM TEMPVS is towerd tid: *stabo* ic stande nu rihte oððe on sumne timan.

> *Futurum tempus* is the future (coming) tense: *stabo*: I stand, just now or at a certain time.[92]

At this date, Old English used the present tense to express both present and future actions, so Ælfric added extra adverbs to clarify his translation.[93] Even so, Latin *stabo* (I will stand) and his rendering of English *ic stande* were not exactly equivalent. Such contortions indicate the fundamentally ancillary role of the vernacular within the text. Nevertheless, Ælfric's decisions as a translator and teacher also drew attention to the fact that English was capable of communicating every linguistic nuance of the Latin, subtly redefining its status to suggest that it was worthy of grammatical analysis in its own right. He stated explicitly that the *Grammar* was intended for the study of both languages:

> Ne cweðe ic na forði, þæt ðeos boc mæge micclum to lare fremian, ac heo byð swaðeah sum angyn to ægðrum gereorde, gif heo hwam licað.[94]

> I do not say by any means that this book can help a great deal in learning, but that all the same, it will provide some introduction to each language, if it pleases anyone.

Fifteen manuscripts of the *Grammar* survive, a rate which implies its usefulness in the classroom.[95] Significantly, there is evidence that post-Conquest readers continued to find it valuable, not only for its pedagogical programme, but also for its innovative application of Latin grammatical models to the vernacular. Two manuscripts from the second half of the eleventh

century both contain twelfth-century glosses in Latin, English, and Anglo-
Norman.[96] Both include heavily annotated sections on verb conjugation,
and these importantly extend Ælfric's Old English explanations to include
French equivalents for the relevant Latin verbs ('*amabo*: jo amerai/*amabis*:
tu ameras', etc.).[97] The *Grammar*'s structure was encouraging students to
examine English and French in a new level of detail.

Anglo-Saxon authors had already begun to direct their grammatical gaze
beyond Old English and towards other vernaculars, albeit in a very fragmentary manner. The monk and scholar Byrhtferth of Ramsey wrote his
Enchiridion in 1010–1012.[98] This commentary on the Computus (a set
of tables used to calculate dates in the liturgical year) was intended for
monks, priests, and minor clerics. For his mixed audience of beginners and
experts, Byrhtferth provided analysis in both Latin and Old English.[99] The
Enchiridion also included a significant amount of grammatical information, which he considered 'wundorlic and eac beheflic to cunnanne' ('wonderful and also necessary to know'): like Ælfric, he explained this in Old
English, similarly translating the Latin grammatical terminology to create
further coinages of his own.[100] However, Byrhtferth extended his consideration of Old English to include an example taken from French:

> Se ðe his agene spræce awyrt, he wyrcð barbarismum, swylce he cweðe 'þu
> sot' þær he sceolde cweðan 'þu sott'. Se ðe sprycð on Frencisc and þæt ne can
> ariht gecweðan, se wyrcð barbarolexin, swylce he cweðe, 'inter duos setles
> cadet homo' þonne he sceolde cweðan, 'inter duos sæles'.

> He who corrupts his own language commits a barbarism, as if he said *þu
> sot* ['you soot'] where he should say *þu sott* ['you fool']. He who speaks in
> French but cannot speak it correctly commits *barbarolexis*, as if he said *inter
> duos setles cadet homo* ['the man falls between two seats'] where he should say
> *inter duos sæles* ['between two seats'].[101]

Byrhtferth's view is idiosyncratic: he seems to consider that a barbarolexis
is a barbarism committed in a foreign language. In contrast, for Isidore
of Seville, barbarolexis merely constituted 'foreign words [...] brought
into Latin speech' ('barbara verba latinis eloquiis inferuntur', I.xxxii.2): to
employ such borrowings did not necessarily constitute the stylistic error of
a barbarism, defined by Isidore as 'a word pronounced with a corrupted letter or sound' ('verbum corrupta littera vel sono enuntiatum', I.xxxii.1).[102]
Byrhtferth's choice of languages leaves his point about French ambiguous.
The substitution of Old English *setl*, 'seat', for Old French *seles*, 'stools, sad-
dles, motions' provides an example of borrowing in French; by respectively

including a French and English word, the two clauses each themselves further provide an example of borrowing in Latin.[103] Yet his comparison of the correctness of the two might also suggest that he saw the difference between *setles* and *sæles* as a form of barbarism, similar to his juxtaposition of Old English *sōt* ['soot'] and *sott* ['fool'].[104] His broader point is not lost: it is as possible to make mistakes in French and English as it is in Latin. The vernaculars have their own standards of linguistic correctness. Given the connections of Ramsey Abbey with traditions of continental learning, we might even see this reference to French as an example of the prestigious linguistic esoterica valorised both in the *Enchiridion's* Greek title, and in Byrhtferth's stylistic employment of rare words in Latin and English.[105] The works of Ælfric and Byrhtferth were both the products of an environment which saw vernacular languages as worthy of academic study; Ælfric's grammatical texts in particular facilitated the continuance and expansion of these scholarly traditions after 1066.

Conquest and Multilingual Identities

Twelfth-century sensitivity to Britain's complex linguistic history reflected a consciousness of the linguistic and political changes stemming from the Norman Conquest: this consciousness was perhaps sharpened by the precedent of the Scandinavian Conquest in the early eleventh century. The twelfth-century writings discussed here are certainly not the earliest evidence of interest in the island's past languages. We might think of the vernacular etymologies in Bede's *Ecclesiastical History*, or of the short ninth-century German tract on the genesis of alphabets and secret writing which is indebted to Anglo-Saxon material.[106] It would also be misleading to claim that such an interest was universal: many works which included historical details were not concerned with language in any way. However, the surviving twelfth-century treatments of language history do exhibit an unusual depth of scrutiny, diversity of approaches, and awareness of language's literary potential to demonstrate the passing of time. Patristic views of the close links between language and ethnicity ensured that the growth, decline or displacement of a language was widely thought to correlate with the political fortunes of its speakers. As invasion was a key mechanism for language change, many twelfth-century discussions of the linguistic past directly or indirectly explored the implications of the act of conquest itself.

The intellectual framework which informed medieval perceptions of multilingualism emphasised the intimate connection between ethnic and linguistic heritage. In contrast to some monolingual paradigms developed in late-eighteenth-century Europe, individuals were not necessarily imagined to have a single first language; nor were political, cultural, and linguistic boundaries imagined as coterminous.[107] Patristic authors tended to link language formation with genealogical descent, relating it to the genesis of ethnic groups. The primary term used for this linguistic community was *gens*, 'people': language was hence more indicative of biological descent than of the political unity implied in modern uses of the term 'nation'.[108] Augustine influentially posited that the division of languages at Babel (Genesis 11) had precipitated the division of Noah's descendants into peoples by their languages (Genesis 10).[109] The creation of multiple languages had caused a natural segregation between linguistic communities, which then ultimately developed into the different peoples of the earth. In this view, language was what brought about the formation of each ethnic group, suggesting that every people had only one speech. However, whilst language was seen as a catalyst for the creation of ethnicity, it was clear to Augustine that there was no one-to-one correlation between people and language in the late antique world. The sons of Noah produced seventy-three descendants, and Augustine assumed that, with one exception, each of them had been assigned their own speech at Babel, creating seventy-two languages in total.[110] Noticing that there were now more than seventy-two ethnic groups, he argued that the peoples of the earth had multiplied so that they outnumbered the languages.[111] Arnobius Junior's fifth-century consideration of this topic built on Augustine's description to explain the presence of Latin across Europe:

> Verbi gratia, cum una lingua Latina sit, sub una lingua diuersae sunt patriae Bruttiorum, Lucanorum, Apulorum, Calabrorum, Picentum, Tuscorum, et his atque huiusmodi similia si dicamus.[112]

> For example, although Latin is a single language, there are under this single language diverse nations of Bruttii, Lucani, Apuli, Calabri, Picentes, Tusci and others of their ilk, if I may say so.[113]

His discussion was popular with medieval authors (amongst them Bede, Henry of Huntingdon and Gervase of Tilbury), who sometimes updated the ethnic groups involved in Arnobius's description to reflect contemporary reality.[114] However, though Augustine's views were well-placed to explain the spread of languages like Latin across Christendom, his work did not fit so neatly with other aspects of multilingualism. The idea that language was responsible for the formation of peoples suggested that each people should speak only one language. Moreover, the total number of languages in the world was presented as being unaltered since Babel, offering no allowance for language death, or for the creation of new languages.

Patristic material also challenged later readers with its portrayal of the relationship between language and location. In the sixth century, Isidore of Seville, influenced by Augustine, insisted that peoples arose from languages, and not languages from peoples ('ex linguis gentes, non ex gentibus linguae exortae sunt', IX.i.14). He argued that there was an equal number of both: seventy-two (IX.ii.2–3). Language therefore gave rise to ethnicity even more straightforwardly than in Augustine's reading of Genesis, where there are seventy-three descendants, but only seventy-two languages. However, for Isidore, the character of peoples was also shaped by their geographical environment:

> Secundum diversitatem enim caeli et facies hominum et colores et corporum quantitates et animorum diversitates existunt.

> People's faces and colouring, the size of their bodies, and their various temperaments correspond to various climates. (IX.ii.105)

These shared characteristics could then affect language. The Saxons are named from *saxosus* ('stony') 'because they are a hard and very powerful kind of people, standing out above the other piratical tribes' ('quod sit durum et validissimum genus hominum et praestans ceteris piraticis', IX.ii.100). Isidore also noted that some suspected that the Britons were so named in Latin 'because they are brutes' ('eo quod bruti sint', IX.ii.102). Climate shapes the characteristics of a people, and these characteristics are in turn expressed by the names of their ethnicity and their speech. Sometimes, geography has a more direct influence on etymology, as with the Vandals, named for the river Vindilicus (IX.ii.96). Although some of these names are in Latin, others taken from local vernaculars suggest a closer consonance between land and language. As a frontier people, the Burgundians draw 'their name from their location' ('nomen ex locis sumpserunt') by deriving their name from their vernacular word for 'forts' ('burgos') (IX.ii.99). There is thus a latent connection here between tongue and landscape. Isidore's grouping of linguistic families by location implies that there may even be a more direct link between the two:

> Omnes autem Orientis gentes in gutture linguam et verba conlidunt, sicut Hebraei et Syri. Omnes mediterraneae gentes in palato sermones feriunt, sicut Graeci et Asiani. Omnes Occidentis gentes verba in dentibus frangunt, sicut Itali et Hispani.

> All the nations of the East – like the Hebrews and the Syrians – crunch together their speech and words in their throats. All the Mediterranean nations – like the Greeks and the people of Asia Minor – strike their speech on the palate. All the Western nations – like the Italians and Spaniards – gnash their words against their teeth. (IX.i.8–9)

Although never directly theorised, Isidore seems to suggest that just as every people is influenced by its location in the world, so too is every language.

Whilst Augustine's and Isidore's understandings of the relationship between language, location, and ancestry continued to exert a significant influence, later authors appear to have been unconcerned by the evident discrepancies between patristic theory and medieval polyglossia, and made comparatively little effort to formulate a coherent theory of the place of language within their communities. Language was still recognised as an important means of distinguishing ethnic identity. In the twelfth century, when Bishop Bernard of St David's wrote to Pope Innocent II to argue that Wales should have its own, separate archdiocese, he pointed out that 'the peoples of our province are distinct in nation, language, laws and customs, judgements and manners' ('populos nostre provincie natione, lingua, legibus et moribus, iudiciis et consuetudinibus discrepare').[115] This consonance between people and language remained the underlying norm in discussions of insular multilingualism. Bede's *Ecclesiastical History* (completed 731) began by enumerating Britain's five languages.[116] Twelfth-century authors drawing on this account either continued to portray the island as multilingual,[117] or adapted Bede's work to celebrate the island's many peoples.[118] These alternative readings suggest that language continued to imply ethnicity. Bede's account, part of a long description of Britain's location and natural resources in the tradition of Orosius, was formative: he emphasised that linguistic plurality could only be a meaningful concept in relation to the boundaries of a particular area.[119] The geography of the island formed the parameters against which multilingualism was measured.[120]

Ideas of place similarly exerted a subtle influence on understandings of both the Welsh and the English language. It was widely accepted that the presence of English and Welsh in Britain was the result of immigration. When the ninth-century *Historia Brittonum* argued that the Britons were descended from a Trojan prince, Brutus, it gave details from the 'brittannico sermone', suggesting that their language had also originated in Troy.[121] This connection between migration and language is made clearer in one of the most important foundation myths of the English, recorded in Gildas's sixth-century *De excidio Britanniae*. Gildas states that, when the Saxons first arrived from the continent, they came in 'three *keels*, as they call warships in their language' ('tribus, ut lingua eius exprimitur, cyulis, nostra longis navibus').¹²² The inclusion of the Old English word, *cēol*, implicitly links the movement of peoples to the movement of languages.¹²³ However, though it was clear that English and Welsh had not arisen from the landscape, to a limited extent they were still seen as connected to it. Language was an important factor in shaping a sense of England. Bede did not distinguish between the different dialects of territories such as Mercia and Northumbria, instead considering all forms to be representative of English.¹²⁴ This perception that the early Anglo-Saxon kingdoms shared a language can be seen as an important 'unifying element' which facilitated the gradual coalescence of the kingdoms into a single realm, England.¹²⁵ The terminology for language, ethnicity, and place may also have strengthened a sense of integration.¹²⁶ By the eleventh century, both the people and the language were referred to as *Englisc*, and their country was *Englalond*, suggesting that the English tongue occupied a specific location within the world.¹²⁷ Perceptions of English, then, were framed by an understanding of its history as the language of one particular people and one particular place.

These considerations of language, history, and identity manifest themselves in the writings of one of the most observant linguists of the twelfth century: Gerald of Wales (*c.*1146–1220/23). In 1188, Baldwin, Archbishop of Canterbury, travelled around Wales preaching the Cross. He was accompanied by Gerald, at this time Archdeacon of Brecon. Their tour resulted in the composition of two related treatises on Wales: Gerald's *Itinerarium Kambriae*, an account of the journey and its points of interest, and his *Descriptio Kambriae*, a pioneering ethnographical work which describes the customs and land of the Welsh.¹²⁸ Both texts were filled with digressive details which ranged across subjects including local politics, fauna, demonology, music, and the history of the religious orders. As part of this discursive style, Gerald included several discussions of vernacular language history. One anecdote reported a child's discovery near Swansea of an underground realm where the Trojan language was still spoken, as if the linguistic roots of Welsh in Trojan extended beyond the figurative and into the soil.¹²⁹ Sensitive to the political threat of native resurgence, Gerald chose to finish his *Descriptio Kambrie* with an 'oddly unambitious' statement of the right of the Welsh people to the land:¹³⁰

> Nec alia, ut arbitror, gens quam haec Kambrica, aliave lingua, in die districti examinis coram Judice supremo [. . .] pro hoc terrarum angulo respondebit.

> I do not think that on the Day of Direst Judgement any race other than the Welsh, or any other language, will give answer to the Supreme Judge of all for this small corner of the earth.¹³¹

This pronouncement is spoken by a former Welsh soldier, 'who had joined the King's forces against his own people, because of their evil way of life' ('qui contra alios tamen vitio gentis eidem adhaeserat, super exercitu regio').[132] Its muted tone partly derives from links to wider pejorative descriptions of the Welsh as arising from the landscape: in the 1150s, the author of the *Gesta Stephani* noted that Wales 'breeds men of an animal type' ('hominum nutrix bestialium').[133] These views exploited a discourse of 'geographic determinism', ultimately traceable to Aristotle and often establishing the superiority of the civilised ethnographer over his savage subjects.[134] Yet whilst Gerald may have been implying that the Welsh were intellectually confined by the land they inhabited, in other ways this intense link between territory and language seems stubbornly resistant to Norman colonial endeavour. No other language could have a connection of similar depth to the landscape of Wales. It is clear that the terrain of Britain exerted an intangible and often unexamined influence on conceptions of its languages. Gerald of Wales's ambiguous presentation of the future of Welsh emanates from this ideological nexus to portray the bond between people, language, and territory as divinely appointed.

Perhaps the strangest twelfth-century depiction of insular language was included in an anonymous Latin catalogue of the wonders of Britain:

> Tricesimum primum sunt aves in littore maris nidificantes in rupibus magnis; veniat aliquis ante fossam ubi nidus illius avis sit aut prope aut de longe, ita ut vox sua usque ad fossam audiri possit, et clamet Anglice vel Britannice et dicat, Es illuc intus? Si vero avis fuerit in fossa respondebit eadem lingua et dicet, Etiam, quis es et quid vis? Et dices, Veni huc foras et occidam te. Et exclamabit avis quasi tristis et lacrymans, 'Vae mihi misero, ad quid factus sum, quando nunc moriar ?' Et veniet ad te cito.[135]

> The thirty-first marvel is the birds nesting on the seashore in great cliffs. One should come before the burrow where the nest of this bird is found, either nearby or far away, so that his voice can be heard from the burrow, and call out in English or British and say 'Is anyone in there?'. Then, if the bird is indeed in the burrow, it will respond in the same language and say 'Now who are you and what do you want?' And you will say, 'Come here outside and I will kill you'. And the bird will exclaim as if sad and weeping, 'Woe is me, what am I reduced to, when now I will die?' And it will come to you soon.

The author does not seem entirely convinced by the story of the talking seabird, and is vague on the details of its language. However, this vagueness is itself of interest. The account assumes that the bird was addressed in English or British, and then replied in the same tongue. This might reflect a preference for using languages learned in infancy to speak to animals; expectations may also have been shaped by Bestiary-lore which described parrots as mimics.[136] Yet it is noticeable that the author does not include French amongst the potential vernaculars which the bird could understand. English and British seem to be the languages most natural to Britain.

Authors depicting French in the context of Britain's multilingualism also responded to these latent connections between language and location, and were similarly interested in linking French to the insular landscape. The Normans themselves did not fit well into Augustine's and Isidore's portrayals of the links between ethnogenesis and language, but, far from being a cause for anxiety, this was frequently celebrated as an indication of their outstanding military prowess. Sometime between 996 and 1015, Dudo of Saint-Quentin wrote an origin myth for the Normans where their founder, Rollo, had a prophetic vision of a flock of different birds peacefully washing themselves together, interpreted as a sign of his triumphant future rule over men of different ethnicities.[137] This vision implies linguistic diversity: Dudo's wider history of the Normans depicted them as formed from Scandinavian and Frankish groups, respectively speaking the *dascica lingua* (Norse) and the *romana lingua* ('Roman'/Romance).[138] In Dudo's myth, the early bilingualism of the Normans became a mark of identity in itself, of a piece with their perceived exceptionalism.[139] The Normans' bellicosity also made them more difficult to link to a single location. Although Normandy remained conceptually important as the birthplace of their people,[140] the Normans' ambition ('tenorem [...] ambitionis') ensured that they were not confined to any one territory.[141] Their language was similarly widespread across Europe. By the eleventh century, Dudo's Norman readers were no longer bilingual, and spoke only the northern French *langue d'oïl*: this vernacular was used not only in lands the Normans had conquered, such as England and Sicily, but also by their immediate neighbours and rivals in northern France. Dudo's portrayal of the *romana lingua* linked the Normans to an even wider 'Roman' linguistic community. By framing Romance as an oral form of Latin, the *langue d'oïl* was depicted as part of a spectrum of dialects which stretched into Spain and Italy.[142] In the decades after the Conquest, other terminology was used in England which indicated the French provenance of the language more closely: besides the *lingua romana*, commentators referred to a *lingua francigena*, or *gallica*.[143] These terms found parallels in the vernacular *romanz*,[144] and *franceise*.[145] If a subjective sense of ethnic identity is facilitated by the presence of 'a contrasting other', it thus becomes clear why language did not feature strongly in a *Normannitas* which partly defined itself in opposition to the French crown.[146] The comparatively late emergence of the Romance vernacular as a written language also influenced perceptions of its relative importance to the history of the Norman people: unlike the long insular tradition of Old English as a language of literature and government, the Normans had almost exclusively written in Latin before the Conquest, leaving the historical importance of the oral 'lingua romana' far less evident.[147]

Perhaps because of these factors, the advent of the French language in England does not seem to have attracted much sustained attention in contemporary accounts of the Norman Conquest. In Guy of Amiens's *Carmen de Hastingae proelio* (written in 1067 or soon after), he noted that there were two identical speeches exhorting the people to affirm William as their king during his coronation, one addressed to the 'famous men of France' ('famosis Gallis'), and one said 'in English' ('lingua [. . .] Angligena').[148] Although the presence of a new community of vernacular French speakers in England could be adduced here, linguistic factors were not emphasised. There may have been another, more pragmatic reason for Guy's reticence: language marked the ethnic separation of the Normans from the existing English population. As William's grip on the country became more assured, authors felt emboldened to include further linguistic details to their accounts of his coronation. Between 1071 and 1077, William of Poitiers wrote the bulk of his *Gesta Guillelmi*, an extended biography of William I designed to show the legitimacy of his succession to the English throne.[149] Like Guy of Amiens, he included a discussion of the crowning of the king, complete with the affirmation of his rulership in Westminster Abbey by the Normans and the English. However, darker events connected to the arrival of French in England were now revealed. He described the consequences of the 'joyful assent' ('hilarem consensum') of the English to confirm William as their lord:

> Ceterum, qui circa monasterium in armis et equis praesidio dispositi fuerunt, ignotae <linguae> nimio strepitu accepto, rem sinistram arbitrati, prope ciuitati imprudentia flammam iniecerunt.

> But the men who, armed and mounted, had been placed as a guard round the minster, on hearing the loud clamour in an unknown tongue, thought that some treachery was afoot and rashly set fire to houses near to the city.[150]

Linguistic incomprehension has provided a stimulus for violence, implicitly foreshadowing further antagonism between the Normans and the English. Writing before 1123/24, and mindful of his own English ancestry, Orderic Vitalis embellished the scene still more.[151] The heavy-handed response of the invaders to the English cries of acclamation not only indicates ethnic mistrust but has incited permanent hatred: we are told that the English 'never again trusted the Normans who seemed to have betrayed them, but nursed their anger and bided their time to take revenge' ('postea Normannos semper suspectos habuerunt, et infidos sibi diiudicantes ultionis tempus de eis peroptauerunt').[152] If Dudo presented multilingualism as a triumphant indication of successful conquest, by the twelfth century, it was also understood to be a troubling marker of ethnic difference.

The putative connections between language, land, and ethnicity enabled twelfth-century writers to explore the ways in which the Normans and their language might be connected to their newly acquired insular territories. Differing views of multilingualism as a witness to both conquest and assimilation created a tension which generated new considerations of the place of the Normans within Britain. Given the growth of a sense of Englishness amongst francophones in the twelfth century, some historians have understandably characterised the connection of language to perceptions of contemporary national identity as 'fairly weak'.[153] Others stress that a multilingual environment encourages the creation of multiple identities, which are assumed in differing linguistic contexts. Discussing new speakers of Latin in the provinces of the Roman Empire, Andrew Wallace-Hadrill has emphasised that there is no need to assume that multilingual individuals maintained a single, constant identity. He quotes Aulus Gellius (*c.* A.D. 123–170):

> Quintus Ennius tria corda habere sese dicebat, quod loqui Graece et Osce et Latine sciret.

> Quintus Ennius used to say he had three hearts, because he knew how to speak in Greek and Oscan and Latin.[154]

For Wallace-Hadrill, Ennius's *tria corda* imply that ancient identities could be 'parallel and coexistent': 'populations [. . .] can sustain simultaneously diverse culture-systems, in full awareness of their difference, and code-switch between them'.[155] This study considers the question of contemporary identities in the twelfth century only indirectly; it is instead centrally concerned with the impact of language on perceptions of ancestral identity. Language formed only one element of medieval assessments of ethnicity amongst other factors such as customs, genealogy, and law.[156] Wallace-Hadrill's model of simultaneously held identities is of interest here:

twelfth-century individuals in Britain could claim descent from various ethnic and linguistic groups, whether as a direct consequence of mixed ancestry, or more obliquely as inhabitants of an island with a multilingual heritage. Particularly when looking back to the past, this allowed different strands of ethnicity to be deployed in response to the varying demands of social and political circumstances. Manipulations of linguistic data can reveal the ways in which authors wished to remember the past of their ancestors, and the aspects of their familial and cultural inheritance that they wished to emphasise. Although primarily investigating the effect of the study of language history on perceptions of the vernacular, this book hence necessarily considers the ways in which literary treatments of historic language were shaped by considerations of ancestral memory. Medieval engagements with language history were implicitly or explicitly linked to the changing political circumstances of Britain's different communities.

Summary of Chapters

This study ranges across a wide variety of genres and languages in order to demonstrate the striking breadth of interest in language history across different social groups, and the complex multilingual culture from which it grew. Authors concerned with the linguistic past addressed monastic, administrative, royal, and noble audiences of both sexes. Occasionally, their works also portrayed discussion of place names taking place amongst the wider community: although these depictions of locals probably do not always reflect the fruits of factual enquiry, they nonetheless demonstrate that the literate considered them to be plausible. The apparently universal appeal of language history ensured that it was depicted in multiple genres including romances, histories, legal translations and forgeries, charters, poetry, practical manuals, and hagiographies. Writers and scribes evoked the linguistic past in several different ways: by directly discussing the development of Britain's vernaculars, or by including archaic language, etymologies, or portrayals of ancient documents. This generic breadth ensures that portrayals of the linguistic past are found across several different languages. French, English, and Latin works are discussed here as the major languages of record in twelfth-century England. However, Anglo-Norman authors themselves were concerned with a much larger range of vernaculars. Twelfth-century Britain was routinely polyglot: whilst alive to the literary heritage of individual languages, writers did not treat them in isolation. Appeals to linguistic history responded to the imaginative and stylistic possibilities of multilingualism, and themselves form a multilingual topos in their own right.

The diversity and also the subjectivity of interest in historical vernacular language during the twelfth century have led me to approach the subject through a series of detailed case studies. Rather than providing a comprehensive survey, these aim to reconstruct the circumstances surrounding the composition of selected texts. Broadly moving from the earlier to the later twelfth century, works have been chosen to represent particular themes which emerge from imaginative engagements with English, Brittonic, and French linguistic history: the importance of ancient documentation and etymology; sensitivity to pre-Conquest English; explorations of Britain's 'Trojan' linguistic heritage; lexical demonstrations of administrative and legal developments; and the links between language and conquest.

Chapter 1 develops the themes of the introduction by outlining some of the main approaches to archaic language in the twelfth century. It stresses that interest in the linguistic past was heightened by a pressing need to authenticate monastic holdings and liberties with Anglo-Saxon documentation, as institutional privilege was subjected to new scrutiny after the Conquest. Focussing on the sophisticated manipulation of expectations of ancient language in the *Gesta Abbatum Monasterii Sancti Albani*, a twelfth- and thirteenth-century history of the Benedictine monastery of St Albans, it examines the ways in which classical paradigms of linguistic interpretation were modified when applied to the vernacular. The text was part of a co-ordinated programme of forgery which influenced the creation or copying of Latin and vernacular charters, histories, and saints' lives. Its portrayal of the recovery of historical linguistic data through the archaeological retrieval of ancient documents and etymology forms a commentary on the pressures and insecurities involved in historical interpretation.

Chapter 2 discusses perceptions of the literary inheritance of Old English in the twelfth century, examining Henry of Huntingdon's Latin translation of a poem from the *Anglo-Saxon Chronicle* (the 'Battle of Brunanburh'), and the Old English gloss to the trilingual Eadwine Psalter, produced at Canterbury. It uncovers a variety of levels of concern about the changes to written English after the Conquest, suggesting that the authors of the texts were more interested in allying their work with the prestigious history of the Old English literary tradition than in dwelling on linguistic difference. At the same time, due to the rapidity of post-Conquest linguistic development, their explorations of historical texts inevitably brought them into contact with older forms of orthography, lexis, and grammar: such differences drew attention to language change, and its potential to illuminate history. These texts indicate that Old English literature was copied as much from a desire to re-interpret the past as to preserve it. However, they also demonstrate a keen awareness of the prestige of this vernacular literary heritage:

the chapter argues that this awareness lay behind the surge in appeals to the authority of archaic language during the twelfth century.

Chapter 3 examines a key manifestation of this new interest in the authenticating power of the linguistic past, discussing the impact of Geoffrey of Monmouth's claim that his *Historia regum Britanniae* was a translation from a 'very ancient book', written in the early 'British' language. It shows that Geoffrey's exploitation of 'British' alerted his twelfth-century readers to the potential of archaic vernacular languages to substantiate depictions of history. This is traced through the commentaries on some other supposedly British texts: Geoffrey's *Prophetia Merlini* and associated Latin translations of Brittonic prophecies. The chapter suggests that, in order to prove that the prophecies were ancient writings, commentators were obliged to demonstrate the historically specific nature of their vernacular style. Geoffrey's unprecedented appeals to the authority of his 'British' sources invited critical appraisal, leading to their evaluation by Latin scholars. For the first time, vernacular texts (albeit in Latin translation) became the object of academic scrutiny.

Chapter 4 is the first of two chapters which discuss francophone responses to the history of Britain's languages. It charts the response of Norman authors to the unique body of pre-Conquest laws which were recorded in Old English. Unparalleled in Europe, this corpus of written vernacular law offered an important repository of linguistic information for those who wished to demonstrate the longevity of twelfth-century government. In order to emphasise the continuity of English law between Edward the Confessor and William I, Old English was widely employed to authenticate post-Conquest legal works. This recognition of the potential of historical language to support portrayals of institutional history prompted new investigations of the lexical fields associated with other aspects of Norman government. Richard fitz Nigel's Latin *Dialogus de scaccario* featured innovative etymological discussions of the French and English coinages of the exchequer. These were employed to frame the institution's development both in the context of his own family, and in the context of the Normans more widely. Prompted by contact with Old English, twelfth-century French speakers were beginning to extend their gaze to the history of their own vernacular.

The final chapter (chapter 5) explores a further aspect of the ways in which interest in the development of French was heightened by exposure to insular vernaculars. It investigates francophone depictions of the language in the context of broader portrayals of multilingual Britain. Through a discussion of Wace's *Brut*, the Latin works of Gervase of Canterbury, and the anonymous *Roman de Waldef*, it demonstrates that insular multilingualism was understood as the product of a succession of conquests by the Trojans, English, and Normans. At the same time, it charts a simultaneous, conflicting desire to see language as influenced by its geographical location: these portrayals of multilingualism obliquely explored the tensions and insecurities inherent in attempts to locate insular French in the British landscape. The chapter shows that whilst the Latin origins of French were almost never explicitly stated by twelfth-century writers, they were much more eager to depict English and British as the language's insular precursors. By the early thirteenth century, it seems that the vernacular predecessors of French in Britain constituted its most important historical and ideological inheritance. Discussions of language history hence provided an opportunity to unravel the anxieties and hopes surrounding conquest, ancestry, and belonging.

CHAPTER I

Methods and Motivations for Studying the Vernacular Linguistic Past

Twelfth-century authors inherited a range of biblical, classical and insular models for considering language history. Discussions of sacred languages often sought to elucidate the eternal, searching lexis for traces of the divine. As post-Conquest historical imperatives quickened a desire for vernacular evidence, the exegetical paradigms of the *tres linguae sacrae* were more fully extended to other types of linguistic data. The application of these paradigms to sources and lexis shaped by the ephemerality of vernacular language created alternative perspectives on the value of the transient. Such evidence could still be used in attempts to reconstruct the truths embodied in language by God at Eden (in many etymologies), or as an eternal witness to divine glory through the possession of land (in many charters). However, at other times, authors focussed more on recovering a given historical moment than on divine intention. Through the lens of a single text, this chapter examines how the impermanence of the vernacular reshaped the parameters of two key methods for portraying language change: etymology and the discovery of archaic source materials.

The evocation or imitation of ancient documents in the languages of pre-Conquest Britain presented an obvious means for substantiating portrayals of history. Uncertainties about ownership and tradition arising from the Norman Conquest had accelerated interest in the demonstration of institutional entitlement. In the main, convincing evidence came from documentation, both genuine and forged: this emphasis on writing drew attention to the importance of old manuscripts, and sometimes to the linguistic detail of charter diplomatic. The bilingual, sophisticated scribal traditions of Anglo-Saxon England influenced the direction of later attempts at archival preservation and manipulation. Latin was the language of Anglo-Saxon diplomas (royal charters recording perpetual grants of land): the scope and authority of these prestigious documents attracted intense attention in subsequent attempts to defend monastic privileges through copying, embellishment or forgery. The types of document written in English often made less

comprehensive bids for property and rights, and were hence less susceptible to later alterations: in the pre-Conquest era, the language tended to be
employed in private documents like wills and leases. However, information
preserved in English still repaid careful consideration from post-Conquest
readers. In the pre-Conquest archive, it was used in boundary clauses and
in sealed royal writs (where the king alerted officials and interested parties to new grants of land, property or privilege). Responses to language
history were not shaped by forgery alone: any post-Conquest assessment
of existing Anglo-Saxon records (in Latin or in English) necessitated close
engagement with the writing strategies of previous centuries. Given the
vernacular focus of this volume, treatments of Old English documents will
be examined in more depth here than Latin ones; however, both languages
offered readers substantial and mutually complementary opportunities to
incorporate archival evidence within depictions of institutional history.

Interest in the material evidence of Old English also stimulated broader
enquiries into how the vernacular could be employed to locate texts in geographically and temporally specific contexts. Even as it encouraged increasingly nuanced depictions of the written word, the use of vernacular evidence also entailed a return to oral sources. Late antique methods of Latin
etymology offered an important template for the recovery of lost contexts
through language, but unlike Latin, later forms of the vernacular continued
to be spoken by the island's twelfth-century population. This created a subtle challenge to textual and social hierarchies: for place names, the linguistic
knowledge inherited by peasants from their forefathers often outweighed
other forms of authority.

Here, these concerns will be explored through an examination of the role
played by vernacular language in the spectacularly successful manipulation
of archival material at the Benedictine monastery of St Albans after the
Norman Conquest. After a brief excursus on the place of Old English documentation within the monks' wider arguments for exemptions and privileges, the chapter turns to two episodes in the *Gesta Abbatum Monasterii
Sancti Albani*, a twelfth- and thirteenth-century chronicle of the abbots of
St Albans. The first passage tells of the Anglo-Saxon discovery of a history
of Alban's martyrdom in the British language, which dramatically crumbles
to dust when translated into Latin. Part of a broader framing of the past
within the *Gesta Abbatum* to combat the abbey's critics, the incident was
more a response to the exigencies of contemporary polemic than a factual
narrative. Although its concerns were germane to the wider emphasis on
written testimony at St Albans, the text was self-conscious in its employment of literary topoi designed to demonstrate the British book's authority.

A second episode of the *Gesta Abbatum* employed etymologies drawn from local memory to verify archaeological discovery: it was similarly alert to tensions between the vernacular's potential to provide historical evidence, and the ways in which the recovery of such evidence had been shaped by imagination and desire. It is argued here that these episodes formed an oblique commentary on how the vernacular subtly modified some Latinate standards of linguistic and documentary proof. Unlike the eternal truth embodied in the etymological details of the *tres linguae sacrae*, the historical value of the vernacular derived from its impermanence in some instances: the unique specificity of its testimony had been shaped by external circumstances of time and place.

Creating Documentary Evidence in English

Ecclesiastical archives became the object of fresh consideration after the Conquest, in response to the threats posed by the systematic replacement of English bishops by Normans; by the reversion of estates to the king in the event of a vacancy in a bishopric; and by incursions into Church holdings by lay magnates.[1] Charters, and particularly royal charters, provided the strongest means of demonstrating ownership: in the course of being copied anew, many documents were judiciously interpolated to update or augment existing privilege. The ubiquity of this practice suggests that the defence of monastic property did not merely reflect administrative and pecuniary pressures. Rather, religious institutions sought to secure the present and future glorification of God by ensuring the continuity of their status, holdings, and rights.[2] Faced with pre-Conquest charters which were inadequate to the increasingly stringent standards of documentary proof required in the twelfth century, many scribes altered them to reflect what they believed would have been the original donors' intentions: although it was understood to be a crime, forgery's status as a sin was more ambiguous.[3]

When they replicated the conventions of Anglo-Saxon documentation, scribes were obliged to pay attention both to its material form, and to the particularity of its phraseology. This entailed a substantial engagement not only with Latin but also with the vernacular at a time when administrative written Old English was gradually becoming more unfamiliar. Soon after the Conquest, royal scribes largely ceased to use the language: probably in 1070, Latin became the preferred idiom of William I's writs.[4] However, the employment of English by Anglo-Saxon kings testified to its previous status: pre-Conquest documents recorded a period when it was a prestigious language of institutional memory. Although the earliest

Anglo-Saxon charters are preserved in Latin, sealed royal writs appeared in English from at least the reign of Cnut. From the ninth century onwards, English was also used with increasing frequency for private documents, including wills, leases, and other agreements.[5] In some cases, this reflected the practical necessity of creating records easily understandable by the laity, or of recording an oral statement precisely.[6] Elsewhere, it entailed a tacit recognition of the particularity of vernacular language. Some of the most prominent forms of Latin charters display an evolving awareness of the value of English. The Latin diplomas which commemorate land grants to the Church feature a boundary clause, outlining the geographical extent of the estate under discussion: the earliest examples appear in the eighth century, where vernacular place names are integrated within Latin compass directions.[7] By the first half of the ninth century, these clauses were becoming a more involved description of the land in question; perhaps in response to a need for greater specificity, some began to be composed entirely in English.[8] By the early tenth century, they stopped being written in Latin at all, and appear exclusively in the vernacular after this point.[9] When encountered by post-Conquest scribes, the clauses offered an important witness to Anglo-Saxon perceptions of the advantages of the vernacular when discussing regional geography.[10] Ancient, royal, yet local, Old English provided a key model for later readers interested in contesting institutional claims through portrayals of language history.

Approaches to the Latin and vernacular texts within an archive varied widely, and included the copying, adaption, translation, and deletion of material. When shaping archives to meet the demands of contemporary circumstances, textual modification did not necessarily seem out of place: charters were narrative documents, designed to record a preferred version of events which the monastery intended future generations to remember.[11] These concerns were manifested in the *Liber benefactorum* of Ramsey Abbey, which offered one of the fullest twelfth-century discussions of the reasons for archival preservation. The text was produced *c.* 1170 in order to provide a permanent memorial to the abbey's benefactors; however, when commemorating their donations, it silently augmented the rights and possessions which they granted to Ramsey.[12] Citing the anxieties of the Anarchy and the troubled abbacy of Walter (1133–1160), the compiler aimed to protect the abbey's holdings from future depredations:

> Cujus dispersionis, quae rerum fere omnium dissipationem secuta est, nos, utcunque collectae reliquiae, et nubilosa tandem caligine per clementiam divinam in serenitatem conversa, cartarum nostrarum privilegiorum quoque

et cyrographorum cedulas de antiquitatis strue recollectas, omnes in volu-
men unum, (quae Anglice scriptae fuerant in Latinum ydioma conversas,)
ad cautelam futurorum et legentium notitiam censuimus congerendas.[13]

We, the reassembled remnants of that scattering which followed the destruction of nearly everything, have somehow been gathered together. Now that
cloudy gloom at last has been turned to fair weather through divine mercy,
we have decided to reclaim from the heap of antiquity all the regathered
scraps of our charters, privileges and chirographs into one volume (having
translated those which were written in English into the Latin language) as a
safeguard and account for future readers.

Significantly, the compiler's strategy of archival protection was one of translation, and based on the problems experienced by the community in com-
prehending Old English. His sensitivity to these difficulties seems to derive
from personal experience, but was framed as a response to a legacy of political uncertainty.[14] Emphasising the linguistic disruption caused by the Conquest, he stated that 'after the rule of the Normans in England, letters
of this kind were less used and less comprehended' ('post dominationem
Normannorum in Anglia hujusmodi apices minus usitati, minus cogniti
habentur').[15] Translating vernacular charters into Latin became an increasingly popular strategy in cartularies, as pre-Conquest English gradually
became more distant from twelfth- and thirteenth-century usage (compare British Library, MS Cotton Nero D.i below). However, translation
could also provide a veil for archival manipulation. Admitting that some
English documents at Ramsey had been lost through age or carelessness,
the compiler argued that this was unimportant, as the benefactions they
recorded were anyway included in the confirmation charter of Edgar the
Peaceable.[16] As Edgar's charter is forged, the lost documents may not have
existed.[17] They have been invoked not out of a desire for historical accuracy,
but in order to augment the authority of the Latin charter: the *Liber Benefactorum* acknowledged the power of 'extremely old documents written in
English' ('vetustissimis scedulis Anglice scriptum') to silence contemporary
scepticism.[18]

In other cases, pre-Conquest English documents were not merely
evoked, but created anew. At Bury St Edmunds in the eleventh century,
the abbey fabricated a Latin charter of Cnut with an accompanying Old
English version in order to claim a significant range of privileges.[19] These
forgeries necessitated a close study of Bury's existing archive: the vernacular text was concocted by borrowing large portions of its phraseology from
a bilingual writ of Edward the Confessor.[20] It may have been intended to

serve as evidence in a dispute between Abbot Baldwin and the Bishop of
East Anglia, which was finally settled in favour of Baldwin in 1081, following his display of written *praecepta* from Edward and Cnut, amongst
others.[21] It is unclear why an Old English version was thought to be necessary: it may seek to reflect the bilingual form of its model, Edward's writ.[22]
The text illustrates both the attention paid to the language and conventions of vernacular texts, and the forgers' assumptions that English formed
an integral part of some pre-Conquest royal charters.[23] By the twelfth century, it seems that some readers of Bury's vernacular texts felt that authority
was transmitted via minute linguistic detail. Richard Sharpe notes the care
with which a Latin writ-charter of William Rufus translates the language of
its English exemplar from William I: Bury preserved several sequences of
these documents, which showed successive kings re-confirming the rights
granted by their predecessors to the abbey for the duration of their own
reigns.[24] Although the importance of reproducing the form and content
of previous textual models was clear, the writer also attempted a very close
replication of the writ-charter's linguistic idiosyncrasies, often producing
calques of vernacular idioms. Bury's scriptorium gave its Old English materials unusually intense attention.[25] However, these scribal interests were
also manifested in archives elsewhere to differing degrees. As monasteries
attempted to validate privileges via the preservation or fabrication of documentary evidence, they became increasingly sensitive to the potential of
Old English (alongside Latin) to embody traditions and rights.

As elsewhere, St Albans abbey sought to protect its possessions in the
climate of uncertainty which followed 1066: it launched an ambitious
campaign with notable success, resulting in a significant rise in its post-
Conquest status and revenues.[26] The efforts to support or augment the
abbey's standing were sustained across a variety of texts and genres, including several works which employ or evoke vernacular documentation. It
seems likely that St Albans abbey had a very small pre-Conquest archive:
its unsettled early history before its refoundation in the late tenth century
probably resulted in the loss of key documents, perhaps aggravated by a
failure to preserve a written record of benefactions at the time they were
granted.[27] The surviving charters account for less than half the holdings of
the monastery as recorded in the Domesday survey.[28] These obvious lacuna
were a source of concern to its medieval community, and steps were taken
to remedy the deficiency. Julia Crick has demonstrated that St Albans in the
mid-twelfth century was a centre of 'hands-on antiquarianism': the scriptorium produced a series of forged or interpolated pre-Conquest Latin documents which were designed to demonstrate the monastery's ancient claims

to exemption from royal and episcopal interference.[29] As this campaign
sought to create supposedly ancient rights anew, as much as to preserve
them, St Albans acquired exceptional status by the end of the twelfth century: the geographical boundaries of its liberty were unusually extensive,
growing from the zone of exemption of fifteen churches defined in 1157
to encompass most of south-west Hertfordshire.[30] The extent of its juris-
dictional immunity was similarly far-reaching: the monastery was exempt
from visitation by the Diocesan bishop, had the power to exclude the king's
officials, could refuse to pay some taxes, and had various judicial rights.[31]
This self-perception as the rightful holder of an ancient Anglo-Saxon privilege was responsible for a carefully co-ordinated archival programme of the
preservation and selective updating of pre-Conquest documents. The community realised the value of their special status, and carefully maintained
it through the judicious manipulation of written record.

Old English played a significant role in the presentation of the St Albans
archive to the world beyond the monastery, and stimulated a deeper imaginative engagement with the opportunities offered by vernacular data. Aside
from three single sheets, our knowledge of all the charters of St Albans
now derives from one cartulary, which was completed after 1156 and probably before the second quarter of the thirteenth century.[32] Although the
manuscript itself is now lost, its contents can be reconstructed via several sources, the fullest of which is a seventeenth-century Bollandist copy
discovered by Simon Keynes.[33] The lost cartulary offered readers carefully selected windows into St Albans's pre-Conquest history, knowingly or
unknowingly using layers of forged material to frame its core contentions.
Some of these textual modifications may be the work of the twelfth-century
compilers themselves. The cartulary featured three copies of an earlier,
forged diploma of the house's founder, King Offa (d.796), two of which
were augmented with material from the papal bull of 1156 which definitively
created the liberty of St Albans.[34] In preserving and shaping the archival
inheritance of St Albans, the compilers of the lost cartulary directed the
abbey's later defenders to texts which connected present privileges to the
ancient past. Significantly, they felt that the vernacular offered an important way to make this connection tangible. The lost cartulary featured an
unusual amount of Old English material (copied from material earlier than
the twelfth century, and very largely genuine); the scribes also retained insular characters in proper names.[35] Its close attention to language and script
formed only one aspect of a broader awareness that material artefacts could
provide historical evidence to substantiate the abbey's contentions regarding the priority of its traditions.

The necessity of replicating, translating or modifying pre-Conquest English material encouraged further experiments with the ways in which the vernacular could encode historical detail. The *Gesta Abbatum Monasterii Sancti Albani* explores the dialogue between the preservation and augmentation of vernacular evidence which shaped the compilation of monastic archives. It now survives only as part of the *Liber additamentorum*, produced by Matthew Paris in the mid-1250s: a separate quire now bound with the manuscript contains the charters of the lost cartulary in abbreviated form, which has been annotated in his hand.[36] Moving away from the attention to Old English displayed in the lost cartulary, Matthew Paris preserved the charters in Latin alone and edited out the vernacular. This probably reflected the same concerns about comprehension shown earlier at Ramsey: a confident reading knowledge of pre-Conquest English was a rare skill by the mid-thirteenth century. However, the versions of the lost cartulary and the *Gesta Abbatum* in the *Liber additamentorum* (British Library MS Cotton Nero D.i) both offer Matthew Paris's thirteenth-century response to the twelfth-century literature of St Albans, and its interest in the vernacular. In the absence of a prior copy of the *Gesta Abbatum*, it is unclear how far his text altered his earlier sources. Cotton Nero D.i contains a note on the top margin of the opening page, which states that the work was compiled:

> Secundum antiquum rotulum Bartholomaei Clerici qui cum Domino Adam Cellarario diu fuerat, serviens ei, et ipsum rotulum sibi retinuit, de scriptis suis hoc solum eligens.[37]

> According to the ancient roll of Bartholomew the clerk who was with Adam the Cellarer a long time, serving him, and kept this roll for himself, choosing this one alone from his writings.

Adam was active *c.*1140–1176, so the roll would already have been old when read by Matthew Paris.[38] This ambiguously phrased acknowledgement is open to several interpretations, but Mark Hagger has recently made a convincing case that Bartholomew's roll provided the underlying narrative structure for the *Gesta Abbatum* up to the mid-twelfth century, even if Matthew Paris continued to embellish the text.[39] Significantly, the lost cartulary also contained material which was connected to the office of the cellarer. The two interpolated copies of the diploma of Offa (discussed above) were incongruously separated from each other by accounts concerning the monks' kitchen, dating from the abbacy of Geoffrey de Gorham (1119–1146);[40] information taken from these accounts was also included in the *Gesta Abbatum*'s narrative of the time of Geoffrey.[41] It is hence possible that Adam the Cellarer was involved in the genesis of both works, which shared an interest in the ways that historical forms of the vernacular affirmed broader portrayals of the past.[42] This complex text offers two layers of responses to the history of St Albans. Firstly, twelfth-century writers gave their perspective on the pre-Conquest period in the source materials for Matthew Paris's *Gesta Abbatum*. Secondly, Matthew's own version of the text responded to these twelfth-century perceptions, which also reflected his own views of the abbey's early history. Here, both layers will be considered as a whole: although the existing form of the work has doubtless been shaped by Matthew, it is also likely to encode twelfth-century interests in the presentation of the past via ancient language and documents.

Like the cartulary, the *Gesta Abbatum* attempted to furnish arguments for those wishing to defend the abbey's status, this time in response to threats from Ely and Bishop Robert of Lincoln.[43] Though the claims it made were prompted by wider imperatives of litigation and prestige, it may have been primarily intended for circulation amongst an internal readership.[44] If so, then its authors spoke more to a favourably inclined St Albans audience than the house's external critics: this allowed them to move beyond the verifiable and the probable to focus on the desirable. The text sought to strengthen the community's institutional identity by recording an idealised version of its history for future generations; it offered a partisan narrative which often preferred historically alluring scenarios to factual accuracy. Yet we might ask whether the laboured elaborateness of some of these explanations deliberately invited, if not disbelief, then at least a heightened sense of the constructed nature of historical argument. By straining the limits of credibility, the text encouraged readers to consider the tensions and elisions involved in the writing of institutional history, even whilst emphasising the triumphant continuity of St Albans traditions in the face of adversity. The *Gesta Abbatum* thus becomes a literary space for the dramatisation and dismissal of anxieties concerning the absence of historical proof.

Whilst the lost cartulary replicated the details of its Old English exemplars in order to convince readers that it recorded genuine charters, the *Gesta Abbatum* created imaginary depictions of the vernacular evidence capable of substantiating its startlingly ambitious historical claims. Two important episodes both related to archaeological investigations into the Roman foundations of the town. A strange blend of the factual and the fantastic, these revealed a disused dragon cave alongside the Roman artefacts which corroborated the existing saints' lives of Alban. The text's idealised portrayals of documentary and etymological vernacular testimony will be examined here in order to trace some of the opportunities perceived by twelfth-century writers (in dialogue with Matthew Paris in this instance) when approaching language history.

The Impermanence of Textual Sources

Issues surrounding evidence, textuality, and belief crystallised in one episode which related the discovery of an ancient book written in British (portrayed by Matthew Paris as occurring in the tenth century). Like much of the Anglo-Saxon material in the *Gesta Abbatum*, this section was a late elaboration designed to cover significant gaps in the monastic archive.[45] The narrator stated that in the course of archaeological investigations, a hollow in a wall was found, containing several small books and scrolls, and with them an unknown volume:

> [D]um fossores muros et abscondita terrae rimarentur, in medio civitatis antiquae cujusdam magni palatii fundamenta diruerunt, et cum tantorum vestigia aedificiorum admirarentur, invenerunt in cujusdam muri concavo, deposito quasi armariolo cum quibusdam minoribus libris et rotulis, cujusdam codicis ignotum volumen, quod parum fuit ex tam longaeva mora demolitum. Cujus nec littera nec idioma alicui tunc invento cognitum, prae antiquitate, fuerat; venustae tamen formae, et manifestae litterae, fuerat; quarum epigrammata et tituli aureis litteris fulserunt redimiti. Asseres querni, ligamina serica, pristinam in magna parte fortitudinem et decorem retinuerunt. De cujus libri notitia cum multum longe lateque fuerat diligenter inquisitum, tandem unum senem, jam decrepitum, invenerunt sacerdotem, litteris bene eruditum, nomine 'Unwonam': qui, imbutus diversorum idiomatum linguis ac litteris, legit distincte et aperte scripta libri praenominati.[46]

While diggers were investigating the walls and the hidden things of the earth, in the middle of the ancient city they excavated the foundations of a huge palace, and when they were admiring the remains of such large building works, they found in a hollow of a wall, as though left in a book box, with lesser books and rolls, an unknown volume in the form of a codex, which so protracted a space of time was insufficient to destroy. Due to its antiquity, neither its script nor language were known to anyone then found there; however, it was of ancient appearance and clear letter forms; its inscriptions and titles shone, adorned with golden letters. Its oak boards and silken bands largely retained their former strength and beauty. Information about these books was diligently sought far and wide amongst many. At last they found an old, even decrepit, priest, very learned, Unwona by name: who, instructed in the languages and scripts of many different tongues, read clearly and accurately the writings of the aforementioned book.

The volume was found to contain a history of the protomartyr St Alban, agreeing in all respects with that provided by Bede in the *Ecclesiastical History*.[47] As the other books contained pagan rites of Apollo and Mercury, the abbot caused them to be burnt, but consigned the *Historia Sancti Albani* to the cathedral treasury, where it was translated by Unwona, in order that its events could be disseminated more widely through preaching. Yet this Latin translation superseded the vernacular testimony of the original text, whose obsolescence was soon dramatically indicated:

> Cum autem conscripta historia in Latino pluribus, ut jam dictum est, innotuisset, exemplar primitivum ac originale, – quod mirum est dictu, – irrestaurabiliter in pulverem subito redactum, cecidit annullatum.[48]

> But when the written history in Latin had made itself known to many, as has already been described, the original and primitive exemplar, – a thing marvellous to relate – was suddenly reduced to dust irrevocably, and fell to nothing.

Whilst the episode closely reflects a monastic desire to possess conclusive and permanent written evidence, the status of this evidence is complicated by the literal and figurative instability of the vernacular.

The description of the incident has been shaped by the literary conventions of the *Schriftauffindung*, a topos which employs the discovery of an old book to support narrative contentions.[49] Whilst this tells us little about Anglo-Saxon St Albans, it offers much more information about medieval perceptions of the ability of documents to verify history. The account is reminiscent of the biblical depiction of the discovery of the Torah scrolls during the restoration of the Temple in 2 Chronicles 34:14. Just as this prompts the Israelites to return to the formerly lost teachings of God's laws, the finding of the British text similarly seems to promise renewal through ancient knowledge. Other monasteries also found the trope to be persuasive. While copying the annals up to 1121 at Peterborough, the scribe of manuscript E of the Anglo-Saxon Chronicle interpolated a similar story of the discovery of ancient documents under the year 963, which led to the monastery's refoundation by Æthelwold:

> Syððon com se biscop Aðelwold to þære mynstre þe wæs gehaten Medeshamstede ðe hwilon wæs fordon fra heðene folce. Ne fand þær nan þing buton ealde weallas 7 wilde wuda; fand þa hidde in þa ealde wealle writes þet Headda abbot heafde ær gewriton: hu Wulfhere kyng 7 Æðelred his broðor hit heafden wroht, 7 hu hi hit freodon wið king 7 wið biscop 7

wið ealle weoruldþeudom, 7 hu se papa Agatho hit feostnode mid his write 7 se arcebiscop Deusdedit. Leot wircen þa þet mynstre . . . [50]

Afterwards the bishop Æthelwold came to the monastery which was called *Medeshamstede*, which was formerly ravaged by heathen people, [and] found nothing there but old walls and wild woods; then found, hidden in the old walls, writings that Abbot Hedde had earlier written, as to how King Wulfhere and Æthelred, his brother, had constructed it, and how they freed it from king, and from bishop, and from all worldly service; and how the pope Agatho confirmed it with his writ – and the archbishop Deusdedit. Then he had the monastery constructed . . . [51]

This intervention was part of a series of twenty passages which aimed to situate the claims of Peterborough's earlier Latin charters within the Chronicle's historical narrative.[52] The 'writes' of Abbot Hedda apparently refer to a version of the *Relatio Hedde Abbatis*, which now survives only in Peterborough's earliest cartulary, the *Liber Niger*, probably dating from the second quarter of the twelfth century.[53] A 'judiciously constructed origin legend', the *Relatio* was perhaps produced during the abbacy of Ernulf (1107–1114).[54] It purported to be Hedda's seventh-century Latin account of the monastery's foundation *c.*654–655 (thereby placing it earlier than its neighbour, Ely), and was followed by the confirmation of several key privileges in a dossier of 'breathtaking' forgeries.[55] By creating an entry for Hedda's discovery of the documents, and by translating their contents, the compilers of the *Chronicle* were participating in the broader integration of the *Relatio* across Peterborough house histories.[56] Yet these insertions also exploited the continuous tradition of composition evinced by the *Chronicle*. The text's ancient origins lent credence to the claims made by the *Relatio*; its employment of Old English emphasised its connection to the pre-Conquest past.

As at Peterborough, the St Albans *Gesta Abbatum* employed the discovery of a prestigious vernacular work in order to authenticate the historical contentions of key Latin texts. The account of Alban's martyrdom in the British book was ostensibly confirmed by Bede's *Ecclesiastical History*. However, the book's authoritative status allowed it, in turn, to provide important confirmation for Bede. The *Ecclesiastical History* was unequivocal about Alban's status as Romano-British, rather than English, placing his death at the hands of the Romans during the persecutions of Diocletian, and thus ensuring the saint's primacy as the earliest Christian martyr in Britain.[57] This chronology formed the foundation of the monastery's claims to privilege; but in the later twelfth century, the house's unbroken connection with Alban seemed under threat due to controversy over the final resting place of the relics of St Alban. By the composition of the *Liber Eliensis* in the 1170s, Ely's chapter were claiming that the relics had been brought to Ely in secret after the Norman Conquest, and buried next to their own patron saint, Ætheldreða.[58] Rather than simply refuting these claims, the authors of the *Gesta Abbatum* inserted a complicated counterstory, asserting that the bones had never left the abbey, and that Ely had merely received a false, decoy set given to them at the time of Cnut's invasion in order to fool the Danes into thinking that Alban's relics had been sent elsewhere.[59] Further stages of verification were added later in the text. Whilst the account of the recovery of the British book from the ruins of Roman St Albans in the *Gesta Abbatum* did not testify to the presence of Alban's relics in the twelfth-century monastery, it verified Bede's account of their original burial, lending further weight to the monks' arguments for primacy.

The authors' employment of the vernacular arose from a desire to demonstrate the ancient, yet local roots of Alban's cult, and its unbroken continuity. This was part of a larger interest in setting of the martyrdom, and in the kinds of source texts which might yield information on the subject. Such interest had undoubtedly been stimulated by the appearance of a new history of Britain in the late 1130s, which provided a wealth of previously unknown detail on the island's earliest inhabitants: Geoffrey of Monmouth's *Historia regum Britanniae*. Importantly, the text explained its deviation from authorities on early Britain such as Bede and Nennius by claiming to be a translation from a new, vernacular source text: 'a very old book in the British tongue' ('Britannici sermonis librum uetustissimum').[60] Like many others, those at St Albans saw the text's considerable potential to enhance the status of their own patron saint, both in the details of Geoffrey's narrative, and in his broader use of the British vernacular. In 1177, the monks had staged the miraculous recovery of the body of Alban's companion from a burial site on their land at Redbourn, before translating his relics to a shrine within the abbey church.[61] This new saint, Amphibalus, was a shadowy figure whose name ultimately reflects Geoffrey's misreading of a graecism for 'mantle', either in Gildas or in a now-lost gloss of Bede.[62] But Geoffrey may also have been making a subtle joke about the saint's provenance: the name can be read as a Greek adjective meaning 'ambiguous' or 'doubtful'.[63] The St Albans community chose to overlook these incongruities: it seems that the new details on Alban's martyrdom were too appealing to be questioned. Moreover, the putative language of Geoffrey's source fitted well with an increasing post-Conquest stress on Alban as England's earliest martyr. Descriptions of the saint as *protomartyr Anglorum* were augmented to *protomartyr Britanniae* in post-Galfridian texts.[64] The lost work in the 'British tongue' offered a tempting new perspective on the house's early history, which the monks were eager to emphasise.

Yet this alertness to the potential of ancient Latin and vernacular documents in constructing the past also suggests an unspoken awareness of their significance to enterprises of forgery. It is unclear how far the first monks to promote the cult of Amphibalus were fully convinced by the *Historia regum Britanniae*. Geoffrey of Monmouth occupied an ambiguous position amongst twelfth-century scholars: whilst many found it expedient to believe in his startling reassessment of Britain's early history, others were more sceptical.[65] Although highly sensitive to the linguistic nuances of British, the *Gesta Abbatum* does not necessarily depict its interpretation as an entirely innocent activity. The name chosen for the book's translator, Unwona, emphasised his role as a witness to the miraculous, recalling earlier house traditions. At the same time, it may have pointed subtly to a nexus of concerns about archival research and falsification. It is likely that the authors came across this extremely rare name in some of the abbey's oldest documents. The lost cartulary included Bishop Unwona of Leicester (i.e. Unwano/Unwana, active *c*.780) in the witness list of several of the earliest charters from the reigns of Offa and his son Ecgfrith: these confirmed some of the abbey's most important rights.[66] Unwona's name probably indicates a continental Germanic provenance, and there is no reason to doubt his historical authenticity.[67] He remained an influential presence in house histories. The *Vitae duorum Offarum* is an innovative Latin biography of King Offa II (whom the *Gesta Abbatum* portrays as the abbey's founder), which explores his links to his ancestor King Offa I (who first vowed to establish the abbey).[68] It is preserved in Cotton Nero D.i amongst other manuscripts, and may have been written by Matthew Paris or an anonymous twelfth-century author. Here, Unwona is depicted as Offa's chancellor, and a key witness to the miracle which allowed the king first to locate Alban's relics, and then to translate them into a new reliquary.[69] Yet Unwona's name also had other resonances. There is a small chance that, on the strength of comparison with Welsh *un*, 'one', it was considered to be a suitable example of British.[70] However, to English ears, the name was reminiscent of another word: *unwon(e)*, 'unaccustomed, unprecedented'.[71] If this drew attention to the rarity of Unwona's linguistic skills, it also signalled the potential artifice of the account. We are invited to overcome any suspicions through faith: the less credible the events seem, the more miraculous the history of the house appears. Our doubts are raised, only to be triumphantly quelled by directing us to the might of St Alban, his wonder-working powers, and the monastery's long tradition as a witness to his miracles.

The conspicuously uncertain provenance of Unwona and his British book might encourage us to read this episode as an oblique commentary on the nature of forgery itself. Monika Otter classes the account amidst other twelfth-century Latin narratives of historical and archaeological discovery which invite their own literary decoding:

> They seek and find, unearth and open up the historical past, and in that sense describe their own function; they both describe and *are* the originary moment of their textual communities' self-understanding.[72]

This enactment of self-referentiality is particularly evident in the *Gesta Abbatum*'s portrayals of linguistic ancientness. Its authors were aware that historically contingent language could indicate wider circumstances of composition, making full use of the British book's putative linguistic details to establish its age. Yet beyond this pragmatic exploitation of the vernacular, the *Gesta Abbatum* also includes a literary depiction of the significance of linguistic mutability. The value of vernacular evidence, marked by time and place, is manifested in the material qualities of the British book. In the moment of its own divinely ordained destruction, it miraculously witnesses the veracity of the British text it contains: paradoxically, it forms an eternal monument to Alban's sanctity through its own ephemerality.

Like other presentations of ancient language at St Albans, the account has been created largely for practical purposes. The authors of the *Gesta Abbatum* offer a nuanced presentation of British, which systematically employs linguistic detail as a means of grounding the life of Alban in a particular place and time:

> Erat enim littera qualis scribi solet tempore quo cives Werlamecestram inhabitabant, et idioma antiquorum Britonum, quo tunc temporis utebantur.[Aliqua tamen in Latino, sed hiis non opus erat.][73]

> For the script was such as was accustomed to be written in the time when people lived in Werlamecestra, and the language was that of the ancient Britons, in which they then spoke. [However, others spoke in Latin, but it was not used in these writings.]

This may betray an awareness of vernacular dialect variations: unlike standardised Latin, the text's British idiom allows its first reader, the priest Unwona, to locate its origin in 'Werlamecestra' or Verulamium, the Roman city of St Albans.[74] Whilst this emphasis on ancient place names again responded to Geoffrey of Monmouth, in other ways, it sought to move beyond British linguistic data to consider the vernacular past as a whole. The text's inclusion of this name was part of its evocation of both English and British vernacular testimony: as well as its references to the British language, it employed the Anglo-Saxon names given by Bede for 'Verulamium', 'which the English now call either *Uerlamacæstir* or *Uæclingacæstir*' ('Uerolamium, quae nunc a gente Anglorum Uerlamacaestir siue Uaeclingacaestir appellatur').[75] This willingness to use linguistic detail from both English and British enlarged the work's historical frame of reference. Significantly, at the point when the book was translated by Unwona, an element of linguistic uncertainty appeared: it was now described as written in 'the ancient English, or British language' ('antiquo Anglico, vel Britannico, idiomate').[76] The authors of the *Gesta Abbatum* situated the ancient volume in both ancient Britain and Anglo-Saxon England.

We might see the authors' vagueness about the volume's language as an appeal to the prestige not only of British, but of English historical documents. A closer inspection of other St Albans engagements with the vernacular reveals that Old English texts provided an influential model for depictions of ancient sources. There are further parallels with another St Albans work which employed an equally sophisticated approach to the authenticating power of vernacular language. Writing around 1178, William of St Albans created a Latin prose narrative of the martyrdoms of Alban and Amphibalus.[77] His text was also portrayed as a translation of vernacular source, this time of 'a book written in the English language' ('liber Anglico sermone conscriptus').[78] However, William's account introduced a further historical layer: in a second prologue, the English book was in turn depicted as a transcript of writings still visible on the ruins of St Albans.[79] These writings contained an account of Alban's martyrdom. The English-speaking author in this second prologue was transcribing the Roman text a substantial period later, but still before the widespread conversion of the country to Christianity. Here, the vernacular was used, not to situate the text in the British past of the protomartyr, but to create the voice of a historically authentic witness to the physical evidence remaining of Alban's martyrdom in Anglo-Saxon times. Yet whilst acknowledging the importance of vernacular evidence, both texts did not locate its value in its durability. As with the British book of the *Gesta Abbatum*, William explained the absence of his Anglo-Saxon narrator's source text through its impending disintegration:

Cives quondam Verolamii, ob elationem cordis sui declarandam qualiter passus sit beatissimus Albanus in muris suae civitatis sculptum reliquerunt:

quam sc[ul]pturam, longo post tempore, in muris eorum, jam ruinosis et ad
ruinam inclinatis, inveni[.][80]

The former citizens of Verulamium, in order to make known their hearts'
exaltation at the suffering of blessed Alban, left behind engravings on their
city walls. I found these carvings long afterward on the same walls, now
ruinous and decaying.[81]

By heightening a sense of its antiquity, such a portrayal paradoxically verified the testimony given by the original text even as its self-destruction put
it beyond the reach of scholarly enquiry.

These displays of self-consumption challenged some models of textual
evidence as eternal witness which were valorised in the cartularies of St
Albans. In his study of Anglo-Saxon diplomas, Scott Thompson Smith
argues that: 'by making timeless claims for land in a sacred environment,
the Anglo-Saxon diploma attempted to fix possession and to refuse change-
ability, and these affirmations of permanence were driven in part by resilient
fears of imminent conflict and reversal'.[82] The proems to such diplomas often appealed to the durability of the written word, even whilst
acknowledging the transience of human possession.[83] The archive at St
Albans contained a version of this trope in a charter of Æthelred II (dated
996):[84]

> Licet regalium dignitatum decreta et antiqua priorum temporum priuilegia
> permanente integritatis signaculo fixa iugiter ac firma perseuerent, attamen
> quia plerumque tempestates et turbines seculi fragilem humane uite cur-
> sum pulsantes contra superna dominice sanctionis iura illidunt, iccirco stili
> officio renouanda et cartarum suffragiis sunt roboranda, ne forte successura
> posterorum progenies, ignorato precedentium patrum cyrographo, inextri-
> cabilem horrendi baratri uoraginem incurrat, nec inde libera exire queat
> donec iuxta ueritatis sententiam cuncta usque ad nouissimum quadrantem
> debita plenissime reddat.

> It is lawful that the royal charters and ancient privileges of former ages shall
> endure, fixed and affirmed perpetually with the seal of integrity; however,
> since many storms and whirlwinds of time, battering the fragile course of
> human life, dash against heavenly laws of sacred binding force, with the
> help of writing they must therefore be renewed and by means of charters
> strengthened, lest perhaps future descendants of later generations, having
> no knowledge of the chirograph of their preceding ancestors, may rush into
> the inextricable chasm of fearsome hell; nor can they leave free from thence
> until they shall entirely fulfil the judgement of truth in all debts even unto
> the last farthing.

This proem is likely to be genuine, and contains substantial verbal parallels with a diploma of Æthelred's father, Edgar.[85] Here, the charter was portrayed as the outward sign of an eternal grant to God's church. In spite of the fact that its material form might decay or perish, the property transfer which it recorded remained eternally valid. By echoing the Sermon on the Mount (Matthew 5:25–26), the proem conflated earthly and divine transgression, situating retribution with Christ, the ultimate judge. Probably after 1107, later readers at St Albans exploited its rhetoric of renewal, inserting a new immunity clause which purported to confirm the privileges contained in an old charter of Offa.[86] This may have been intended to support wider documentary manipulation: around the same time, the monks fabricated a diploma of Offa from earlier sources, which laid claim to the core endowment of the house.[87] Yet if these alterations show a belief in the charter as a permanent monument to the monastery's possessions, they also suggest anxiety about the vulnerability of written record to indifference and decomposition. The forgers' actions reflect a wider pattern of late Anglo-Saxon and post-Conquest concerns: from the late tenth century onwards, the extant charters which demonstrated St Albans's title to its contemporary holdings were felt to be insufficient. Noticing that the documents of previous generations had decayed, been destroyed, or simply never been written, the monks decided to supplement the archive with their own creations. They were aware that endurance of the charter as a witness was threatened by dangers of neglect, corrosion, and forgetfulness.

Under these circumstances, the destruction of the British book provides a different perspective on textual instability. Just as the mutability of the vernacular becomes an advantage when locating works in their historical and geographical context, the fragility of the material text also becomes paradoxically advantageous. The *Gesta Abbatum* offers a fantasy to readers concerned with the preservation of monastic documents. In contrast to charters, the corrosive effects of time do not threaten the witness of the British book. Rather, the very source of its strength lies in its mutable nature. Far from interfering with its ability to testify to God's will, when the British book crumbles to dust, it confirms that its narrative of Alban's life is a divine revelation. The book enacts the value of vernacular impermanence.

Testimony to the Truth: Vernacular Etymologies

If in many ways the episode of the British book represents the apotheosis of vernacular textuality, the authors of the *Gesta Abbatum* were also aware of the potential of etymological testimony to promote the cult of Alban. In the passage immediately preceding Abbot Eadmer's excavations, they depicted prior archaeological research into ancient Verulamium. This laid the foundations for the British book's later confirmation of Bede's account, but here, the finds were validated by the linguistic witness of local inhabitants. Increasing interest in grounding evidence in a particular period and area transformed perceptions not only of the worth of vernacular written records but also of oral evidence. These re-evaluations of impermanent language encouraged an expansion of the types of vernacular data subjected to scholarly scrutiny, and a modification of the etymological paradigms employed in its interpretation. The vernacular's appeal was situated in the mutability which allowed it to be shaped by its temporal and geographical surroundings.

The *Gesta Abbatum* stated that Eadmer's predecessor, abbot Ealdred, ordered excavations to be carried out within the remains of the Roman city, based on unspecified *antiquae scripturae*. The finds included anchors, shells, sand, and parts of ships, suggesting the prior existence of a large body of water. Material evidence was able to establish the authority of earlier martyrdom narratives on Roman Verulamium: the authors commented that the miracle by which the large river became a small one was narrated in full in the *Historia de Sancto Albano*.[88] This may have been intended as a reference to Unwona's British book; or to an episode in William's hagiography where the Ver miraculously dries up in response to a prayer from Alban.[89] Given that, according to Bede, Alban's miracles also involved parting the waters of the river and temporarily relocating it to the top of a hill, the saint's power was rendered far more impressive to a medieval audience by emphasising that the Ver had been navigable in Roman times.[90] Yet, significantly, a further layer of confirmation was felt to be required. As the excavations continued, the diggers unearthed previously forgotten linguistic tradition:

> Unde nomina locis ubi talia repererunt incolae, haec videntes, vel imposuerunt, vel retulerunt se a veteribus relata meminisse: utpote, Oistrehulle, Selleford, et Ancrepol.[91]

> When the local inhabitants saw these things, either they bestowed new names on the locations where they had been discovered, or otherwise they were prompted to remember the names they had been told by their forefathers: like Oysterhill, Shelford and Anchorpool.

Matthew Paris seems to have found this passage a convincing demonstration of the longevity of local memory. In his manuscript, he augmented the list of names, adding in a marginal gloss: 'Fishpol, – nomen vivarii regii ex reliquiis aque diminute' ('Fishpool – the name of the royal fishpond made out of the remains of the diminished waters').[92] The evidence of the *incolae* is only employed as a prelude to the appearance of the British book, suggesting that the volume's miraculous discovery ultimately carries greatest conviction. Yet, if playing a supportive role, oral material is not in competition with the written. Rather, it is uniquely placed to connect text with the historical landscape.

This creative use of oral data to provide geo-historical evidence offers a subtly different perspective on some existing social and epistemological hierarchies. Rather than stressing aristocratic or ecclesiastical authority, it draws more heavily on the perceptions of local knowledge implied by practices of boundary perambulation when delineating estates. Elisabeth van Houts has analysed the widespread use of oral sources in twelfth-century historiography, arguing that authors had a stratified understanding of such testimony. As well as privileging eyewitness accounts, they were also concerned with the status of the witness: information from high-ranking men was preferred.[93] According to their lowly social status, the oral testimony of peasants should have held little authority. However, the *Gesta Abbatum*'s treatment of vernacular evidence is part of a wider trend which encourages us to re-interpret such testimony. As their ability to move away from a particular estate was often subject to restrictions, peasant language was perceived to have evolved within a specific local area.[94] This connection to the landscape, stretching back over several generations, was exploited by twelfth-century authors seeking to situate narratives within local geography. Not all chose to convince their readers via an emphasis on the vernacular. Boundary clauses were copied less frequently in the period: although in part, this was due to difficulties or anxieties surrounding the continued comprehension of Old English, other models of linguistic prestige were also available.[95] However, the use of vernacular evidence from oral sources presented a fundamental challenge to those who thought linguistic expertise to be founded on grammatical and social training. Instead of investing the educated or the aristocratic with the greatest authority, it offered a startlingly egalitarian perspective: knowledge of a given vernacular was available to anyone in contact with the relevant speech community. When employing oral testimony to root historical arguments in a landscape, language which displayed local idiosyncrasies was often more highly prized.

Interest in these idiosyncrasies encouraged a reassessment of previous methods for studying language history, drawing attention to the exegetical opportunities presented by the ephemeral instead of the eternal. As discussed in the introduction, Isidore of Seville remained the central medieval authority on Latin etymology, for whom reality was 'primarily a verbal structure which could be comprehended by the analysis of words'.[96] However, not all vocabulary offered the potential for a Neo-platonic recovery of divine intention. Isidore explicitly included vernacular words in his comprehensive catalogue of etymological techniques, although he noted possible difficulties of comprehension:

> Sunt autem etymologiae nominum aut ex causa datae, ut 'reges' a regendo et recte agendo, aut ex origine, ut 'homo', quia sit ex humo, aut ex contrariis ut a lavando 'lutum', dum lutum non sit mundum, et 'lucus', quia umbra opacus parum luceat. Quaedam etiam facta sunt ex nominum derivatione, ut a prudentia 'prudens'; quaedam etiam ex vocibus, ut a garrulitate 'garrulus'; quaedam ex Graeca etymologia orta et declinata sunt in Latinum, ut 'silva', 'domus'. Alia quoque ex nominibus locorum, urbium, vel fluminum traxerunt vocabula. Multa etiam ex diversarum gentium sermone vocantur. Unde et origo eorum vix cernitur. Sunt enim pleraque barbara nomina et incognita Latinis et Graecis.

> Etymologies of words are furnished either from their rationale, as 'kings' from ['ruling' and] 'acting correctly'; or from their origin, as 'man' because he is from 'earth', or from the contrary, as 'mud' from 'washing', since mud is not clean, and 'grove', because, darkened by its shade, it is scarcely 'lit'. Some are created by derivation from other words, as 'prudent' from 'prudence'; some from sounds, as 'garrulous' from 'babbling sound'. Some are derived from Greek etymology and have a Latin declension, as 'words', 'home'. Other words derive their names from names of place, cities, [or] rivers. In addition, many take their names from the languages of various peoples, so that it is difficult to discern their origin. Indeed, there are many foreign words unfamiliar to Latin and Greek speakers. (I.xxix.3–5)

Amidst this extensive list, Isidore left no place for the derivation of words created 'by whim' ('secundum placitum'), arguing that: 'etymologies are not to be found for all words, because some things received names not according to their innate qualities, but by the caprice of human will' ('omnium nominum etymologiae non reperiuntur, quia quaedam non secundum qualitatem, qua genita sunt, sed iuxta arbitrium humanae voluntatis vocabula acceperunt', I.xxix.2–3). He did not explain why such coinages were unsuitable for etymological scrutiny: presumably because, rather than offering insights into the divine force which shaped both word and referent in Eden, they instead reflected only human concerns.

When exploring vernacular data, the emphasis of etymological study was altered. Rather than seeing names created in recent historical circumstances as ephemeral and hence unworthy of analysis, such names became a central scholarly focus. The transience of vernacular language rendered them uniquely valuable, because they recorded local responses to specific events. This type of etymology was particularly common in hagiographical and historical writing, drawing on pre-Conquest insular interpretative traditions.[97] When reworking an earlier Hiberno-Latin life of St Modwenna, Geoffrey of Burton was at pains to emphasise that his additions reflected the 'trustworthy and reliable report of truthful men, who had knowledge of them from their elders or witnessed them at first hand' ('ueracium ualde uirorum, qui uel didicerunt a maioribus uel ipsi uiderunt atque affureunt presentes, fidelissima et probatissima narracione').[98] His source, Conchubranus, had described the miraculous resurrection of a drowned girl through the intercession of St Modwenna, as witnessed by nearby shepherds.[99] Geoffrey retained the account, but was careful to include a further passage which described the oral dissemination of the story, and its subsequent etymological commemoration:

> Diuulgatum est autem circumquaque istud tam grande miraculum, prius quidem per ora pastorum qui presentes fuerant ac deinde relacionibus quam plurimorum, et fluuius in quo uirgo submersa est Anchora dicitur et illa pars aque ubi ceciderat, quia fuerat sanctimonialis Osid, ad testimonium ueritatis ab incolis loci illius sermone publico usque hodie Nunnepol appellatur.

> Reports of this great miracle spread far and wide, first from the mouths of the shepherds who were present and in the accounts of many others. The river in which the virgin drowned is called the Anker and, because Osgyth was a nun, that part of it where she fell is still called 'Nun's Pool' to this day by the inhabitants of the place as testimony to the truth.[100]

The appeal of etymology lay in its ability to transform each member of its audience into a type of eyewitness: we can confirm the author's etymological interpretation through our own knowledge of the word under discussion. Geoffrey's consideration of this place name was able to demonstrate something more. Like the authors of the *Gesta Abbatum*, who depicted the locals bestowing new names on places found in the course of the excavations, he assumed that toponyms were often created to mark noteworthy occurrences. Here, twelfth-century audience members beyond the immediate vicinity of the river Anker may well have been unable to verify the etymology through their general knowledge.[101] However, by using the testimony of local inhabitants, Geoffrey could provide a group of contemporary witnesses whose knowledge was strengthened by a substantial linguistic inheritance: their authority stemmed from the length of their ancestral association with the land. Not only did the *incolae* attest to the persistence of the name into the twelfth century; they affirmed that their predecessors thought Osgyth's rescue from the waters sufficiently miraculous to mark the spot with a new toponym. This kind of etymology does not directly pursue the recovery of an atemporal, divine truth through close linguistic analysis. Rather, it reconstructs the climate of local wonder prompted by the miracle as historical occurrence. Although this helps to verify that the event took place, which in turn vouchsafes the presence of God on earth, its primary goal is to situate a particular event in time.

Whilst these employments of etymology to recreate the temporally particular sought to modify trans-historical trajectories of language, other aspects of the Isidorean legacy remained influential. In their use of vernacular evidence to substantiate broader arguments, twelfth-century authors were closely informed by contemporary interest in etymology as a technique for rhetorical exegesis. Peter Helias (c.1100–c.1166) wrote:

> Ethimologia ergo est expositio alicuius vocabuli per aliud vocabulum, sive unum, sive plura magis nota, secundum rei proprietatem et litterarum similitudinem ut 'lapis' quasi 'ledens pedem', 'fenestra' quasi 'ferens nos extra'. Hic enim et rei proprietas attenditur et litterarum similitudo observatur.[102]

> Therefore, etymology is the exposition of one word through another word or words which are more familiar, according to the property of the thing and the similarity of letters, such as stone, as it were wounding the feet, window, as it were carrying us outside. Here indeed, the property of the thing is respected and the similarity of letters is observed.[103]

This model continued to follow Isidore by stressing the elucidation of a word's divine inner force (vis): deriving etymology from ethimos (true) and logos (word), Peter noted that 'he who etymologises describes the true, that is the first, origin of the word' ('qui ethimologizat veram, id est primam, vocabuli originem assignat').[104] However, his emphasis on exposition and association shows a growing sense of the ways in which etymology could also be used to provoke new perspectives.

Increasingly, lexical study was seen as a mechanism as much for generating eloquence as linguistic investigation. Peter's definition has been influenced by the grammatical technique of derivation (derivatio): already outlined by Isidore, in the twelfth century this was seen as part of, or related to, the discipline of etymology. The technique aimed 'to create families of terms, of which one was considered as the original and all the others as "derivations" or terms derived from the original one'.[105] In his influential

Liber derivationum, Osbern of Gloucester (*fl.*1148) provided a characteristic treatment of *rivus:*

> Rivus vi, inde hic rivulus li, et rivosus a um, et hic rivalis is .i. ille qui cum alio tenet unam uxorem, unde Terentius in eunucho militis ego rivalem recipiendum censeo. Et per compositionem derivo as, unde derivator, derivatus, derivatio, et derivatim adverbium, sicut dicimus hec pars derivatim dicitur ab illa .i. secundum ordinem derivandi. Item ab hoc nomine quod est rivus et pluraliter hi renes num quia ab eis rivi cenosi humoris dirivantur, et inde hic renunculus li diminutivum, et his reno nis .i. pellicia circa renes, et hoc renale is .i. zona circa renes, et hic rien enis .i. porcellus.[106]

> *Rivus, -vi* ('river'), whence *rivulus, -li* ('rivulet'), and *rivosus, -a, -um* ('endowed with streams'), and *rivalis, -is* ('rival'), which is one who shares a wife with another, hence Terence in *The Eunuch*: 'I suggest [you] accept the rival of the soldier'. And through compounding: *derivo, -as* ('I derive'), whence *derivator* ('deriver'), *derivatus* ('derived'), *derivatio* ('derivation'), and the adverb *derivatim,* just as we say 'this word is said derivatively from that', i.e. according to the order of deriving. Also from the noun *rivus,* in the plural: *renes, -num* ('kidneys'), because from them the filthy streams of humour are drawn off, and whence as a diminutive *renunculus, -li* ('a little kidney'), and *reno, -nis* ('a fur garment'), which is a thing made of skins [wrapped] around the kidneys, and *renale, -is* ('renal'), which is the area around the kidneys, and *rien, -enis,* which is a piglet.

Osbern's presentation of the allusive connections between words created several pathways in parallel, which did not direct readers to any single perspective. Instead, his work aimed to facilitate interpretative plurality. The prologue stated that although beginners may select 'slight and scarce words' ('tenues [. . .] et perraras partes'), experts would 'extend themselves in multiple streams in multiple ways of deriving' ('in multiplices se derivandi rivos multipliciter extendunt').[107] Rather than depicting the linear development of lexis, *derivatio* provided a rhetorical method of linking several ideas and arguments together through language. This form of verbal exegesis was less concerned with tracing historical filiation, than with composition.

The production of twelfth-century vernacular etymologies was therefore poised between sensitivity to the historical specificity of language, and awareness of the discursive possibilities afforded by linguistic interpretation: whilst etymological data could afford unique insights into popular perceptions of language history, it was equally shaped by the imperatives of clerical narration. In one sense, the depiction of language in the *Gesta Abbatum* exemplified the ways in which the study of vernacular linguistic

history offered a counterpoint to presentations of the past which emphasised the timeless exemplarity of God's providential plan.[108] The British
language attested to the Roman date of the *Vita* of St Alban; the historical
witness of place names was confirmed, not via the Edenic reverberations
contained in Isidorean etymologies, but in peasant memory. Yet this historicity was complicated by a simultaneous awareness of linguistic exegesis
as a site for ludic, rhetorical constructions of meaning. Even whilst appealing to the authoritative testimony of ancient languages, the *Gesta Abbatum*
unravelled this authority by raising doubts over the relationship between
linguistic interpretation and desire: etymology, like the discovery of ancient
writings, was driven by the demands of imagination as much as fact.

The last place name given in this passage of the *Gesta Abbatum* explores
the tension between exposition and rhetorical extrapolation: as with the
British book, this episode provides a commentary on the emotional motivations which influence the writing of history. The place names remembered
by the locals impressively substantiate archaeological discovery, connecting the newly uncovered landscape to communal memories of the ancient
past. But the final English toponym supplied in this context exposes the
extent to which such names arre based on hopes for a type of evidence
capable not only of corroborating, but of penetrating and illuminating the
historical subject. We are told that during his excavations, Abbot Ealdred
found the subterranean remnants of Verulamium to be a haunt of thieves
and prostitutes. He therefore decided to raze as much of the remains as was
practicable, although retaining any Roman materials suitable for ecclesiastical construction projects. The last vernacular name provided in the passage
occurs in this context, when the abbot discovers the signs of an abandoned
dragon's lair:

> Specum quoque profundissimum, monte continuo circumseptum, cum
> spelunca subterranea, quam quondam draco ingens fecerat et inhabitavit,
> in loco qui 'Wormenhert' dicitur, in quantum potuit, explanavit; vestigia
> tamen aeterna habitationis serpentinae derelinquens.[109]

> Also he flattened (insofar as he could) the deepest cave, enclosed by the
> unbroken rock, with the underground den which once a huge dragon had
> made and inhabited, in the place which is called 'Wormenhert'; but he left
> behind the still-remaining traces of a serpent's dwelling.

Isidorean etymology purports to reveal the 'innate qualities' ('qualitatem,
qua genita sunt') of any given object.[110] Ealdred's entry into the deepest
cave mirrors this process of etymological penetration. His archaeological
act rejects the recovery of material evidence in favour of the linguistic.

Here, the word itself becomes an artefact. He emerges not only with knowledge of the serpent's den, but with a rationale for its name: the dragon can now be shown to have lived at the heart of the hill. If the historical impulse behind etymological enquiry is dramatised here, the authors did not directly employ etymological methods to elucidate the connection between the dragon's cave and its name. Rather, readers must analyse its onomastic significance for themselves, recreating Ealdred's prior act of toponymic recovery. Other aspects of the name's origins remain suggestively ambiguous: the reasons behind the decision to call the cave 'Wormenhert' are left opaque. Although this could be a freshly bestowed name, the text leaves open the possibility that Ealdred's discoveries has prompted the locals to recollect another archaic epithet previously used by their ancestors. The vernacular is depicted as a repository of material which is both tangibly connected to a semi-fabulous past, and latent in the most ancient recesses of the landscape: etymological investigation proves capable of bringing to light names and things which previously appeared to be buried beyond the reach of memory. Yet as coincidences and correspondences accrue, the narrative's comprehensive fulfilment of the demands of linguistic recovery raises questions concerning its status as fact or fiction. In providing a total (rather than partial) verification of the St Albans past, the authors surpass the limited parameters of what can be verified historically: instead, the narrative becomes what ought to have been true. The more successful the abbot's investigations, the greater our suspicions of the account's veracity become. The *Gesta Abbatum* emphasises the tension between a wish to believe in comprehensive linguistic proof, and the extent to which such credulity can be stretched: it offers a too-perfect correspondence between the type of historical arcana we desire, and that which is supplied. If the account's improbabilities invite us to fantasise about language's power to recover the seemingly lost, they also invite us to consider the implications of our own enjoyment of such historically improbable details. The authors require us not only to be complicit in their fantasy of linguistic recovery, but to explore the reasons why we would wish to be so. Vernacular language history provides a site to evaluate motivations for the creation and consumption of imaginative literature.

Portrayals of Britain's vernaculars offered authors a way to manifest the concerns which lay behind a growing interest in history and written records in the twelfth century. In discussing the motivations behind the sudden florescence of miracle collecting in the post-Conquest era, Rachel Koopmans has rejected the premise that a written dossier was necessary to secure the status of native saints. Rather, she suggests that the compilers of the

seventy-five or so surviving collections were more concerned with potential forgetfulness: 'What they were seeking to defend themselves against
with these texts, it appears, was the weight of time and the fragility of
human memory'.[111] Anxiety over the endurance of remembrance rendered
the past a burden: the compilation of cartularies, the creation of histories, the search for ancient source texts and the tracing of vernacular etymologies all provide examples of the ways in which the twelfth century
was preoccupied with loss. Yet whilst monastic authors were most vocal
in their awareness of the precarious nature of transmitting past traditions,
they also tacitly took advantage of the opportunities destruction brought to
re-shape institutional legacies. The earliest major post-Conquest historian,
Eadmer (c.1060–1126 or after) wrote an elegiac description of Anglo-Saxon
England, enumerating the pre-Conquest cathedral church at Canterbury
as he knew it as a small boy before its destruction by fire in 1067. But his
poignant reconstruction of a vanished era also provided a crucial excuse
for the absence of Christ Church's ancient charters, supposedly destroyed
in the blaze.[112] Between 1070 and 1123 a series of forged papal letters and
privileges were created in the monastery, designed to cement its claim to
primacy over every church in Britain.[113] They were included by Eadmer as
part of an extended assertion of Canterbury's rights in his *Historia novorum in Anglia*: while he may or may not have known of their provenance,
the scriptorium more widely did not scruple to take advantage of their
purported archival losses to fabricate new texts.[114] The interpretation of
Britain's linguistic history in the St Albans *Gesta Abbatum* was situated at
the centre of this awareness of the issues and options created by decay.
Its authors explored the dual need to preserve the past, and to present it
to future generations. The vernacular provided a locus for thinking about
change: although language could be interpreted as a penitential exemplar of
eternal mutability, its instability also allowed writers to consider the different ways in which this historically contingent material could be deployed
to situate texts in specific time periods, or in a more mythical past. As with
earlier insular scholarship, twelfth-century portrayals of Britain's linguistic
history were hence almost never straightforward attempts to recover the
verbal testimony of previous ages. Instead, creative concerns intersected
with the factual, as authors interpreted the vernacular in the light of ambitions, disappointments, and dreams.

CHAPTER 2

Perceptions of English Linguistic and Literary Continuity

Whilst new scrutiny of institutional archives in the post-Conquest period drew attention to vernacular documents as potential evidence of the past, twelfth-century authors were also exploring other types of Old English text to reconstruct prestigious Anglo-Saxon legacies. If some readers seem to have found the written norms of pre-Conquest English increasingly distant from their own idiom, problems of comprehension did not prevent them from situating ancient and modern words on the same spectrum of linguistic continuity. Reading earlier texts encouraged audiences to look for lexical similarities with contemporary language, drawing attention to the development of the vernacular. Several recent studies have convincingly demonstrated the unbroken vitality of English literary culture in the post-Conquest period, partly based on the markedly innovative nature of some of the new compositions, but primarily with reference to the continued adaptation, annotation, and circulation of Old English texts. In response to earlier discussion of twelfth-century English as the product of nostalgic antiquarianism, the weight of investigation in some of these analyses has lain with the connections of English to contemporary culture.[1] This chapter emphasises a different facet of twelfth-century engagements with pre-Conquest vernacular texts by considering how far later readers of Old English were aware of its linguistic and literary past.[2]

Over two hundred manuscripts compiled between 1066 and 1220 survive with some writing in English, ranging from a few lines of marginalia to new compositions and copies of pre-Conquest works.[3] The Old English literary texts whose composition can be securely dated to the twelfth century are comparatively scanty, but there continued to be a strong demand for pre-Conquest texts, especially those with religious content. The audience of Old English was not confined to those reading it for education or enjoyment. Pre-Conquest Latin and vernacular texts were assessed with a pragmatic eye to their pastoral, historical, or legal value: Mark Faulkner has emphasised the engagement of post-Conquest precentors with the earlier manuscript holdings of their institutions, which were identified and catalogued in an 'appraisal of Anglo-Saxon books [which] was one of the major bibliographical achievements of the Anglo-Norman period'.[4] Whilst the examination of pre-Conquest manuscripts was partly motivated by utilitarian considerations, many readers also remained sensitive to the continuing cachet of the Anglo-Saxon literary legacy. This dual awareness of the practical and the prestigious is particularly apparent in twelfth-century engagements with English traditions of law-making. As discussed in the previous chapter, the preservation of pre-Conquest legal records (largely royal writs) formed one of the most pressing motivations for the copying of Old English.[5] Yet the Anglo-Saxon legal corpus was valued as much for its historical authority as for any direct relevance to twelfth-century administration. Several collections of Anglo-Saxon royal legislation were compiled after the Conquest, preserved in the original Old English or in Latin translations. Although they aimed to be comprehensive, their practical application is not immediately obvious: Anglo-Saxon and Anglo-Norman law were both primarily implemented with recourse to custom, rather than written precedent.[6] However, at his coronation, William I had sworn to uphold the laws of Edward the Confessor: these 'legal encyclopaedias' testify to the continuing symbolic importance of the Anglo-Saxon inheritance.[7] Twelfth-century readers remained highly aware of the historical context of pre-Conquest literature, and some were also sensitive to the potential of linguistic detail to embody such context. Divergence between pre- and post-Conquest orthographic and linguistic norms ensured that the twelfth-century disseminators of English implicitly positioned their own language in relation to the diction of earlier texts. Such positioning was shaped both by considered and by less considered responses to a variety of influences. It could reflect scribal preferences for conservatism or modernisation, as well as other educational and environmental factors like scribal training and the linguistic practices of the local area. Older forms of English could be used strategically in order to accentuate, or to attenuate a sense of linguistic continuity.

Confidence in reading pre-Conquest English varied widely, influenced by the age of the text under consideration and the linguistic expertise of its reader. For some, the language seems to have presented little difficulty. As part of his historical research, William of Malmesbury (c.1090–1142 or after) consulted a wide range of pre-Conquest vernacular sources, including some now lost.[8] Of mixed Norman and English ancestry, he was able to read the language well, producing at least one translation.[9] Despite his reservations about the sound of Old English, William was able to make innovative deductions about the history of the language based both on wider historical knowledge, and on his own linguistic observations.[10] He noted the similarities in patterns of naming amongst the Franks and the English:

> Nepos Faramundi fuit Meroueus, a quo omnes post eum reges Merouingi uocati sunt. Eodem modo et filii regum Anglorum a patribus patronomica sumpserunt, ut filius Edgari Edgaring, filius Edmundi Edmunding uocentur, et ceteri in hunc modum; communiter uero athelingi dicuntur. Naturalis ergo lingua Francorum communicat cum Anglis, quod de Germania gentes ambae germinauerint.

> Faramund's grandson was Merovech, from whom all subsequent kings were called Merovings. In the same way the sons of English kings took patronymics from their fathers' names: Edgar's son is called Edgaring, Edmund's Edmunding, and so on, while in general they are named æthelings. Thus the native tongue of the Franks is related to English, because both races germinated from Germany.[11]

William's discussion was grounded in a historical tradition stretching back to Gildas, who had first depicted the arrival of the Angles, Saxons and Jutes from the continent, along with the English language.[12] However, direct considerations of the genesis of English were extremely rare, and William's support of his position via a comparison with Frankish is unique. Despite the pioneering nature of his assessment, his interest in the origins of the language was fleeting: he was more enthused by certain aspects of the English literary tradition, devoting extensive attention to Bede's and Alfred's translations.[13]

Whilst William could read Old English confidently enough to speculate on its origins, for others, the language was becoming increasingly opaque. A significant amount of Old English was translated into Latin or French in the twelfth century. In part, this was to reach wider, non-Anglophone audiences: portions of the *Anglo-Saxon Chronicle* were translated into Latin by John of Worcester and Henry of Huntingdon, and into French by Gaimar.[14] However, Latin translations of English charters, wills and other documents may also betray anxieties about the continuing comprehension of written Old English, even amongst native speakers.[15] Differences between modern and older forms of the language had become more apparent after the Conquest. As early as the second half of the tenth century, texts began to display some of the distinctive phonological changes which would ultimately lead to a radical simplification of the Old English case system.[16]

However, the changing nature of spoken English was largely not reflected in the manuscripts produced in the century before 1066. Regardless of their location, late-tenth- and eleventh-century scribes widely employed a regularised written form of late West Saxon dialect, Standard Old English.[17] This standardised orthography gradually fell into disuse after the Conquest, following William I's decision to issue the vast majority of royal writs in Latin, rather than in English (probably in 1070).[18] Perhaps because there was less of a royal incentive to maintain these spelling conventions, scribes once more began to reflect contemporary language, to varying degrees. Not only did this increased freedom of orthography allow them to experiment with modernising their source texts, it also drew attention to the ways that spoken language had continued to evolve during the period of the ascendancy of Standard Old English.

The new developments in English could present the twelfth-century readers of earlier texts with difficulties. Grammar and lexis were gradually diverging from the written norms of the pre-Conquest era. The twelfth century was a period of transition from late Old English to early Middle English, and approaches to written language were not uniform: influenced by their education and geographical location, scribes exhibited varying levels of linguistic innovation and conservatism.[19] Over the course of the century, the Old English vowel system underwent significant changes, leading to a reduction in the number of vowel inflections available to indicate grammatical case, which in turn had far-reaching implications for syntax.[20] At the same time, English took on many new loanwords, notably from French; words derived from Norse also began to appear in written texts to a much greater extent.[21] These linguistic developments affected comprehension: by the early thirteenth century, the 'Tremulous Hand' glosses of one Worcester scribe indicate that for some, Old English was only partially intelligible.[22] As the challenges of reading pre-Conquest English grew, those exploring earlier vernacular literature were confronted with a body of material written in an increasingly ancient style. This chapter examines two different interpretations of the past literary language of England, considering how far this language was presented as continuous with contemporary speech, and how far its less modern features were emphasised in order to create an impression of age. It discusses contrasting levels of anxiety about language change, and the ways in which these anxieties could influence authorial decisions concerning the treatment of pre-Conquest English language and literature. First situating Henry of Huntingdon's translation of the 'Battle of Brunanburh' in the context of wider twelfth-century engagements with Old English poetry, it then considers the approach to vernacular traditions of Psalm glossing displayed in the Eadwine Psalter.

Henry of Huntingdon: Perceptions of Language Decay in the *Historia Anglorum*

Henry of Huntingdon's thoughtful and admiring responses to Old English verse were partly shaped by an interest in Latin metrics and by his larger engagements with the *Anglo-Saxon Chronicle*. However, he also shared a widespread belief in the close connections between languages and peoples.[23] For Henry, the Anglo-Saxons' valour and nobility was fittingly encoded in their vernacular poetry. But these perceived links between the fortunes of languages and peoples also made him unusually sensitive to the future prospects of Britain's vernaculars. Noticing that both the Picts and Pictish had died out since the time of Bede, Henry did not assume that any of the island's peoples or languages would endure forever.[24] This keen sense of language's historical contingency informed his unusual perspective on English poetry. Rather than searching for linguistic continuities with post-Conquest verse like many of his contemporaries, Henry's depictions of Old English prosody instead emphasised the ancient. Whilst his pioneeringly close translation strategy in the 'Battle of Brunanburh' was designed to encapsulate Anglo-Saxon achievement, this desire to inspire readers' awe through archaic language also influenced the presentation of his source text in other ways. He may have omitted to include the vernacular original of 'Brunanburh' alongside his Latin translation from concern about the future comprehension of Old English. However, it is more likely that he sought to reduce opportunities for readers to make connections between modern usage and the poem's diction. Henry innovatively transplanted the accustomed rhythms of 'Brunanburh' into a quasi-vernacular Latin alliterative metre. Whilst some readers might well have known Old English poetry, the diction and prosody of 'Brunanburh' seems unfamiliar when transposed into Latin. This heightened sense of difference created a far more imposing portrayal of the original text's age, encouraging the perception of ancientness via a process of linguistic alienation.

Henry began to write the *Historia Anglorum* in or after 1123, encouraged by his patron, Alexander, Bishop of Lincoln. He produced five different versions of it over the next thirty years, the last being in 1154.[25] Henry was eager to follow Alexander's recommendation to make extensive use of Bede (p.6). He opened his work with a description of Britain which was heavily indebted to the *Historia Ecclesiastica*, recounting the natural fecundity of Britain, with its rich grazing, pearls, whelks, jet, and other familiar *topoi* of Bede's vision of plenty. Completed in 731, the *Historia Ecclesiastica* listed five languages used in Britain: English, British, Irish, Pictish, and Latin.[26] These existed 'just as the divine law is written in five books, each in its own way devoted to seeking out and setting forth one and the same knowledge of sublime truth and true sublimity' ('iuxta numerum librorum quibus lex diuina scripta est, [. . .] unam eandemque summae ueritatis et uerae sublimitatis scientiam scrutatur et confitetur').[27] Whilst it is perhaps unnecessary to seek an explanation for the five-volume structure of the *Historia Ecclesiastica* here, for Bede the model of the Pentateuch remained suggestive of created perfection.[28]

Yet by the twelfth century, the languages of Britain had changed. This provided troubling and incontrovertible proof that the divine perfection visible to Bede was capable of being eroded by time. The relevant passage of the *Historia Ecclesiastica* elicited different reactions. Concerned more with the credible than the factual, Geoffrey of Monmouth decided to update Bede's now-obsolete description. In his *Historia regum Britanniae*, he instead spoke of the Saxons, Normans, Picts, Scots and Britons, and by extension, of their languages.[29] However, Henry of Huntingdon was more sensitive to the implications of the linguistic differences between Bede's time and his own. He noticed that the Picts were no longer extant (Pictland having been eclipsed by its Gaelic neighbours in the second half of the ninth century).[30] Whilst retaining Bede's assertion that 'five languages are used in Britain' ('quinque [. . .] linguis utitur Britannia', p.24), immediately afterwards he remarked that the race and language of the Picts subsequently appeared to have passed away entirely:

> Quamuis Picti iam uideantur deleti, et lingua eorum omnino destructa, ita ut iam fabula uideatur, quod in ueterum scriptis eorum mentio inuenitur. Cui autem non comparet amorem celestium et horrorem terrestrium, si cogitet non solum reges eorum et principes et populum deperiisse, uerum etiam stirpem omnem et linguam et mentionem simul defecisse?

> The Picts, however, appear to have been annihilated and their language utterly destroyed, so that the record of them in the writings of the ancients seems like fiction. Who will not espouse love of celestial things and dread of worldly things, if he considers not only that their kings and princes and people have perished, but also that at the same time their whole racial stock, their language and all remembrance of them have disappeared? (pp.24–25)

In one sense, as Henry was quick to point out, the demise of Pictish showed history's power to teach by example, through 'the recorded deeds of all peoples and nations, which are the very judgements of God' ('in rebus gestis omnium gentium et nationum, que utique Dei iudicia sunt', pp.4–5), which could 'encourage worldly men to good deeds and reduce their wickedness' ('seculares ad bona sollicitant et in malis minuunt', pp.4–5).

This pedagogical emphasis ultimately stemmed from an Augustinian stress on the historical sense of the Scriptures, where God teaches man through his created works.[31] At the same time, language death posed a profound threat to this understanding of history grounded in the eternal, divine truths contained within an essentially unchanging natural world. Henry stated that the extinction of the Picts was capable of making all historical record of them seem 'like fiction' ('ut [...] fabula').[32] This may be because his definition of the value of history relied on its contemporary relevance: it 'brings the past into view as though it were present, and allows judgement of the future by representing the past' ('Historia igitur preterita quasi presentia uisui representat, futura ex preteritis imaginando diiudicat', pp.4–5).

For Henry, the most disturbing aspect of the disappearance of the Picts from Britain remained the extinction of their language:

> Et si de aliis mirum non esset, de lingua tamen quam unam inter ceteras Deus ab exordio linguarum instituit, mirandum uidetur.

> And if there were nothing surprising in other respects, yet it must seem amazing as regards their language, which was one of those established by God at the very beginning of languages. (pp.24–25)

In his belief that the seventy-two languages established by God correspond with the seventy-two nations after the building of the Tower of Babel, Henry here adhered to an influential idea first propounded in the fifth century by Arnobius Junior, cited by Bede and, in turn, cited in full elsewhere in the *Historia Anglorum*.[33] To Henry, then, the fate of Pictish did not invalidate the account of its origins. Presumably his assumption that it was one of the seventy-two original languages stemmed from the precision of Arnobius's allocation of twenty-seven, twenty-two and twenty-three languages to each of the respective territories governed by the sons of Noah: Shem, Ham, and Japeth. This concept of the rigidity of the historical difference between languages builds on the account of Babel in Genesis 11:1–9 discussed in the introduction to this volume. This likewise left no room for a gradual evolution of language, merely remarking that: 'ibi confusum est labium universae terrae'.[34] Finally, Bede's portrayal of the five languages of Britain as divinely ordained may well have led Henry to conclude that Pictish must have been one of the originals. Having established to his satisfaction that it was there 'ab exordio linguarum', its disappearance from the cosmic structure of history was all the more disquieting. Far from upholding the fixed order of creation instituted by God from the beginning of the world, the death of Pictish indicated that languages were capable of decline as well as growth.

How far did Henry's keen awareness of the mutability of languages affect his perceptions of other vernaculars? Although confident in contemporary English, he pushed the limits of his knowledge by engaging with historical source material: this may have quickened an alertness to language change. The exact source of his proficiency is unclear. His father, Nicholas, archdeacon of Huntingdon, was a member of the Norman Glanville family, although his mother may have been English.[35] Henry appears to have spoken the language from boyhood, mentioning that he heard very old men speak of the St Brice's day massacre in 1002 when he was a child. ('De quo scelere in puericia nostra quosdam uetustissimos loqui audiuimus' (p.340).) He was comfortable explaining the etymologies of place names. For example, 'Huntingdon' is correctly glossed as 'mons uenatorum' ('hill of the hunters').[36] He seems to have had a good reading knowledge of older forms of English, using a text closest to the Peterborough version E of the *Anglo-Saxon Chronicle* as one of his main sources.[37] These older forms sometimes caused him problems. Diana Greenway has noted a number of minor errors of translation made by Henry or his scribes. Occasionally they made mistakes in transcribing Old English letters such as eth and wen (although these difficulties may equally have stemmed from their exemplars).[38] More importantly, Henry sometimes misunderstood the Old English: *mære*, 'border' was treated as a place name (pp.224–225); *gesæt*, 'resigned', was translated as *factus est*, 'was made' (pp.252–253); and *binnan þam gatum*, 'within the gates' was translated as *portam [. . .] fregerunt*, 'broke through the gate' (pp.306–307). However, these small slips were not widespread, and Henry was capable of manipulating his material so that it made grammatical sense. Understandably, he sometimes misidentified names, as when *in ceastre*, 'in the city', was translated as *in Ceastre* 'at Chester' (pp.252–253). Significantly, the *Anglo-Saxon Chronicle*'s ancientness seems to have been an intrinsic part of the text's attraction for Henry: he consistently referred to it as the 'scripta ueterum'.[39] Not least, this perception may have arisen from his enjoyment of decoding linguistic uncertainties through translation.

Henry's unusual attention to the historical specificity of pre-Conquest English poetic language seems influenced by an awareness of his sporadic problems of comprehension. The *Historia Anglorum* does not include any examples of poetry in the original English, but instead features Latin translations which are unusually concerned with preserving the style, tone, and alliterative metre of their vernacular sources. In this chapter, Henry's longest and most ambitious translation, the 'Battle of Brunanburh' is situated in the context of other treatments of English poetry within the *Historia Anglorum*, and of wider twelfth-century engagements with the English poetic corpus. The prestige of ancient language may have heightened Henry's interest in the replication of English poetic idiom.

Henry was an appreciative reader of vernacular poetry, including Latin translations of isolated Old English verses at six points in his history.[40] Due to the thematic links between the extracts, which all concern battles, these may well be from the same work.[41] Whilst Henry gave no indication of the language in which these lines were originally written, merely introducing them with 'whence it is said' ('vnde dicitur'), this was not the case for his full translation of one of the poems in the *Chronicle*, 'The Battle of Brunanburh', which made explicit his admiration for Old English literature. The poem is included in the A, B, C, and D versions of the *Chronicle* entry for 937, and treats of the battle between an alliance of Mercians and West Saxons, under Æthelstan and his younger brother, Edmund, and an alliance of Scots, Norsemen, and Strathclyde Welsh led respectively by Constantine II, Anlaf, king of Dublin, and Owain of Strathclyde.[42] A. G. Rigg has argued that Henry attempted to reproduce not only the poem's subject matter, but also its scansion, suggesting that, although copied into the *Historia* as continuous prose, the poem can be divided into word patterns that resemble the Old English four-stress line.[43] Henry was careful to reproduce other features of the poetry, too, such as the kennings: Æthelstan remained a 'ring-giver' ('torquium dator', pp.310–311).[44] This was in keeping with his translation strategy of near-total fidelity to the language of his original. Henry wrote concerning 'Brunanburh':

> De cuius prelii magnitudine Anglici scriptores quasi carminis modo proloquentes, et extraneis tam uerbis quam figuris usi translatione fida donandi sunt. Vt pene de uerbo in uerbum eorum interpretantes eloquium ex grauitate uerborum grauitatem actuum et animorum gentis illius condiscamus.

> The English writers describe the magnitude of this battle in a kind of song, using strange words and figures of speech, which must be given a faithful translation, rendering their eloquence almost word for word, so that from the solemnity of the words we may learn of the solemnity of the deeds and thoughts of that people. (pp.310–311)

His decision to pursue an almost literal translation, 'pene de uerbo in uerbum', suggests deep respect for the unique forms of expression possible in Old English poetic diction.

Henry's translation of 'The Battle of Brunanburh' is only one example of his wider experimentation with the composition of metrically innovative

Latin poetry.[45] However, whilst he was eager to embrace new Latin verse
forms, his tastes in Old English verse seem to have been more conservative. This radically influenced his approach to the literal reproduction of
vernacular tropes. Although the *Chronicle* included many other poems and
poetic passages besides 'Brunanburh', the only one translated by Henry was
the 'Rime of King William', an elegy for William the Conqueror preserved
in version E's entry for 1087.[46] The author made extensive use of rhyme as
a way of structuring his text:

> Castelas he let wyrcean 7 earme men swiðe swencean. [. . .]
> He sætte mycel deorfrið, 7 he lægde laga þærwið
> þet swa hwa swa sloge heort oððe hinde, þet hine man sceolde blendian.
> [. . .]
> Swa swiðe he lufode þa headeor swilce he wære heora fæder.[47]

> He had castles built and wretched men oppressed. [. . .] He set up great
> game-preserves, and he laid down laws for them, that whosoever killed hart
> or hind[,] he was to be blinded. [. . .] He loved the stags so very much, as
> if he were their father.[48]

Seth Lerer has argued that the author's interest in rhyme stemmed from
a desire to emulate the techniques of French and Latin poetry.[49] Others
locate his work within the context of the *Chronicle*: Thomas Bredehoft
emphasises earlier employments of rhyme in poems found in the annals
for 975, 1036, and 1067.[50] If the end-rhyme does not represent a radical
departure from Old English tradition, it nonetheless does not conform to
the alliterative patterns favoured in the majority of the corpus. Its subject
matter, too, could be situated as much in the context of twelfth-century
complaints about forest law, as in the earlier *Chronicle* royal elegies.[51] Since
it is located at a juncture of old and new literary traditions, the work does
not follow the patterns of classical Old English versification in the same
way as 'Brunanburh'. The author's more modern approach to poetry does
not seem to have been appreciated by Henry, who was far less interested in
tailoring his translation of the 'Rime' to the stylistic demands of his English
source:

> Ad castella solus omnes fatigabat construenda. Si ceruum caperent aut
> aprum, oculos eis euellebat, nec erat qui obmumuraret. Amauit autem feras
> tanquam pater esset earum.

> He went beyond everyone else in castle building. If anyone caught a stag or
> a boar, he put out his eyes, and no one murmured. He loved the beasts of
> the chase as if he were their father. (pp.404–405)

This rendering is frequently a loose paraphrase, often mixing the order of the information given in the *Chronicle*. It gives a rough reproduction of the sense, rather than the sound of the text. Henry's lack of interest in recreating the formal characteristics of the English elegy contrasts with the many examples of his own Latin compositions in the genre, scattered throughout the *Historia*.[52] There were hence major differences between Henry's careful and creative replication of the language of 'Brunanburh' and his paraphrase of the more innovative versification in the 'Rime'. His enjoyment of the 'grauitas' of 'Brunanburh' may have stemmed in part from the way it exemplified traditional techniques of English poetry.

Henry's treatment of 'Brunanburh' was unusually concerned with recreating specifically English poetic patterns. He frequently aimed to recapture alliterative effects, for example in the first line: 'Rex Adelstan, decus ducum' (p.310). This could lead to conflicts between the demands of poetry and his commitment to a 'de uerbo in uerbum' translation: whilst Henry has 'decus ducum', 'ornament of leaders', 'Brunanburh' has 'eorla dryhten', 'leader of warriors' (p.93.1).[53] Here, considerations of language outweighed those of literalism. He made a concerted effort to preserve the poem's imagery, as in 'heardes hondplegan', ('hard handplay'/'fighting') (p.93.25), which he translated accurately as 'duro manus ludo' (pp.312–313). He was aware of the impact of time on poetic practice, changing his style radically to incorporate the metrical and lexical effects of his source text. This stress on linguistic idiosyncrasy offered an alternative perspective to the *Historia Anglorum*'s portrayals of history's overarching moral exemplarity. Far from having 'no interest in the pastness of the past', his approach to 'Brunanburh' instead explored the ways in which bygone heroic ideals could be evoked through minute details of poetic language.[54]

By the 1120s, Henry's interest in pre-Conquest verse was comparatively rare. Late eleventh- and twelfth-century scribes sometimes included Old English poetry if they came across it embedded within a Latin work. *Cædmon's Hymn* appeared in seven English marginal glosses to Bede's Latin version in the *Historia Ecclesiastica*,[55] and the English text of 'Bede's Death Song' is preserved in seven copies and one reworking of Cuthbert's *Epistola de obitu Bede*.[56] One Old English poem was circulating independently: 'De situ Dunelmi', an English encomium to Durham, was copied twice in the twelfth century, but it cannot be securely dated to before 1066.[57] In one manuscript, it formed part of a larger dossier of works, arguably compiled at Durham *c.*1188 in order to demonstrate the monastic chapter's right to control their own property and revenues.[58] In the early twelfth century, Symeon of Durham already considered its testimony on the cathedral's relics to be authoritative, although he did not quote from it directly.[59] Whilst plausibly shaped by Anglo-Norman concerns, its choice of form also drew attention to the richness of Durham's Anglo-Saxon inheritance: the English poem was evidently found to be a fitting monument to Durham's natural and spiritual wealth. 'De situ Dunelmi' is a reminder of the problems inherent in dividing twelfth-century poetry into starkly defined categories of 'ancient' and 'contemporary', and in distinguishing between pre- and post-Conquest verse. For medieval readers encountering poems in manuscript, in some cases, it was impossible to ascertain the date of composition. Moreover, the literary form, language, and context of many late Old English works have also been shaped by a mixture of the traditional and the more innovative. Henry's sensitivity to 'Brunanburh' as a piece of specifically ancient poetry was uncommon.

Henry seems to have been aware that his translation pursued an unusual strategy by seeking to replicate the particularity of vernacular language. The *Historia Anglorum* also includes Bede's Latin translation of the Old English poem, *Cædmon's Hymn*. Bede did not try to reproduce the metre of the Old English (assuming that the surviving Old English gloss to the relevant passage in the *Historia Ecclesiastica* represents the original, rather than a translation of the Latin). There was likewise little attempt to include alliteration. Henry may well have noticed the differences in their approaches. Bede, finishing the translation, commented apologetically:

> Hic est sensus, non autem ordo ipse uerborum, quae dormiens ille canebat; neque enim possunt carmina, quamuis optime conposita, ex alia in aliam linguam ad uerbum sine detrimento sui decoris ac dignitatis transferri.

> This is the sense, but not the order, of the words which he sang as he slept. For it is not possible to translate verse, however well composed, literally from one language to another without some loss of beauty and dignity.[60]

Henry did not incorporate the entirety of this statement into his own work, omitting the first clause concerning Bede's self-confessed rearrangement of word order. This may have been due to the variation of their translation practice. Unlike Bede, he was prepared to utilise the fluidity of Latin syntax to a certain extent in order to capture some of the English effects of 'Brunanburh'. He carefully retained the position of the initial verb in 'geslogon æt sæcce' 'struck [...] in strife' (p.93.4) as 'percusserunt in bello' 'struck in battle' (pp.310–311). These considerations of word order may well have influenced his choice of translation strategy. Henry quoted part of St Jerome's famous recommendation that translating 'word for word' ('verbum e verbo') was the best technique for tackling the syntax of the

Bible, where 'the order of words is a [divine] mystery' ('verborum ordo mysterium est').[61] Whilst 'Brunanburh' was far from being included in the numinous mystery of the Christian Word, Jerome's recommendations for difficult syntax remained a widely accepted formulation of the best standard of translation.[62] Henry's evocation of this standard, then, was a statement of his respect and admiration for the diction of 'Brunanburh'. For him, the unique value of the Old English poetic tradition lay not only in the 'grauitas' of the virtues it depicted but in its manipulation of the language itself.

His determination to preserve both the literal meaning and the literary experience of reading 'Brunanburh' is all the more remarkable given Henry's sporadic difficulties with the poem's tenth-century speech patterns. He sometimes misunderstood its West Saxon poetic diction.[63] 'Se froda', 'the aged' (p.94.37) and 'guðe', 'in battle' (p.94.44) were rendered as the names 'Froda' and 'Gude' (pp.312–313). A kenning describing swords, 'hamora lafan', 'with hammers' leavings' (p.93.6) was translated as 'domestice reliquie' 'those who were left of the family' [*or* household] (cf. 'hām', 'house') (pp.310–311). Perhaps perplexed by the kenning, Henry did not associate *hamora* with twelfth-century English 'hamer', choosing instead 'hām'.[64] In general he was confident identifying Old English genitives, although his flexible translations may indicate occasional uncertainty: this is consistent with the increasingly streamlined morphology of twelfth-century English.[65] There may have been underlying difficulties with his manuscript source. Textual issues probably resulted in Henry's misidentification of 'feld dunnade', 'the field darkened' (p.93.12) as 'colles resonuerunt', 'the hills resounded' (p.312–313, cf. 'dynian', 'to resound').[66] He has then assumed that the next line is the beginning of a new sentence, but has had to alter the grammar accordingly: 'secga swate', 'with soldiers' blood' [*or* 'sweat'] (p.93.13) becomes 'sudauerunt armati', 'the warriors sweated' (p.312, my translation). The surviving Old English also has lines that Henry made no attempt to translate, most notably:

> sweordes ecgum, þæs þe us secgað bec,
> ealde uðwitan [. . .]

> [B]y the sword's edges, [. . .] as books tell us, old authorities.[67]

Given that he painstakingly reproduced the rest of the poem, it seems unlikely that this omission is due to incomprehension.

Henry was only mildly interested in producing a strictly literal translation. Whilst he preserves some features of the language faithfully, other aspects of his translation suggest intelligent guesswork based on verbal

resemblances to twelfth-century vocabulary. These sought more to evoke
the atmosphere of Old English poetry, than to untangle unfamiliar lexis.
Paradoxically, his attempt to recapture the spirit of ancient verse could
sometimes lead to unconscious modernisations of the text which reflected
twelfth-century expectations of composition. Examining Henry's insertion
of a classical group of mourning mothers and women (the idea of weeping
perhaps extrapolated from 'wæpengewrixles', 'mixing of weapons', p.94.51),
Kenneth Tiller has drawn attention to the way that some of Henry's linguistic extrapolations can lead to the reframing of Old English imagery as
Latinate epic grandeur.[68] However, this disjunction between intention and
achievement does not imply that Henry's approach to the English text was
a failure.[69] His advocacy of literal, or near-literal translation may not have
been strictly representative of his intended strategy. Rather, as a rhetorical
device, it allowed him to create a fiction: Latin's capacity to recapture the
English original's style and sense in full. He was eager to minimise any difficulties of comprehension stemming from the differences between past and
present forms of English. At the same time, his emphasis on the original
text's 'strange words and figures of speech' ('extraneis tam uerbis quam fig-
uris') located much of its value in its difference from twelfth-century poetic
diction.

Even within the select group of those who demonstrate an interest in
the history of earlier English verse, Henry's insistence on the ancient language of his vernacular source remains unusual. Two twelfth-century historians chose to give the original English text alongside their Latin translations of Anglo-Saxon (or supposedly Anglo-Saxon) poems. Both made no
comment on the diction of their sources. Symeon of Durham's history of
Durham (composed 1104 × 1109) included a version of 'Bede's Death Song'
in West Saxon dialect, as part of his edition of Cuthbert's *Epistola de obitu
Bede*.[70] His insertion of an accurate translation shows that he understood
the poem well, even though he did not expect a similar level of comprehension from the entirety of his audience. However, Symeon's decision to
retain the vernacular original implies that he expected at least some of them
to appreciate the poem's language, despite the fact that Bede died in 735.
A different approach was taken in the *Liber Eliensis*, completed sometime
between 1173 and 1177.[71] The work united various documents confirming
the property and privileges of the monastery at Ely. Its author drew attention to the fact that he translated many of these from the vernacular,[72] but
only Edward the Confessor's confirmation of the abbacy of Wulfric (1044
× 1066) was included in both its original English form and in Latin translation.[73] He also quoted the English for the first stanza of a song which is

claimed to have been composed by King Cnut (d.1035) as he approached Ely by boat:

> Merie sungen ðe muneches binnen Ely
> ða Cnut ching reu ðer by.
> Roweþ cnites noer the lant
> and here we þes muneches sæng.

> Quod latine sonat: 'Dulce cantaverunt monachi in Ely, dum Canutus rex navigaret prope ibi. Nunc, milites, navigate propius ad terram et simul audiamus monachorum armoniam'.[74]

> This is how it sounds in Latin: 'The monks sweetly sang in Ely, when King Cnut rowed near there. Now knights, row closer to the land and let's hear the song of the monks'.

The language of the verse reflects several twelfth-century developments, but the author does not seem to feel that this was inconsistent with the date of its supposed origins.[75] This may be because Cnut's song has been deliberately recorded in its twelfth-century incarnation: the author noted that 'this and the remaining parts that follow are up to this day sung publicly by choirs and remembered in proverbs' ('et cetera que sequuntur, que usque hodie in choris publice cantantur et in proverbiis memorantur').[76] Alternatively, he may have considered these forms to be continuous with those of pre-Conquest English, and therefore a convincing representation of the words Cnut may have sung. Both Symeon and the *Liber Eliensis* did not dwell on the putative antiquity of the language of these poems, and did not expect their age to prevent the anglophone members of their audiences from understanding them. They relied on context to convey a sense of the early date and historical significance of their sources.

In contrast, although his translation paid far greater attention to the tone and style of the English, Henry did not include his vernacular original. This may be because he did not expect his immediate Norman audience to comprehend the language. This portion of the history was dedicated to Alexander, Bishop of Lincoln (pp.2–8). A later letter was addressed to Warin the Breton,[77] and at Bec, Robert of Torigni made his own personal copy of the text.[78] Other dedicatees included Henry I (p.502), and Walter, Archdeacon of Leicester.[79] For all of these men, Latin was the most familiar written idiom. It was also less susceptible to language change, perhaps making it seem a more permanent form of record. Given his own dark view of the history of Britain as a series of successive plagues, Henry's lack of interest in including his English source might express doubts about the future comprehensibility of the language.[80] However, it also has another effect. Henry's careful rendering of the poem's 'strange words and figures of speech' aimed to evoke an archaic grandeur. By leaving out the English text, he did not allow anglophone readers the opportunity to search for the linguistic continuities between their own dialect and the diction of 'Brunanburh' in the way that they could with Symeon's edition of 'Bede's Death Song'. Instead, the poem's remoteness from the norms of Latin versification was underlined. The omission of the English source with its familiar stress patterns left Henry's emphasis on the extreme ancientness and *grauitas* of the language unchallenged.

For Henry, the Battle of Brunanburh was 'the greatest of battles' ('preliorum maximum', p.310), and Æthelstan's victory marked an important moment in the history of the English people.[81] Tiller's recent work has emphasised the way that Henry's poetic choices responded to the poem as a humbling of the prideful *Normanni*: the defeat of the pagan Norsemen of Dublin pointed forward to the potential chastisement which God would one day inflict on the Normans.[82] Henry's vision of 'history unambiguously based on divine providence' influenced his translation.[83] We might see his focus on the ancient itself as part of this subtle reshaping of 'Brunanburh' into a definitive depiction of the English people: the text is designed to be an impressive witness to their righteousness when acting in accordance with God's will. The translation represents an important acknowledgement of the authority of ancient documentation, and the ways in which vernacular language can be used to authenticate presentations of the past.

Continuity and Community in the Eadwine Psalter

Others were more reluctant to distinguish between ancient and contemporary forms of English. The language of earlier times remained comprehensible to many, and literary traditions could be presented as ongoing as well as old. Henry's translation of 'Brunanburh' can be seen as anticipating the interest in the history of English apparent in the early-thirteenth-century poetry of Laȝamon or the glosses of the 'Tremulous Hand'.[84] However, he himself depicted the poem more as a monument to the past literary and military successes of the Anglo-Saxons than as an inspiration to future vernacular writers. Although he exemplifies the ways in which Old English alliterative poetry continued to be appreciated into the twelfth century, Henry's decision to omit the original text of 'Brunanburh' suggests that he primarily saw the work through the lens of his own historical project. Translating Anglo-Saxon poetry formed part of a wider enterprise of the reconstruction, preservation, and dissemination of England's past, as Henry introduced the lessons and pleasures of insular history to an international, Latinate audience. The Eadwine Psalter adopted an alternative emphasis: its scribes were much less interested in communicating ancientness, modernising the language of their exemplars to varying degrees. However, they laid far greater stress on past and future traditions, presenting the composition and compilation of vernacular religious literature as a prestigious feature of the history of scholarship at Christ Church, Canterbury.

Although in many ways, the focus of literary production after the Conquest at Christ Church had shifted towards the Latin of new writers like Eadmer, Osbern of Canterbury, and Nigel Wireker, twelfth-century Canterbury retained a strong interest in English. Some twenty-four volumes dating from *c*.1040–*c*.1210 in English or with English annotations survive which have been attributed to Christ Church; twenty-one manuscripts which included English were mentioned in two Christ Church book-lists dating from *c*.1175 and *c*.1300.[85] These texts continued to be authoritative: Richard Pfaff suggests that two of the typological windows added to the eastern end of the cathedral after the fire of 1174 drew on Ælfric's homilies.[86] As well as copying and adapting older material, the scriptorium also experimented with the creation of new works. Christ Church is the likely provenance of British Library, MS Cotton Vespasian D.xiv, a mid-twelfth-century anthology of English prose texts which features nine items composed between 1075 and 1150 and uniquely attested there.[87] These include translations of two Latin theological works from the circle of Anselm (d.1109): a homily on the Virgin Mary by Ralph d'Escures, and extracts from Honorius of Autun's *Elucidarium* and *Speculum ecclesiae*.[88] The manuscript also contains a life of St Neot, which George Younge argues was probably composed at Canterbury at the beginning of the twelfth century.[89] Dense with verbal echoes of the works of earlier authors such as Ælfric, the text employed older diction with care in order to create a stylistic connection to earlier vernacular traditions of hagiography, even as it used the figure of King Alfred to explore 'post-Conquest anxieties about governance'.[90] The compilers of the Eadwine Psalter similarly combined a consciousness of the stylistics of the past with a desire to attest to the new vibrancy of Christ Church's contemporary multilingual culture.

Some key features of the manuscript will be outlined first, before examining the English gloss and its implications for twelfth-century perceptions of linguistic continuity in more detail. The Psalter, Cambridge, Trinity College MS R.17.1, was assembled around 1155–1160 in Christ Church Cathedral, Canterbury.[91] Its huge size (the leaves measure 455 × 326 mm) suggests that the manuscript was intended to be a work of reference: fourteenth-century records indicate that it was kept in a book box ('armariolum') in the cloister, presumably for the purpose of study.[92] The patron who commissioned it remains unknown, but seems to have been concerned with producing a work as comprehensive as possible.[93] In addition to multiple texts of the Psalms, the Eadwine Psalter incorporates the *Parva Glosatura* attributed to Anselm of Laon, a calendar, and other liturgical material such as the Canticles; it is lavishly illustrated throughout.[94] It includes all three of St Jerome's Psalm translations: the *Romanum*, the *Gallicanum* and the *Hebraicum* (Figure 1).[95] The *Romanum* was based on the *Vetus Latina* translation of the Psalms. It was the version most widely used in Anglo-Saxon glossed psalters, and was also glossed in English by the Eadwine scribes. The *Gallicanum*, Jerome's other revision of the *Vetus Latina*, was the version used in twelfth-century England in the liturgy; here it was given the Latin biblical gloss attributed to Anselm of Laon. For his third translation of the Psalms, the *Hebraicum*, Jerome purported to rely on Hebrew texts rather than the Latin. It was glossed here with insular French. Hence the *Gallicanum*, the version in day-to-day liturgical use, was the only version not to receive a vernacular gloss, suggesting that the French and English translations were not intended to be study aids for those with insufficient Latin.

The English gloss to the Psalter is of particular interest to an examination of twelfth-century awareness of language change. For some twentieth-century scholars, the gloss was characterised by 'extraordinary blunders'.[96] The main exemplar, which was used for Psalms 1–90.14, 92.1–2, 95.3–142.7 and 142.9–150, appears to have had poor word separation. This created difficulties for the original glossator, who had little knowledge of Latin (for clarity, this uncorrected exemplar is designated *Ead* hereafter). Appropriate translations from the Old English Metrical Psalms were inserted to fill *lacunae* in *Ead*'s gloss. The Canticles were also glossed, partly from *Ead*, partly from other sources, including a D-type psalter (i.e. one related to the tenth-century Regius Psalter (London, British Library, MS Royal 2 BV)).[97] After the initial gloss had been copied into the Eadwine Psalter, a scribe with considerable knowledge of Old English made extensive corrections to Psalms 1–77, but no further, perhaps because the manuscript was still lying unbound in two halves at this point.[98] The complexity of the sources of the Eadwine gloss can be conveniently summarised in a table (Figure 2):[99]

This patchwork of sources has been seen as testament to the *ad hoc* nature of the English gloss. One of the strongest proponents of this view has been

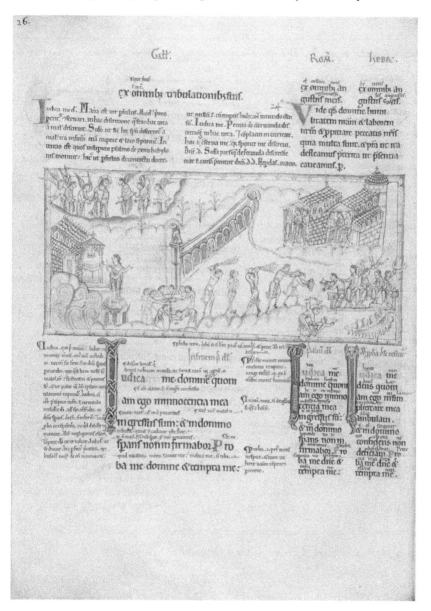

Figure 1. The Eadwine Psalter, Cambridge, Trinity College, MS R.17.1, fol. 43v. Three versions of Psalm 25 (left to right): *Gallicanum* with Latin biblical gloss attributed to Anselm of Laon, *Romanum* with English gloss, *Hebraicum* with insular French gloss.

Text	Source of the English Gloss	Notes
Psalms 1–90.14, 92.1–2, 95.3–142.7, 142.9–150	*Ead*, an unknown psalter with Old English gloss.	Glosses to Psalms 1–77 corrected extensively with reference to a second psalter with Old English predominantly D-type gloss.
Psalms 90.15–91.16, 92.3–95.2 and 142.8	Old English Metrical Psalms	The text was probably consulted in order to fill *lacunae* in the manuscript of *Ead*, although the reasons behind the choice of the Metrical Psalms over another Psalm translation remain unclear.
Canticles 1–7	*Ead*	
Canticle 8	Unknown Old English source	Shares a common ancestor with the eleventh-century Old English gloss to this canticle in the Vespasian Psalter (London, British Library, MS Cotton Vespasian A I).
Canticles 9–12	Unknown gloss related to that found in the Regius Psalter (London, British Library, MS Royal 2 BV, composed s.x med.).	O'Neill suggests this D-type source may be the same as that used to correct Psalms 1–77.
Canticles 13 and 14	Unknown Old English source	Vernacular translations of the Credo and Pater Noster were widespread in Anglo-Saxon England, perhaps encouraging scribes to supply their own translations.
Canticle 15	Unknown D-type psalter	Same source as Canticles 9–12.
Psalm 151 (extra-canonical)	Unknown contemporary source	Probably copied from a translation composed specifically for the Latin text employed in the Eadwine Psalter.

Figure 2. Sources of English Gloss in Cambridge, Trinity College, MS R.17.1.

Patrick O'Neill, who suggests that the selection and copying of the initial exemplar (*Ead*) was 'bungled', forcing other scribes to correct its *lacunae* and its occasionally erroneous translations.[100] This could imply that less care was given to this aspect of the project than others, and that understanding of earlier English texts was diminishing at Canterbury. However, it is important to place this element of the gloss in its wider temporal and multilingual context. In retrospect, the scriptorium recognised that **Ead* had been a problematic exemplar, but they sought to amend it: the first eighteen of thirty-six quires in the Eadwine manuscript (comprising Psalms 1–77) were corrected very thoroughly. Moreover, **Ead*'s selection may not have been casual. Its copying was well organised, with major changes of scribes occurring half-way through the Psalter, and other changes occurring at the ends of quires.[101] Most strikingly, similar patterns of copying and correction can be detected in the insular French gloss: the initial exemplar of Psalms 1–124 seems to have been 'a very imperfect and defective translation' which featured substantial *lacunae*.[102] This portion of the text was partially corrected using a second, more skilful translation, which also provided the French for Psalms 131–148. The gloss has still been left with significant gaps: no text was ever inserted for Psalms 125–130 and 149–150, and many smaller omissions remain. This is because the corrections were never completed: the first of two principal correctors focussed on Psalms 1–110, intervening only sporadically after this point; the second principal corrector seems to have been employed to review the work of the first, but only revised Psalms 1–44.[103] Like the English gloss, the French scribes reconsidered their initial choice of exemplar; like them, the corrections were never fully finished. These shared difficulties may reflect the exigencies of manuscript production for a high-status patron. The two vernacular versions may have been adversely affected by a need for haste or other pressures now lost to us: in both cases, early decisions were rethought later, but never fully remedied.

The English and French translations form a central aspect of the lavish visual impression created by the manuscript, which eloquently displays Canterbury's past and present splendour. The Psalter was carefully shown as the culmination of previous traditions. Its illustrations imitated the Carolingian ninth-century Utrecht Psalter, one of the most valuable manuscripts in the twelfth-century library of Christ Church, Canterbury: this had already been copied there once in the eleventh century, creating the Harley Psalter (London, British Library, MS Harley 603). The Eadwine Psalter both paid tribute to the Utrecht Psalter's achievements, and portrayed itself as heir to the intellectual climate in which it was produced.[104] In some ways, its depiction of this climate was conservative. The compilers opted for classic works of scholarship over the more experimental: they chose to include the *Parva Glosurata*, which adhered closely to standard patristic exegesis, rather than to reflect more recent theological developments.[105] Much of the project focussed on the consolidation of existing study, weaving together the varying strands of Christ Church's responses to the Psalms in one volume. However, this attempt to create the *sine qua non* of reference works was itself an innovative rejoinder to the latest trends in prestige manuscripts: it can be seen in the context of other large, *de luxe* twelfth-century books such as the Dover Bible, the Winchester Bible and Psalter, and the Bury Bible.[106] The Eadwine Psalter, then, was both a monument to the past achievements of Canterbury and a statement of its present magnificence.

An assessment of the place of the English gloss within the manuscript's overall scheme reveals how far its presence there is similarly poised between an awareness of the prestigious history of the language at Canterbury, and its role in forming future traditions of multilingual exegesis. English becomes a medium of linguistic continuity: the Psalter's boundaries encompass pre- and post-Conquest Psalm translations, sacred and vernacular etymology, and different written forms of English in the twelfth century. This sense of continuity should inform our assessments of the varying levels of competence in reading earlier forms of English which the gloss displays. In several ways, the Psalter demonstrates that the understanding of Old English in the scriptorium remained high. Its scribes included the very competent individual, designated by Teresa Webber as OE4, who made the majority of the extensive, skilfully incorporated corrections in the first half of the manuscript.[107] Additionally, the insertion of the Metrical Psalms to fill *lacunae* in *Ead shows that Old English works were still being widely consulted at Christ Church in the mid-twelfth century. However, some scribes were less confident with earlier forms of the language. On one hand, the Metrical Psalms may have been deliberately chosen for the translation's poetic qualities by an avid vernacular reader.[108] On the other hand, the scribe who copied them, OE1, seems to have had 'very little idea what he was doing', failing to correct simple mistakes.[109] He was also mainly responsible for the copying of *Ead as main exemplar, but did not attempt to rectify its errors.[110] One interpretation of these difficulties might link them to an eroding mastery of Old English, and the Eadwine Psalter's position as the final example of a complete interlinear Old English Psalm translation. It is unlikely that members of the scriptorium would have shared this perception. Further Psalters with English glosses may have been envisaged: Jane Toswell has recently suggested that the Paris Psalter (an unfinished triple Psalter produced at Christ Church, Canterbury *c.*1180–1190 with reference to the Eadwine Psalter) was originally intended to include an English translation.[111] The Psalms were seen as a continuing legacy, to be read, remembered, and adapted.

The compilers sought to emphasise the place of their gloss within the literary lineage of the vernacular. By selecting the *Romanum* as lemma, they made evident the prestigious history of the pre-Conquest Church and the role of Old English within it. The *Romanum* had been the Psalter of the English Church from its inception until the Benedictine Reform, its prestige enhanced by the knowledge that it was the Psalter used at Rome.[112] It was also the version of the Psalter particularly associated with Old English glossing: Mechthild Gretsch notes that in spite of the widespread adoption of the *Gallicanum* in Britain along with other customs of continental Benedictine houses during the tenth century, seven of fourteen surviving glossed psalters took the *Romanum* for their Latin text.[113] This version was particularly associated with Christ Church, Canterbury. When copying the Utrecht Psalter to create the Harley Psalter, the Christ Church scribes changed the text of the Psalms from the *Gallicanum* to the *Romanum*.[114] The tenth-century Bosworth Psalter (London, British Library MS Additional 37517), also potentially from Christ Church, similarly translated from the *Romanum*.[115] Furthermore, Old English Psalm glossing was specifically associated with the Benedictine Reform: a disproportionately high number of surviving glossed psalters emanate from Winchester, probably from the school of St Æthelwold.[116] Particularly given the growth of alternative monastic orders such as the Cistercians in Britain in the first half of the twelfth century, to include the English gloss may have been to emphasise the specifically Benedictine context of the Eadwine Psalter as a whole.

This interest in traditions of Psalm translation might also have influenced the initial selection of the poor-quality main exemplar, **Ead.* The uncorrected gloss contains perplexing errors, largely caused by difficulties in discerning where one Latin word ends and another begins. For example, 'Seon regem amorreorum [. . .] et og regem basan' ('Seon, king of the Amorites [. . .] and Og the king of Basan') is glossed as 'Seon kining lufu hiræ 7 þet ewed bæson' ('Seon, king of their love and Basan the flock'), where 'amorreorum' has been read as 'amor eorum' and 'og regem' as 'o gregem'.[117] The compilers' initial selection of it is all the more surprising given that the tenth-century Regius Psalter (London, British Library, MS Royal 2.B.V), known for the excellence of its translation, is amongst the exemplars likely to have been at Christ Church.[118] However, given the overall ambition of the project, it is possible that the choice of exemplar was not random. A factor in the compilers' decision may have been consideration of the age of **Ead.* Whilst it is no longer tenable to assume that the gloss originated in late-seventh-century Mercia,[119] if the text did indeed suffer from poor word separation, this would have given it a superficially ancient appearance: in insular Latin manuscripts, separation prevailed by the eighth century.[120]

Perhaps due to its high status, some of *Ead*'s erroneous glosses were retained even after the text had been corrected. Scribe OE4 was largely responsible for a subtle and thoroughgoing programme of revision. He was confident reading and reproducing earlier vernacular material: seamless and careful alterations have been made with recourse to the conventions of Standard Old English. Where possible, he preserved *Ead*'s original reading, although in many cases he also wrote his own gloss beside it, and linked the two using the conjunction *uel*. The corrector wished to bring the gloss closer to his preferred exemplar, a manuscript closely related to the D-type Regius Psalter, and many of his alterations were designed to restore D-type readings. Where these did not conflict with the original text, he retained both glosses. It is possible that OE4 did not expunge some of these syllabic readings because he saw them as etymological puns with heuristic potential. He has not rectified the gloss to Psalm 59.9, although he has erased approximately two letters from the end of 'kynig':

> Meus est galaad et meus est manasses et effrem fortitudo capitis mei Iuda rex meus.

> Galaad is mine, and Manasses is mine, and Effrem is the strength of my head, Judah my king.

> Min is helm 7 min is to wunienne 7 to onfonne strengðo heæfedes mines Iudæ kynig min.

> The helmet is mine, and mine is to remain and to receive the strength of my head, Judah my king.[121]

The original glossator apparently mistook 'galaad' for 'galea', 'helmet', and thought 'manasses' to stem from 'manere', 'to remain'. His interpretation of 'effrem' is somewhat less clear, but he perhaps considered the second syllable to be a part of 'ferre', 'to carry'.[122] These glosses could be read via Isidorean etymological traditions, punning on the Latin in order to reflect the Psalmist's metaphor about the protection of the head. The corrector may have kept the passage in this form because he considered it to reveal something of the true nature of the divine reality attached to the names. He was interested in interpretations according to the spiritual sense of the Scriptures: two verses later he inserted the D-type gloss 'on ða eorðlican þing' over 'in Idumeam' ('into Edom'), following Jerome's gloss of 'Idumea'

as 'terrena'.[123] Although from the perspective of a word-for-word translation, *Ead*'s value at Psalm 59:9 is minimal, its approach to the language
of the Psalms was clearly of interest to the corrector. By expounding the
Hebrew through its specious similarities to the Latin, vernacular translation itself becomes a kind of etymological practice, able to uncover the
hidden significance of sacred language.

Even whilst pointing to the long history of English Psalm glossing, and
exploring its richness as a scholarly tool, the scribes also situated more
recent written forms of the language in the context of these traditions.
They adhered to patterns of Standard Old English to a greater or lesser
degree, but all included some twelfth-century English innovations. Some
extended passages of more modern forms may indicate the need for spe-
cially composed material in the absence of suitable exemplars. The final
Psalm, 151, was extra-canonical, and is hence glossed only once elsewhere,
in the eighth-century Vespasian Psalter: this version bears no relation to the
Eadwine translation.[124] The Latin text of Psalm 151, however, does occur in
several Old English glossed psalters.[125] Its treatment in the Eadwine Psalter
was thus a departure from the norm, and a testament to the desire of the
glossators for a comprehensive translation that matched and even exceeded
the interpretative ambitions of its literary predecessors. It also witnessed the
degree of exegetical freedom which the trilingual psalter afforded the vernacular reader. The Psalm was prefaced with a stern warning concerning
the dangers of apocryphal material, but only in the Eadwine Psalter was
this translated into English and French:

> Hic psalmus proprie scribitur dauid & extra numerum cum pugnauit cum
> goliath. Hic psalmus in ebreis codicibus non habetur sed nec a seputaginta
> inquit interpretibus additus est & iccirco repudiandus.

> Þes ilca psalm is iwriten bi seoluan dauide 7 is wiðutan ðere tale of ðan
> hundrede 7 fifti psalman. 7 ðeosne ilcan he machede ða he feath wið goliam.
> Þes psalm nis nawiht on hebreisse bocan hach ða hund seouenti biqueðeres
> othðe latimeres hine habbað idon to þan heoðran 7 forþi he is to ascunianne.

> Ceste salme demeniement est escrite de dauid e si est defors le numbre des
> cent cinquante salmes. Ceste fist il quant il cumbatit oð goliam. Ceste salme
> es ebreus liures nen est heue meis des setante entrepreturs est aiustet e pur
> ceo seit a refuser.

> This Psalm is written by David himself when he fought with Goliath and it
> is outside the number of the 150 Psalms. This Psalm is not in the Hebrew
> books but was added by the seventy translators, the Septuagint, and hence
> is to be set aside.[126]

Intriguingly, the English gloss appears to have taken precedence in this quotation: it was initially copied before the French, which was squeezed underneath in the first line. At 'goliath', the English scribe switched to glossing directly above the Latin, leaving no room for the French scribe, who was then forced to write above, rather than below him. When the text of the Psalm proper began, they reverted to the order of glosses assumed in the Canticles, with French closest to the Latin, followed by English above the French. This unusual sequence of events may even suggest this preface was glossed *ad hoc* by the scribe, offering a view of his own language unmediated by any exemplar.[127]

This scribe was OE2: he offered a noticeably contemporary form of English, which may have been a conscious linguistic preference. OE2 was responsible for modernisations of language in the main gloss to the Psalms, which mainly occur in the half of the work uncorrected by OE4.[128] Amongst other features, the passage above includes French-derived lexis ('latimeres') and orthography (the substitution of <qu> for English <cw> in 'biqueðeres'). OE2 wrote the prefix <ge-> as <i-> ('idon') and used the definite article to indicate an inflected noun ('to þan heoðran'). Only one erasure was made in the English gloss to Psalm 151, but its implications are significant. On fol. 281v, David states of Goliath that he 'cut his head off', 'achearf his heauod off'. Above the 'u' of 'heauod', an ascender has been erased, suggesting that the gloss originally read 'heafod'. OE2 has mistakenly included an old-fashioned orthographical variant: in Old English foot-medial /v/ was generally written as <f>, whereas by the mid-twelfth century, it tended to be distinguished as a separate phoneme, written as <v>.[129] This erasure suggests that either OE2, or someone else involved with the project, was prepared to make corrections to bring the text closer to a favoured form of English. Amongst several potential motivations, this may have been because he perceived it as more up to date than other language in the Psalter, or because it seemed closer to his own speech. Given the variety of approaches to English displayed in the gloss, contemporary innovations do not appear to have been thought incompatible with pre-Conquest English. Rather, this juxtaposition of different forms implicitly places mid-twelfth-century Psalm translations as the harmonious equal of much earlier material.

Instead of exclusively making a statement about the continuity of traditions of English at Christ Church, the compilers of the Eadwine Psalter were also attempting to found a tradition of their own. By creating a resplendent setting in which to unite their newly multilingual scholarship, they sought to emphasise the productivity of the cultural fusions taking place in the Christ Church scriptorium. The second half of this book explores the ways in which this process of fusion not only influenced perceptions of the future legacy of contemporary literature, but also reshaped perceptions of its linguistic inheritance: enquiry into Old English sources drew attention to the historical potential of other vernacular materials, leading to investigations of languages such as French and Welsh.

In the case of the Eadwine Psalter, reframing the English gloss in a trilingual context offered a new presentation of its literary past and future. Such a reframing anticipates the future confluences between English and French Psalm translation. As with Henry of Huntingdon's 'Brunanburh', Old English traditions were envisaged as continuing not only through the English of the twelfth century, but through other languages. But it is possible that this reframing also sought to invite a fresh consideration of the history of Psalm glossing. By juxtaposing the French text with the English, readers of the Eadwine Psalter were encouraged to situate it amidst an illustrious and durable practice of vernacular exegesis which extended over centuries of Canterbury scholarship. More speculatively, the scribes may have been inspired by this awareness of English tradition to point to the accelerating pace of Psalm translation in French. The Eadwine gloss to the *Hebraicum* displays vernacular literary histories which are now lost to us: it was copied from at least two earlier translations.[130] Prestigious manuscript projects elsewhere had previously incorporated French material. Oxford, Bodleian Library, Douce MS 320, offers an Anglo-Norman version of the *Gallicanum* which was translated directly from the Latin text of the St Albans Psalter (completed within a decade of 1130).[131] The Canterbury scribes could have known of this Psalter and its linked French translation: the two houses enjoyed close connections, the iconography of some elements in the St Albans and Eadwine Psalters derives from a shared source, and the text of Douce 320 was widely disseminated.[132] In one of their most ambitious collaborative ventures, the scriptorium sought to align their house traditions of vernacular study with different types of linguistic inheritance. The Eadwine Psalter's translations constructed a hermeneutic arc of sacred meaning which stretched from the Hebrew Psalms via Latin to English and French. But they also offered other historical pathways into Anglo-Saxon and Anglo-Norman England, connecting both vernaculars to a continuity of Benedictine scholarly innovation. As they passed on Old English literary traditions to future generations of readers, both Henry of Huntingdon and the Eadwine compilers knew that the memory of the past could shed new light on the present day.

CHAPTER 3

Explorations and Appropriations of British Linguistic History

The existence of prestigious and ancient documents in Old English not only encouraged new evaluations of the Anglo-Saxon past, but drew attention to the historical testimony provided by material in other languages. Over the course of the twelfth century, interest in the history of the Brittonic vernaculars increased exponentially amongst Norman audiences. Most Latin commentators had at best an imperfect knowledge of these languages (understood today as Welsh, Cornish and Breton, but most often referred to inclusively as 'British' in the Middle Ages). Their reconstructions of Brittonic language history therefore tended to incline more to the imaginative than to the philological, revealing much about readers' expectations of the authorising potential of the ancient. Almost all of these twelfth-century discussions were occasioned by the innovative decision of Geoffrey of Monmouth (d.1154/55) to portray two works as translations from British: the *Historia regum Britanniae* and the *Prophetia Merlini*. In particular, the *Historia*'s claim to be based on a 'very old book in the British tongue' ('Britannici sermonis librum uetustissimum') gave rise to a new awareness of the vernacular linguistic past, and of the ways in which this past could be exploited.[1] The advent of Galfridian historiography may thus be seen as the catalyst which initiated a series of transformations in Anglo-Norman attitudes to the history of the Brittonic languages.

Geoffrey's works were influential precisely because of his expert manipulation of wider post-Conquest anxieties, especially those concerning authentic documentation, and its absence. These pressures had already led clerical authors to extend their gaze beyond Anglo-Saxon England to ancient Britain. In the late eleventh and early twelfth centuries, charters from Christ Church, Canterbury were made to portray the cathedral's archbishops as exercising authority over the whole of the island.[2] Sometime between 1100 and 1107, monks there also commissioned a Latin and English version of the *Anglo-Saxon Chronicle* (MS F). The work began with the arrival of the Britons from Armenia, and their rule over Britain's southern regions.[3] Others drew more directly on historical material from early Wales. In an attempt to protect his diocese from the depredations of Norman settlers, Bishop Urban of Llandaff commissioned the *Liber Landavensis* sometime between 1119 and 1134.[4] This magnificent liturgical manuscript (which also contains saints' lives, charters and papal bulls) was designed to prove the continuous existence of the episcopal see of Llandaff from the fifth century.[5] Although the cartulary as a whole is a twelfth-century fabrication, Wendy Davies has shown that the charters are copies of much earlier works, manipulated to favour the claims of Llandaff.[6] Stylistic analysis indicates that the charters and saints' lives were compiled by the same person, who John Reuben Davies suggests may have been the twelfth-century hagiographer, Caradoc of Llancarfan.[7] In the *Historia regum Britanniae*, Geoffrey stated jokingly that he would leave writing the history of the Welsh kings after Athelstan to Caradoc (p.280).[8] It is hence possible that he knew some individuals who were closely connected to the *Liber Landavensis*. All these projects looked to the earlier Brittonic past in varying degrees of depth, but Geoffrey's approach also responded to other aspects of monastic cartulary culture. The trope of the British book coincided with a broader sense of the ways in which archaeological and antiquarian discoveries could be used to validate various political and poetic agendas. His focus on linguistic detail can be paralleled in forgers' similarly careful deployments of Old English material: the British language (and linguistic history more generally) offered another means of embellishing and adapting the past to meet contemporary concerns.

The Discovery of British: Geoffrey of Monmouth's Romance of Language

Geoffrey's *Historia* led considerations of the Brittonic vernaculars in an important new direction by alerting twelfth-century readers to their potential for substantiating historical claims. Earlier Latin literature had featured few accounts of the development of Welsh, Cornish, and Breton. Bede glossed some Celtic words in the *Historia Ecclesiastica*, but he seems to have been most familiar with the languages of Northern Britain.[9] Some Welsh place names appeared, and British was included alongside English, Irish, Pictish and Latin in his description of the country's five languages, which he compared approvingly to the books of the Pentateuch.[10] Later authors were unfavourably impressed by the belligerence of the British, which in turn affected portrayals of their tongue. The eighth-century hagiographer Felix claimed that St Guthlac was attacked by a horde of demons, who spoke to each other in the British language, described as a speech (*loquela*) which was *barbara* ('barbarous') or 'strimulenta' (the latter is a *hapax legomenon*, but seems to have a pejorative sense).[11] By the twelfth century, this distrust of the British had intensified, as the Normans sought to secure their hold on Wales, periodically meeting fierce native resistance. Authors increasingly portrayed the British as barbarians, a portrayal that sometimes extended to their language (although Felix's *Vita Guthlaci* indicates that this was also found in some Anglo-Saxon perceptions of British).[12] Geoffrey's emphasis on etymology and his use of the *liber uetustissimus* drew attention to the history of the Brittonic languages, and the possibilities inherent in the elucidation of such history.

In the *Historia regum Britanniae*, Geoffrey created a controversial narrative which radically reinterpreted the historical potency of the island's British inhabitants. He endowed them with Trojan ancestry, importantly shifting forward the date when the governance of the island was transferred from the Britons to the Anglo-Saxons.[13] Heavily inspired by the eighth-century Welsh *Historia Brittonum*, his work significantly rejected pre-Conquest English scepticism concerning the Trojan origin myths of Welsh and continental ruling dynasties.[14] This major departure from precedent was supported by new and creative strategies for conveying a sense of historical authenticity. Geoffrey used language both to give the appearance of conventional historiographical analysis, and to elude it. Whilst his etymologies sought to uncover clues to the British past hidden in contemporary usage, he eschewed critical examination by framing his work as a translation from a *liber uetustissimus*, locating his sources beyond the scrutiny of other historians. For Geraldine Heng, romance is characterised by the 'structure of desire' which drives its narratives: we might thus see Geoffrey's work not only as one of the earliest romances of conquest, but also of language.[15] The *liber uetustissmus* offered insular readers a linguistic fantasy: to recover an archaic vernacular tongue which demonstrated ancestral entitlement to a particular territory. Therefore, the *Historia* did not seek to seduce by depicting the Latin text's triumphant effacement of its British source. Rather, Geoffrey subverted expectations of linguistic hierarchy, alerting his audience to the vernacular's potential to be an object of scholarly analysis. After discussing Geoffrey's linguistic qualifications as a possible translator, this chapter traces the extent of the authority lent by British to his Latin history. It then explores the wider consequences of his reassessment of the British language's value, examining scholarly commentaries on two texts which claim to be Latin translations of Merlin's vernacular prophecies. Both arcane and archaic, the prophecies were of uncertain provenance. This made interpreters anxious to increase the text's credibility by emphasising its origins in the ancient past of Britain, even whilst their exegesis effaced any sense of that past's linguistic difference. The British language was perhaps of greatest literary value in the moment of its own evanescence.

Much critical analysis of the *Historia regum Britanniae* has inevitably focussed on evidence for the *liber uetustissmus*, and on Geoffrey's ability to comprehend the language of this putative Brittonic source text. The *Historia* begins with a startling claim to be translated from 'a very old book in the British tongue' ('Britannici sermonis librum uetustissimum'), which had been given to Geoffrey by Walter, archdeacon of Oxford (pp.4–5). Whilst literary historians have shown it to be most unlikely that this statement about the *liber uetustissimus* was a disingenuous reference to some single source, certain elements of the text may still have been influenced by Brittonic material. Geoffrey did have a degree of understanding in Welsh: he correctly translated some very common words such as *kaer* (fortress) and *pen* (head).[16] He also described Trojan as 'crooked Greek' ('curuum Graecum', pp.28–29). Translated into Welsh, this would derive *Cymraeg* (Welsh) from **camroeg* (cf. *cam*, 'crooked' and *Groeg* 'Greek'). If this was indeed Geoffrey's own etymology, then it suggests that he had some knowledge of Welsh initial consonantal lenition.[17] However, T. D. Crawford considers Geoffrey's unorthodox orthography to reduce the likelihood that he was familiar with written forms of the language.[18] He may still have drawn on some Brittonic material in a fragmentary manner: Stuart Piggott has pointed out the similarities between early medieval Welsh lists of pedigrees and the seemingly extraneous genealogical data included in the part of the *Historia* which describes the pre-Christian rulers of Britain.[19] Some form of connection with Welsh literature is further suggested by the Anglo-Norman historian Gaimar, who in the epilogue to his *Estoire des Engleis* (probably composed 1135 × 1159) described one of his sources as a translation made for Robert, Earl of Gloucester, from certain books about the kings of Britain which belonged to the Welsh.[20] This translation is unlikely to have been anything else but Geoffrey's *Historia*. The *Estoire* corroborates Geoffrey's claims about his own sources: Gaimar stated that he improved the text by adding extra material directly from the good book of Oxford which belonged to Archdeacon Walter.[21]

All the linguistic and literary traces left by Geoffrey's *liber uetustissimus* suggest that it may have been Welsh, if it existed at all. But the *Historia regum Britanniae* itself did not provide clear information about its own origins. Geoffrey stated that the book was brought 'ex Britannia' by Walter, archdeacon of Oxford (p.280). This was an ambiguous term, which pre-Conquest writers employed to signify both the whole island of Britain, and specific British territories.[22] Occurring without a qualifier such as 'maiore', here it should perhaps be translated as 'from Brittany'; but at this date it could still refer to any of the British lands, including Wales.[23] Even if Geoffrey had only a passive competence in Breton, it seems odd that no linguistic details survive in the *Historia*.[24] Biographically, too, a Welsh source seems a likely scenario. Although Geoffrey spent most of his adult life in Oxford, he called himself 'Monemutensis'. In 1151 he became Bishop of St Asaph's, but may never have visited his see due to the uncertain political situation in North Wales.[25] All these discrepancies have led some critics to dismiss entirely the possibility that a British book ever existed. However, if so, it was very bold of Geoffrey to implicate Walter in his deception: Michael Curley notes that 'the office of archdeacon was a very public one'.[26] Furthermore, the two men were known to each other.[27] It is true that they could have concocted a story together. But given Walter's status, the simplest explanation is that he did give Geoffrey some form of documentation relating to ancient British history.

The single most suspicious aspect of the *liber uetustissimus* is the sheer convenience of its existence. At the end of the *Historia*, Geoffrey based his arguments for the uniqueness of his work on his privileged access to Walter's British book, an access which was linguistic as well as logistic. He stated:

> Reges autem eorum qui ab illo tempore in Gualiis successerunt Karadoco Lancarbanensi contemporaneo meo in materia scribendi permitto, reges uero Saxonum Willelmo Malmesberiensi et Henrico Huntendonensi, quos de regibus Britonum tacere iubeo, cum non habeant librum illum Britannici sermonis quem Walterus Oxenefordensis archidiaconus ex Britannia aduexit.

> The Welsh kings who succeeded one another from then on I leave as subject-matter to my contemporary, Caradoc of Llancarfan, and the Saxon kings to William of Malmesbury and Henry of Huntingdon; however, I forbid them to write about the kings of the Britons since they do not possess the book in British which Walter, archdeacon of Oxford, brought from Brittany. (pp.280–281)

Geoffrey's British source effectively placed the *Historia* beyond the intellectual scrutiny of his critics. By portraying this source as the sole conduit for the history of the Britons, Geoffrey legitimated his own narration of past events. However, he also made a powerful statement for the importance of the British language to historical research. For one of his most vehement detractors, William of Newburgh, this valorisation of British sources through their translation into Latin was one of the most shameful aspects of Geoffrey's historiography. He wrote in the preface to his *Historia rerum anglicarum* (composed between 1196 and 1198):

> Fabulas de Arturo ex priscis Britonum figmentis sumptas et ex proprio auctas per superductum Latini sermonis colorem honesto historiae nomine palliavit.

> He has taken up the stories about Arthur from the fictitious accounts of the Britons, has added to them himself, and by embellishing them in the Latin tongue he has cloaked them with the honourable title of history.[28]

Geoffrey's translation practice was more even radical than William's accusations suggest. Not only did the *Historia* implicitly insist that a history written in the British language was worthy of translation, but Geoffrey also inverted assumptions about the relative rhetorical merits of the Latin and British texts. He stated that his British source was written in an 'excellent style' ('perpulcris orationibus'), whereas the literary merits of his own Latin text were modest in comparison (pp.4–5). Similarly, he claimed that he himself wrote in a 'poor style' ('uiliori dictamine') that would 'appear to spoil' ('uidear [...] maculare') subject matter that the historian Gildas was able to describe well (pp.30–31). Although Geoffrey's protestations largely represented a conventional modesty topos – he was, in fact, an accomplished Latinist – their effect was revolutionary, prompting a twelfth-century re-evaluation of the significance of the Brittonic vernaculars.[29]

   This re-evaluation encompassed perceptions of the language of the Trojan era. Geoffrey's presentation of the stylistic integrity of his ancient text was in marked contrast to the projected primitivism of the language of one of his major sources. The *De excidio Troiae historia* is the single text most frequently found alongside Geoffrey's *Historia* in manuscripts.[30] A late antique Latin narrative of the Trojan war, it is supposedly the eyewitness account of one Dares Phrygius.[31] The text is based on a Greek source, but the *De excidio* is not a word-for-word translation by the Latin biographer, Cornelius Nepos, as its prologue claims.[32] To convince its audience that the text was older than Homer, the style of the *De excidio* had to confirm classical preconceptions of archaic language: Nepos was made to stress that he had chosen to write truly and simply ('vere et simpliciter') in order to replicate the language of the original text.[33] For this author, the antique equated to the primitive. He avoided complex sentence structure, and repeated lexis and grammatical constructions.[34] In contrast, Geoffrey's insistence on the literary integrity of British encouraged his audience to re-imagine the language of the past as stylistically sophisticated, not as a more simplistic proto-form of contemporary speech.

Perceptions of the ancient British were transformed by Geoffrey's emphasis on the complexity of their vernacular literary endeavours. A major part of the *Historia*'s impact lay in its favourable assessment of the significance of British history, and by extension, British culture. Based on the influential allegations of Gildas that the British were continually 'ungratefully rebelling, stiff-necked and haughty' ('erecta cervice et mente [. . .] ingrata consurgit'),[35] Bede determined that the reason for the invasion of Germanic tribes was the 'slackness' ('segnitia') of the Britons.[36] Derogatory attitudes persisted into the twelfth century. The lack of extant British historical records seemed to confirm their bestiality: for Henry of Huntingdon, the act of historiography chiefly 'distinguishes rational creatures from brutes' ('distinguat a brutis rationabiles').[37] To Norman observers of the slow conquest of Wales over the late eleventh and twelfth centuries, the fact that the British were without written history thus seemed especially apt. John Gillingham has explored a 'growing fashion for dismissing the Celtic peoples as barbarians', particularly as exemplified in the writings of William of Malmesbury.[38] These opinions were widespread: even Geoffrey seems partially to subscribe to the view of British barbarity promulgated by William. In the closing paragraphs of the *Historia regum Britanniae*, he noted that:

> Barbarie etiam irrepente, iam non uocabantur Britones sed Gualenses, uocabulum siue a Gualone duce eorum siue a Galaes regina siue a barbarie trahentes.

> As their culture ebbed [lit. 'with barbarianism having been slowly introduced'], they were no longer called Britons, but Welsh, a name which owes its origin to their leader Gualo, or to queen Galaes or to their decline [lit. 'to their barbarianism']. (pp.280–281)

Even whilst the *Historia* encouraged the Normans to reassess their perceptions of the ancient British as being brutish in their lack of history, Geoffrey reaffirmed the justice of their attitudes towards the current inhabitants of Wales.

The *Historia* contradicted a widespread assumption: that the undesirable cultural characteristics of England's neighbours were also manifested in their languages. Perceived differences in the cultural weight of Gaelic and English played an important role in William of Malmesbury's vision of a civilised Norman-centred culture surrounded by barbaric lands to the North and West.[39] His treatment of a passage in Bede is particularly revealing, where King Oswald translates Bishop Aidan's Scottish Gaelic sermons into English for his congregation. Whereas Bede simply described the Gaelic language as 'linguam Scottorum', William preferred to construct a dichotomy between the obvious and the obscure, the familiar and the barbaric.[40] He stated that Oswald 'made plain in his native tongue what had been wrapped up in a barbarian language' ('barbari sermonis inuolucrum patria lingua expediret').[41] Geoffrey's *Historia* cast British in a different light. He not only endowed the Britons with a much fuller history than had previously been available, but located the significance of that history in their language.

Besides Geoffrey's insistence on the stylistic excellence of its source material, the *Historia* also demonstrated at length that the British language was worthy of scholarly etymological study. Sharing the widely prevalent medieval belief, influentially stated by Isidore of Seville, that 'one's insight into anything is clearer when its etymology is known' ('nam dum videris unde ortum est nomen, citius vim eius intellegis'), Geoffrey included much detail culled from the vernaculars.[42] His etymologies were taken from Welsh, Latin or English, but he rarely specified which: the reader was either expected to be able to identify the language and to follow his reasoning, or to accept his authority without investigating further. He sometimes situated a single place name across several languages. Many of the etymologies based on Welsh relied on a crude juxtaposition of the word *kaer* ('city, fortress, camp') with the name of the founder of the town, or with a distinguishing epithet, such as *Kaerleir* (Leicester, 'Leir's town') or *Kaerbadum* (Bath, 'town of baths') (pp.36–37).[43] As in the latter example, Geoffrey calls the depth of his linguistic proficiency into question through his use of Latin to supplement his Welsh. However, these inconsistencies do not seem to have troubled him: using his understanding of English, he suggested that *Seftonia* (Shaftesbury) was originally called *oppidum montis paladur*, using the Latin *oppidum*, 'town' (cf. Old and Middle English *burh*), *mons*, 'hill', and the Welsh *paladr*, 'shaft' (pp.36–37).[44] It is unclear why Geoffrey included the hill: perhaps to reflect the geography of Shaftesbury. The specificities of the data provided by English, Latin, and Welsh are merged in order to produce a single, coherent, inter-lingual account. Rather than necessarily indicating gaps in Geoffrey's knowledge then, his multilingual etymologies may instead reflect patterns of linguistic enquiry shaped by code-switching.

Geoffrey's etymologies radically departed from classical precedent in their focus on the vernacular, encouraging his audience to reconsider the intellectual value of British. Unlike Isidore's etymological derivations, which were based on Latin, or, occasionally, on Greek, for Geoffrey, the evidence provided by the indigenous British language could sometimes be a more reliable indicator of the island's history than the tongues of its conquerors. Vernacular etymologies not only preserved the former inhabitants' perceptions of the British landscape, but also furnished clues to the lives of those inhabitants themselves. Speaking of Queen Guendoloena's decision to throw her step-daughter Habren into the river 'now called the Severn' ('nunc Sabrina dicitur'), Geoffrey noted that Guendoloena was responsible for its name, as 'she wanted Habren to enjoy immortality since her own husband had been the girl's father' ('uolebat etenim honorem aeternitatis illi impendere quia maritus suus eam generauerat', pp.34–35). He continued:

> Vnde contigit quod usque in hunc diem appellatum est flumen Britannica lingua Habren, quod per corruptionem nominis alia lingua Sabrina uocatur.

> Hence the river is called Habren in British even today, although in the other tongue this has been corrupted to Severn. (pp.34–35)

This 'alia lingua' was presumably English, or perhaps even Latin. In identifying this as a *corruptio nominis*, a linguistic corruption, Geoffrey hinted at an inversion of the discourse of British barbarianism. For Isidore, a word 'pronounced with a corrupted letter or sound' ('corrupta littera vel sono enuntiatum') was a 'barbarism' ('barbarismus'). He explained:

> Appellatus autem barbarismus a barbaris gentibus, dum latinae orationis integritatem nescirent. Vnaquaeque enim gens facta Romanorum cum opibus suis vitia quoque et verborum et morum Romam transmisit.

> It is called 'barbarism' from barbarian peoples, since they were ignorant of the purity of the Latin language, for some groups of peoples, once they had been made Romans, brought to Rome their mistakes in language and customs as well as their wealth. (I.xxxii.1–2)

By suggesting that the English (or Latin) language was also capable of corruption, Geoffrey portrayed the speakers of this 'other tongue' as barbarians, making 'mistakes' through their ignorance of the native idiom. This portrayal of ancient British offered substantial challenges to assumptions about the relatively low status of the twelfth-century Brittonic languages. For an Anglo-Norman audience, it may also have raised troubling questions about the degree to which cultural and linguistic assimilation was possible or desirable for those conquering new territories.

Whilst seeking to reframe the dignity of British, Geoffrey nonetheless sharply circumscribed its prestige by exclusively stressing its historical significance. His description of the origins of British transformed it into the only language which preserved the perpetual memory of a classical hero:

> Denique Brutus de nomine suo insulam Britanniam appellat sociosque suos Britones. Volebat enim ex diriuatione nominis memoriam habere perpetuam. Vnde postmodum loquela gentis, quae prius Troiana siue curuum Graecum nuncupabatur, dicta fuit Britannica.

> Brutus named the island Britain after himself and called his followers Britons. He wanted to be remembered for ever for giving them his name. For this reason the language of his people, previously known as Trojan or 'crooked Greek', was henceforth called British. (pp.28–29)

For late-twelfth-century francophones, this stress on Greek antecedents might have recalled the connections between their language and Latin. This enhanced the *Historia*'s combative portrayal of the *liber vetussissimus* and its excellent style: the status of British rivals not only Latin, but French.[45] However, this status remained carefully circumscribed. As Welsh speakers alone could call to mind the parallels between *camroeg* ('crooked Greek') and *Cymraeg* ('Welsh'), Geoffrey situated the evidence for his derivation beyond the ken of most of his readers.[46] This occluded the full significance of the name 'crooked Greek', passing over in silence the etymological evidence it provides for the connections between the Trojan language and contemporary Welsh. Instead, Geoffrey emphasised the links between Brutus and the language of the ancient British, ensuring that the classical heritage of the Welsh remained firmly in the past. As in the broader scheme of his work, this simultaneously strengthened and dissolved the Britons' hopes of a later resurgence. Even though a high proportion of the evidence for the historical and linguistic links between British and the tongue of Brutus had been assembled from medieval Welsh, the language's entire value was located in its Trojan history. Its contemporary linguistic forms coalesced with those of Geoffrey's *liber uetustissimus*, since the etymological information Geoffrey claimed to be taken from ancient British was in fact from Welsh. He implicitly suggested that the main significance of the twelfth-century language lay in its etymology. Geoffrey hence made a case that the British vernacular was as worthy of prolonged scrutiny as the sacred languages of antiquity, and that, like them, it was capable of yielding up the secrets of history.

The British Language and the Prophetic Past

In another Latin work, the *Prophetia Merlini*, Geoffrey encouraged his audience to engage with the language of his supposedly British source far more intensely than elsewhere. The text is primarily known for sparking international interest in Merlin as a vatic figure. However, it is an equally significant point of origin for the academic study of vernacular tropes. Both Geoffrey's putative translations seem to offer readers a unique connection to the British language, but with differing degrees of immediacy. Whilst comments in the *Historia* apparently invite further study of its vernacular source, the claim to have discovered an ancient book simultaneously deflects more detailed investigations. Geoffrey's portrayal of the text as a translation defers linguistic analysis, directing the reader's close attention away from the *Historia* and towards the chimerical *liber uetustissimus*.[47] In contrast, the *Prophetia Merlini* also purports to be a translation from British, but one which invites a perusal attentive both to its language, and to its historicity. The text survives in over eighty manuscripts, a testament to widespread and careful study. Besides many copies which feature interpretative glosses on the prophecies, there are also several full-length commentaries. Some of these run into thousands of words. For Geoffrey's contemporaries, the opacity of the prophecies relating to future times did not invalidate their testimony. Instead, it suggested that the text had further potential to reveal unknown truths, if one could only interpret them correctly. Extensive efforts were made to subject the work to detailed examination: commentators recognised that the text's secrets lay hidden in the specificities of Merlin's figurative language. These concerted attempts to unlock literature via the techniques of Latinate scholarly analysis were part of a much wider twelfth-century trend which sought to re-interpret major authors such as Virgil and Ovid. But another aspect of these works was profoundly innovative: these commentaries on Merlin's prophecies are some of the earliest attempts to describe and discuss vernacular literary style, albeit in Latin translation.

The *Prophetia Merlini* comprised the seventh book of the *Historia regum Britanniae*, and was supposedly a translation of the prophecies which Merlin Ambrosius made to Vortigern in early Britain.[48] However, whilst it was included within the *Historia*, the *Prophetia Merlini* also seems to have circulated independently in advance. Orderic Vitalis knew the prophecies before Henry I's death in 1135, and included a version in his own *Historia Ecclesiastica*.[49] Geoffrey's text was equipped with its own dedicatory epistle addressed to Alexander, who was Bishop of Lincoln from 1123 to

1148.[50] The epistle confirms that the work was published early by popular demand (pp.142–143). Geoffrey stressed to Alexander that, like the *Historia*, the work was a translation 'from British into Latin' ('de Britannico in Latinum'):

> At tamen, quoniam securus eram ueniae quam discretio subtilis ingenii tui donaret, agrestem calamum meum labellis apposui et plebeia modulatione ignotum tibi interpretatus sum sermonem.

> All the same, because I was sure that the discernment of your subtle mind would grant me pardon, I have put my rustic pipe to my lips and, to its humble tune, have translated the tongue which is unknown to you. (pp.142–143)

In both the *Historia* and the *Prophetia*, Geoffrey used this *sermo ignotus* to reinforce his position as privileged interpreter of a text otherwise rendered linguistically inaccessible to the reader.

Geoffrey's fictions of translation seem to have been an important factor in his success. Like the *Historia*, the *Prophetia Merlini* does not appear to be a straightforward rendering of an earlier text. The work may have had some connection to vernacular literature: the theologian John of Cornwall made a Latin translation of an alternative, related text of the *Prophetia Merlini* which featured some Brittonic glosses (discussed further below). A more diffuse parallel is found between the zoomorphic imagery of the *Prophetia* and the animal epithets bestowed on Welsh warriors by native chroniclers.[51] Nonetheless, if influenced by earlier vernacular traditions, the *Prophetia Merlini* has also been extensively adapted for the political concerns of a twelfth-century audience. Geoffrey did not portray his third Latin work, the *Vita Merlini*, as a translation. It is, however, the most unambiguously reliant on Welsh sources, both in its depiction of Merlin as a wild man and in its inclusion of the bard Taliesin.[52] Geoffrey stated explicitly that the *Vita* had been designed with entertainment in mind, inspired by a 'jovial muse' (*musa jocosa*).[53] This focus on fun might explain why he did not feel it necessary to frame it as a British text, worthy of translation into Latin because of the international significance of its content. The reception history of the *Vita Merlini* suggests that audiences did not respond favourably to this explicitly imaginative literature with no ultimate textual authority. The work survives in its full form in only one manuscript, and as extracts in another six, compared with over two hundred witnesses of the *Historia*, and around eighty of the *Prophetia Merlini*.[54] The popularity of Galfridian works was strikingly affected by whether or not a text was depicted as a vernacular translation.

The *Prophetia Merlini* were not only widely reproduced, but widely believed. Several leading intellectuals were convinced that the prophecies were worthy of close consideration. Abbot Suger remarked around 1140 that he found them to be elegant and truthful, whilst Herbert of Bosham complained to the pope that Henry II had used them to threaten Thomas Becket. If, in 1169, John of Salisbury thought Merlin to be a prophet of 'no authority' ('futilem [. . .] auctoritatem'), he himself had cited the prophecies in 1166 with reference to political developments in Brittany.[55] Some responses were more ambiguous: Wace omitted the *Prophetia Merlini* from his translation of the *Historia regum Britanniae*.[56] Whilst this may suggest that that he was unconvinced by them, he did not explicitly condemn Geoffrey. The omission may instead intimate that Anglo-Norman readers took their political content seriously enough to be concerned about the personal consequences of transmitting them: Henry of Huntingdon, otherwise an admirer of Geoffrey's work, failed to mention them in his *Letter to Warin the Breton* (where he recounted discovering a text of the *Historia regum Britanniae* at Bec) or to record them elsewhere.[57] Orderic Vitalis seems to have been equally intimidated. After his abrupt inclusion of the *Prophetia Merlini* within his own *Historia Ecclesiastica*, he began to interpret them up to the reign of Henry I, before he fell silent, noting that 'after this fashion wise men may clearly decipher the rest' ('Sic cetera sophistae liquido discutiant').[58] Alan Cooper suggests that Orderic was afraid of Henry I's influence, and chose to say nothing, rather than to expound the rest of the prophecies in a light unfavourable to the king.[59]

Why did this array of sophisticated readers find the text credible? In part, its pretensions to accuracy rested on a coded portrayal of events up to the 1130s which seemed to suggest that future truths were yet to be revealed. However, the distinctive language of the text also offered confirmation of its authenticity. Medieval detractors isolated one aspect of Geoffrey's linguistic strategy. They recognised that by framing his text as a translation, Geoffrey was able to make a powerful case for the textual authority of his work. Writing in 1196–1198, William of Newburgh considered the aim of Geoffrey's translation not only to be one of self-valorisation, but also to encompass the valorisation of the British. This formed one of his main criticisms of Geoffrey's historiography:

> Qui etiam majori ausu cujusdam Merlini divinationes fallacissimas, quibus utique de proprio plurimum adjecit, dum eas in Latinum transfunderet, tanquam authenticas et immobili veritate subnixas prophetias vulgavit.

> More audaciously still he has taken the most deceitful predictions of a certain Merlin which he has very greatly augmented on his own account, and

in translating them into Latin he has published them as though they were authentic prophecies resting on unshakeable truth. (I.28–29)

Clearly, for William, the Latin language itself guaranteed the veracity of a text to a certain extent. The stylistic conventions of the classical tradition are implicitly compared to the 'old fictitious accounts of the Britons' ('priscis Britonum figmentis'): their *neniae* ('nursery rhymes' or 'incantations') reflect the primitive, infantile and superstitious state of their own culture, with its credulous hopes of the future return of Arthur.[60] William may have seen Geoffrey's sources as intrinsically unreliable simply because they were British. Gildas influentially portrayed the Britons as having a 'hatred of truth and its champions, and [a] love of falsehood and its contrivers' ('odium veritatis cum assertoribus amorque mendacii cum suis fabricatoribus').[61] William quoted Gildas's assertion that the Britons were neither 'brave in war nor trustworthy in peace' ('nec in bello fortes fuerint nec in pace fideles', I.28–29).Despite the fact that Gildas was himself one of these untrustworthy Britons, William saw his fierce condemnation of their 'many evil traits' ('multa [. . .] mala', I.28–29) as proof of the historical reliability of his testimony. In contrast, he accused Geoffrey of having an 'uncontrolled passion for lying' ('effrenata mentiendi libidine', I.32–33). William did not clarify whether this *libido mentiendi* merely reflected Geoffrey's own authorial practice in presenting fiction as history, or whether it also extended to his employment of the falsehoods found in British sources. William insisted that Merlin's prophecies must have stemmed from Satanic inspiration. But instead of criticising their content first of all, he focussed initially on Geoffrey's portrayal of these 'most deceitful' (*fallacissimae*) predictions (I.28–29). William seems to imply that the act of translation endows its object with authority by implicitly portraying it as worthy of dissemination. However, he may also have been concerned that the medium of Latin was itself a guarantee of veracity. Readers encountering a Latin text would make positive assumptions about its credibility that a British text would not warrant.

William's assessment of the linguistic appeal of the *Prophetia Merlini* is supported by the surviving commentaries. Geoffrey's work attracted widespread and protracted attention: it received at least four full-length commentaries in the twelfth century alone, as well as extensive interpretative glossing.[62] The apparently ancient and vernacular imagery of the prophecies fascinated twelfth-century readers and writers, even whilst they attempted to transform the text's distinctively obscure tropes into more conventional lexis. For many, the authority of the *Prophetia Merlini* did not reside in its Latinity, but in its opaque idiom: this seemed to confirm the early date of the prophecies and their mysterious origins. Such language presented the commentator with an irresistible interpretative challenge. Orderic stated that: 'the prophet Merlin predicted the course of things to come in the northern isles, and preserved it in writing in figurative language' ('Iamdictus uates seriatim quae futura erant insulis septemptrionis predixit, tipicisque locutionibus memoriae litterarum tradidit').[63] He posited a disjunction between the prophetic truth as revealed to Merlin, and the ambiguous manner in which it was recorded for posterity. Merlin's manner of discourse is what Lesley Coote has termed a 'hermeneutic language': it both invites and defies interpretation.[64] Orderic did not question that the allegorical imagery veiled a self-evident political meaning, 'clearer than daylight' ('luce clarius'). Significantly, the decoding of such allegory required a thorough understanding of the past. He stated of Merlin that: 'Men well read in histories can easily apply his predictions' ('Historiarum gnari eius dicta facile poterunt intelligere').[65] Political prophecies necessarily portray themselves as ancient texts, so that the contemporary writer can construct a series of retrospective predictions which conform sufficiently closely to historical events to convince readers of the prophet's future accuracy. They are both archaic, and immediate. This is of particular interest with regard to the function of translation within the *Prophetia Merlini*. The British language rendered the prophecies linguistically inaccessible to Anglo-Norman readers, endowing their contents with an air of mystery. However, readers were also encouraged to believe that such opacity might be penetrated through the powers of interpretative analysis born of a Latin education. Commentators located linguistic authority in Merlin's supposedly British idioms, but simultaneously attempted to smooth away this ambiguous language into academic prose. Whilst their efforts to explain the text's idiosyncratic language recognised its unique authority, they sought to reduce its historical particularity to a transparent Latin medium.

The commentaries hence display a tension between drawing attention to obscure language, and resolving the issues of comprehension such language presents. This is apparent in the longest of them, by an otherwise unknown Alanus, who expounded the *Prophetia Merlini* in seven books between 1167–1174.[66] In his prologue, he wrote that after careful scrutiny of the text, 'nothing finally seems strange that I am interpreting either by its own literal meanings, or by images and customs of speech in metaphors' ('nihil denique, quod a propriis vocum significationibus, vel a figuratis & usitatis verborum translationibus peregrinum videatur').[67] Alanus was eager to stress that despite its elaborate language, on closer examination, nothing in the text need be considered *peregrinus*, 'strange' or 'foreign'.[68]

The interpretation of the text becomes a means of exerting linguistic control: the *Prophetia Merlini* invites the reader to decipher the British past according to the Anglo-Norman present, an exegesis mirroring the prior act of translation from British to Latin. The text's recondite, supposedly vernacular stylistic features bring a sense of mystique to the prophecies, heightening the reader's feelings of triumph and empowerment in their interpretation. It encourages the performance of a translation from the figurative to the literal which parallels that of British to Latin: this performance re-enacts the translator's mastery of the vernacular, even whilst that vernacular remains unknown to the reader. The vatic and historical significance of the British language is made immanent at the same time as its linguistic specificity recedes.

Although scholarly interest in vernacular style remained closely tied to decoding the content of the prophecies, it nonetheless inspired unprecedented analysis of British as a literary idiom. The *Prophetia Merlini* offered an exegetical opportunity to re-inscribe the meaning of its vernacular source through commentary. But if this act of allegoresis enabled 'the displacement of the original text and the investment of the new text with an originary authority', it equally endowed the original text with an authority of its own.[69] Geoffrey's *Prophetia Merlini* was certainly not the first Latin secular text to inspire a commentary tradition. Important classical works such as Virgil's *Aeneid* captured the attention of Anselm of Laon and other twelfth-century biblical scholars.[70] In contrast, vernacular texts had received a very limited amount of such treatment. We might think of Notker Labeo's comments on the grammatical structure of his Old High German translations of Latin texts at St Gall in the late tenth and early eleventh centuries. However, the Old High German here remained subservient to the Latin insofar as it was designed to illuminate the source text, rather than to be the object of commentary itself.[71] In Old English, yet more diffuse parallels are found in Bede's remarks on *Cædmon's Hymn*, or perhaps in Byrhtferth of Ramsey's early-eleventh-century *Enchiridion*, which employed both Latin and Old English as vehicles for instruction.[72] Although all these works incorporated elements of the commentary tradition, no vernacular text had yet received a sustained exegetical treatment in its own right. The commentaries on Geoffrey's *Prophetia Merlini* were thus unusual, even unique, in their object's claim to be a translation from a vernacular language. By encoding political information within supposedly British rhetorical tropes, the *Prophetia Merlini* prompted new considerations of vernacular literary style. It depicted a British work as worthy of close scholarly attention, marking an important milestone in Anglo-Norman attitudes to the vernacular.

Brittonic Interpretations of Merlin's Political Allegories

In spite of the revolutionary nature of the relationship between these Latin commentaries and the vernacular, both Geoffrey and his twelfth-century readership retained a certain ambivalence towards British. The language was seen as unsuitable for academic scrutiny, even whilst encapsulating the historical and prophetic data that necessitated the attention of the scholar. This ambivalence is clearly visible in the only commentary on a version of the prophecies of Merlin which seems to bear any tangible trace of a Brittonic source: the Latin translation and commentary by John of Cornwall. Although the text shares a proportion of its lines with Geoffrey (see below), most of John's work appears to derive from a different source, and it also includes six Brittonic glosses: this may perhaps indicate that John and Geoffrey were both translating from a common text. John stated that he wrote at the request of 'R.', Bishop of Exeter: this is most likely to have been Robert Warelwast, who was in office from 1138–1155, and was of Norman extraction.[73] Internal references within John's commentary (especially the absence of an unambiguous mention of the coronation of Henry II in 1154) led Michael Curley to date the work tentatively to the years 1153 × 1154.[74] The palaeography of the sole surviving manuscript, Vatican City, Vatican Library MS Ottobian Latinus 1474, suggests that it was copied somewhat later, between the last third of the twelfth century and the first quarter of the thirteenth.[75] The single hand displays English features.[76] Although influenced by Geoffrey of Monmouth, John's translation does not seem to derive from him exclusively, and his commentary also incorporates six vernacular glosses, some of which are definitely Welsh, some Cornish, and others which could be from any P-Celtic language. The work is thus of double interest in its presentation of an alternative text of Merlin's prophecies, and in the insight it offers into their reception amongst speakers of Brittonic languages. After examining John's treatment of the literary language of his source or sources, this section will compare his responses to the political sensitivity of Merlin's language with those of his acquaintance, Gerald of Wales.

In commissioning John to translate a text of vernacular prophecy, Bishop R. may have been motivated by a curiosity concerning the basis of legends already circulating in his diocese, a curiosity heightened by the enthusiastic reception of Geoffrey of Monmouth in Cornwall.[77] The *Historia regum Britanniae* featured much discussion of 'Cornubia': it endowed the region with a Trojan founder, Corineus, whose prowess in wrestling giants was much vaunted by Geoffrey (pp.28–29). He gave the Cornish their own etymology (from their chief, Corineus), stressing their outstanding bravery: 'in every battle [they] proved more helpful to Brutus than the rest' ('Bruto in omni decertatione prae ceteris auxilium praestabat', pp.20–21). Geoffrey's portrayal of Cornwall was highly flattering, culminating in an emphasis and embellishment of Arthur's close links with the region.[78] Moreover, the area south of Exeter seems to have had a native tradition of Arthurian myth prior to the *Historia regum Britanniae*: in 1113, canons from Laon journeying through 'Danavexeria' (South Devon and Cornwall) were told that they were in 'the land of Arthur' (*terra Arturi*) and shown natural features described as Arthur's seat and his oven.[79] In Bodmin, a member of their party became involved in a fight with a local who asserted that Arthur was still alive, a characteristically British belief later ridiculed by William of Malmesbury.[80] At least one of the twelfth-century Cornish was eager to exploit the prestige accrued by this Galfridian inheritance. In Johannes de Hauvilla's Latin hexametric poem, the *Architrenius*, written around 1184, much was made of the supposedly Trojan ancestry of his Cornish patron, Walter de Coutances, Archbishop of Rouen; Gerald of Wales went so far as to claim that Walter was a direct descendant of Brutus.[81] John's version of the *Prophetia Merlini* thus fitted well with wider patterns of literary interest in Cornish oral tradition.

Both scholarly and local concerns influenced John's portrayal of his text. He was a theologian by training, eventually rising to become archdeacon of Worcester. Nothing is known of his early life, although his name and interests indicate a Cornish background. By the 1150s, he had already studied in France in the school of Thierry of Chartres; later in life he was to attend the University of Paris, under Peter Lombard.[82] His educational experiences seem to have influenced his approach to the *Prophetia Merlini*: he added interlinear glosses and a commentary for the first 134 lines of his verse translation. The final thirty-three lines were left unglossed. The presentation of the text suggests that John considered it to be worthy of serious critical attention. The L-shaped layout of the commentary around the main text of the prophecies and the differentiation of the scripts used for each recalls the standard *mise-en-page* of early-twelfth-century glossed manuscripts intended for the academic study of the Bible and of the liberal arts.[83] E. K. Chambers was led by John's subject matter to conclude that he had merely produced a shortened verse paraphrase of Geoffrey's *Prophetia Merlini*, but later examination has shown that only 38 prophecies out of the total 139 can be derived in this way. Several of these exhibit minor variants which may point to a common source, rather than to direct copying.[84] Certainly, the commentary does not purport to focus on

Geoffrey, although the *Historia* is mentioned.[85] However, the Galfridian version of the *Prophetia Merlini* remained the main impetus behind John's project: the translation was presumably requested because Bishop R.'s interest in Brittonic prophecy had been piqued by Geoffrey. John never stated that he used Galfridian prophetic material, instead portraying his work as a translation from a British original. In his dedicatory preface, he used the possessive pronoun to emphasise that he had been chosen to translate the prophecies due to his status as a native speaker of the language: 'iussus [...] prophetiam Merlini iuxta nostrum Britannicum exponere' ('having been ordered to expound the prophecies of Merlin according to my British' (vv.3–4)).

John never specified exactly which language he intended 'Britannicus' to signify. Based on survival rates for other Brittonic prophetic texts, the balance of probability lies strongly in favour of a Welsh source: this has been augmented with further Cornish oral or written material.[86] John's commentary, however, adapted the text to the interests of his Exeter audience: the diocese had jurisdiction over the entirety of Cornwall, and John largely interpreted the poem according to Cornish events, although Welsh and Breton details were also included in the commentary to a lesser extent.[87] This international perspective suggests that the text was more pan-Brittonic than proto-nationalistic in its affiliations, a hypothesis supported by the six glosses which John has chosen to include.[88] Some of them are certainly from Welsh, others from Cornish, and others potentially from Welsh, Cornish, or Breton: due to the early date, confused scribal copying, and limited scope of the material, the languages cannot be conclusively differentiated in some cases. The uncertainty has been compounded by the activity of the scribe in the only surviving manuscript, who does not appear to have had any knowledge of the languages in question, producing very rough approximations of the original glosses. This may provide further confirmation that John's audience was primarily composed of non-native speakers.

Given this potential audience, we might ask whether John intended the glosses to be understood at all: Curley has suggested that their presence primarily served to demonstrate the translator's linguistic credentials as the interpreter of an authentic vernacular text.[89] John included six Brittonic phrases in his commentary, along with some place names. Only one of these glosses is unambiguously Cornish: *pemp bliden warn ugens ha hanter* ('twenty-five and a half years', v.190), two could be Cornish or possibly Breton: *goen bren* ('high moor', vv.266–267) and *guent dehil* ('winnowing wind', v.241), and another could be derived from any of the Brittonic languages: *awel garu* ('bitter wind', v.271).[90] Two appear to be closest to Welsh: *castel uchel coed* ('the fortification of the high wood', v.282) and *michtien luchd mal igasuet* (v.247). The interpretation of the latter is very unclear.[91] If it does indeed correspond to the Welsh poetic image of *mechdeyrn llwyd mal i gassec*, 'the chief as white as his mare',[92] then the gloss may have been displaced from its lemma elsewhere (cf. vv.140–143). In the poem's current form, John offers it as a translation for 'canus adoptatus Perironis obambulat ortus' ('the adopted grey-haired man [. . .] shall walk back and forth in front of the springs of Periron', v.91).[93] It is uncertain whether this seemingly misplaced gloss has implications for John's understanding of the poem: other sources attest to his capabilities as a translator. According to his friend, Gerald of Wales, his linguistic expertise was a factor in his nomination for the bishopric of St David's in 1176 by Gerard Pucelle, canonist and sometime Bishop of Coventry. Gerald of Wales added that one of the royal secretaries told Pucelle that this would be seen by the Normans as a disadvantage.[94] The anecdote was primarily recounted for satirical effect, but there seems little reason to doubt that John did not have at least a passive competence in one or more Brittonic languages: Gerald and John knew each other personally.[95]

This probable knowledge of Welsh and Cornish sources suggests that John himself did not feel the need to distinguish between the differing provenances of glosses, designating them all as *Britannicus*. Whilst this may be a conscious fusion of different traditions into a single unitary entity, it is more likely that John was not particularly concerned with the issue of language differentiation, and did not think it necessary to make the diverse sources of his translation apparent to his Latin readers.[96] He may also have augmented or adapted glosses from an earlier text: the Cornish ones do not seem to be of a uniform date.[97] Writing in 1193/94, Gerald of Wales saw the degree of intelligibility between Cornish, Welsh, and Breton as evidence of their shared Trojan roots:

> Cornubia vero, et Armorica Britannia, lingua utuntur fere persimili; Kambris tamen, propter originalem convenientiam, in multis adhuc et fere cunctis intelligibili. Quae, quanto delicata minus et incomposita magis, tanto antiquo linguae Britannicae idiomati magis, ut arbitror, appropriata.

> In both Cornwall and Brittany they speak almost the same language as in Wales. It comes from the same root and is intelligible to the Welsh in many instances, and almost in all. It is rougher and less clearly pronounced, but probably closer to the original British speech, or so I think myself.[98]

Significantly, here it is the Cornish/Breton language (still seen by Gerald as being essentially the same tongue) which has preserved the more authentically ancient idiom. We could, perhaps, posit a scenario whereby the varying Brittonic languages used in John's glosses were all seen as relevant to

the reconstruction of an earlier British text. This must necessarily remain
highly conjectural: the evidence afforded by the glosses is ambiguous, the
scribe's infelicities compounded by the inconsistencies and vagueness of
John's own linguistic testimony. Whether the glosses reflect a single main
source or a scattering of phrases selected from a variety of textual and oral
traditions, they bear witness to the importance John attached to the information contained in the British language.

If, for us, the glosses' varied provenance obfuscates our picture of John's
sources, he himself seems to have had a clearer idea of their intended effect
on his readers. All the glosses were inserted to provide examples of what
John calls 'our language' ('nostra lingua', v.266): when John did contextualise them, he related them to a Cornish background. This included a
gloss likely to come from Welsh, *michtien luchd mal igasuet*, which John
connected to the white-haired man from Periron (v.247). In Welsh literature from the *Armes Pryddein* (*c.*930) onwards, *Periron* was the name for
a major river, although its precise location is unknown.[99] John, however,
chose to see *Periron* instead as the stream in Cornwall on which the castle
of Dindaiol (probably Tintagel) was situated (vv.247–249). His commentary often interpreted the text according to Cornish history, even though
there is only one direct reference to 'Cornubia' in the prophecies (v.104)
and another to the river Tamar (v.107). John considered a third, *Brenti-
gia*, to refer to Fowey Moor (v.108, 265–267). In contrast, there are several
references common in Welsh poetic diction, including the plain of Rheon
(vv. 80, 148); Anglesey (v.95); and Caerleon (v.160). There are also three
Welsh names for rivers: the Tywi (v.146); Periron (vv.91, 141); and Sabrina,
the Severn (v.145). When these were included in the portion of the poem
encompassed by John's commentary, they were sometimes dealt with in a
much more perfunctory fashion, or were passed over in silence, or were
assimilated to the Cornish tradition, as in the case of Periron. This may
be because of gaps in John's knowledge: he did include information on
the Welsh name for Anglesey (vv.249–255), suggesting that he sought to
elucidate his source material where he could. The location of John's audience is more certain. Readers were expected to be able to enlarge his references to earlier Cornish feuds with their own background knowledge,
and John tactfully did not dwell on the stealing ('depredationem') perpetrated by those from Devon in Cornwall ('apud nos') for fear of seeming
'contumelious' ('ne contumeliosus uiderer') (vv.231–233).[100] At the same
time, John stated that he chose to focus only on historical events from the
Norman Conquest onwards, leaving out what went before because it had
been covered adequately ('satis') by previous commentators (vv.8–11). The

vernacular text only seems to exist insofar as it is relevant to the twelfth-century reader. John's role in the selection and interpretation of such relevant material allows him to re-inscribe himself in the role of author. His commentary brings the text into being a second time by deciding which aspects are of vatic significance.

Like other commentators on Merlin's prophecies, John singled out their figurative language as a justification for the potentially reductive nature of his allegorical exegesis. Such language, for him, was specifically Brittonic (or perhaps Cornish); it occurred 'very often in our poetry' ('sepissime [. . .] in nostris cantilenis', vv.203–204). This style provided confirmation of the text's authenticity and antiquity, whilst paradoxically permitting and, indeed, inviting interpretation according to contemporary events and concerns:

> *Solium*, id est, Cornubia que in hystoria appellatur domus Coronei, ideo scilicet quia Coroneus iste sorte Bruti eam antiquissime obtinuit; appellatur etiam domus solium Arcturi, eo quod ipse maximus regum inibi est ortus (vv.215–218).[101]

> *The throne*, that is Cornwall, which in the history is called the house of Coroneus, because Coroneus obtained her in an allotted portion from Brutus in most ancient times; the house is also called the throne of Arthur, because the greatest of kings arose from there.

Such passages show the influence of the *Historia regum Britanniae*, although, as we have seen, an allegiance to King Arthur seems to have been a feature of Cornish culture from at least the second decade of the twelfth century. John used the information given by Geoffrey of Monmouth to embellish the text's historical diction with data which could be verified by a twelfth-century Latin audience. The imagery affirms the historical integrity of the work, but given the conglomeration of Welsh and Cornish elements that the text contains, this integrity may well be something of a fiction. It was therefore all the more important for John to emphasise the potency of its testimony, a potency heightened by an awareness of the text's age. He contextualised the gloss in historical terms:

> Eo enim tempore uentus tam uehemens insaniuit, ut frustrata relinqueret uota cultorum. Hoc malum nominat ipse in Britannico *guent dehil*.

> For in that time a wind raged which was so violent that it left the prayers of the priests disappointed. He [Merlin] calls this evil in British *guent dehil.* (vv.239–241)

If not explicitly theorised, John still seems to have had a definite sense that his text was rendered valuable both through its language, and through the age of that language.

John's acquaintance, Gerald of Wales, discussed the authenticating power of archaic language more fully in the preface to his own Latin translation of a version of the *Prophecies of Merlin*. He originally expected this translation of the *Prophecies* to form the third book of his *Expugnatio Hibernica*. However, only his translator's preface survives: Gerald claimed that the translation itself was never begun, perhaps due to an unfavourable political environment (discussed further below). The preface emphasised Gerald's selective strategy of translation:

> [C]unctis moderni sermonis composicionem redolentibus quasi reprobatis et abiectis, sola veritatis amica sermonis antiqui rudis et plana simplicitas diligenter excepta mentem allexit.

> Therefore all those [prophecies] in which the style suggests that of more modern writings have been rejected, and the rough and unvarnished simplicity of the older idiom has been carefully distinguished from the rest, and has won our favour as being the only true friend of truth.[102]

Gerald deliberately edited the text, stating that 'the jealous profession of the bards has falsified nature, and added to the genuine prophecies many others of their own invention' ('bardorum ars invida naturam adulterans, multa de suis tamquam prophetica veris adiecit').[103] For Norman readers, the authority of the translation was actually increased by this selection process. Gerald's text refused to credit the accretions of subsequent Welsh commentators with any ideological validity, instead seeking to pare back the text to the original vatic truth. A key criterion for the discernment of such 'truth' was its historicity. The text's stylistic idiom became a guarantee of its own authenticity.

As with other twelfth-century commentators on the *Prophetia Merlini*, both John and Gerald were very anxious that their work should not appear subversive to those in authority. Gerald refused to translate the *Prophetia* at all, and John declined to comment on the final thirty-three lines. Jean Blacker has suggested that John's failure to explain the significance of the end of the prophecies, with their treatment of the reigns of Conan and Cadwaladr, indicated an awareness of the importance of these figures to hopes of a British resurgence.[104] Gerald did not even begin his translation of the prophecies, fearful that the truth 'should burst forth prematurely and perilously into the light of day, thereby offending those in power' ('in lucem cum maiorum offensa prepropere pariter et periculose prorumpat').[105] Although this could be a parody of Geoffrey's shadowy British source text, it is equally likely that Gerald was aware of the controversial nature of the material. He was involved in the excavation of Arthur's remains at Glastonbury in order to demonstrate the fact of his death to the Welsh, Cornish, and Bretons, and made efforts to distance himself from the interpretations of Galfridian history open to Arthur's return.[106] Given the hanging of the prophet Peter of Pontefract in 1213, and the threats of Gerald's own relatives to draw the attention of the authorities to the treasonous utterances in his writings, Gerald's systematic excision of references to prophecy in his revised edition of the *Expugnatio Hibernica* may suggest anxiety about the potential repercussions of prophesying in the reign of John.[107] Whilst their ostentatious silence signalled Gerald and John's refusal to engage with the text's potentially subversive content, this silence was also a powerful testament to their belief that such predictions might ultimately be fulfilled.

Both authors drew attention to aspects of vernacular language which were able to confirm the text's authority. They were aware that British linguistic detail could be employed to authenticate political allegories. This awareness may have provided one reason for John's ambiguous treatment of the literary qualities of the text. It has not been previously noted that his presentation of the language of his British poem may be inviting scorn in order to deflect an imagined official eye. Seemingly participating in the medieval trend for protestations of authorial modesty, John wrote humbly to Bishop R. that he had composed the work in a 'puerile style' ('puerili stilo', v.6). However, this may also have been a broader comment on the language of the text. The *Rhetorica ad Herennium* discusses the figures of *homoeoptoton* and *homoeoteleuton*, where two or more words, with the same case or indeclinable ending respectively, appear in the same clause. The author cautioned the reader against their overuse, noting that they can lessen the orator's 'credibility, impressiveness and seriousness' ('fides et gravitas et severitas'). He stated: 'If then, we crowd these figures together, we shall seem to be taking delight in a puerile style' (Quomodo igitur, si crebo his generibus utemur, puerili videmur elocutione delectari).[108] John chose to translate the poetry of his source into Leonine hexameters: each line features monosyllabic internal rhyme on the first half of the third foot with the last syllable of the sixth foot, hence employing both *homoeoptoton* and *homoeoteleuton* in their reliance on similar endings. His claim to translate 'word for word' ('pro uerbo uerbum', vv.7–8) might suggest that his work aimed to reflect the original vernacular metre of Merlin's prophecies.

Evoking a 'puerile style' lessens the *gravitas* of the text, and perhaps casts doubts on the vatic credibility of his British source. Gerald of Wales framed his work with an even clearer sense of linguistic hierarchy, writing that 'I have illumined the darkness of a barbarous tongue with the clear light of Latin' ('barbare lingue tenebras Latini luce sermonis illustravi').[109] John and Gerald's concern with the literary qualities of the British prophecies indicated their desire to engage with the text on its own terms. Yet at the same time, these works were also triumphant demonstrations that they had mastered the latest techniques of Latin scholarly analysis, a mastery which could elucidate even the most obscure of vernacular texts.

Given the ambivalence displayed here, it is clear that if Geoffrey of Monmouth initiated a new interest in the Brittonic languages, we should not consider this to be a simple narrative of the growing valorisation of the vernacular. The politically sensitive context which motivated interest in the British language simultaneously encouraged the denigration of Welsh and Cornish pretensions to literary authority, even as commentators used all available techniques of Latin critical scrutiny to uncover the hermetic information concealed within British stylistic tropes. We might even see the emphasis on these texts' vernacularity as a way to assure readers of their intellectually negligible contents. The pre-Anglo-Saxon past remained politically potent. If the British language was only valuable insofar as it enabled access to that past, and to the future that it adumbrated, twelfth-century interest in Merlin's prophecies shows that this alone was a sufficient incentive for the investigation of Brittonic vernacular literature. However, it would be wrong to see the impetus behind the creation of these commentaries as exclusively utilitarian. The Latin critical apparatus which accompanies many copies of the *Prophetia Merlini* also testifies to the challenge and pleasure of deciphering the text's allegorical language. Not only did Geoffrey's work alert twelfth-century readers to the potential of archaisms and etymology for validating narratives of continuity and possession, it also introduced the literary appreciation of vernacular texts to an international audience.

Gerald of Wales and Linguistic Archaeology

Geoffrey of Monmouth's stimulating treatment of language history drew attention to the literary possibilities inherent in etymological excavation, inspiring elaborate narratives which sought to dramatise the process of linguistic discovery. Returning to Geraldine Heng's formulation of romance as a 'structure of desire', we might consider that Geoffrey offered his readers not only a fantasy which demonstrated historical entitlement through language, but also one which demonstrated an unbroken connection with the linguistic past.[110] Yet attempts to retrace such connections also served to emphasise the intangibility of Trojan heritage. This chapter concludes by examining an anecdote of linguistic excavation in the work of Gerald of Wales. The episode responds to Galfridian fictions of language history, and to the sense of rupture, loss, and absence which such fictions exacerbate.

Gerald's *Itinerarium Kambriae* was an account of a journey around Wales which he made in 1188 with Baldwin, Archbishop of Canterbury, in order to preach the Third Crusade. A related work, his *Descriptio Kambrie*, provided an innovative ethnographical discussion of Welsh customs using material collected during the journey. At the same time, these texts also recounted Gerald's exploration of the Welsh language: they were saturated with the results of his linguistic enquiries, discussing the history of several different vernaculars and many topographical etymologies. His work provided one of the fullest considerations of vernacular language history available in the twelfth century. The largest category of information was devoted to Welsh place-name etymologies, but he also included further material on Welsh, English, French, Irish, Low German, Latin, Greek, Scots Gaelic, and Norse (with varying degrees of accuracy).[111] Even more unusually, Gerald was able to apply his breadth of multilingual vocabulary to questions concerning the evolution of Britain's vernaculars. The works included unique discussions of the development of English, French, Welsh, Breton, and Cornish, and demonstrations of the relationship between some Welsh words and those in Latin, Greek, and other Western European languages. Far exceeding the descriptive demands of a travel narrative, the *Itinerarium* and the *Descriptio* constitute highly sophisticated explorations of the Welsh language's history, and the linguistic connections of Wales to the wider world. Ostensibly scornful of Geoffrey, Gerald's perception of Welsh remained deeply influenced by Galfridian historiography. Whilst a search for the linguistic roots of the Trojan past seems to have provided a significant impetus for his investigations, the uncertain political context of the *Historia* precluded him from exploiting the connections between the Welsh and the Trojans to their fullest extent.

Gerald's ethnographic gaze was far from dispassionate. Both his works were profoundly marked by the Norman struggle for control of Wales. Violent anecdotes of kin slayings, massacres, and castrations abound, arising both from the attempted imposition of Norman rule, and from Welsh internal strife.[112] Gerald's own perspective was complicated by his family background. His father and both grandfathers were Norman, but his maternal grandmother, Nest, had been a Welsh princess; Gerald remained proud of his kinship with the descendants of Rhys ap Tewdwr.[113] An idealistic view of former glory complicated the pragmatic desire for self-aggrandisement evident in his writings on Wales. He frequently denigrated the Welsh, but did not reject their pretensions to an august Trojan pedigree. As discussed above, Henry II was eager to discredit Geoffrey of Monmouth's depiction of Arthur's potential return, particularly when reasserting Angevin rule in Wales after the losses incurred by Stephen. Gerald was present in 1190 when the monks of Glastonbury staged an exhumation of Arthur and Guinevere's bones, having been told by Henry where to dig.[114] If this seemed to prove the accuracy of Geoffrey's *Historia* in one sense, it also demonstrated that Arthur was well and truly dead, along with Welsh hopes of eventual victory. Prompted by political expediency, Gerald hence affected to despise the *Historia*, mocking Geoffrey's historical pretensions. The work was mentioned by name only in the context of a certain Meilyr, gifted with second sight: Gerald claimed that when the *Historia* was placed in his lap, Meilyr saw demons dancing all over it.[115] This heavy-handed satire was designed to signal the author's political distance from a vision of the Welsh future which was portrayed as risible, or even Satanic.

However, Gerald's scorn for Galfridian material was not sustained throughout the text. Given his own Welsh ancestry, he found the *Historia*'s putative Trojan genealogy very attractive, even as he remained reluctant to associate himself with Geoffrey's work. Without acknowledgement, he discreetly incorporated many Galfridian details into the *Itinerarium* and the *Descriptio*.[116] Although it valorised this aspect of his ancestry, his discussion of the language did not unambiguously ally him with his Welsh contemporaries. Gerald's extensive display of linguistic knowledge was designed to demonstrate a profound understanding of Welsh culture (although occasional errors of interpretation suggest that he was less fluent than he claims).[117] Such knowledge augmented his authority by asserting his familiarity with his ethnographical subjects. Yet the authority which came from this linguistic mastery was paradoxically built on critical distance. Even whilst emphasising his close acquaintance with Welsh, by adopting the role of ethnographer, Gerald simultaneously set himself apart from the objects of his enquiry. Although keen to embrace his putative Trojan heritage, he was not interested in Geoffrey's depiction of a future Welsh renaissance. His own vision was far less inflammatory: the Welsh would merely continue to rule 'the least attractive corner' ('angulo pessimo') of the island of Britain.[118] Gerald used language as a nuanced tool for the reconstruction of ethnic history, and the exertion of scholarly authority over others. Linguistic study was capable both of augmenting the past status of the Welsh, and of cementing their current domination by the Normans.

One episode of the *Itinerarium* particularly explored the tensions between views of Trojan ancestry as derisory and desirable. Gerald gave an account of a priest, Elidyr, who, when around the age of twelve and learning to read, ran away from the beatings of his teacher by hiding in a hollow place in a river bank.[119] Two tiny men appeared to him and took him to a beautiful land through a tunnel under the bank – the boy became a frequent visitor there, but continued to return to his mother, who one day asked him to bring her back a present. The boy stole a golden ball, but the little men pursued him and on the threshold of his mother's chamber, it slipped from his hand. They snatched the ball away with scorn, and, although he spent hours searching for the entrance, the boy was never able to return to their land. Gerald's attention was primarily captured by the linguistic interest of this story. We are told that the protagonist could still remember a large number of the words which the little people spoke, and which were very like Greek:

> Salem requirentes dicebant, *Halgein ydorum*, id est, salem affer. *Hal* vero Graece sal dicitur, et *haleyn* Britannice. Lingua namque Britannica, propter diutinam quam Britones, qui tunc Trojani, et postea Britones a Bruto eorum duce sunt vocati, post Trojae excidium moram in Graecia fecerant, in multis Graeco idiomati conformis invenitur.

> When they wanted salt they said 'halgein ydorum', which means 'salem affer' [bring salt]. Salt is ['hals'] in Greek and 'halen' in Welsh. The Britons stayed a long time in Greece after the fall of Troy and then took their name from their leader Brutus, so that the early Welsh language is similar to Greek in many of its details.[120]

Imperceptibly, Gerald has slipped from talking about the language of the little people to speaking of Welsh: both are related to Greek, and Elidyr speaks them both when eschewing the Latin teaching of his schoolmaster. In one sense then, the connections between Welsh and this fairy language were a means of parodying Galfridian theories of the Greek roots of Welsh, stemming from notions of their Trojan ancestry. Gerald seems to imply that the connections between Greek and Welsh are as fantastical and unproven as those between Greek and the language of the little people, only believable to those as credulous as children.

However, there is another side to the anecdote: even as Gerald derided the *Historia*, Geoffrey's linguistic theories stimulated serious enquiry. In his *Descriptio Kambriae*, a description of Wales composed around the same time as the *Itinerarium*, he continued his discussion of the origins of Welsh.[121] Without acknowledgement, he included Geoffrey's etymology of *Cymraeg*, 'Welsh', as 'crooked Greek', *kam Graecus*, filling out the linguistic details omitted in the *Historia* but ultimately disagreeing with it in favour of another Galfridian interpretation, where Cymry/Cambria was linked to Camber, son of Brutus.[122] He also contradicted Geoffrey's derivation of the name 'Wales' from Queen Gwendolen, explaining it instead with recourse to the 'barbarous terms' ('barbara nuncupatione') of the Saxons:

> Saxones enim, occupato regno Britannico, quoniam lingua sua extraneum omne Wallicum vocant, et gentes has sibi extraneas Walenses vocabant.

> In their language the Saxons apply the adjective *Wallicus* (? <*wealh*) to anything foreign, and, since the Welsh were certainly a people foreign to them, that is what the Saxons called them.[123]

If based on English *wealh* ('foreigner, Briton, Welsh person, slave'), this etymology is consonant with modern understandings of the derivation of 'Welsh'.[124] The most spectacular instance of Gerald's linguistic awareness occurs in the discussion of the word for 'salt', which ends the tale of Elidyr in the *Itinerarium*. Gerald noted that 'salt' had cognates in several languages:

> Hic autem mihi notabile videtur, quod in uno verbo tot linguas convenire non invenio, sicut in isto. *Hal* enim Græce, *Halein* Britannice, *Halein* similiter Hibernice; *Halgein*, *g* interposita, lingua praedicta. Item *sal* Latine – quia, ut ait Priscianus, in quibusdam dictionibus pro aspiratione ponitur *s* [. . .] – *Sel* Gallice, mutatione *a* vocalis in *e*, a Latino; additione *t* literae, *salt* Anglice, *sout* Teutonice. Habetis ergo septem linguas, vel octo, in hac una dictione plurimum concordantes.

> It seems remarkable to me that I do not find so many languages agree so much over any other word as they do in this: [*hals*] in Greek, *halen* in Welsh, *halgein* in Irish, where *g* is inserted, and *sal* in Latin, where, as Priscian tells us, *s* replaces the aspirate in some words.[. . .] In French the word becomes *sel*, the vowel *a* changing to *e* as it develops from Latin. In English a *t* is added to make *salt* and in German[ic] the word is *sout*.[125] In short, you have seven languages, or even eight, which agree completely over this word.[126]

Even though some of the linguistic details are wrong or approximate, Gerald displays remarkable powers of observation which anticipate the discovery of Indo-European, and also provides a very early mention of the relationship between Latin and French.[127] He used the *Historia regum*

Britanniae to explain the fact that 'all the words in Welsh are cognate with either Greek or Latin' ('verba linguae Britannicae omnia fere vel Graeco conveniunt vel Latino'). This allowed him to claim that the Welsh alone (unlike the French- and Italian-speaking descendants of Antenor and Aeneas) had retained their linguistic, and, by implication, cultural connection to the Greek-influenced dialect of the early Trojans.[128] For Julia Crick, 'expediency, conviction and self-interest' dictated Gerald's shifting stance towards Galfridian historiography, which was endorsed only insofar as it related to the glorious past of the Welsh, rather than to their future.[129] The *Historia regum Britanniae*'s interest in language sparked Gerald's own linguistic enquiries into the origins of Welsh, but Geoffrey's politicisation of the ancient British past necessitated dismissing the conclusions of Gerald's observations.

CHAPTER 4

The Vernaculars of Ancestral Law
Royal Administration and Linguistic Authority

Geoffrey of Monmouth's *Historia regum Britanniae* responded to the prestige of the Anglo-Saxon textual corpus, exploring the potential of archaic vernacular texts to validate portrayals of insular history. This aspect of Geoffrey's work developed previous employments of ancient documents, building on wider interest in the authoritative vernacular witnesses of pre-Conquest rule. Whilst his work drew attention to the potential of the vernacular as a site of scholarly commentary, it also offered an important new framework for the interpretation of Britain's languages in other ways: Geoffrey employed place name etymology to portray the transfer of power between peoples. This etymological method for exploring linguistic inheritance across conquests heavily influenced many late-twelfth-century discussions of the history of insular French. Although some authors such as Gerald of Wales were able to deduce that French came from Latin, most were far more concerned with exploring its place within Britain via Galfridian paradigms. Before considering how these paradigms shaped francophone perceptions of the relationship between language and conquest, this chapter explores etymological depictions of another type of linguistic inheritance: the royal vocabulary of Anglo-Saxon and Anglo-Norman government.

Richard fitz Nigel's twelfth-century manual of fiscal practice, the *Dialogus de scaccario* (*Dialogue of the Exchequer*), offered a nuanced exploration of Norman ancestral and administrative language. The text was begun in 1177 and was still being revised in the mid-1180s or later; it was shaped by a climate where traditions of Old English legislation remained of major ideological significance.[1] Although Richard's *Dialogus* has received extensive critical attention as a source for fiscal and governmental history, its importance in relation to twelfth-century perceptions of vernacularity has been largely overlooked. His work incorporates a novel and sophisticated treatment of the interaction between Latin and the vernacular languages which is integral to the success of his historical project. The source of Richard's linguistic innovation is paradoxically located in a valorisation of patrimonial heritage. By using the language history of the Normans and the English to trace the distinguished past achievements of his own family, Richard constructed Latin etymologies which innovatively explored the development of vernacular administrative vocabulary. After surveying Norman responses to Old English legislation, the chapter examines how this context influenced Richard's view of the twelfth-century exchequer and its lexical history.

The Normans' exposure to Anglo-Saxon law had profound consequences, which stimulated both new legal developments, and new linguistic approaches. Whilst the government of the Anglo-Saxons employed written Old English extensively, the government of the pre-Conquest Normans was not strongly associated with a vernacular. Their earliest historian, Dudo of Saint-Quentin, portrayed the early Normans as speaking the Norse and 'Roman' tongues, but their language of written record was Latin.[2] Furthermore, in the twelfth century there were no widely available early vernacular texts to stimulate critical enquiry into the history of either Norse or Romance.[3] Perhaps due to this, surviving evidence for awareness of the Norman vernaculars' development is scanty and fragmented: it is often necessary to reconstruct it with recourse to a wider literary and historical context. However, the Normans were inspired by Anglo-Saxon precedents when creating their own legislation. These precedents can be traced in the formation of the common law, a legal system unique to England. In F. W. Maitland's foundational analysis, this was a major new direction in English jurisprudence, and largely the product of the late-twelfth-century innovations of Richard fitz Nigel's contemporaries under Henry II.[4] Later reassessments have placed greater emphasis on the Anglo-Saxon contribution to Norman legislation, stressing its incremental development over the course of the twelfth century.[5] Engagements with pre-Conquest law drew attention to the potential of vernacular languages as a witness to royal power. As they developed new legal and administrative concepts, the Normans also experimented with new terminology, and new ways of depicting its history. The first legal text written in insular French, the *Leis Willelme*, dates from the reign of Henry I or Stephen: its vernacular treatment of the law of William I responded to Anglo-Saxon royal law codes written in Old English, several of which had been translated into Latin in the twelfth century.[6] However, the text is also an important new experiment in portraying French as major language of Anglo-Norman government. Richard fitz Nigel's treatise represents a further development of this interest in the history of legal and administrative language, which he connects not only to Anglo-Saxon England, but to the more recent Anglo-Norman past.

Like England's laws, insular Norman identity in the 1170s was shaped by a sense of both English and Norman contributions. Having been very strong in the late eleventh and early twelfth centuries, by the reign of Henry II, this Norman identity was gradually beginning to be subsumed into a larger sense of affinity with England.[7] It is impossible give an exact date for the decisive demise of *Normannitas*: whilst John Gillingham has seen 'a developing sense of Englishness' in the writings of William of Malmesbury and Henry of Huntingdon from the 1120s to the 1150s, Hugh Thomas has drawn attention to a continuing awareness of continental Norman identity in the mid-thirteenth-century writings of Matthew Paris.[8] Individuals could, of course, adopt aspects of identities from several different communities simultaneously. Thomas notes that 'both the English and the Normans were capable of displaying hostility toward other groups and working with or even assimilating those groups at the same time'.[9] If the extent to which individuals defined themselves as Norman or English in the late twelfth century remains opaque, it is clear that a sense of history was a key element of their constructions of identity.[10] Some have seen the rejection of *Normannitas* as a crucial part of becoming English. Emily Albu writes: 'Everywhere the Normans had gone, they were dissociating themselves from their Norman past and aligning themselves with the peoples of their new homelands'.[11] However, the slow adoption of an English identity over the course of the twelfth century was not incompatible with a continuing awareness of Norman ancestry. The long insular tradition of Old English vernacular literature stimulated unprecedented thinking on the subject of language history, as the invaders sought to authenticate Norman institutions and innovations with recourse not only to Old English, but also to French.

Richard was eager to explore the ways in which the cultures of Normandy and England were intertwined. He famously stated that the extent of intermarriage amongst free people ensured that 'today one can scarcely distinguish who is English and who is Norman' ('uix decerni possit hodie [...] quis Anglicus quis Normannus sit genere', pp.80–81). This is often cautiously adduced as evidence for the assimilation of the Normans into insular society.[12] Yet in other ways, this assimilation seems less assured. Richard's employment of vernacular linguistic data sought to portray the exchequer as a Norman institution, linking its development to the successful careers of his father and uncle. He rejected speculation concerning the exchequer's English origins, instead arguing that it was brought from

Normandy by William I, after the Conquest. However, whilst the *Dialogus* was primarily concerned with emphasising the Norman contribution to English government, it remained informed by perceptions of the authoritative nature of English vernacular legislation. Richard used etymology to construct an institutional history for the exchequer which, like English law, was grounded in vernacular language. Yet the text also dismissed some English vernacular testimony in favour of new versions of history which stressed the potency of Angevin rule: Richard was interested in the development of the vernaculars only insofar as it served to confirm his own view of the exchequer.

The next section situates the *Dialogus* in the context of Richard's contemporaries. Widespread interest in vernacular legislation encouraged some authors to authenticate depictions of legal history with recourse to Old English. Others denied the existence of English written law in order to emphasise the ultimate authority of the king. Pre-Conquest vernacular legislation was central to twelfth-century understandings of English government, encouraging attempts to render its testimony compatible with Angevin policy.

Leges Non Scriptas: Norman Responses to Old English Law

The Normans were avid consumers of Old English legal literature, perhaps due to the comparative absence of similar material in their own culture: although very little evidence has survived relating to the pre-Conquest legislation of the dukes of Normandy,[13] the Anglo-Saxon kings preserved an extensive body of vernacular documentation relating to their laws, from the seventh century onwards.[14] More importantly, this textual corpus remained of direct relevance to Norman ideas of government. On his accession to the English throne, William the Conqueror's early charter to the people of London undertook to uphold the laws of the land as they were on the day that Edward the Confessor died, an avowal later repeated in the coronation charter of Henry I and Stephen's charter of promises to his barons.[15] Although these Old English legal texts had undisputed ideological value, it is less clear how far they were intended to have a practical function. In Anglo-Saxon England written law may have borne little relation to contemporary legal practice, decided largely according to a combination of custom and current exigency.[16] The Normans quickly introduced further innovations.[17] Their interest in Anglo-Saxon law paradoxically diminished the degree of its implementation in post-Conquest England, as kings adapted existing law to suit their political priorities. However, their legal practice continued to be self-consciously rooted in the Anglo-Saxon era. Even though post-Conquest law 'remained to a large degree oral and therefore flexible', strong motivations still existed for recording and translating Anglo-Saxon law codes.[18]

The desire to create a symbolic continuity between Anglo-Saxon and Anglo-Norman law is most extensively portrayed in an anonymous but widely disseminated legal text, the *Leges Edwardi Confessoris*. Written sometime between 1096 and 1175, it purports to be the record of a council held by William I after the Conquest, when he summoned men from every county who were 'wise and learned in their law' ('sapientes et lege sua eruditos') so that he might learn the laws and customs of the land.[19] This fiction of a king eager to recognise English law had some potency. Orderic Vitalis even portrayed William as trying to learn Old English in order to be able to follow court procedure.[20] The vision of unity between the king and the English nobility depicted in the *Leges Edwardi* reaffirmed that the Norman administration continued the traditions of pre-Conquest government. William himself was eager to enhance these perceptions of continuity, vowing at his coronation to maintain Edward the Confessor's laws. This reassurance offered by this portrait was a welcome one. The *Leges Edwardi* survives in more than forty manuscripts, and the council scene created by the author was only exposed as a fiction in 1685.[21] The author was not heavily reliant on textual sources, and seems to have made little use of the existing wealth of texts describing pre-Conquest law.[22] This does not necessarily deprive the *Leges Edwardi* of its claims to authority: Patrick Wormald suggests that the elements of the work which do not come from reading are 'likely to derive from experience'.[23] It therefore did not simply reproduce earlier sources, but synthesised various legal texts and contexts into a single document designed to demonstrate William's affirmation of Anglo-Saxon law.

The author of the *Leges Edwardi* was not unusual in his sensitivity to the linguistic potential of pre-Conquest legislation. His judicious employment of vernacular terminology parallels the etymologies in Richard's *Dialogus de scaccario*. The text is scattered with elucidations of English words, designed to convey an impression of the author's familiarity with English usage.[24] Etymology was used to enhance the historical prestige of English legal custom: the author derived *wapentake*, another word for 'hundred', from the practice of confirming (*taccare*) the reeve at his investiture with weapons (*wapa*).[25] The author's most ambitious etymology, however, is the one he gave for the word 'reeve' itself, *greeve*:

> Et uidetur nobis compositum esse e grit Anglice, quod est pax Latine, et ue Latine, uidelicet quod debet facere grit, id est pacem, ex illis qui inferunt in

terram ue, id est miseriam uel dolorem (summa auctoritate domini nostri
Ihesu Christi dicentis: Ue tibi Bethsaida, ue tibi Corozaim).

It seems to us to be composed of *grit* in English, which is peace in Latin,
and woe [*ue*] in Latin, that is to say what ought to make *grit*, that is peace,
from those who would introduce woe, that is misery or pain, into the land
(by the highest authority of our Lord, Jesus Christ, who said, 'Woe to you
Beth-saida, woe to you Chorazin!').[26]

He went on to contextualise the word geographically and temporally. The
author pointed out that the Frisians and Flemings had counts called *mere-
graves* 'because [they are] greater or good, peaceful men' ('quasi maiores
uel bonos pacificos'); in the past they were called *aldermen*, 'not because
of their age, but because of their wisdom' ('non propter senectutem, sed
propter sapientiam').[27] Through the construction of this rhetorically ambitious etymology, the author created an extremely flattering portrayal of an
unpopular job, transforming the reeve into a Christ-like figure who struggles for peace.[28] The *Leges Edwardi* was characteristic in its emphasis on the
connections of English terminology to the history of pre-Conquest vernacular legislation. In exceptional cases, other texts portrayed legal lexis
as Norse to draw attention to the prestigious judicial traditions stemming
from King Cnut.[29]

Pre-Conquest legislation was not only of ideological importance: its
guidance on past practice became more valuable as England's laws grew in
their reach and sophistication. The impetus for legal research was felt particularly widely with the increased efficiency of royal administration under
Henry I. Officials sought to clarify the authority of the various, potentially competing jurisdictions present in the Henrician legal system, and
their relationship to the laws of Edward.[30] For the Normans, this often
necessitated the codification and translation of existing Anglo-Saxon literature. The most ambitious of these enterprises was the so-called *Quadripartitus*. This work was originally envisaged in four parts, beginning with the
Anglo-Saxon laws translated into Latin, and continued to the present day.
After the completion of the first section, it seems likely that the author
re-imagined the project, resulting in the amalgamation of the second,
third and fourth parts into the work surviving today as the *Leges Henrici
Primi*.[31] Although the *Leges Henrici* was largely concerned with contemporary legal practice, it still translated a significant amount of the Old
English legal corpus that the author found of continued relevance.[32] As
discussed earlier, monastic scriptoria increasingly made efforts to preserve
relevant Old English documentation when defending their rights after the
Conquest through careful attention to charters and archives. Pre-Conquest

vernacular legal texts sometimes also provided relevant evidence. The *Textus Roffensis* offers an ambitious example of this trend. This law book and cartulary was created in the 1120s.[33] The compiler amassed Old English legal material relating to Rochester Cathedral Priory, much of which was preserved in its original language. His interest may have been stimulated by the possibility of the aggrandisement of Rochester's heritage. He could well have known Bede's belief that the early Anglo-Saxon king and law-maker Æthelberht had founded the priory at Rochester.[34] In the earlier twelfth century, then, interest in Anglo-Saxon law was hardly confined to antiquarians.

In the later twelfth century, royal concern increased over the growing influence of the precedents provided by written law.[35] Officials sought to maintain the flexibility of contemporary legal custom by directing attention away from England's prior legislative traditions. By the reign of Henry II (1154–1189), it seems that the importance of research into Old English legal texts had become a controversial issue. Interest in English legal history had, if anything, increased, with late-twelfth-century historians like Roger of Howden choosing to include legal texts in their works for the first time.[36] However, unlike most of his Norman predecessors, at his coronation Henry II had sworn to uphold the laws of his grandfather, Henry I, rather than Edward the Confessor, and in the early years of his reign, new legislation forbade Englishmen (*Anglici*) from pursuing a claim founded on the seisin (justified enjoyment of a possession) of an ancestor from any time earlier than the death of Henry I in 1135.[37] These concerns were articulated in one of the most important manuals of Angevin governance: the *Tractatus de legibus et consuetudinibus regni Anglie*, once thought to have been written by Henry II's justiciar Ranulf Glanvill, and datable to 1187 × 1189.[38] The text provides a rare overview of contemporary legal practice, and reflects the latest developments in legal reasoning.[39] As a pragmatic member of the privileged coterie of administrators close to the king, we might not be surprised to find the author somewhat dismissive of the long Anglo-Saxon tradition of written law. However, he went beyond the dismissal of this tradition in favour of an outright denial of its existence, stating that 'the laws of England are not written' ('leges [. . .] Anglicanas licet non scriptas').[40] This may be part of a broader strategy pursued by the author in valorising his own work. He emphasised the difficulty of his project by stating that it was 'utterly impossible for the laws and legal rules of the realm to be wholly reduced to writing in our time, both because of the ignorance of scribes and because of the confused multiplicity of those same laws and rules' ('Leges autem et iura regni scripto uniuersaliter concludi nostris temporibus omnino quidem impossibile est, tum propter scribentium ignoranciam tum propter eorundem multitudinem confusam'). However, there were still 'some general rules frequently observed in court' ('quedam in curia generalia et frequentius usitata') which he was happy to record.[41] This obliteration of previous traditions of English written law conveniently endowed his *Tractatus* with an originary authority. He may also have thought that English legal history was not relevant to his enterprise: much of the text's significance lies in the author's decision to describe contemporary legal practice. For R. C. van Caenegem, the author's position thus represents a polemical defence of unwritten custom's importance to English common law, as opposed to the codified legal systems based on Roman law.[42]

Bruce O'Brien sees the text as a conscious negation of written precedent's importance in response to the early, decisive rift between Henry II and Thomas Becket over the Constitutions of Clarendon (1164).[43] Convinced that the Church had encroached on the limits of royal authority as enjoyed by Henry I, the king sought the advice of legal experts to prove that royal law did not conflict with divine law.[44] He aimed to define the exact extent of Henry I's historical power. Thus, in delineating the privileges of the king, the Constitutions of Clarendon claimed to be a record of 'the customs which are called grandfatherly (*or* ancestral)' ('consuetudines quas avitas vocant').[45] Whilst their bid to represent the laws of Henry I was 'very broadly' accurate, several clauses sought to enlarge the scope of these laws, making significant incursions into ecclesiastical jurisdiction in England.[46] Henry's decision to set down these customs in writing laid them open to the considered scrutiny of Thomas's supporters, who pursued a similarly recursive strategy of historical counter-argument, often with recourse to the same legal texts used by Henry.[47] Whilst the *Tractatus* was composed about twenty-five years after the events sketched here, the concessions made by Henry in the aftermath of Becket's murder (1170), and the rebellion of 1173–1174, had 'subtly changed the legal environment', forcing Henry to negotiate with the papacy to a greater extent.[48] In a loyal affirmation of royal authority over historical precedent, the *Tractatus* author quoted Justinian's *Institutes:* 'what pleases the prince has the force of law' ('quod principi placet, legis habet uigorem').[49] This rejection of written legislation may reflect that documentary evidence had not been sufficient to ensure the success of the king's attempt to consolidate the rights of his grandfather. Twelfth-century authors were hence alert to the potential of Anglo-Saxon vernacular law to support contemporary arguments; they often employed linguistic details to demonstrate specific aspects of their contentions. This engagement with archival material itself heightened awareness that views of the past could differ, clash, or compete. The Becket conflict in particular underlined the polemical possibilities of historical interpretation, and the malleability of documents in substantiating alternative claims.

Richard responded to these pressures and opportunities by using vernacular etymologies to construct a narrative of the exchequer's history which was closely tied to his own family. He was inspired by contemporary interest in England's legal institutions, and highly aware that written presentations of their genesis could be shaped to favour a particular historical slant. However, his work also advanced these preoccupations in a new way. It did not focus on the laws of the past, but on the more recent history of Anglo-Norman fiscal innovations. This creative focus on the exchequer reflected developments in the genre of biography, as new groups claimed the status associated with possessing a past. Over the twelfth century, the range of subjects considered worthy of historical enquiry was enlarging in scope beyond the royal and the hagiographical. Notably, the lives of aristocrats increasingly received sustained attention. Biographical works from the *Gesta Herwardi* (1109 × 1131) to the *History of William Marshal* (1224–1226) preserved the memory of contemporary chivalric deeds; romances such as Thomas's *Horn* (?*c*.1171–1172) emphasised the glamour of the nobility's English roots.[50] Other depictions of aristocratic identity began to focus more closely on lineage. Genealogies became more elaborate, and from 1100, shield designs became increasingly distinctive: these proto-heraldic patterns were being passed on to descendants from the third quarter of the twelfth century. Shared family armorial devices also began to appear on seals.[51] Richard's depiction of the exchequer can be seen as an important further step in this expansion of biography to encompass new subjects and new ways of depicting ancestral identity. But it also ingeniously circumvented the personal problems which this social trend created for Richard. As stress on lineage grew, those of humble origin in prominent positions of power (including his great-uncle, Roger of Salisbury) were considered by some with disfavour. In linking his family to the administrative innovations of the exchequer, Richard created a new form of genealogical prestige which did not depend on a long line of illustrious ancestors. The *Dialogus* hence offers a highly innovative form of double biography: bureaucratic and familial.

Ancestral Neologisms in Richard Fitz Nigel's *Dialogus de Scaccario*

Although the pioneering nature of Richard's treatise as the first description of the exchequer has been widely recognised, its importance as a literary source for perceptions of Anglo-Norman administrative language has been previously overlooked.[52] Here, the implications of Richard's nuanced portrayal of the relationship between vernacularity and Latinity will be explored. He emphasised that the language employed in the *Dialogus* needed to reflect the usage of the exchequer in order to be of practical value; his work is full of lexis culled from both Anglo-Norman and English. In an unprecedented move, Richard attempted to explain some of the philological processes behind these vernacular borrowings, providing potential evidence for an early consideration of the relationship between Latin and French, and shifting the reader's focus from the novelty of his diction to its venerable roots. Turning from the Isidorean project of the recovery of the divine intention behind Latin discourse, Richard used etymology instead as a tool for the recovery of ancestral agendas.

Like the work of the *Tractatus* author, Richard fitz Nigel's *Dialogus de scaccario* located the king as the centre of fiscal and legal authority, producing a guide to contemporary royal administration for practical use in government. In different ways, the two works both negated the importance of written sources in their efforts to emphasise Henry's power. However, the *Tractatus* author was extremely unusual in his explicit denial of the significance of previous collections of English written law. Richard adopted a different approach: by adapting his historical and legal sources, he was able to explain the exchequer's development through stressing the importance of the Normans, not least his own ancestors. John Hudson has shown that, whilst offering a detailed description of financial practice to be a model for future generations, Richard simultaneously attempted to recover the motivations of his father, great-uncle, and the Normans more widely in their projected establishment of the exchequer.[53] Notoriously, this portrayal of the exchequer's Norman foundation necessitated certain historical elisions, as Richard emphasised the success of Norman government at the expense of the Anglo-Saxons. Less reliant on written sources than he claimed, Richard enlisted the help of etymology in this construction of Norman pre-eminence, seeking a rationale for the current *status quo* in a highly innovative exploration of bureaucratic terminology.

Begun in 1177, and written and revised into the mid-1180s or later, Richard fitz Nigel's *Dialogus de scaccario* is a practical manual on the workings of Angevin fiscal administration at the exchequer.[54] The *Dialogus* initiates the neophyte into the exchequer's intricacies, purporting to be a realistic record of a conversation between a master and a student. The author was a well-qualified guide to these matters. Although his identity is not stated explicitly within the *Dialogus*, its attribution to Richard by Alexander of

Swerford (the thirteenth-century compiler of the Red Book of the Exchequer) places the text at the heart of the Angevin government.[55] Richard was the son of Nigel, Bishop of Ely and treasurer to both Henry I and Henry II. He was the great-nephew of Roger, Bishop of Salisbury and principal administrator of Henry I. Richard himself does not seem to have displayed any outstanding abilities: the monks of Ely thought that Nigel had paid the king £400 to secure the office of treasurer for his son. He had to wait until after the king's death for his appointment to the bishopric of London in 1189, having been passed over as a candidate for the see of Lincoln in 1186. If there are some indications that Henry II was not overly convinced of Richard's capabilities, he still retained the office of treasurer for nearly forty years, from around 1160 to his death in 1198.[56] There is also evidence of his legal expertise. Richard served as an itinerant justice in 1179, and as a royal justice at Westminster.[57] Perhaps because of his comparatively modest political career, he had leisure to pursue an interest in history. In his youth, he wrote the *Tricolumpnis*, 'on the threefold history of the kingdom of England under the illustrious king Henry II ('de tripartita regni Anglie historia sub illustri Anglorum rege Henrico secundo', pp.40–41)'. Whilst a traditionalist in his financial practice, in literature Richard was already more innovative. The *Tricolumpnis* employed an unusual structure, arranging material in three columns according to its ecclesiastical, royal or legal relevance (pp.40–41).[58] He had a sense of the future historical significance of the present day. The *magister* enjoins the *discipulus* that:

> Hic si forte in manus tuas inciderit, caue ne te effugiat. Vtilis enim esse poterit futuris forte temporibus, et iocundus his qui de regni statu sub predicto principe solliciti fuerint.

> If this book should fall into your hands, don't let it get away. For it could be useful to posterity and enjoyable for those who are interested in the state of the realm under the said prince. (pp.40–41)

Although the *Tricolumpnis* itself does not survive, these concerns also seem to have informed the *Dialogus*, a self-conscious clarification of the arcane recesses of the exchequer carried out under the projected scrutiny of future generations. Richard's emphasis on the practical uses of his work to future researchers suggests that he himself had frequent recourse to historical records in the business of government.

Richard's historical interests did not stop with Anglo-Saxon law and its language, but extended to a more recent vernacular: Anglo-Norman. He aimed to produce a treatise which was couched in the terminology used daily by the royal administration, intending the work to be of primarily practical value. Richard was not alone in expressing his commitment to constructing a form of Latin which reflected everyday official usage, even at the expense of rhetoric. The *Tractatus de legibus et consuetudinibus regni Anglie* (discussed above) was similar in its aims to the *Dialogus*, providing an overview of contemporary legal practice. The author stated that he was: 'adopting intentionally a commonplace style and words used in court in order to provide knowledge of them for those who are not versed in this kind of inelegant language' ('stilo uulgari et uerbis curialibus utens ex industria ad eorum noticiam comparandam eis qui in huiusmodi uulgaritate minus sunt exercitati').[59] It was not uncommon to borrow vernacular lexis, especially when there was no equivalent Latin word. Many other administrative works 're-Latinized' contemporary vernacular terminology.[60] Found alongside Richard's *Dialogus de scaccario* in all its three manuscript witnesses, the *Constitutio domus regis* set out the allowances for the peripatetic household which travelled with Henry I (in a form datable to *c*.1136, but incorporating earlier material). Although written in Latin, much of its vocabulary was inspired by the Anglo-Norman used at court.[61] Likewise, the Domesday Book betrays its vernacular genesis in its coinage of terms to describe 'culturally specific phenomena', such as *soca*, from Old English *socn*.[62] Richard fitz Nigel and the author of the *Tractatus* were unusual, not for their employment of lexis derived from the vernacular, but for their explicit discussion of it.

The language of these works reflects an anxiety to avoid the potential misunderstandings which could arise in the routinely multilingual administration of twelfth-century England. Translators responded creatively to these concerns about clarity: Richard could have chosen several different methods beyond the coinage or selection of Latin words which closely mirrored their vernacular equivalents. Some alternative techniques are exemplified in twelfth-century Latin translations of Anglo-Saxon legal literature. Many translators simply retained and glossed such characteristic Old English terminology as *healsfang* (a form of wergild).[63] Others created calques designed to reflect the etymological elements of the word: the author of the *Consiliatio Cnuti* translated the compound *healsfang* literally as 'collicipium', 'a seizing of the neck'.[64] There was also a need for texts which met the linguistic demands of contemporary judicial administration: whilst English probably remained the standard language of the hundred and shire courts, it is likely that the language of the higher law courts was Anglo-Norman.[65] The late twelfth century saw the creation of the first surviving trilingual glossary of legal terms, designed to help its readers tackle the oral challenges which the courts presented. In some manuscripts this was attributed to Richard's uncle, Alexander, Bishop of

Lincoln.[66] Richard's linguistic approach was therefore only one of a variety of innovative strategies. Hence, rather than seeing texts like the *Dialogus de scaccario* as literary failures (although, as discussed below, Richard is worried that we will adopt such a perspective), we might instead think of his interlingual style as a 'desired target'.[67] These works used vernacular borrowings to reflect the linguistic circumstances of their composition as closely as possible.

If the language of Richard's *Dialogus* was largely aimed at a bureaucratic audience, its subject matter was also tailored to their concerns: the work seems to have achieved a comparatively limited circulation, primarily amongst readers interested in fiscal procedure. It survives in four thirteenth-century manuscripts, notably in the Red and Black Books of the Exchequer, two extensive compilations of texts and records relating to the exchequer. Its other two witnesses also pair it with administrative and legal works.[68] However, if his readers had a pragmatic approach to the text, Richard's own literary aims were more ambitious. The work was peppered with quotations from the Bible and an impressive selection of classical, patristic, and medieval authors, stressing the text's connections to wider Latin culture.[69] Moreover, Richard emphasised that some aspects of the exchequer could be interpreted as 'symbols' ('figura') of the last judgement (p.38–39), gesturing towards other prestigious secular works read as Christian allegories by medieval scholars. The text's indebtedness to the vernacular was also explored from a literary perspective. The *Dialogus* claimed to be an account of a conversation held between a master (*magister*) and a student (*discipulus*), beginning in a realistic setting with Richard sitting 'by the window of a tower next to the river Thames' ('ad fenestram specule que est iuxta fluuium Tamensem', pp.6–7). By framing his work as a dialogue, Richard located it in the broader context of a distinguished genre which included examples by Gregory the Great, Donatus, and Boethius. He may have chosen to employ the form for its fusion of the oral and the written, which enabled him to discuss the implications of his linguistic borrowings in relation to the work's Latinity.

The text begins with the student passionately defending Richard's right to use the everyday terminology of the exchequer. He flares up irritably ('succensus in iram') at Richard's protestations that such a contemporary description could only be composed 'with plain speech and simple words' ('rusticano sermone et communibus loqui uerbis', pp.8–9). The student argues that:

> Artium scriptores ne multa parum scisse uiderentur et ut ars difficilior cognitu fieret, multa conquisierunt et uerbis incognitis palliarunt. Tu

scribendam artem non suscipis set quasdam consuetudines et iura scaccarii,
que quia communia debent esse, communibus necessario utendum est uerbis ut sint cognati sermones rebus de quibus loquimur. Preterea quamuis
plerumque noua liceat nomina fingere, rogo tamen si placet ut usitatis rerum
ipsarum uocabulis, que ad placitum sunt, uti non pudeat, ne noua difficultas
ex insolitis uerbis oborta amplius perturbet.

Writers in the liberal arts take many subjects and wrap them up in obscure
language, to avoid seeming to know too little about many things, and so
that the arts will seem more difficult. You won't be writing about the liberal
arts, but about the customs and laws of the exchequer, for which one must
use ordinary words, so that these things may become common knowledge,
and so that the language used is related to the things under discussion. And
while it's fine to invent new expressions, please don't be embarrassed to use
the conventional names of things, so that unfamiliar words don't produce
new difficulties. (pp.8–9)

Richard employed this linguistic strategy to justify his inclusion of many
terms which were taken from the vernacular. He drew attention to his anxiety about this, asking later in the work for mercy from his potential detractors, since he had not 'insisted on an elegant mode of speech or made-up
names' ('exquisito uerborum scemati, uel confictis nominibus duxerimus
insistendum', pp.68–69). Reassured by the student that he has no desire for
'strange new words' ('nouitas insueta', pp.70–71), the *magister* continues to
fret, worrying at the beginning of the second book that the silent student is
'about to burst out laughing at [his] rough style' ('propter agrestem stilum,
diu suppressus cachinnus succuteret', pp.104–105). Although these protestations of stylistic ineptitude formed part of a standard modesty topos in
the twelfth century, Richard's terminology is of interest here.[70] *Agrestis*,
'rural', and by extension 'boorish', 'wild' and 'coarse' relates directly to the
'plain' or 'country' speech ('rusticano sermone', pp.8–9) which the *magister*
promised his *discipulus*.[71]

Richard's language is certainly innovative, incorporating an extensive
range of words taken from French and English. He included many French
terms, such as: *forulus*, 'sack' (pp.12–13, cf. Anglo-Norman *forel*); *baro*,
'baron' (pp.14–15, cf. Old French *ber, baron*); *bernarius*, 'berner' or 'keeper
of hunting dogs' (pp.30–31, cf. OF *brenier*); *perdonum* 'pardon' (pp.74–75,
cf. AN *perdone*); and *bailliuus*, 'bailiff' (pp.118–119, cf. OF *bailiff*). There
were also some words from English, including *danegeldum*, 'Danegeld'
(pp.84–85, cf. Old English *Denegēld*), and two terms for units of land: *hida*,
'hide' (pp.72–73, cf. OE *hīd*) and *hundredus*, 'hundred' (pp.98–99, cf. OE
hundred).[72] Richard took advantage of existing Latin technical terms where
possible, employing common vocabulary in very specific senses to reflect

the specialised discourse of the exchequer in terms like smelter (*fusor*), knight silverer (*miles argentarius*) and teller (*computator*) (pp.18–19). Occasionally, he had recourse to his own ingenuity here. The *Dictionary of Medieval Latin from British Sources* lists him as the first instance of some of these loan-translations, as in *censēre* 'to assess rents' (pp.46–47, cf. Classical Latin *censēre* 'to tax, assess, rate, estimate'),[73] and *dealbare*, 'to 'blanch' payment of a farm'[74] (pp.128–129, cf. Classical Latin *dealbare*, 'to whitewash', and Richard's term for a 'blanch farm', a 'firma blanca' from OF *blanc*, 'white').[75] He may also have coined his own words from the vernacular: the *Dialogus* provides the first recorded usage of the noun *essaium*, 'assay', from Anglo-Norman *essai* or Old French *essaie* (pp.16–17).[76] Although ostensibly composed in Latin, the text was saturated with French and English vocabulary; Richard's lexical choices relied on the reader's prior knowledge of vernacular terminology to convey their meaning, creating a kind of mutual inter-linguality where French and English loanwords were shaped by Latin grammar.

Richard's interest in the history of the vocabulary connected to the exchequer is one of the most distinctive features of his linguistic approach. He included some speculation on the etymology of some ten Latin terms, and one English term:[77]

> *comes* ('earl', 'count', < Classical Latin *comes*, 'companion', p.98);
> *comitatus* ('county' < CL *comitatus* 'company, retinue', p.98);
> *danegeldum* ('Danegeld', < Old English *Denegēld*, p.84);
> *foresta* ('forest', < Late Latin *forestis*, p.92);
> *murdrum* ('murder' < Middle English *murder, morther* < OE *morþor*;
>   Old French *murdre, mordre* < Frankish, p.80);
> *scaccarium* ('exchequer', 'chessboard' < Medieval Latin *scacca*
>   'chess piece' + -*arium*, pp.8–10);
> *scutagium* ('tax paid to king on knight's fee in lieu of military service'
>   < CL *scutum* 'shield' + -*agium*; cf. Anglo-Norman *escuage*, p.80);
> *thesaurus* ('treasury', 'treasure' = CL *thesaurus*, p.94)
> *uastum* ('waste land' < CL *vastus* 'devastated', p.92)
> *uicecomes*, ('sheriff', cf. CL *comes*, OF *vicomte*, p.98)
> *Domesdei* (English 'Domesday', p.96)

Comparatively few of these words were explicitly labelled as vernacular. Richard described *scutagium, murdrum* and *danegeldum* as 'barbara', 'barbarous terms' (pp.78–79), and he noted that the Domesday Book was called *Domesdei* 'by the natives' ('ab indigenis', pp.96–97). Many words were introduced more simply with a variation on 'this is called' or 'is named' ('dicitur', 'nominatur', or 'nuncupatur'): these formulations were largely used for the administrative and legal jargon connected with the exchequer, perhaps drawing attention to their oral context.[78] In the *Dialogus* as a whole, Richard described some twelve other terms as being said 'commonly' ('uulgo' or 'usitatius'); again, all these words were examples of specific exchequer terminology.[79] He also included discussion of differences in oral usage over time, briefly noting changes in the expressions 'at the exchequer' (pp.10–11) and 'hundred' (pp.98–99). The language of his contemporaries was of equal interest: he considered some alternative opinions on the correct employment of 'cess' and 'farm' (pp.46–47). The *Dialogus* was therefore as much a guide to exchequer language as it was to exchequer procedure.

Richard's work was motivated by a desire to elucidate unfamiliar exchequer terminology, combined with an unusual interest in the historical development of such language. The pedagogical emphasis of the *Dialogus de scaccario* partly accounts for his inclusion of etymologies, following Isidore of Seville's stress on their value as an educational tool.[80] Twelfth-century monastic writers also recognised etymology's significance as a mnemotechnical aid.[81] They were influenced by contemporary belief in the partial ability of language to encapsulate the physical qualities of its referent. John of Salisbury thought that: 'While grammar has developed to some extent, and indeed mainly, as an invention of man, still it imitates nature, from which it partly derives its origin' ('Sed licet haec aliquatenus immo ex maxima parte ab hominum institutione processerit, naturam tamen imitatur, et pro parte ab ipsa originem ducit').[82] Etymology, by reconstructing the motivations behind the bestowal of this language, allowed one an insight into the true nature of the object under discussion. Yet twelfth-century authors were aware that etymology could also be manipulated so that this putative repository of truth strengthened their own historical and political narratives.

Richard's interest may have been sparked by Isidore initially: he quoted his etymology for *thesaurus*, 'treasury' (pp.94–95). However, his scrutiny was not confined to classical Latin words. The *Dialogus* can also be situated in the context of Geoffrey of Monmouth's and Gerald of Wales's innovative etymological treatments of vernacular place names, or of the English etymologies given in the *Leges Edwardi*. Some of Richard's etymologies were explicitly given for 'barbarous terms' ('barbara', pp.78–79), derived from Anglo-Norman and English. Other etymologised lexemes seem to hover somewhere between Latin and the vernacular. Unusually, Richard gave the putative background for two of these Anglo-Norman loanwords: *uastum* ('waste')[83] and *foresta* ('forest'), deriving *uastum* from 'uastatum' ('devastated') and *foresta* from 'feresta' ('a place for wild animals') (pp.92–93).[84] Richard included unprecedented consideration of the mechanisms by which these linguistic changes may have taken place, stating that *uastum* had come about through abbreviation, or syncope ('per sincopam'), whilst the 'o' of *foresta* had been changed from an 'e' ('e mutata in o') (pp.92–93). His descriptions of the emergence of these words recall the terminology of the Latin grammarian, Donatus, but significantly, they apply not only to the medieval Latin derivatives, but also to their Anglo-Norman equivalents.[85]

If Richard was thinking of the history of the Romance words here, his interest would be extremely unusual. Serge Lusignan has located the first explicit discussion that French came from Latin significantly later, in the writings of Pseudo-Robert Kilwardby (mid-thirteenth century).[86] However, this dawning perception of the links between Latin and Romance did not necessarily begin in the thirteenth century. When sharing its written form with Latin, speakers may have felt that Romance and Latin were different registers of the same language anyway. This seems to have been the case before Alcuin's reforms in the eighth century,[87] and in the tenth century, Dudo of Saint-Quentin still referred to the vernacular speech of Rouen as the 'Roman' language ('lingua romana').[88] To the interested reader, the connections between Latin and French may well have been self-evident from the vernacular's earliest appearances as a distinct written language.[89] There are several indications which suggest that we should locate an awareness of the relationship between Latin and French earlier than Pseudo-Kilwardby. Any work which gave both the Latin and French names for the object under discussion must have invited comparisons between the languages. The first French version of the Lapidary of Marbode of Rennes (written before *c.*1250) gave some etymologies which covered both the French and the Latin lexeme:

> *Hyaenia De Hyena*
> Hyene naist en la prunele
> D'une beste: piere est mult bele.
> La piere apelent par sun num,
> Kar la beste hyene a num.

> The *hyaenia* is born in the pupil of the eye of an animal: it is a very beautiful stone. They call the stone by its name because the animal is called a hyena.[90]

Readers were not obliged to choose whether they understood this etymology as referring to *hyaenia/hyena* or *hyene/hyene*: it is valid in both cases.

More explicit evidence of the perceived Latin foundations of French was offered by Adelard of Bath (d. *c*.1152) in his treatise on falconry:

> Cum autem ad locum quietis pervenerint, dum infirmi sunt et nondum super perticam sedere possunt, casam eis sine trabe fieri oportet, quam vulgo firmam dicunt, eo quod in ea penne firmantur.

> Once [the birds] arrive at the resting place, as long as they are weak and cannot sit on a perch, one should provide for them a small shed without a beam, which they call a 'firma' in the vulgar language, because it is in this that they get firm feathers.[91]

Adelard did not have a rigid sense of the boundaries between Latin and the vernacular, which remain linguistically permeable: 'firma' seems to be assimilated to Latinity through its association with 'firmantur'.[92]

Some claims were more audacious: the earliest Anglo-Norman Bestiary (1121 × 1135), written by Philippe de Thaon for Adeliza of Louvain, sought to etymologise some French words according to the other two sacred languages, deriving *pantere*, 'panther', from the Greek 'pan', 'all', and, far less plausibly, 'Adeliza' from Isidore's etymology for Hebrew 'alleluia', 'God's praise'.[93] Philippe calculated that Adeliza would be flattered by her name's connection with the most ancient of the *tres linguae sacrae*, a feat only possible if his intended audience believed that this Hebrew derivation were likely. Although twelfth-century francophones, then, had no trouble in understanding that French words were constructed from a variety of sources, none of the etymologies offered here included discussion of the philological processes by which this French lexis was created. As mentioned in the previous chapter, in his *Itinerarium Kambriae*, Gerald of Wales stated in a survey of the cognates of the word 'salt' that 'in French the word becomes *sel*, the vowel *a* changing to *e* as it develops from Latin' ('*sel* Gallice, mutatione *a* vocalis in *e*, a Latino'). However, this was written slightly after the *Dialogus*, between late November 1190 and October 1191.[94] Richard's potential speculations concerning the precise details of the evolution of Latin into French would therefore be novel, though according well with a broader interest in etymology shared by his contemporaries.

Richard's methodology was often indebted to Isidore of Seville, but when he extended his linguistic scrutiny beyond classical Latin, he was obliged to adopt a more innovative approach. Isidore's *Etymologies* was cited twice by Richard, and he included his explanation of *thesaurus*, 'treasury' (pp.94–95). This suggests that he attempted to research the etymological origins of at least some exchequer language. However, his treatments of 'uastum' and 'foresta' illustrate his understanding that other words required a different response. This can be traced most clearly in Richard's etymology for the titular *scaccarium*, with which he chose to begin his work. The first chapter of the *Dialogus* has the *discipulus* requesting the 'reason' (*ratio*) for the name of the exchequer (*scaccarium*), which Richard initially locates in its resemblance to a chessboard ('quia scaccarii lusilis similem habet formam', pp.10–11). However, the student rejects this as superficial, and so the master offers a further explanation:

> Discipulus: Numquid antiquorum prudentia pro sola forma sic nominauit? Cum et simili ratione posset tabularium appellari.
> Magister: Merito te scrupulosum dixi. Est et alia set occultior: sicut enim in scaccario lusili quidam ordines sunt pugnatorum et certis legibus uel limitibus procedent uel subsistunt, presidentibus aliis et aliis precedentibus, sic in hoc quidam president quidam assident ex officio, et non est cuiquam liberum leges constitutas excedere, quod erit ex consequentibus manifestum. Item, sicut in lusili pugna committitur inter reges, sic in hoc inter duos principaliter conflictus est et pugna committitur, thesaurarium scilicet et uicecomitem qui assidet ad compotum residentibus aliis tanquam iudicibus ut uideant et iudicent.

> Student: Do you think that was the only reason our wise ancestors gave it that name? Because they could just as well have called it a checkerboard.
> Teacher: I was right to call you meticulous. There is another, less obvious reason. For just as in a chess game the pieces have a certain order and move or stand still according to certain laws and within certain parameters, some ranking higher and some leading the way, in the same way, at the exchequer, some preside and others have seats because of their official positions, and no one is free to act outside the established rules, as will be clear from what is to follow. Also, just as, in chess, battle is joined between the kings, so at the exchequer there is basically a competition and struggle between two individuals, namely the treasurer and the sheriff who makes his account to the others sitting there as arbiters, so that they may see and judge. (pp.10–11)

The persistent requests of the student emphasise Richard's belief in the pedagogical value of etymologies. The student's 'meticulous' requests lead to the uncovering of several layers of motivation behind the naming of the exchequer. Consideration of its etymology moves our thoughts beyond the initial visual resemblance between the exchequer table and the chessboard, accounting both for the antagonistic nature of the exchequer's business, and its rigid hierarchy.

Richard's etymologies did not simply mimic Isidore's methods: he explained terminology not only with reference to divine will, but also with reference to Anglo-Norman predecessors. Isidore was influenced by the patristic belief that Hebrew was the language used by Adam to name the animals in Eden, a language in which the disjunction between sign and referent was hence uniquely absent, and the language from which all others were descended after Babel. He argued that the Latin alphabet was derived from the Greek, which in turn was derived from the Hebrew: this demonstrated by extension that Latin vocabulary could be traced to its Hebraic, Adamic roots (I.iii.4). Etymology hence became an enterprise which sought to recover the divine intention behind the impositions of these names.[95] However, for Isidore: 'etymologies are not to be found for all words, because some things received names not according to their innate qualities, but by the caprice of human will' ('omnium nominum etymologiae non reperiuntur, quia quaedam non secundum qualitatem, qua genita sunt, sed iuxta arbitrium humanae voluntatis vocabula acceperunt', I.xxix.2). He implied here that it was impossible to produce etymologies for words which did not have a basis in the pre-Lapsarian language constructed by God. Richard thought differently: aside from his borrowing from Isidore of *thesaurus*, 'treasury', from 'thesis auri', 'the placing of gold', he was exclusively interested in the use of etymology as a tool to reconstruct the motivations of those establishing words in the recent past (pp.94–95).[96] His etymology for 'exchequer', *scaccarium*, emphasised that an examination of the terminology used to designate ephemera could reveal a rich history. He largely used etymology as a means of elaboration and elucidation of the concepts he considered either to be of major interest, or a source of confusion to the neophyte. Many of his etymologised terms were hence coined for use in a specific administrative context. However, in a significant departure from Isidore's interests, this history did not provide the enquirer with an insight into the mind of God, but into that of 'our wise ancestors' ('antiquorum prudentia', pp.10–11). Richard did not question their power to create names that were equally capable of mirroring the intrinsic qualities of the onomastic object, a power that was not confined to Latin, but also manifested itself in the vernaculars.

Per Traducem: The Linguistic Legacy of the Exchequer

Although the *Dialogus* was subtly inventive in ways beyond its treatment of language, Richard preferred to portray the text as a conservative continuation of existing traditions. He was aware of the innovative nature of his overall project, pleading for clemency from his future detractors by reminding them in the closing passages of the book that he had written 'without a guide or example' ('duce carens et exemplari', pp.192–193). But if he professed himself content to lay his axe to 'wild and untouched woodland' ('intacta [. . .] rudique silua', pp.192–193), the originality of his enterprise was not motivated by a disregard for the past. He himself ruled out the possibility that his book would allow for the 'discovery of interesting novelties' ('iocunda nouitatis inuentio', pp.6–7). Given Richard's determination to write of useful, rather than subtle things ('non subtilia set utilia', p.8), M. T. Clanchy has argued that this represents a self-conscious opposition of his work against the *moderni*, the new breed of upwardly mobile schoolmen.[97]

Despite this self-declared preference for the traditional, Richard's depiction of the exchequer was shaped by comparatively modern bureaucratic developments. Much of the material that he self-consciously opposed to 'novelties' was, in fact, of fairly recent origin, if grounded in more ancient custom. Some form of tax collection seems to have been a feature of the English political scene in Anglo-Saxon times, but the exchequer itself appears to be an institution of comparatively recent foundation. Judith Green identifies 1110 as the first year when its activity is clearly visible, although it was then a bi-annual audit of royal revenue whose personnel were shared with the royal household.[98] Nor does the institution of the exchequer seem to have been brought from Normandy, as Richard claimed: though a centralised court of audit was established in Normandy by the 1130s, by the reign of Henry II its development seems to have lagged behind its English counterpart, if indeed it had been in continuous existence until that time.[99] Richard fitz Nigel is likely to have accompanied Henry's exchequer official, Richard of Ilchester, to Normandy in 1176 on a mission to reorganise Norman finances: only from this time do explicit references to an exchequer sitting at Caen survive.[100] Probably due to Stephen's arrest of Richard's great-uncle Roger of Salisbury, who had been responsible for the exchequer under Henry I, he also sought to minimise any sense of competent administration during Stephen's reign, stating that the knowledge of the operation of the exchequer was then 'almost entirely lost' ('pene prorsus abolitam', pp.76–77).[101] Although there is some evidence for the continued activity of the exchequer during the civil war, Richard argued instead that the 'whole order of its procedure' ('totius descriptionis eius formam', pp.76–77) was only revived by his father, Nigel, after Henry II's accession.[102] At the same time, he glossed over the many changes which had taken place after the anarchy. The role of treasurer under Henry II was far more restricted than it had been in the time of Roger of Salisbury, with Richard now rarely at court.[103]

Rather than depicting institutional continuity across the Conquest, the *Dialogus* was far more concerned with recording Norman contributions to the exchequer; Richard's own family received particular attention. He noted that some considered the exchequer's origins to be Anglo-Saxon:

> Sunt etiam qui credant usum eius sub regibus Anglicis extitisse, hinc sumentes rei huius argumentum quod coloni et iam decrepiti senes fundorum illorum qui corone annominantur, quorum in his cana memoria est, optime nouerint a patribus suis edocti quantum de albo firme pro singulis libris soluere teneantur.

> Some people believe it existed under the Anglo-Saxon kings, supporting this with the argument that the peasants who are now decrepit old men on the crown lands, whose memory in these matters goes all the way back, know very well, because they were taught by their fathers, how much they were liable to pay for each pound to blanch the farm. (pp.20–21)

However, Richard rejected this possibility, preferring instead to present it as being instituted by William the Conqueror, and modelled on the Norman exchequer (p.20). This involved a certain amount of contortion. The author made a valid point that folk memory of the procedure of blanch farm (where a set weight of the coin collected as tax revenue would be melted down to remove its impurities and weighed again to find out how much silver was proportionally lacking from the overall payment) only provided evidence for the pre-Conquest existence of this procedure, rather than for the exchequer as a whole. More controversially, he chose to eliminate any doubt over this matter by stating that the Domesday Book made no mention of blanch farm ('nulla prorsus de albo firme fit mentio', pp.20–21). This is one of Richard's most famous errors, which, R. L. Poole argues, arises from a poor knowledge of the contents of the Domesday Book, in spite of Richard's exploitation of its symbolic power as a repository of fiscal data.[104] Another view would posit that his treatment of the Domesday Book was part of a deliberate strategy to enhance the reputation of his great-uncle, Henry I's administrator, Roger of Salisbury, whom Richard claimed to be the first person to have instituted the procedure of blanch farm at the exchequer (pp.64–67).[105] Etymology was used to underpin his historical arguments. He correctly interpreted the English word *Domesdei* as 'day of judgement' ('dies iudicii'), stating that 'when recourse is made to the book, its word cannot be denied or set aside without penalty' ('cum uentum fuerit ad librum, sententia eius infatuari non potest uel impune declinari', pp.96–99). This etymology emphasised that Domesday Book's testimony was authoritative, even infallible: his assertion that the work made no mention of blanch farm thus supported his own contention that Roger of Salisbury implemented the procedure.

Historical accuracy was overshadowed by the demands of Richard's literary material as Norman panegyric, as he sought to link contemporary policy with the ancestral past. He was concerned with the counterpoint the material offered between contemporary practice and ancestral inheritance, rather than with its intrinsic historicity. As we have seen, he had a selective attitude to historical research: John Hudson has stated that he clearly spent 'much time poking around in archives', but Richard's inaccurate reading of the Domesday Book is only one of his odd oversights.[106] Some have felt that the error concerning blanch farm is so glaring that Richard cannot have made the claim himself, and that this passage must be an interpolation by a later, less knowledgeable hand.[107] However, Richard's most recent editor has argued persuasively for the integrity of the text as a whole, suggesting that its inconsistencies are a product of Richard's revisions over a number of years.[108] This is supported by the fact that this treatment of the evidence of the Domesday Book strengthened Richard's presentation of the procedure of blanch farm as the brainchild of his great-uncle, Roger of Salisbury. Hudson has stated that Richard's work 'provides a history, a biography, even a genealogy, for his kin and for the exchequer, promoting his own and their importance'.[109] Richard may have been seeking to augment more conventional kinds of aristocratic genealogy with this bureaucratic legacy. Roger of Salisbury was an egregious example of one of the common men whom Henry I and Henry II controversially raised above the nobility by appointing to administrative posts.[110] Richard himself stated defensively that his great-uncle was 'unknown (but not ignoble)' in his youth ('ignotus non tamen ignobilis', pp.64–65). Yet he also sought the aggrandisement of Norman administration and innovation more widely. Blanch farm (and hence the exchequer) was shown as a legacy of William the Conqueror. This flattered not only his great-grandson, Henry II, to whom the *Dialogus* is dedicated, but all those with Norman ancestry. The description provided by Richard of the contemporary workings of the exchequer was accurate and detailed. But the presentation of his historical and linguistic material was influenced by a desire to magnify the importance of a Norman and familial legacy.[111]

Throughout the *Dialogus*, Richard was preoccupied by ideas of ancestral bequests. He stressed the influence of Roger of Salisbury on the work, stating that: 'from the overflowing of his knowledge have I received, as an inheritance, the little that I know' ('de cuius stillicidiis nos quoque modicum id quod habemus per traducem accepimus', pp.64–65). There is a clear sense of the exchequer as the history of the future: Richard has a moral duty to record his inherited expertise for the generations after him so that they will be able to imitate the good financial practice bequeathed to him by his family. Even this was a concern stemming from his father, Nigel of Ely, Henry II's treasurer, about whom Richard wrote that:

> Credidit sane uir prudens satius esse constitutas ab antiquis leges posteris innotescere quam sua taciturnitate ut noue conderentur efficere. Vix enim modernitas in questu pecunie mitiora prioribus iura dictauit.

> This wise man sensibly believed it better to write down for posterity the laws established from ancient times than to let his silence cause new ones to be invented. For in seeking money the modern age has hardly created more moderate laws than earlier times. (pp.76–77)

Given that the reign of Henry II saw the birth of important developments in inheritance law such as the assize of *mort d'ancestor*, we might perhaps see such language as a subtle way to aggrandise this further aspect of Norman administrative innovation.[112] To employ the lexical field of inheritance is itself a kind of Norman legacy: John Hudson has traced the growth and increasingly precise use of the language of heritability in the Norman legal system over the early twelfth century.[113] Richard demonstrates a sensitivity to differing historical usage, discussing archaic terms for 'hundred' seen in Anglo-Saxon charters (pp.98–99). It is uncertain how much he knew about the historical nuances of this inheritance language. However, in scrutinising technical terminology in order to demonstrate the Norman origins of the exchequer, Richard seems to consider that the language of bureaucracy is an inheritance in itself: the etymological methods demonstrated in the *Dialogus* can only yield valid data if the administrative impact of the Norman government is accepted to be inseparable from its linguistic legacy.

The Normans and English Genealogy

For all the stress on inheritance in the *Dialogus*, the nature of the legacies left by the Anglo-Normans and Anglo-Saxons remains profoundly ambiguous. In some ways the two groups seem to merge ethnically, linguistically, and historically; but Richard was also subtly concerned with emphasising Norman bureaucratic excellence over competing versions of exchequer history based on Anglo-Saxon achievement. Ostensibly, the text was committed to a harmonious vision of intertwined peoples. When explaining the

origins of the murder fine, Richard was eager to stress that the penalty
was designed to correct social circumstances which had long since passed.
He saw the term as originating in post-Conquest guerrilla war, when the
English had the Normans 'clandestinely murdered' ('clanculo iugulabant',
pp.80–81) in remote places. If the identity of the murderer could not be
established, the local community would be fined collectively. His etymology explained:

> Murdrum proprie dicitur mors alicuius occulta cuius interlector ignoratur.
> Murdrum enim idem est quod absconditum uel occultum.

> Murder is the name for the secret death of someone whose killer is unknown.
> For 'murder' means something concealed or hidden. (pp.80–81)

In one of the most widely quoted passages of the *Dialogus*, he continued:

> Cohabitantibus Anglicis et Normannis et alterutrum uxores ducentibus uel
> nubentibus, sic permixte sunt nationes ut uix decerni possit hodie, de liberis
> loquor, quis Anglicus quis Normannus sit genere; exceptis dumtaxat ascrip-
> titiis qui uillani dicuntur, quibus non est liberum, obstantibus dominis suis,
> a sui status conditione discedere. Ea propter pene quicumque sic hodie
> occisus reperitur, ut murdrum punitur, exceptis his de quibus certa sunt
> ut diximus seruilis conditionis indicia.

> With the English and the Normans living side by side and intermarrying,
> the two peoples are so mixed that today one can scarcely distinguish who is
> English and who is Norman – among free persons, that is, for it is different
> with those unfree persons who are called villeins, of course, who are not
> able to change their condition without permission from their lords. For that
> reason, today, if anyone is found to have been killed, it is treated as murder,
> except in the case of those who, as I said, are proved to be unfree. (pp.80–83)

From one linguistic perspective, this intermarriage is mirrored in the
semantic transfers witnessed by the etymology of *murdrum*. The Anglo-
Saxon offence of *morðor*, 'an unatonable killing or betrayal of one's lord'
has acquired the sense of its French cognate, *mordre*, 'assassination or secret
murder'.[114] But Richard himself did not emphasise this dual etymological background. He could have considered the term to be exclusively Old
French in origin: he described the murder fine as a post-Conquest development instituted by William I (in contrast to other twelfth-century writers
who attributed it to Cnut).[115] The profound and often imperceptible linguistic connections between English and French lexis illustrate Richard's
comments with some serendipity. Yet in the *Dialogus* more widely, his

contention that differences between the two peoples were scarcely distinguishable seems less secure. Richard remains a problematic witness to post-Conquest perceptions of ethnicity: his assertion of unity is somewhat belied by the care with which he constructs the exchequer as a product of Norman culture.

Particularly with regard to the inheritance of personal wealth, it seems that divisions between the English and the Normans continued to be felt. Whilst Richard stressed Norman and familial inheritance in the *Dialogus*, the English did not receive a comparable patrimony. In his account of the post-Conquest land settlement obtained from the 'natives' (*indigeni*), he emphasised that they 'could not claim anything for themselves by hereditary right from the time of the Conquest' ('nomine successionis a temporibus subacte gentis nichil sibi uendicarant', pp.82–83). For Richard, this was both an instance of William I's clemency in allowing the English to possess anything at all, and a desirable way to ensure their continuing subordination:

> Quod quidem quam discreta consideratione cautum sit, manifestum est, presertim cum sic modis omnibus, ut sibi consulerent, de cetero studere tenerentur deuotis obsequiis dominorum suorum gratiam emercari.

> It is certainly clear how prudent this decision was, especially since from then on, in their own interests, they would always be bound to seek the favour of their lords through loyal service. (pp.82–83)

Like many of Richard's adaptations of legal history, this was only partially true. In fact, this was a situation no different for Norman subjects, whose feudal succession was also theoretically confirmed by their lord (although by the reign of Henry I the right of a tenant's heir to succeed was seldom disputed in practice). This 'considerable security of tenure' was further cemented by Henry II's land law reforms such as the assizes of *novel disseisin* (1166) and *mort d'ancestor* (1176).[116] Rosalind Faith has located Richard's account in 'fictitious "social memory"', stemming from a desire to provide 'some kind of justification of the depressed status' of the English.[117] We might thus see it as motivated by Norman guilt about the continuing consequences of the Conquest, even whilst English subjugation is transformed into further proof of Norman greatness.

Whilst Richard's depiction of the two peoples elided their social and financial inequalities, this favourable perspective on their unity finds parallels elsewhere in literature connected to Henry II. The king was undoubtedly eager to portray himself as both English and Norman, and to emphasise his English ancestry through his maternal grandmother, a great-great niece of Edward the Confessor. Aelred of Rievaulx wrote a *Vita* of Edward dedicated to Henry, which showed him as the triumphant fulfilment of a prophecy. In a deathbed vision, Edward saw a green tree which, having been cut down and set apart for the space of three yokes of land, flowered again and brought forth 'fruit' ('fructum').[118] Comparing this vision with the twelfth-century royal succession, Aelred interpreted this 'fruit' as Henry, 'the cornerstone', where 'the two walls of the English and Norman peoples have met' ('in quem velut lapidem angularem Anglici generis et Normannici [...] duos parietes convenisse').[119] Richard seems less confident about the genealogical restoration and renewal posited by the 'green tree' prophecy. English was certainly a vital part of the linguistic testimony he exploited to provide evidence of the history of the exchequer. 'Domesday' (*Domesdei*) and 'Danegeld' (*danegeldum*) merited etymological elucidation amongst several other borrowings such as 'hide' (*hida*) and 'hundred' (*hundredus*). Moreover, he used a variety of English oral sources, perhaps including his mother. A description of English post-Conquest tenurial rights was taken 'from the natives themselves' ('ab ipsis indigenis', pp.82–83), and he was familiar with the pre-Conquest accounts of blanch farm heard by 'peasants who are now decrepit old men' ('coloni et iam decrepiti senes', pp.20–21).[120] However, for Richard, the economic contribution of the English to their descendants could in no way match this linguistic bequest.

These profound uncertainties over inheritance not only coloured Richard's portrayal of the English but influenced his painstaking construction of Norman heritage. In *Etymologies and Genealogies*, Howard Bloch has claimed that ideas of lineage were central to medieval understandings of language, and vice versa (although he thinks it impossible to ascertain which discourse first influenced the other).[121] We might consider Richard fitz Nigel's work to be an exploration of etymology *as* genealogy, where proof of heritage is located in linguistic descent. However, this descent is not automatic or unproblematic. Emphasising that the medieval relationship between father and son could only take place if both parties acknowledged their genetic connection verbally, Zrinka Stahuljak has stated that genealogy is 'not a natural blood relationship between father and son', but a 'linguistic tie'.[122] In locating the transmission of English patrimony in the feudal oath between lord and vassal, Richard made this act of linguistic filiation explicit: unlike the Norman transmission of exchequer lore, patterns of English inheritance are distinguished by rupture, not genetic continuity, as each new tenant must be reconfirmed in his tenure by his lord. The Norman legacy of Richard's own work is equally uncertain. His demonstration of the genealogical continuity of exchequer knowledge is

dependent on language, yet the unbroken linguistic thread that the practice of etymology enables us to follow is only traceable through the very
fact of its own mutability. Richard anticipated that his own oral testimony
would also be rendered obsolete by changing circumstances. His advice
would soon be outdated:

> Ex uariis enim et insolitis casibus uel nulla fiet uel adhuc incognita disci-
> plina; unde fit ut detractoriis linguis hinc potius exponar dum, succedente
> tempore, pleraque dubia necdum audita proponi continget.

> For systematic instruction, at least as we know it, cannot cover a miscellany
> of unusual cases; and so I will be criticised by my detractors when, over time,
> many doubtful and unprecedented questions arise. (pp.190–191)

Both genealogy and etymology are united in their focus on the past, but
their value is contingent on a future continuity of descent. If Richard is confident that others will construct a 'royal palace' ('regie domus', pp.192–193)
on the foundations he has laid, the future of the exchequer as a particularly Norman institution seems less clear. As we have seen, many historians
locate the gradual diminishment of the importance of *Normannitas* to the
end of the twelfth century. In its focus on ancestral language, the *Dialogus
de scaccario* implicitly raises questions about a comparable future legacy.

CHAPTER 5

Placing French in Multilingual Britain

This chapter continues to explore Norman understandings of the development of French, and its relationship with the insular past. Twelfth-century perceptions of insular multilingualism were shaped by an awareness that England's languages recorded the passage of dominion from one people to another. If for some this was a troubling reminder of the difficulties of integration, for others, the association of multilingualism with conquest made the presence of French within Britain a satisfying testament to the Normans' successful invasion. As discussed in the introduction to this volume, medieval understandings of the importance of language to ethnic identity transformed treatments of multilingualism into oblique discussions of the transfer of sovereignty. Yet the arrival of languages from the continent as a result of migration or aggression also raised questions concerning how far these new languages could be seen as fully assimilated. This chapter suggests that portrayals of the place of French within Britain represent an important site for anxieties about integration. Through an examination of francophone depictions of place names and insular literary traditions, it argues that these discussions of multilingualism explore how far it is feasible or desirable to place the French language within the British landscape.

Post-Conquest interest in the history of the French of England reflected Norman settlers' increasing ties to the island. The geographical idea of England formed a continuity across the Conquest which encouraged the new settlers to see themselves as participants in insular culture.[1] Even before the loss of Normandy (1204), aristocratic possessions shaped identity. The Conquest precipitated a major redistribution of land in Anglo-Norman England. After William I had rewarded his followers with new territories, the higher echelons of landholders were composed almost exclusively of Normans, and by 1086 only thirteen English tenants-in-chief remained.[2] At a local level, this aristocracy seems rapidly to have become 'particularist': only the greatest continued to retain cross-channel interests into the late twelfth century.[3] Trends in the transmission of land also encouraged a sense of identification with specific holdings. Over the eleventh and twelfth centuries, there was a growing tendency to favour a strategy of keeping the ancestral lands together as a single unit for one son, rather than sharing them out between several descendants.[4] Some of the Normans also adopted toponyms based on their most important estates. Whilst the most prestigious referred to lands in France, English place names were also frequently employed by both Normans and English, not always to indicate lordship as much as a sense of association with a particular settlement.[5] By the late 1150s, the Warenne Chronicler had a particular name for this element of the Norman aristocracy increasingly closely tied to lands in England: *Normananglí.*[6]

As the Norman settlers became ever more financially and emotionally attached to their new territories, they began to evince an interest in the past of the island.[7] The 1120s and 1130s saw the appearance of several important new insular histories like Henry of Huntingdon's *Historia Anglorum*, Geoffrey of Monmouth's *Historia regum Britanniae*, and William of Malmesbury's *Gesta regum Anglorum*.[8] Although intermarriage in the post-Conquest period remained comparatively rare, it is perhaps significant that all three authors were certainly or potentially of varied ethnic stock: to different elements of England's newly mixed population, its past was ancestral, esoteric, or even, perhaps, exotic.[9] By the mid-twelfth century, histories of England were also being commissioned by royalty and the aristocracy in their own language, French.[10] Gaimar's *Estoire des Engleis* may be the earliest surviving example of this trend: the work was tailored to the interests of his patron, Constance fitz Gilbert, the wife of a member of the lower aristocracy with lands in Lincolnshire.[11] Although the portion of the work now extant was primarily translated from an independent copy of the Northern Recension of the *Anglo-Saxon Chronicle*, Gaimar also included long sections which recorded East Anglian folk history; his epilogue stated that the now-lost beginning of the work was based on the *Historia regum Britanniae*.[12] These texts reflected political, as well as local identities. Geoffrey's *Historia* was translated into Old French verse at least seven times in the twelfth century; Wace's *Roman de Brut* is the only complete version to survive, and was by far the most popular.[13] Jane Zatta has argued that these works were shaped by the interests of the insular aristocracy, emphasising the rights and prerogatives of the nobility in the face of encroachments perpetrated by the king.[14] Although the decision to figure aristocratic descent from Normans, British or English is sometimes depicted as a conscious choice between discrete options, in practice, boundaries often overlapped: Gaimar's *Estoire* incorporated British and English material, while Wace wrote histories of the British and the Normans, perhaps both intended for the same royal audience.[15] These histories suggest that insular aristocratic identities could and did draw simultaneously on a range of potential ethnicities, but it is clear that, over the course of the twelfth century, the appeal of Englishness was increasing.

Throughout the later Middle Ages, French facilitated international and intellectual expansion beyond England: francophone expertise ensured participation in cross-continental networks of commerce, diplomacy, and literature. At the same time, Anglo-Norman gradually began to be seen to be differentiated in some respects from other forms of French. In 1113, Philippe de Thaon already saw it as 'our country's spoken language' ('raisun mustree de la nostre cuntree').[16] For one nun of Barking Abbey, composing a *Life of Edward the Confessor* in the 1160s, this insular Anglo-Norman fell short of the standard of French spoken elsewhere:

> Si joe l'ordre des cas ne gart
> ne juigne part a sa part,
> certes n'en dei estre reprise
> ke nel puis faire en nule guise:
> qu'en latin est nominatif
> ço frai romanz acusatif.
> Un faus franceis sai d'Angletere
> ke ne l'alai ailurs [re]quere.
> Vus ki aliurs apris l'ave
> la u mester iert, l'amendez!

> If I do not observe the order of the cases or construe clauses together, I should certainly not be criticised because it is quite impossible for me to do so. What is nominative in Latin, I shall translate as accusative in French. My French is a false French of England, for I have not been anywhere else to acquire it. Those of you, however, who have learnt your French elsewhere should correct mine where it is necessary.[17]

The nun stresses that any translation is obliged to modify the grammar of its source text to some extent. However, rather than simply copying her Latin source, Aelred of Rievaulx's *Vita* of Edward the Confessor, she has chosen to translate it into Anglo-Norman. If French cannot replicate the nuances of Latin grammar, the reverse is also true. Her radical insistence that her French is 'faus' suggests that, as with Latin, there is a widely recognised standard of correctness for the vernacular. Although her modesty topos implies that this particular text has failed to attain such correctness, her use of grammatical terminology nonetheless draws attention to the prestigious potential of French as a vehicle for linguistic scholarship and literary composition.

By 1175–1185, Thomas of Kent was proud of the idiosyncrasies of his insular French, at the same time as his lexical choices revealed the inherent fluidity of Anglo-Norman's notional linguistic boundaries.[18] In his versified *chanson de geste* of the life of Alexander the Great, he included much information on the marvels of the East. These featured a mountain in India so high that for those living at its base:

> Ne piert qe quinze jors en l'an septentrion;
> Ces sunt les esteilles qe nos Charle Wain nomon.
> Char l'apellent Franceis; diray vos l'achaison:
> Quatre sunt come roes e troys al temon.

> The Plough only appears for fifteen days in the year; these are the stars we call Charles's Wain. The French call it the Chariot; I'll tell you the reason: four are the wheels and three are the shaft.[19]

Charles's Wain is an Old English name, *Carleswæn*, first attested before 1000 in Ælfric's *De temporibus anni*;[20] Anglo-Norman *char* seems to be derived from 'carriage, cart, waggon or chariot', translating an idea similar to 'wain'.[21] Ian Short has hence concluded that Thomas 'is inscribing himself within the bilingual French- and English-speaking community of England while at the same time distancing himself from the French speakers of France'.[22] However, although the *Anglo-Norman Dictionary* includes an entry for 'Charle Wain', Thomas provides the only citation.[23] It seems likely that he himself saw the term as English. Thomas's comment could therefore be read differently: rather than inscribing himself within a bilingual community, his French is conceptually aligned with English. Ardis Butterfield has explored the 'porous' nature of the boundaries between the two languages in the later Middle Ages, and we might productively extend this idea to linguistic categories in the twelfth century.[24] On a lexical level, Thomas's quotation illustrates the fluidity of 'French', where the language's own insular identity is strengthened by encompassing English terms. French was not monolithic: its incorporation of different dialects, territories and socio-economic groups across Europe created fluctuating opportunities for a nuanced and subjective range of cultural alignments. Thomas's discussion hence took place within a profoundly cosmopolitan context: even as they continued to look towards the continent, the Normans were also becoming more interested in seeing their tongue as part of a multilingual dialogue between the peoples of Britain.

Accounts of the history of French were therefore shaped by the factors traced above: to a certain extent, it was set apart from the other languages of Britain by its recent history. But this also placed it within a broader insular framework of successive conquests. Although it may appear at first glance that francophones only began to consider the development of their language in a sustained way during the thirteenth century, by hunting for information that relates exclusively to French, it may be that we have been searching in the wrong places.[25] Rather than exploring the history of French in isolation from other insular languages, most medieval writers situated it against the multilingual past. Etymology provided the most significant means of tracing the connections which the languages of Britain had to each other, and to the landscape. However, authors also considered the historical implications of French's presence in Britain, and its relationship to English traditions of vernacular literary composition. Three such attempts to locate French are examined here: Wace's *Brut*, the works of Gervase of Canterbury, and the anonymous *Roman de Waldef*. All three authors explored the problems and potential inherent in the language's arrival with the Normans at the Conquest, grounding French in the growth of multilingualism in Britain. Wace and Gervase were both writing new recensions of Galfridian history by adapting the same two versions of Geoffrey of Monmouth's *Historia regum Britanniae*; the author of *Waldef* responded to the British setting of Wace's *Brut*. These texts hence offer three related perspectives on the challenges of integrating the Normans into Geoffrey's history of insular language, where etymologies record the transfer of rule from one linguistic group to another. For all three authors, Britain's multilingual heritage allows them to portray the advent of French in the island as the culmination of a pre-existing historical pattern. Even at the moment of their conquest, the Normans are marked out as future natives.

Multilingualism in Wace's *Brut*

Geoffrey of Monmouth's *Historia regum Britanniae* (1123 × 1139) provided one of the most sensitive negotiations of the complex ideological inheritance of multilingualism. The arrival of Brutus gloriously introduces Trojan British to the island: he renames Albion after himself as Britain, establishing a pattern of Trojan toponyms which commemorate colonisation. Yet with the appearance of the Saxons from the continent, multilingualism becomes a tool for miscommunication and treachery. Linguistic plurality facilitates the passage of dominion from the British to the English: Hengist and Horsa duplicitously take advantage of Vortigern's ignorance of the Saxon tongue in order to slaughter his retinue and claim the island for themselves. Geoffrey's interpretation of British history was unmistakably influenced by contemporary politics, but the Normans were never incorporated into this picture directly. He did include many details borrowed from contemporary place names, but only his discussion of the etymology for Brutus's city of New Troy hinted at Britain's recent past:

> Vnde nominata fuit postmodum Kaerlud et deinde per corruptionem nominis Kaerlundein; succedente quoque tempore, per commutationem linguarum dicta fuit Lundene et postea Lundres, applicantibus alienigenis qui patriam sibi submittebant.

> Later it was renamed Kaerlud, a name afterwards corrupted to Kaerlundein; as time passed and languages changed, it was called Lundene and then Lundres when foreigners landed and conquered the country.[26]

For the most part, the presence of the Normans was intimated through a framework of successive transfers of insular power: this framework found its implicit culmination in the Norman Conquest. Two responses to the *Historia regum Britanniae* will be examined here which seek to incorporate the French language into Geoffrey's Trojan tradition to a much fuller extent: Wace's *Roman de Brut* and Gervase of Canterbury's Latin historical works. Both authors depicted Britain's multilingualism as a clear consequence of the many struggles for the control of the island outlined in the *Historia*. They were more ambivalent about whether this should be interpreted as a symbol of mutability or of the magnificence of Norman rule: multilingualism was simultaneously an index of present glory, and a portent of the future obliteration of its current splendour through other conquests.

Wace's *Brut* was the most popular of at least seven twelfth-century French translations of Geoffrey of Monmouth, surviving in over thirty manuscripts.[27] As discussed above, these works and their reception are often seen in the context of a growing sense of Englishness on the part of the Anglo-Norman aristocracy, reflecting an increasing identification with their newly acquired territory. However, Wace himself does not fit into this narrative in any simple way. Born in Jersey, he spent most of his life in northern France, studying in Paris or Chartres and becoming a 'clerc lisant' at Caen and a canon of Bayeux Cathedral, (although he may have visited southern England at least once).[28] His thirteenth-century Middle English translator, Laȝamon, stated that the *Brut* was presented to Eleanor of Aquitaine: whilst we cannot verify this, we know that it probably found favour with Henry II, who commissioned his next work, the *Roman de Rou*.[29] Henry seems to have envisaged a history of the Normans which stretched from Rollo (*Rou*), their founding father, to the glories of his own kingship. Wace produced an increasingly ambivalent depiction of Norman rule, and eventually an unimpressed Henry II asked a rival historian, Benoît de Sainte-Maure, to attempt the project instead. Although Wace engaged with both the continental and insular history of the Anglo-Norman realm, he identified with neither Britain nor Normandy in a straightforward way. His *Roman de Brut* explored the means by which French could fit into a narrative of the development of Britain's languages, but he did not portray any people or language as wholly connected to the landscape. For Wace, the island was a contested space, and the struggles for the control of it were recorded in its toponyms, which charted a pattern of successive possession and loss: all linguistic dominion was ephemeral.

Although a reminder of the futility of human endeavour, this understanding of possession also provided a possible way of incorporating the Normans into the realm of Britain. If no single *gens* had an inalienable right to the island, invasion could be seen as a morally neutral act. Wace explored this perspective, shaping a favourable portrayal of conquest through a careful approach to source material. The *Brut* included material from the Vulgate (Geoffrey's own text of the *Historia*), but the First Variant formed its main textual foundation. This was an extensively reworded, abbreviated reworking of the *Historia*, created soon after the publication of the Vulgate by someone other than Geoffrey. Often restructuring Geoffrey's *Historia* to give a more coherent narrative, the First Variant is distinguished by the increased morality of its tone, and by its more cautious treatment of the passage of dominion from the Britons to the English.[30] It is unclear whether Wace was using two different recensions of the *Historia*, or a single, composite manuscript which combined elements of both. On one hand, if an author already had access to a First Variant manuscript, it would perhaps not be difficult to obtain and compare this recension with Geoffrey's Vulgate, given its wide availability. Wace's demonstrably meticulous approach to historical research in the *Brut* and the *Rou* makes this possibility attractive.[31] The evidence of the eight surviving First Variant manuscripts suggests that conflation was a common strategy: no less than six of them contain some passages which have been combined with Vulgate readings.[32] This was done either to remedy deficiencies in the original exemplar,[33] or, in one ambitious manuscript, to create a new composite text.[34] On the other hand, the ubiquity of these conflated manuscripts admits the possibility that rather than selecting different readings from different recensions of the *Historia*, Wace was already using manuscript sources which combined the

First Variant and the Vulgate. Two other twelfth-century authors employed both recensions: Johannes de Hauvilla and Gervase of Canterbury.[35] Overall, then, three-quarters of the surviving First Variant manuscripts have Vulgate interpolations, and all three of the authors known to have used the First Variant in the twelfth century also used the Vulgate. Whilst we cannot reconstruct Wace's sources with certainty, it is more likely that he was employing composite sources, rather comparing manuscripts. It is hence perhaps safest to see his use of Galfridian material in terms of the differing emphasis he places on First Variant and Vulgate elements.

Wace's *Brut* was profoundly influenced by the First Variant's stress on Saxon military success. Although previous historical narratives had assigned the passage of dominion from the Britons to the English to the early sixth century at the latest, in Geoffrey's Vulgate, power was decisively transferred to the Saxons only during the reign of Cadwalladr in the later seventh century.[36] The Vulgate further diminished this Saxon victory by depicting Cadwalladr's British in a weakened state, because they had already suffered a significant blow in the second half of the sixth century. This was when the African king, Gormund, gave a substantial part of their territories to the Saxons following his military successes in Britain.[37] Geoffrey made clear that the Britons were primarily defeated by Gormund, rather than the Saxons, whose subsequent seventh-century conquest of the entirety of the island owed much to the prior successes of the Africans. Alarmed at the discrepancies between Geoffrey's account and those of earlier writers such as Bede, the author of the First Variant sought to harmonise them. He placed far greater emphasis on the importance of the donation of Gormund, which was presented as the point when the British lost control of the island.[38] In the Vulgate, the first king to rule over the whole of Loegria was Æthelstan in the tenth century, but the First Variant moved his reign to the seventh century, portraying him as a contemporary of Cadwalladr.[39] The author's approach is only coherent up to a point, as Vulgate material on Cadwalladr was also included which conflicted with the First Variant's depiction of Gormund. Overall, he markedly diminished the length of British rule, toning down Geoffrey's portrayal of the Britons' autonomy after the arrival of the Saxons.[40]

Wace largely followed the narrative outlined in the First Variant, concurring with its portrayal of Gormund, and similarly assigning the reign of Æthelstan to the seventh century.[41] However, he also included a detailed biography of Æthelstan at this point, making it clear that he was the same person as the tenth-century king.[42] This collapsing of temporal distance was part of a larger employment of prolepsis, emphasising the inevitability of the Britons' eventual loss of the sovereignty of the island. The First

Variant's markedly less partisan portrayal of the passage of dominion was further supported by Wace's interjection of comments which anticipated key historical milestones, foreshadowing the decline of British rule. These foretold the loss of Britain's name following the donation of Gormund (13379–13384), and the expulsion of the Britons across the Tamar and the Wye by Æthelstan (13939–13946). Wace's approach to nomenclature heightened a sense of the impending disintegration of British power. After Gormund's invasion, the First Variant called the island *Anglia* once, but subsequently reverted to *Britannia*, which was then employed until the end.[43] In contrast, after the first mention of Gormund, Wace stated that at this point 'Britain lost its name' ('Bretaine perdi sun nun', 13384). After this, he called the island *Engleterre* until the end of the *Brut*. He was hence subtly supportive of Saxon colonisation, augmenting the Anglophile stance of the First Variant with further anticipations of the loss of British dominion. His treatment of the Saxons emphasised their right to deprive the Britons of power, and, consequently, the right of the Normans to do the same to the English. This approach is not unproblematic: a stress on acquisition through conquest cannot grant any weight to the rights accrued through continuity of rule. Wace did not countenance the claim of any single group to the territory. It is military strength which determines possession of the island, rather than divine favour: any dynasty could be displaced by another power. Although his paradigm stressed the might of the Normans, Wace looked beyond them to their ultimate defeat by another contender for the mastery of Britain.

The *Brut* departed from atemporal portrayals of Britain's landscape, stressing its linguistic instability as a textually constructed space. Anglo-Saxon traditions of depicting Britain as contained yet fertile were enthusiastically continued in twelfth-century histories. Gildas and Bede's delineations of the island as a *locus amoenus* attracted further attention from Geoffrey of Monmouth and Henry of Huntingdon in Latin; the *Description of England* (1139 × 1200) offered a French adaptation of Henry's text.[44] Geoffrey's *Historia* began with a *descriptio insulae* characteristic of this tradition:

> Britannia, insularum optima, in occidentali occeano inter Galliam et Hiberniam sita, octingenta milia in longum, ducenta uero in latum continens, quicquid mortalium usui congruit indeficienti fertilitate ministrat. Omni etinem genere metalli fecunda, campos late pansos habet, colles quoque praepollenti culturae aptos, in quibus frugum diuersitates ubertate glebae temporibus suis proueniunt.

Britain, the best of islands, lies in the western ocean between France and Ireland; eight hundred miles long by two hundred miles wide, it supplies all human needs with its boundless productivity. Rich in metals of every kind, it has broad pastures and hills suitable for successful agriculture, in whose rich soil various crops can be harvested in their season. (*HRB*, pp.6–7)

Here, the island was seen as a pre-existing entity, already defined and desired by those who came to it. Wace emphasised the temporality of landscape more heavily, stressing its contingent nature. The beginning of the *Brut* omitted Geoffrey's *descriptio insulae*, instead discussing the sequential transfers of power which had shaped England:

> Ki vult oïr e vult saveir
> De rei en rei e d'eir en eir
> Ki cil furent e dunt il vindrent
> Ki Engleterre primes tindrent,
> Quels reis i ad en ordre eü,
> E qui anceis e ki puis fu,
> Maistre Wace l'ad translaté
> Ki en conte la verité.

> Whoever wishes to hear and to know about the successive kings and their heirs who once upon a time were the rulers of England – who they were, whence they came, what was their sequence, who came earlier and who later – Master Wace has translated it and tells it truthfully. (pp.1–8)

Unlike Geoffrey, the *Brut* did not offer a vision of the landscape as an eternal continuity which outlasted successive linguistic and political regimes. Instead, Wace's perspective seems more closely aligned to that found in the Domesday Book and other administrative documents. In an extraordinarily comprehensive strategy, the compilers of the Domesday survey (1086) sought to document and to exploit England's resources: unparalleled efforts were made to transform dreams of fecundity into the concrete and the taxable.[45] The island was framed as awaiting not only settlers' expansion but future written records: Domesday's densely textual approach to mapping implicitly acknowledged that the landscape as an object of human use was constituted by the act of description. Similarly, in Wace, the land is only made visible through its possession by a particular group of people, and through its existence in writing. Brought into being and perhaps lost again by authors and rulers, territory becomes doubly transient.

Etymology formed a key part of this textually constructed, ephemeral landscape. In several places, Wace modified his source or sources in order to incorporate French into the history of Britain's languages. Whilst the

Historia regum Britanniae's etymologies depicted the transition from British to English, Wace frequently inserted extra information on French into Geoffrey's remarks on the changing place names of Britain. Here, he initiates the first of two discussions on the successive names for New Troy which culminate in London:

> Pur ses anceisors remembrer
> La fist Troie Nove apeller;
> Puis ala li nuns corumpant,
> Si l'apela l'om Trinovant;
> Mais qui le nom guarde, si trove
> Que Trinovant est Troie Nove,
> Que bien pert par corruptiun
> Faite la compositiun. [...]
> Por Lud, un rei ki mult l'ama
> E longement i conversa,
> Fu puis numee Kaerlu.
> Puis unt cest nun Lud corumpu
> Si distrent pur Lud Lodoïn;
> Pur Lodoïn a la parfin
> Londenë en engleis dist l'um
> E nus or Lundres l'apelum.

> In memory of his ancestors he had it called 'New Troy'. Then the name became corrupted, and men called it 'Trinovant'; but whoever looks at the name will find that 'Trinovant' is 'New Troy', which is apparent through the corruption done to the name. [...] From Lud, a king who was very fond of the city and long dwelt there, it was then called 'Kaerlu'. Then they corrupted this name, Lud, and said 'Lodoin' instead. Finally, people call 'Lodoin', 'Londene', in English, and we now call it 'Lundres'. (1223–1230, 1231a-8)

Difficulties of communication between linguistic groups ensure that, far from being replicated, the Trojan names established by Brutus gradually become corrupted when pronounced by successive generations of foreigners, who alter them to suit their own speech patterns. The transfer of meaning between languages is a mechanism for linguistic corruption. This model questions the enterprise of translation. Seen in this light, as a rendering of Latin into French, the *Brut* itself becomes a figure of linguistic decline. The inclusion of French in the *Brut* has obvious penitential emphasis: contemporary language is not exempt from a seemingly universal linguistic and corporeal corruption.

However, the ending of the *Brut* offered a second perspective on linguistic corruption, its implications for the translator, and its implications for French. Wace chose to finish his work with an extensive comparison of Welsh, English and French which became an exploration of the tensions surrounding the translation and temporality of languages. Following the famine and plague which decimate the Britons, the Saxons seize their opportunity to emigrate *en masse*, consolidating their hold on the island:

> Les nuns, les lages, le language
> Voldrent tenir de lur lignage;
> Pur Kaer firent Cestre dire,
> E pur Suiz firent nomer Sire,
> E Tref firent apeler Tune;
> Map est gualeis, engleis est Sune,
> En gualeis est Kaer cité,
> Map fiz, Tref vile, Suiz cunté,
> E alquant dient que cuntree
> Swiz est en gualeis apelee
> E ço que dit Sire en engleis
> Ço puet estre Suiz en gualeis.
> Entre Gualeis uncore dure
> De dreit bretanz la parleüre.

> They wanted to keep the names, laws and language of their race: for 'kaer' they said 'chester', and for 'suiz', 'shire', and they called 'tref' 'tun'. 'Map' is Welsh, the English for it is 'son'; in Welsh 'kaer' means 'city', 'map', 'son', 'tref', 'town' and 'suiz', 'county', and some say a district is called 'suiz' in Welsh and what 'shire' means in English may be what 'suiz' means in Welsh. Among the Welsh the correct way of speaking the British language is still preserved. (14739–14752)

Wace's contention that the Welsh still maintained 'the correct way of speaking the British language' seems to adopt an Augustinian perspective, seeing language as a part of the ethnic customs which are transmitted genealogically between generations.[46] Received as part of the British descent of the Welsh, the contemporary language apparently has not altered across time, as Wace borrows some of its words here as examples of correct British.

Yet if the Welsh were still speaking *dreit bretanz*, this was in stark contrast to their wider cultural decline. Wace stated that:

> Tuit sunt mué e tuit changié,
> Tuit sunt divers e forslignié
> De noblesce, d'onur, de murs
> E de la vie as anceisurs.
> Guales cest nun a Guales vint
> Del duc Gualun, ki Guales tint,

U de Galaes, la reïne,
A ki la terre fud acline.

> The Welsh have quite altered and quite changed, they are quite different
> and have quite degenerated from the nobility, the honour, the customs and
> the life of their ancestors. Wales takes its name from duke Gualo, who ruled
> Wales, or from queen Galaes, to whom the land was subject. (14851–14858)

The exemption of language from this overarching cultural degeneration
seems improbable, especially as Wace explicitly treated it as an aspect of
ethnic custom ('costume'; 'usage') elsewhere in the *Brut* (see vv.3193, 13659).
Many medieval readers appear to have been unconvinced by this vision
of the Welsh preservation of British linguistic purity. The statement that
'among the Welsh, the correct way of speaking the British language is still
preserved' (14751–14752) has been omitted from nine manuscripts, including the only complete twelfth-century witness.[47] Wace himself may have
been aware of the inconsistencies of his approach. In his discussion of the
names of London, he described further internal changes to British which
happened 'through corruption' ('par corruptiun', 1229). Moreover, the very
name of the language belied any suggestion that it was unaffected by time:
instead of British, it was now called Welsh. The *Brut* therefore ended with
a vision of Welsh, *dreit bretanz*, as a continued source of linguistic purity.
Yet this insistence on its correctness conflicted with other Galfridian etymologies, which aimed to trace insular place names back through successive corruptions to their original purity of their Trojan roots. Wace hence
offered two interpretations of potential linguistic correctness: whilst the
Brut acknowledged the importance of the Trojan sources of Welsh, it also
emphasised that later forms of the language could have their own authority.

Wace's contention that correctness can be preserved despite linguistic
change has important implications for the *Brut*'s portrayal of translation.
His revisionary approach to his source texts suggests that he did not intend
his work merely to replicate Geoffrey of Monmouth's depiction of British
history, but also to expand, clarify, and adapt it. He depicted the *Brut* as
an authoritative text in its own right, in spite of its status as a translation.
Although he owned that his work was a rendering of earlier material, Wace
framed the *Brut* as primarily shaped by his own labour. He did not identify
any particular source text for his British history, stating only that 'Master
Wace translated it' ('Maistre Wace l'ad translaté', 7). In place of a conclu-
sion mentioning Geoffrey or the British book, he wrote that 'Master Wace
made this narrative' ('Fist mestre Wace cest romanz', 14866). He also gave
the date here, 1155, encouraging readers to look no further into the past for

the inception of the work (14865). Unlike the Vulgate and the First Variant, Wace noted that the 'story of the British' had ended ('Ci falt la geste des Bretuns', 14859), but refused to give any specific details concerning his sources. He eliminated all references to Geoffrey of Monmouth and his claim that the *Historia* was a translation from a British *liber uetustissimus*. Wace rejected the recursiveness of Geoffrey's original history, where textual authority was eternally situated beyond the Latin in an inaccessible British book. Here, the *Brut* itself becomes the most significant point of reference for those interested in the British past. If linguistic correctness can still be found in Welsh, the most recent form of the Trojan language, then translation, itself a kind of renaming, can similarly relocate authority in itself, rather than in its source texts.

As with translation's refiguring of earlier sources, the French etymologies which refigure the earlier names of Britain could also be seen as simultaneously correct and corrupt. Wace presented all etymological forms as valid, and all worthy of preservation in writing. Significantly, this emphasis on preservation also valorised the enterprise of historiography. In his *Roman de Rou*, composed and revised between 1160 and 1174, Wace depicted the historian as the guardian of etymological memory.[48] A long and poetic passage on the inexorability of mortality concluded that a man's fame would not endure 'unless it is set down in a book by a cleric' ('si par clerc nen est mis en livre').[49] After an extended consideration of changes in place names from Scotland to Bethlehem, Wace reminded his audience that:

> Des tresturnees de ces nuns,
> e des gestes dunt nus parluns,
> poi u nïent seüssum dire
> si l'um nes eüst feit escrire.

> Concerning the twists and turns of these names and the deeds of which we are speaking, we would have been able to say little or nothing if someone had not had them written down.[50]

We might thus see his interest in toponymy as a subtle way of drawing attention to the vital role of the historian in disseminating knowledge, or as a way to arrest the devastating effects of mutability by preserving linguistic information in a permanent record. Wace does not present any single answer to the questions raised by the existence of insular French in multilingual Britain. French is portrayed as the glorious culmination of the layers of languages which witness the differing possessors of the island, a tradition of naming which points back to a Trojan past and forward to an Anglo-Norman future. However, this history of invasion is quickly revealed as a precarious process of decay and decline. Yet even whilst etymologies emphasise the inevitability of corruption, they also testify to the power of the historian in enabling future generations to recover lost linguistic data.

Gervase of Canterbury and the Genesis of Multilingual Britain

Wace had an exceptional sensitivity to language history, and his nuanced consideration of the place of French in England is likely to have been one of the more sophisticated responses to the implications of multilingualism. Other readers of Geoffrey of Monmouth shared some aspects of Wace's conclusions, whilst embellishing or rejecting others. Gervase of Canterbury's portrayal of multilingualism used similar sources to Wace, hence offering a comparable perspective on the linguistic issues arising from Galfridian etymologies. Both authors were sensitive to the ways in which the different languages of Britain recorded its subjugation by foreigners. However, unlike Wace, Gervase did not only consider the ways that the etymological continuities between Britain's past and present place names witnessed invasion: he also offered extremely unusual direct discussion of the perceived connections between conquest and multilingualism. Here, Britain's linguistic plurality was seen as a testament both to the punishments sent by God in the form of invasion, and to the divine grace which favoured the island with uniquely diverse natural resources.

Gervase was made a monk of Christ Church, Canterbury in 1163, when he was probably around eighteen; he spent his entire career in the monastery until his death in or soon after 1210.[51] Although most famous for his *Chronica*, a history of Christ Church from the time of St Augustine to 1199, Gervase was also an avid reader of Geoffrey of Monmouth. He included a condensed paraphrase of the *Historia regum Britanniae* in his *Gesta regum*, a political history of England which ran up to his own time.[52] Galfridian material also formed the basis of his later *Mappa mundi*.[53] Rather than being a pictorial map, this was a brief historical description of England, followed by an ecclesiastical survey of each county with a list of its religious houses, and finally a list of foreign bishoprics. It was completed soon after 1201: this is the only attempt at such a survey made before the seventeenth century.[54] It has not previously been noticed that Gervase, like Wace, was either using both the Vulgate and the First Variant text of Geoffrey's *Historia regum Britanniae*, or a composite manuscript. In passages derived from the First Variant, Gervase mentions the loss of Britain's name following the Saxon conquest; St Augustine also comes to preach Christianity in the First Variant's *Anglia*, instead of the Vulgate's *Britannia*.[55] As both authors are responding to the same two versions of the *Historia*, Gervase's work provides an alternative commentary on the views of Galfridian multilingualism presented in the *Brut*.

Wace and Gervase adopted different stances towards the conjectured factuality of Geoffrey's *Historia*. For Wace, Arthur's adventures were 'the stuff of fiction' ('fable', 9792): 'not all lies, not all truth, neither total folly, nor total wisdom' ('Ne tut mençunge, ne tut veir,/Ne tut folie ne tut saveir', 9793–9794). He repeatedly and ostentatiously drew attention to the gaps in his historical knowledge by refusing to pronounce judgement on apparently trivial details, encouraging his readership to question the completeness of his sources. Geoffrey's etymologies were not exempt from his scrutiny. He wrote that he did not know ('jo ne sai', 1528) the reason why Maiden Castle (*Chastels des Pulceles*) was not called Ladies' Castle (*de dames*) or Handmaidens' Castle (*d'anceles*), prompting an elaborate, and seemingly excessive avowal of ignorance (1529–1530):

> Ne me fu dit ne jo nel di
> Ne jo n'ai mie tut oï
> Ne jo n'ai mie tut veü
> Ne jo n'ai pas mie entendu,
> E mult estovreit home entendre
> Ki de tut vuldreit raison rendre.

> I was not told, nor did I invent it, nor have I heard all about it, nor have I seen it all, nor have I understood all about it, and a man who wants to give an account of everything must have a good understanding. (1531–1536)

Whilst Wace drew attention to the arbitrary, and perhaps even literary, aspects of the choice of names recorded in the *Historia regum Britanniae*, Gervase approached Geoffrey's etymologies as a repository of historical information, rendered problematic only by the changeful effects of time. He lamented contemporary scepticism concerning Geoffrey's records of the deeds of Arthur and the prophecies of Merlin, which he ascribed to the fact that no physical evidence survived:

> Fere omnia illa magna et miranda temporibus istis risui digna videntur, quia visibilia non sunt; credendum tamen est plurima ex illis bellico strepitu et hostili furore, quibus vix aliquando misera vacavit Anglia, disparuisse, et in nostrum, ut dicam, nichilum redacta fuisse.[56]

> Nearly all those great and marvellous things now seem worthy of laughter, since they are not visible; however it is necessary to believe many of them to have disappeared from the clash of war and the fury of enemies, from which

wretched England has scarcely ever been empty, and in our day, so I will say, to have been reduced to nothing.

Although names were not exempt from this devastation, their changes could provide historically important evidence: for Gervase, Geoffrey's etymologies were a crucial means of linking the past to the present day.

His treatment of Britain's toponyms complemented Wace's, but also extended it. We have seen that at key points in the transfer of power from the British to the Saxons, Wace inserted comments into the *Brut*'s narrative which anticipated the island's change of name from Britain to England. He was inspired by a comment in the First Variant, where, after the African king Gormund conquers a substantial part of the island and gives it to the Saxons, the narrator remarks that the English then called the country England, and the land lost the name of Britain. Gervase similarly drew on the passages of the First Variant which emphasised the loss of Britain's name, stating that when the Saxons invaded the island, the name of Britain itself was erased, and that it was called England from the English.[57] A strategy of modernising names was pursued to an even fuller extent than in Wace, and several further asides and insertions into Geoffrey's work were made in order to link present places to their British predecessors. He first collapses the distance between the British past and the Norman present by stating that Brutus landed in *Anglia*, then known as Albion, before noting that he had come ashore near *Cambria*, at Totnes.[58] The first attestation of *Cambria* in the sense of 'Wales' is by Geoffrey of Monmouth, who provides an etymology linking it to Brutus's son, Camber.[59] Gervase's employment of the term anticipates the later victories of Brutus and Camber portrayed in his own history, and the term's future use in the twelfth century. Further attempts were made to update past names of the island with present ones. In addition to Geoffrey's own discussions of contemporary names, he linked others such as Richborough, Chester, Mercia, and Sandwich to their British precursors: this makes Saxon dominion seem even more inevitable.[60] For both writers, toponymic control equates to political control of the island.

In other ways, Gervase's response to Geoffrey of Monmouth was very different to Wace, because he chose to minimise the linguistic discrepancies between his sources and the present day. Although fascinated by the changing names of Britain, he was reluctant to see such changes as the result of the process of linguistic corruption outlined in Geoffrey's *History*, and explored in Wace's *Brut* to its fullest possible extent. Eager to accept the idea that the names of cities revealed the presence of their founder, he sometimes manipulated his sources in order to create a closer correlation between the two. For Geoffrey and Wace, the gradual renaming of Brutus's Trinovant to Kaerlud to London took place through corruption, but Gervase ingeniously avoided this by inventing an extra ruler, Landanus, who bestows his name on London.[61] This links contemporary language more closely to the past, minimising the discrepancies between the initial toponym and its current form. Overall, then, we can see that Gervase was heavily influenced by the same Galfridian vision of language linked to colonisation which marked Wace's work, although he found the linguistic legacy of invasion to be less problematic.

Significantly, these Galfridian views of the multilingual past shaped Gervase's understanding of the present state of the country. He thought of himself as a francophone, calling French 'nostra lingua' ('our language').[62] As with Wace, the French language was the culmination of a chain of conquests stretching back to Brutus. When describing the Norman invasion in 1066, he stated that William I brought to England 'a new form of living and speaking' ('novam vivendi [...] formam et loquendi').[63] In his *Mappa mundi*, he related these invasions to Henry of Huntingdon's penitential vision of five successive plagues of Britain: the Romans, Picts and Scots, English, Danish and, finally, the Normans.[64] However, Gervase built on Henry to use these plagues in a unique explanation of Britain's ethnic and linguistic diversity:

> His itaque fatigationibus et plagis factum est, ut quatuor nationibus et linguis misceatur; habet enim linguam Britannicam, Anglicam, Normannicam, quae et Gallica est, et Latinam quae solis patet litteratis.

> So by these vexations and afflictions it has come about that four peoples and languages are mixed: there is the British language, the English, the Norman, which is also French, and Latin, which is only understood by the learned.[65]

His characterisation of French as the 'lingua normannica' is very rare, and may well be borrowed from its first recorded citation in William of Malmesbury's *Gesta regum Anglorum*, a work extensively consulted by Gervase. William's attestation occurs in the context of the Conquest's immediate aftermath.[66] An interpreter with knowledge of the *normannica lingua* translates from the Old English defence of Bishop Wulfstan of Worcester at a council of Norman churchmen. The linguistic divisions between Wulfstan and the rest of the council emphasise his precarious status as the last remaining Anglo-Saxon bishop. William's choice of terminology also stresses the language's links to the *Normannitas* of the conquerors, and their linguistic and political separation from the English. Apparently Wulfstan so convinced the Norman council of his piety, that he was asked by the archbishop of York to conduct visitations in his own dioceses 'in places to which he was afraid to go, either from fear of the enemy or from ignorance of the language' ('quo ipse pro timore hostium uel sermonis ignorantia cauebat accedere'.)[67] Resistance to Norman rule is linked to linguistic division.

If Gervase's potential citation of William subtly drew attention to the circumstances surrounding the advent of Anglo-Norman in Britain, in other ways, the resonance of the 'lingua normannica' was very different. As discussed above, from the 1160s onwards, writers began to differentiate insular French from the French of the continent. Gervase himself had an unusual interest in the observation and description of the world around him: besides his unique list of the religious houses of England in the *Mappa mundi*, he is most famous for his exceptionally detailed record of the architecture of Canterbury Cathedral before its destruction by a dramatic fire in 1174.[68] If his understanding of Anglo-Norman's beginnings in Britain was shaped by its status as a language of invasion, it also found a place in his broader antiquarian enterprise of accurately recording England's history. This antiquarianism valorised the present as much as the past: whilst Gervase recognised that Anglo-Norman began in Britain through conquest, its value was located in the continuity of its contemporary presence in the island. By drawing attention to insular multilingualism, Gervase celebrated its distinctiveness. This discussion forms part of a description of Britain's geographical features in the tradition of Bede, situating the list of sites of religious significance in a larger pattern of the natural abundance bestowed by God on Britain. Although, as with Wace's *Brut*, the linguistic history of the island has been shaped by conquest, Anglo-Norman is not presented as enacting a symbolic triumph by displacing other languages. Instead of being exceptional, it forms only a small part of the linguistic diversity which is one of the natural wonders of Britain.

The accretion of different languages through successive invasions of the realm tended to be celebrated, rather than elided. However, the phenomenon of multilingualism also presented Wace and Gervase with substantial ambiguities for interpretation. Both considered this situation of linguistic flux to indicate what Gervase called the constancy of human fragility, where mutability is the only certainty remaining. Under such circumstances, their attempts to use multilingualism to valorise their own respective enterprises of translation and the description of Britain's geographical and monastic heritage seem ultimately futile. Yet disconcertingly, or, perhaps, attractively, these depictions of multilingualism did not only serve to indicate the vicissitudes of human fortune. In the eleventh century, around the same time as Dudo of Saint-Quentin was emphasising the splendour of the Normans' linguistic and ethnic diversity, on the other side of Europe King Stephen of Hungary scornfully remarked that a kingdom with just one language and one way of life would be weak and fragile.[69] Far from revealing the transience of earthly glory, multilingualism was also a measure of the power of the Angevin polity.

Language Change, *Waldef*, and the Englishness of 'Romans'

Although multilingualism was understood as the product of invasion, successful conquest did not necessarily imply linguistic mastery, or effacement. A different perspective on Wace's depictions of language is offered by the prologue to the *Roman de Waldef*. This Anglo-Norman verse romance was probably produced for an East Anglian patron, in or around the first decade of the thirteenth century.[70] Although highly receptive to Wace's understanding of a Britain shaped by conquest, the author also situated his work amidst wider literary responses to the Anglo-Saxon past: as with other Anglo-Norman and Middle English works, *Waldef*'s French narrative was depicted as the successor to Old English, inheriting and preserving its literary traditions.

Waldef's portrayal of French was shaped by the author's pronounced emphasis on Englishness, an emphasis more unambiguously 'national' than the discussions of England found in twelfth-century insular material.[71] The decade following the turn of the century saw a significant contraction of the Angevin empire. King John lost the vast majority of his continental domains to Phillip II of France in the campaigns of 1202–1204: the ceded territories included Normandy, although he managed to retain Gascony and some parts of Poitou. These setbacks threw the importance of England into greater prominence, not only as a source of fiscal revenue for John's later, disastrous attempts to regain his lands abroad, but also geographically and ideologically.[72] This strengthened insular focus may have fed into the concerns articulated by English barons and clerics in the Magna Carta of 1215, a group expressing common grievances connected to the realm of England. Rosalind Field has noted the 'romance trajectory' of the document in its projected restoration of a 'good old law', harking back to the pre-Conquest relationship between king and barons influentially depicted in the *Leges Edwardi Confessoris*.[73] The concerns of *Waldef* are linked to a group of English romances which 'explore an imaginative response to the insular barony's peculiar situation'.[74] The author was receptive to the romance trope of the 'idea' of Anglo-Saxon England, and this qualified his reading of the British past in Wace's *Brut*.[75] Rather than stressing that the island was a space continually redefined through conquest, the work considered the island's contemporary identity as England to be the constant which underlay its previous incarnations. The English language was similarly the constant which underpinned insular French literature.

Waldef is a romance written for those already in love with the genre, fusing British and Anglo-Saxon material to create a mesh of knowing references to other romance tropes and to insular history. It survives in only one late-thirteenth- or early-fourteenth-century manuscript: Geneva, Fondation Martin Bodmer, MS 168.[76] Although this does not preserve the ending, the remaining portion is already some twenty-two thousand lines long. The work is densely packed with plot. After losing and regaining his rightful inheritance in the first three thousand lines, the eponymous hero spends much time defending his patrimony, but also embarks on a mission to rescue his queen and children from the Saracens. This initiates a series of adventures in Spain, Poitou, Denmark and Ireland. He finally dies offstage, but by this time the focus of the romance has shifted to his two sons, Guiac and Gudlac. There are also several sub-plots featuring Waldef's retainer Florenz, and his son, Lione.[77] All this leaves comparatively little space for the conventions of love: the author claims to be writing for a 'duce amie', whose name he does not initially wish to reveal, but the work primarily concerns itself with action.[78] The past is most strikingly referenced through the names of the characters. The genesis of the work seems to have had no direct relationship with Waltheof, the rebellious Earl of Northumbria beheaded by William I for treason in 1076 and still informally venerated as a saint in the thirteenth century.[79] However, the author's choice of a name for his hero is part of a broader evocation of an Anglo-Saxon ambience. Other important roles are played by Bede and Gudlac (cf. St Guthlac, hermit of Crowland, d.715). Rosalind Field has argued that *Waldef*'s use of names taken from the Galfridian tradition constructs a 'pattern of opposition between the Matter of Britain and the Matter of England': notable villains include Uther and Merlin.[80] This opposition is more complicated than it initially appears. The author's treatment of Galfridian names can certainly be seen as part of a broader strategy which significantly privileges the Anglo-Saxon past. Yet despite its ostensibly negative view of British history, *Waldef* silently refashions much of Wace's work to assimilate it to Old English tradition.

The romance encourages us to see the distant past in English, rather than British terms. Although some of the characters with overtly British connections in *Waldef* are portrayed unfavourably, other literary and geographical elements of the romance's British background are retained and reframed in the context of England. The author's treatment of Wace's *Brut* is ambiguous. The romance is set in pre-Conquest Britain, and the audience was directly encouraged to educate themselves about the historical context of *Waldef* by consulting Wace. In order to find out about the Roman conquest, we are told that one should 'read the Brut' ('lise le Brut', v.24). However, the author subtly refigured Wace's information. As in the *Brut*, Britain in earliest times is ruled by several different kings, but there are many more in *Waldef* than Wace. Every county now has its own ruler, subservient to a high king in London; this social aggrandisement is perhaps intended to evoke and to extend the powers inherent in thirteenth-century baronial control.[81] Wace's treatment of language was similarly reinterpreted. *Waldef* starts with an explanation that:

> Bretaigne esteit dunc apelee
> Qu'ore est Engleterre clamee.

> What is now called England, was then called Britain. (5–6)

Only then does the author anchor us to British history by giving the romance's first reference point, Julius Caesar's invasion. By presenting Wace's information in this order, the author altered its emphasis. Although the changing names of Britain may connote conquest, this conquest does not necessarily create the sense of displacement portrayed in the *Brut*'s symbolic redefinitions of language and politics through etymology. Instead, *Waldef* lays claim to a continuity between the past and the present of England, as embodied in the land. The author's equation of 'Bretaigne' with 'Engleterre' suggests that their territorial boundaries are synonymous.[82] One can be seen as a cipher for the other.

Given the expectations raised by *Waldef*'s initial stress on Wace, the direct references to the *Brut* are surprisingly scanty and imprecise.[83] It seems more likely that the author has drawn our attention to Wace to emphasise his subversion of the *Brut*'s vision of history. In radical contrast to Galfridian narrative, Caesar has displaced Brutus as the earliest invader of the island. His conquest has been effected through the treachery of Androgeus, nephew of the British king: this morally suspect quisling is the most prominent of the very few British characters in the narrative. Even less flattering is the author's decision to include only the passage of dominion from the Romans to the English, rejecting the majority of the *Brut*'s subject matter and robbing the contemporary Welsh of their epic British past. We are told that Caesar made the conquest 'because he greatly desired the land' ('car il desiroit mult la terre', 11): by obscuring his potential political motivations in favour of a consuming wish to possess, the island is transformed into a prize worthy of an emperor. The Romans hold their new acquisition just long enough to institute the Norfolk towns of Caister, Brancaster, and Narborough, but the loss of the country quickly follows. Like Wace, these settlements have an etymological connection to their founders (Castor, Brun, Neron), but *Waldef* does not seem overly attached to Wace's paradigm. The author stresses heavily that Castor's connection to 'Castorie', is 'still [...] remembered' ('Uncor l'avom nus en memorie', 206), heightening its authority by mentioning that he found it in his written source (248). It is also noted that Bruncastre was named after Brun (216–218). Yet just as Neron seems about to bestow his name on Nereburc, the author's attention shifts elsewhere. He moves on without mentioning the connection, comically deflating our assumption that each town will have an etymology stemming from its founder.[84] This apparent loss of interest in the linguistic imprint of Roman conquest is extended in *Waldef*'s offhand treatment of their departure:

> Changa le siecle, changa tens,
> Mururent les reis e les genz,
> Li Rumein perdirent la terre,
> Fust ço en peis, fust ço en gerre.

> The world changed, times changed, kings and peoples died. The Romans lost the land, whether in peace or war (257–260).

Although the removal of references to the British has made a Galfridian discussion of Saxon treachery unnecessary, neither does the author portray this change of regime as a triumphant English victory.

A muted approach to conquest is similarly apparent in the author's exploration of Arthurian leadership. The missing ending of the romance is recorded in a fifteenth-century Latin translation of *Waldef*, which amalgamates some of the narrative with a lost, later Middle English verse version ('in lingua Anglica metrice composita'): here, Waldef's son, Guiac, subdues and rules not only Rome, but also Greece.[85] The surviving portion of the Anglo-Norman *Waldef* only states that Guiac's fledgling imperial ambitions are checked by a palmer, who accurately foretells dire consequences for his presumption in claiming that he will forcibly enter the earthly paradise in the Holy Land at the same time (20711–20798). Guiac seems to be under the erroneous impression that Arthur conquered Rome, drawing attention both to his own ignorance, and to Arthur's failure (in the *Brut* he is obliged by Mordred's treacherous seizure of his queen and lands to turn back just as he is about to advance on the city).[86] He twice cites the king as a model for his own acquisitive vision (15015, 17663), linking Arthur to his own not entirely well-advised desire for empire. After the Romans leave, the barons of the realm collectively decide on a course of action significantly different from the long-suffering endurance of invasion depicted in the *Brut*:

> E li baron puis s'asemblerent,
> En lur conseil puis esguarderent
> Que ne sufferunt mes pur rien,
> Avenist lur u mal u bien,
> Que estrange gent d'altre terre
> Entreuls eüsent mais que fere,
> La terre entreuls departireient
> E entreuls issi la tendreient.

> The barons then assembled. In their deliberations, they then decided that, whether good or ill came of it, they would no longer, on any account, allow foreigners from other lands ever again to have anything to do with them. They would divide the land among themselves and they would thus hold it for themselves. (261–268)

Although the rest of the romance is devoted to the feuding that arises from these rival petty kingdoms, the nobility is nonetheless united by a common purpose, one which pits the English against European attempts to control them. Rather than being a record of successive submissions to foreign powers, the prologue promises to tell us of how the English kings held the land ('com il la terre dunc tenoient', 29). Value is located in the continuing possession of Caesar's prize: the author is not simply challenging the Galfridian tradition's valorisation of British history, but its resigned approach to the loss of land through conquest.

The author's presentation of the Norman invasion of 1066 stressed the endurance of English customs, moving away from Wace's emphasis on the colonial imposition of new manners and languages. His depiction of Englishness as a trans-historical continuum affected his treatment of the romance's sources. Although set in the Britain or England of the *Brut*, the author insisted that his story was an English one, much loved by the English nobility until the time of the Norman conquest ('mult iert amee des Engleis / [....] desqu'a la prise des Normanz', 36, 38). When the Normans arrive, they take the land, but at the same time, take up its heritage in a process that involves both displacement and assimilation:

> Quant li Norman la terre pristrent
> Les granz estoires puis remistrent
> Qui des Engleis estoient fetes,

Qui des aucuns ierent treites,
Pur la gent qui dunc diverserunt
E les languages si changerunt.
Puis i ad asez translatees,
Qui mult sunt de plusurs amees,
Com est le Bruit, com est Tristram,
Qui tant suffri poine e hahan,
Com est Aelof, li bons rois,
Qui tant en fist des granz desrois[. . .]
Ces gestes, qu'erent en engleis,
Translatees sunt en franceis.

When the Normans seized the land, the great *estoires* that the English had
made were displaced in favour of others because of the different population and linguistic change. Since then much has been translated and greatly
loved by many, such as the *Brut*, such as Tristan who suffered such pain
and anguish, such as Aelof, the good king, who performed such impetu-
ous deeds. [. . .] These *gestes* which were in English are now translated into
French.[87]

The *Roman de Waldef* itself was portrayed as part of this tradition. The
author noted that he examined the English *estoire*, and translated it into
French ('L'estoire englesche regardai, / En franceis la translatai', 85–86). A
written source has not yet come to light, and it seems equally likely that
the author was referring to the continuing circulation of pre-Conquest oral
material. He included 'Aelof' in the catalogue of translations: this narrative
is probably related to the twelfth-century romance ('vers del parchemin')
mentioned by Thomas as the precursor to his Anglo-Norman *Romance of
Horn*.[88] This might support the author's claim to be drawing on English
legend. Although it has not survived, Judith Weiss has shown *Horn* to be
descended from a lost pre-Conquest English source which also influenced
the *Gesta Herwardi*, a Latin translation of an English work on Hereward
the Wake.[89] On the other hand, the Anglo-Saxonism of *Waldef*'s other
proposed sources is less readily apparent. The British setting of the extant
twelfth-century narratives in the *Tristan* tradition has led several modern
scholars to suggest a Brittonic provenance; Wace's *Brut* also focusses on
Britain.[90] These British backdrops could have raised doubts amongst some
members of the author's medieval audience about *Waldef*'s assertions concerning the English genesis of *Tristan* and the *Brut*.

It is uncertain how far the audience of *Waldef* would have perceived
British and English literary traditions as being in conflict with each other.
The twelfth-century French author Jehan Bodel's threefold classification
of 'conte' into the *matieres de France, Bretaigne* and *Rome* suggests that

audiences were capable of distinguishing groups of romances by their content.[91] However, there is no evidence for medieval perceptions of a distinct category of 'matter of England' romances.[92] It is hence unlikely that the prologue of *Waldef* sought to emphasise the dominion of English over a separate division of British material. The author may instead have intended to re-adjust the historical perspective of his contemporary audience. When looking back to the insular past from the early thirteenth century, readers were encouraged to see *Tristan* and the *Brut* as proto-English. We might draw parallels between this redefinition of British material and King John's policies in Wales, notably successful in the first decade of the thirteenth century. Through clever exploitation of the role of feudal overlord, John was able to his strengthen his hold on the land by specifying increased obligations for his Welsh vassals.[93] This closer relationship to the king conceptually aligned them with the broader English aristocracy. Ifor Rowlands writes that: 'the Crown increasingly perceived the native Welsh princes as barons of a sensibly English kind; their status was being assimilated to that of English tenants-in-chief'.[94] Anglicisation was also an important strategy in *Waldef*, which similarly sought to re-construe its relationship with Britain. Although not rejecting Brittonic literary traditions, the author preferred to perceive English cultural hegemony as extending back into a past which was less ancient British than pre-Saxon. He encouraged his readers to see the *Brut* and *Tristan* as examples of the Old English literary tradition.

Significantly, this assimilative discourse can be extended into the future, as well as into the past: *Waldef* portrays contemporary Anglo-Norman literary works as Old English, in a move that is both a serious claim to the insular roots of romance literature, and a knowing exploitation of the conventions of translation. *Waldef* participates in an established genre of translators' prologues which grew out of the Latin *accessus ad auctores*, an introductory passage of commentary used to examine and to emphasise the authority of the text under discussion.[95] This authority was often connected to ancientness: Walter Map wrote of his contemporaries' preference for 'old copper' ('uetustum cuprum') instead of 'new gold' ('auro nouello'), noting that 'every age, from the first onwards, has preferred the previous one to itself' ('queuis etas a prima preteritam sibi pretulit').[96] Although French translators radically departed from the structures of Latin prologues, they were similarly concerned with the establishment of authority, and sometimes age.[97] This frequently led to extravagant truth-claims. Some writers chose to portray their texts as translations in order to increase the authority of their own work. Chrétien de Troyes notably participated in this tradition, claiming that *Cligés* was an *estoire* taken from an ancient

book (presumably written in Latin) which he found in the library of St
Peter's Church in Beauvais. The 'intertextual dimension' of Chrétien's work
renders it unlikely that he had any single source.[98] In his comment on the
library, he emphasised the impressive antiquity of the book of Beauvais:

> Li livres est molt ancïens
> Qui tesmoingne l'estoire a voire;
> Por ce fet ele mialz a croire.[99]

> The book which witnesses that the story is true is extremely old; therefore
> it is more greatly to be believed.

Finally, he invoked the topos of *translatio studii*, stating that ancient learning passed from Greece to Rome, and reappeared in France.[100] His putative
Latin source becomes a symbol of the classical inheritance of French literature. Yet this imagined act of translation may suggest a desire not simply
to replicate, but to master the culture embodied by the book of Beauvais.
From its Graeco-Roman inception, the topos of *translatio studii* was often
paired with *translatio imperii*, the transfer of rule, and framed in terms of a
reciprocal cultural conquest:[101] Horace wrote that 'captive Greece captured
the savage victor and brought the arts into rustic Latium' ('Graecia capta
ferum victorem cepit et artis intulit agresti Latio').[102]

Waldef's prologue evoked a similar transfer of cultural and political
sovereignty, drawing on earlier French, and, perhaps, English depictions
of contemporary works based on authoritative Anglo-Saxon sources. The
author's claim is unique amongst Anglo-Norman romances, although others implied that their works were translations from Latin; more diffusely,
Breton lays often depicted themselves as informed by a linguistic and artis-
tic kinship with Breton sources, even if the relationship was not directly
portrayed as translation.[103] Beyond the genre of romance, twelfth-century
authors frequently exploited the prestigious history of Old English literature, particularly when associated with Alfred the Great.[104] Sometimes this
merely led the author to weight the presentation of his or her sources in
favour of Old English elements. Gaimar's *Estoire des Engleis* emphasised its
reliance on the 'ancient' ('ancïan') and 'true' ('vreie') *Anglo-Saxon Chronicle*, whilst passing over the (potentially oral) sources for its interpolated
romance episodes in silence.[105] Gaimar included two extended passages
which extolled Alfred's virtues as the *Chronicle*'s instigator, implicitly figuring the *Estoire* as the heir to this tradition of Old English historiography.[106]
Other discussions of sources seem to have been more deliberate attempts to
accrue prestige. The epilogue to Marie de France's *Fables* depicted her work

as a translation from King Alfred's Old English, which she portrayed as a rendering of Aesop's Latin translation of the original Greek.[107] There was a twelfth-century Latin text of the *Fables* by Alfred the Englishman which may perhaps have provided her with a source. However, Marie's claim to be translating from Old English was almost certainly spurious.[108] She stressed that Alfred's translation was written 'en Engleis': language formed a major element in the authentication of the text.[109] By framing his work as a translation, the author of *Waldef* self-consciously evoked a larger discourse which appealed to the cultural authority of Old English. For him, the Norman Conquest provided a catalyst for the genesis, rather than the effacement of this cultural authority: the events of 1066 allowed the English literary tradition to become the prestigious insular inheritance of francophone authors.

Waldef simultaneously develops and resists the implications of Wace's depiction of language as an indication of conquest. As with Wace, the author drew attention to two major, interlinked consequences of 1066: immigration and linguistic change. Although these were identified as causing the initial displacement of English literature, the author did not follow the *Brut* by presenting the succession of languages of Britain as an index of cultural change. *Waldef* sees the advent of the Normans, not as an opportunity for the imposition of new customs on the island, but for the adoption of old ones. The Normans become English, rather than forcing the English to become Norman. The *Brut*'s discussions of translation focus on the successive place names of Britain, sites where appropriations of culture and territory converge. In contrast, for *Waldef*, translation provides an opportunity for cultural assimilation, rather than annexation. The prologue asks us to believe that this work of French literature is a transparent medium for a work of English history. English becomes a prefiguration of French. In turn, we are asked to read the French of *Waldef* as if we were reading it in English. Melissa Furrow has written of the 'relationship of expectation to language', caused by writing a romance (*romans*) in French (*romans*): '*romans* became and stayed "the kind of story that is told in French", even after that kind of story was also told in English'.[110] *Waldef* subverts such expectations by portraying a romance that is, if not written in English, then written *as* English. French is situated amidst English literature in the profoundest possible sense.

Wace, Gervase of Canterbury, and *Waldef* all accept that the Normans and their language played a significant role in shaping the contemporary polity, but the extent to which French can be seen as fully incorporated into the insular landscape remains ambiguous. Several critics have noted that although Wace's etymologies are designed to illustrate the ebb and flow of the different peoples of Britain, in another sense they become a figure of the permanence of the land, a permanence located beyond language.[111] If heightening our sense of the way that words can be grounded in places, such etymologies also emphasise the fundamental disjuncture between the two: the shifting patterns of naming serve only to indicate the stability of their topographic referents. Language can never be fully connected to the land, but etymology seems to promise the recovery of such a connection, even if this connection forever hovers on the edge of attainment. For David Wallace, locales are 'both geographic sites and ideas, dreams, and feelings about places'.[112] We might see language as a similar locus in which to search for a sense of belonging. *Waldef* in particular evokes an idea of Old English literature as a kind of country intended more to be imagined than explored. Language and landscape are co-extensive, but never contiguous: their dislocations can only be overcome fleetingly, via connections made in the mind.

Conclusion

The phenomenon of language change gave twelfth-century authors an important opportunity to situate their works in historically specific contexts, offering an alternative to approaches to the past that traced an overarching moral exemplarity through the vagaries of historical circumstance. Linguistic detail provided a means of grounding narrative in a particular time and place, recognising that in some ways, the past was unique and irrecoverable.

An interest in the development of Britain's languages is not, of course, ubiquitous in the twelfth-century literary corpus. However, a significant minority of authors engaged sensitively with the history of the vernaculars, and drew perceptive conclusions. Later scholarship has confirmed the accuracy of some of their conjectures, such as Gerald of Wales's discussions of the Norse elements in northern English, and William of Malmesbury's prescient remarks on the shared linguistic heritage of the English and the Franks. Other engagements were concerned more with rhetoric than research, notably Geoffrey of Monmouth's constructions of the Trojan origins of the British language. For all these authors, etymology, archaisms, and treatments of language development were deployed with precision in order to substantiate their portrayals of insular and institutional history. Therefore, even whilst they acknowledge the particularity of the historical moment, discussions of language history can themselves be considered a literary topos.

New questions emerge when such discussions are positioned against the wider sweep of insular and continental literature from the eleventh to the thirteenth century. The importance of the Anglo-Saxon inheritance to twelfth-century considerations of language history is clear. Most evidently, the continued circulation of pre-Conquest English literature meant that a corpus of archaic and prestigious vernacular texts was easily accessible to scholars. This provided an obvious source of inspiration for twelfth-century attempts to draw on the authority of the linguistic past. More subtly, the sophistication of Ælfric's and Byrhtferth of Ramsey's treatments of Old English grammar laid the foundations for later assessments of the development of the vernaculars. Yet if twelfth-century investigations of language history primarily responded to the past, they were in other ways profoundly forward-looking. Notably, they formed the intellectual inheritance of important thirteenth-century engagements with Old English, such as the glosses to Old English manuscripts by the Worcester scribe known as the 'Tremulous Hand';[1] the interest in archaic language found in Laȝamon's translation of Wace's *Brut*;[2] and the author's claim in the AB language *Life of St Margaret* that 'ure ledene' ('our language') is 'ald Englis' ('old English').[3] This material anticipates future linguistic scholarship even as it looks back to previous centuries.

Discussions of the linguistic past also connected the contemporary and the historical in other ways. Medieval attitudes to the lexical innovation arising from multilingualism remain an area for further enquiry. We might question how far the depictions studied here were affected by the increased amount of linguistic borrowing following the Conquest, and by the high number of neologisms apparently created during the period. How did twelfth-century authors position their depictions of archaic language in relation to these new borrowings and coinages? For Horace, the old and the new could, given the right circumstances, be one and the same. As we have seen, the *Ars Poetica* pointed out that even as some words vanish from the language, 'many terms that have fallen out of use shall be born again' ('multa renascentur quae iam cecidere [...] vocabula').[4] The interlocking temporalities of archaism and neologism identified by Horace are also discernible in some of the medieval works considered in this study. Richard fitz Nigel's *Dialogus de scaccario* offered a complicated portrayal of the words created at the exchequer, presenting its coinages as simultaneously modern and ancestral. Wace's etymological discussions were also couched in highly innovative lexis which variously used terms taken from Latin, English, a Celtic language, and the Norse-derived nautical vocabulary of the Normans.[5] New words were employed in order to investigate ancient ones, sometimes themselves becoming the object of linguistic scrutiny.

Borrowings also emphasise the overlapping lexical and geographical parameters of Britain's different languages. Several of the etymological discussions surveyed here concern vocabulary which was initially borrowed from another language. How far were these words differentiated by their linguistic origins? Or were they viewed as part of a 'common stock of lexis' shared between French, English, Latin, and other insular languages, to be deployed when context required?[6] On a broader scale, similar questions can be asked concerning the advent of Britain's languages themselves, and how far they were seen to be separate from or connected to the continent. This study has primarily focussed on treatments of language history in the context of insular culture, but most of these depictions located the roots of Britain's languages abroad. If largely concerned with the island, such portrayals also exemplify the Normans' cosmopolitan understanding of their place in Europe.

The authors discussed here often focus on the history of one particular language, but their work also responds to the exceptionally rich multilingual environment of twelfth-century Britain. Contact with the place names, lexis, and traditions of vernacular composition in a variety of different languages provoked new considerations of the history of Britain's vernaculars, both by applying existing grammatical methodology to new languages, and by situating insular literary heritage in new, multilingual contexts. All the discussions examined here demonstrate that twelfth-century portrayals of vernacular language history were interlinked.[7] They cannot be divided into discrete categories relating to English, British, French, and registers of Latin which emphasised vernacular loanwords and syntax. Rather, depictions of vernacular language history drew on shared perceptions, acknowledging the high status of the ancient and the importance of inherited traditions. Although the tools for charting the development of the vernaculars were primarily borrowed from Latin grammar, this was not the only mutual framework which the languages occupied. Portrayals of linguistic development did not exclusively contribute to the study of any one tongue, but instead deepened a common consciousness of vernacularity and its complex prestige. The authority of insular vernaculars could be grounded in the durability of writing or the transience of the oral: authors drew on both the sophistication of Anglo-Saxon documentary culture and the geo-historical specificity of place names and terminology preserved in local or institutional memory. At other moments, the authoritative was less important than the imaginative. The vernacular's geographic and temporal rootedness provided a conceptual space for literary excursus, allowing writers to offer new perspectives on the emotional weight of the past. Multilingualism did not merely form a backdrop to perceptions of language history in the twelfth century. In their reliance on a shared multilingual collection of literary paradigms, discussions of insular language demonstrated the profound permeability of Britain's vernaculars.

Notes

INTRODUCTION

1 Walter Map, *De nugis curialium: Courtiers' Trifles*, ed. and trans. by M. R. James, rev. by C. N. L. Brooke and R. A. B. Mynors (Oxford: Clarendon, 1983, repr. 2002), pp.28–31 (dating discussed pp.xxiv–xxxii).

2 For other medieval 'wild hunt' stories, see C. S. Watkins, *History and the Supernatural in Medieval England* (Cambridge: Cambridge University Press, 2007), pp.215–217.

3 Ruth Morse, *Truth and Convention in the Middle Ages: Rhetoric, Representation, and Reality* (Cambridge: Cambridge University Press, 1991), p.106.

4 A. J. Minnis, *Medieval Theory of Authorship: Scholastic Literary Attitudes in the Later Middle Ages* (London: Scolar Press, 1984), pp.10–11 (10).

5 R. M. Thomson, *William of Malmesbury*, rev. edn (Woodbridge: Boydell Press, 2003), pp.22–23.

6 Édouard Jeauneau, '"Nani gigantum humeris insidentes": Essai d'interprétation de Bernard de Chartres', *Vivarium*, 5 (1967), 79–99.

7 Peter Damian-Grint, *The New Historians of the Twelfth-Century Renaissance: Inventing Vernacular Authority* (Woodbridge: Boydell, 1999), pp.68–72.

8 William of Newburgh, *Historia rerum anglicarum*, in *Chronicles of the Reigns of Stephen, Henry II, and Richard I*, ed. by Richard Howlett, *RS* 82.1–2 (London: H.M. Stationery Office: 1884), I:308.

9 *The Ecclesiastical History of Orderic Vitalis*, ed. by Marjorie Chibnall, 6 vols (Oxford: Clarendon, 1969–1980), VI.436–437. For further examples, see Watkins, *History and the Supernatural*, p.15.

10 Monika Otter, *Inventiones: Fiction and Referentiality in Twelfth-Century Historical Writing* (Chapel Hill: University of North Carolina Press, 1996), p.5.

11 Simon Keynes, 'The Æthelings in Normandy', *ANS*, 13 (1990), 173–205.

12 C. P. Lewis, 'The French in England before the Norman Conquest', *ANS*, 17 (1994), 123–144 (pp.140–144, 135–136).

13 Ian Short argues that this is the only Old French borrowing in pre-Conquest English ('Another Look at "Le Faus Franceis"', *Nottingham Medieval Studies*, 54 (2010), 35–55 (p.43)); for an alternative perspective, see Helmut Gneuss, '*Anglicae linguae interpretatio*: Language Contact, Lexical Borrowing and

Glossing in Anglo-Saxon England', *Proceedings of the British Academy*, 82 (1992), 107–148 (p.135 n106).

14 On the international scope of eleventh-century literature, see Thomas O'Donnell, Matthew Townend, and Elizabeth M. Tyler, 'European Literature and Eleventh-Century England', in *The Cambridge History of Early Medieval English Literature*, ed. by Clare A. Lees (Cambridge: Cambridge University Press, 2013), pp.607–636.

15 Nicholas Brooks, *Anglo-Saxon Myths: State and Church, 400–1066* (London: Hambledon Press, 2000), p.30.

16 On Norse literature at Cnut's English court, see Roberta Frank, 'King Cnut in the Verse of His Skalds', in *The Reign of Cnut: King of England, Denmark, and Norway*, ed. by Alexander R. Rumble (London: Leicester University Press, 1994), pp.106–124 (108–109).

17 David N. Parsons, 'How Long did the Scandinavian Language Survive in England? Again', in *Vikings and the Danelaw: Select Papers from the Proceedings of the Thirteenth Viking Congress, Nottingham and York, 21–30 August 1997*, ed. by James Graham-Campbell et al. (Oxford: Oxbow Books, 2001), pp.299–312 (302).

18 For a review of previous discussions, see Matthew Townend, *Language and History in Viking Age England: Linguistic Relations between Speakers of Old Norse and Old English* (Turnhout: Brepols, 2002), pp.9–11; Townend's own conclusions are presented on pp.181–211.

19 *The First Grammatical Treatise: The Earliest Germanic Phonology*, ed. by Einar Haugen, 2nd edn (London: Longman, 1972), pp.12–13.

20 On perceptions of these similarities, see Sara Harris, '*Tam Anglis quam Danis*: "Old Norse" terminology in the *Constitutiones de foresta*', *ANS*, 37 (2014), 131–148.

21 For this hypothesis, see Richard Dance, *Words Derived from Old Norse in Early Middle English: Studies in the Vocabulary of the South-West Midland Texts* (Tempe, AZ: ACMRS, 2003), pp.312–313.

22 R. W. Burchfield, "The Language and Orthography of the Ormulum MS", *Transactions of the Philological Society*, 55 (1956), 56–87; Dance, *Words Derived from Old Norse in Early Middle English*.

23 The two exceptions were Alan of Brittany and Eustace of Boulogne: for a full list, see David C. Douglas, *William the Conqueror: The Norman Impact upon England* (London: Eyre and Spottiswoode, 1964), p.269.

24 Ian Short, *Manual of Anglo-Norman*, 2nd edn (London: Anglo-Norman Text Society, 2013), pp.17–21; for an introduction to the *langue d'oïl* and the *langue d'oc* (medieval terms for northern and southern dialectal divisions based on differing words for 'yes'), see R. Anthony Lodge, *French: From Dialect to Standard* (London: Routledge, 1993), pp.71–78.

25 These features include nonpalatalisation of /l/ and /n/ (allowing for rhymes such as *feignent: peignent; merveilles: esteiles*), a general reduction of diphthongs, use of the letters <k> and <w>, and loanwords from English: see further Short, *Manual of Anglo-Norman*, pp.45–46; on Anglo-Norman

and continental French, see David Trotter, '*Deinz certeins boundes*: Where Does Anglo-Norman Begin and End?', *Romance Philology*, 67 (2013), 139–177 (pp.158–168). A note on the vexed question of terminology: I will primarily refer to the Normans' use of the *langue d'oïl* as 'French', reserving 'Anglo-Norman' for discussion of their dialect in an insular context (for a full assessment, see Jocelyn Wogan-Browne, 'General Introduction: What's in a Name: The "French" of "England"', in *Language and Culture in Medieval Britain: The French of England c.1100–c.1500*, ed. by Jocelyn Wogan-Browne et al. (York: York Medieval Press, 2009), pp.1–16).

26 Ian Short, '*Anglice loqui nesciunt*: Monoglots in Anglo-Norman England', *Cultura Neolatina*, 69 (2009), 245–262.

27 Richard Ingham, 'The Persistence of Anglo-Norman 1230–1362: A Linguistic Perspective', in *Language and Culture in Medieval Britain*, ed. Wogan-Browne, pp.44–54; for more detail, see Chapters 6–10 of his *The Transmission of Anglo-Norman: Language History and Language Acquisition* (Amsterdam: Benjamins, 2012).

28 On Gerald of Wales's contact with Flemish settlers in South Wales, see Ad Putter, 'Multilingualism in England and Wales, *c.*1200: The Testimony of Gerald of Wales', in *Medieval Multilingualism: The Francophone World and Its Neighbours*, ed. by Christopher Kleinhenz and Keith Busby (Turnhout: Brepols, 2010), pp.83–105 (102–105). Judith Weiss suggests that the decision to frame the *Lai of Haveloc* as a Breton lay may have been influenced by the colony of Bretons living in South-West Lincolnshire in the late twelfth century (*The Lai of Haveloc*, in Judith Weiss (trans.), *The Birth of Romance in England: Four Twelfth-Century Romances in the French of England* (Tempe, AZ: ACMRS, 2009), pp.155–169 (158–159 n14)).

29 Helmut Gneuss, 'The Origin of Standard Old English and Æthelwold's School at Winchester', *ASE*, 1 (1972), 63–83 (pp.63, 70).

30 This change was perhaps in response to the displacement of Regenbald the priest, the last English *cancellarius*, or due to the fact that the majority of the powerful recipients of the king's correspondence no longer had English as their first language. For discussion, see David Bates (ed.), *Regesta regum Anglo-Normannorum: The Acta of William I (1066–1087)* (Oxford: Clarendon, 1998), pp.48–50. However, note that fifty-five post-Conquest royal charters and ninety-three further documents survive in English from the period of William I to Henry II: David A. E. Pelteret, *Catalogue of English Post-Conquest Vernacular Documents* (Woodbridge: Boydell, 1990).

31 Mechthild Gretsch, 'Winchester Vocabulary and Standard Old English: The Vernacular in Late Anglo-Saxon England', *Bulletin of the John Rylands Library*, 83 (2001), 41–87 (pp.75–83).

32 For an overview of the developments in post-Conquest English, see the essays collected in *The Cambridge History of the English Language: Volume II, 1066–1476*, ed. by Norman Blake (Cambridge: Cambridge University Press, 1992). For some studies of twelfth-century scribal practice, see Andreas Fischer, 'The Hatton MS of the West Saxon Gospels: The Preservation and Transmission of

Old English', in *The Preservation and Transmission of Anglo-Saxon Culture*, ed. by Paul E. Szarmach and Joel T. Rosenthal (Kalamazoo, MI: Medieval Institute Publications, 1997), pp.353–367; Roy Michael Liuzza, 'Scribal Habit: The Evidence of the Old English Gospels', in *Rewriting Old English in the Twelfth Century*, ed. by Mary Swan and Elaine M. Treharne (Cambridge: Cambridge University Press, 2000), pp.143–165; *Old English Homilies from MS Bodley 343*, ed. by Susan Irvine (Oxford: Early English Text Society, 1993), pp.lv–lxxvii.

33 Ian Short, 'Patrons and Polyglots: French Literature in Twelfth-Century England', *ANS*, 14 (1991), 229–249 (pp.230–232). The legacy of this important article is assessed in Elizabeth M. Tyler, 'From Old English to Old French', in *Language and Culture in Medieval Britain*, ed. Wogan-Browne, pp.164–178.

34 In contrast, classic diglossia concerns different varieties of the same language. (Charles A. Ferguson, 'Diglossia', *Word*, 15 (1959), 325–340; Joshua A. Fishman, 'Bilingualism with and without Diglossia; Diglossia with and without Bilingualism', *Journal of Social Issues*, 23:2 (1967), 29–38.)

35 On problems with diglossia as a model, see e.g. J. N. Adams, *Bilingualism and the Latin Language* (Cambridge: Cambridge University Press, 2003), esp. pp. 537–541, 754–755; Alex Mullen, 'Introduction: Multiple Languages, Multiple Identities', in *Multilingualism in the Graeco-Roman Worlds*, ed. by Alex Mullen and Patrick James (Cambridge: Cambridge University Press, 2012), pp.1–35 (24–25).

36 Jane Gilbert and Sara Harris, 'The Written Word: Literacy across Languages', in *The Cambridge Companion to Medieval British Manuscripts*, ed. by Orietta da Rold and Elaine Treharne (Cambridge: Cambridge University Press, forthcoming).

37 John Gillingham, *The English in the Twelfth Century: Imperialism, National Identity and Political Values* (Woodbridge: Boydell, 2000), pp.96–97.

38 Notably, the Irish had a long tradition of interest in the history of their language: see the *Auraicept na n-Éces: The Scholars' Primer*, ed. by George Calder (Edinburgh: Grant, 1917), a treatise on the development of Gaelic composed in sections from the seventh century onwards. Amidst much detailed etymological speculation, glossaries also discussed the history of Brittonic loanwords in Irish (Paul Russell, 'Brittonic Words in Irish Glossaries', in *Hispano-Gallo-Brittonica: Essays in Honour of Professor D. Ellis Evans* (Cardiff: University of Wales Press, 1995), pp.166–182).

39 On francophone linguistic continuity across England and France, see David A. Trotter, '(Socio)linguistic Realities of Cross-Channel Communication in the Thirteenth Century', *Thirteenth-Century England*, 13 (2009), 117–131.

40 E.g. Henry of Huntingdon, *Historia Anglorum*, ed. and trans. by Diana Greenway (Oxford: Clarendon, 1996), pp.24–25.

41 E.g. Marie de France, 'Laüstic', in *Lais bretons (XIIe–XIIIe siècles): Marie de France et ses contemporains*, ed. and trans. by Nathalie Koble and Mireille Séguy (Paris: Champion, 2011), pp.456–469 (vv.3–4).

42 The Latin accounts of the migrations (beginning with Gildas) are collected in Kenneth Jackson, *Language and History in Early Britain: A Chronological*

Survey of the Brittonic Languages, First to Twelfth Century A.D. (Edinburgh: Edinburgh University Press, 1953), pp.12–15.

43 Before 1169, the Normans were already seeking out books from Ireland: Geoffrey of Burton obtained a Hiberno-Latin Life of St Modwenna sometime between 1118 and 1150, described in the twelfth-century Burton library catalogue as a *vita antiquissima* (Geoffrey of Burton, *Life and Miracles of St Modwenna*, ed. and trans. by Robert Bartlett (Oxford: Clarendon, 2002), pp.xi, xiv).

44 These alternative percentages are cited and discussed in Olga Timofeeva, 'Anglo-Latin Bilingualism Before 1066: Prospects and Limitations', in *Interfaces between Language and Culture in Medieval England: A Festschrift for Matti Kilpiö*, ed. by Alaric Hall et al. (Leiden: Brill, 2010), pp.1–36 (12–15 (14–15)).

45 M. T. Clanchy, *From Memory to Written Record: England, 1066–1307*, 3rd edn (London: Wiley-Blackwell, 2013), pp.228–232.

46 The following discussion is indebted to Arno Borst, *Der Turmbau von Babel: Geschichte der Meinungen über Ursprung und Vielfalt der Sprachen und Völker*, 6 vols (Stuttgart: Hiersemann, 1957–1963), III.617–730; John M. Fyler, *Language and the Declining World in Chaucer, Dante, and Jean de Meun* (Cambridge: Cambridge University Press, 2007), pp.1–59; and Eric Jager, *The Tempter's Voice: Language and the Fall in Medieval Literature* (Ithaca, NY: Cornell University Press, 1993), pp.51–98.

47 *Glossa ordinaria in Genesim* 10–11, *PL* 113, col.113ff.; on Gibert's authorship, see Beryl Smalley, 'Gilbertus Universalis, Bishop of London (1128–34) and the Problem of the *Glossa ordinaria*', *Recherches de théologie ancienne et médiévale*, 7 (1935), 235–262 (pp.258–259, 262).

48 Fyler, *Language and the Declining World*, p.49, citing respectively Augustine, *Sermo* 271, and Bede, *Expositio actuum apostolorum et retractatio* 2.4; see also Mary Carruthers, *The Experience of Beauty in the Middle Ages* (Oxford: Oxford University Press, 2013), pp.155–158.

49 Augustine, *De Genesi contra Manichaeos*, ed. by Dorothea Weber (Vienna: Verlag der österreichischen Akademie der Wissenschaften, 1998), pp.123–124. For a fuller explanation of the nature of this 'inner word', see Augustine, *De Trinitate*, CCSL 50–50A, ed. by W. J. Mountain with Fr. Glorie (Turnhout: Brepols, 1968), XV.11.

50 Augustine, *De Genesi ad litteram*, PL 34, cols 245–486 (387).

51 Genesis 1:26. All quotations from the Bible in the text are taken from the Vulgate; all translations from the Douay-Rheims Bible. Augustine, *Confessionum libri XIII*, ed. by Martin Skutella and Lucas Verheijen, CCSL 27 (Turnhout: Brepols, 1981), VII.10.16.

52 Augustine, *De Genesi ad litteram*, cols 400–401.

53 Augustine, *De civitate Dei*, ed. by Bernard Dombart and Alphonse Kalb, CCSL 47–48 (Turnhout: Brepols, 1955), XVI.11.

54 Jager, *Tempter's Voice*, p.54.

55 Genesis 11:6–9.

56 Petrus Abaelardus, *Expositio in Hexameron*, ed. by Mary Romig and David Luscombe, *CCCM* 15 (Turnhout: Brepols, 2004), pp.xi–III (97–101).

57 John of Salisbury, *Policraticus*, ed. by C. C. J. Webb (Oxford: Clarendon, 1909), I.27–28.

58 Augustine, *De civitate Dei*, XVI.6.

59 Borst, *Turmbau*, III.636.

60 Isidore, IX.i.3–4. All future references given in the text are taken from this edition and translation (for bibliographical details, see the list of abbreviations).

61 Irven M. Resnick, 'Lingua Dei, Lingua Hominis: Sacred Language and Medieval Texts', *Viator*, 21 (1990), 51–74.

62 Jerome, Epistola 106.2, *PL* 22, col.838. For an introduction to Hebrew study in high medieval England, see Judith Olszowy-Schlanger, *Les manuscrits hébreux dans l'Angleterre médiévale* (Paris: Peeters, 2003). On Greek, see Walter Berschin, *Greek Letters and the Latin Middle Ages: From Jerome to Nicholas of Cusa*, rev. edn, trans. by Jerold C. Frakes (Washington, DC: Catholic University of America Press, 1988). Maria Mavroudi notes that Sicily, northern Italy and the Crusader lands all provided important opportunities for contact with Greek material; some Anglo-Normans visited and worked in these areas in the twelfth century ('Translations from Greek into Latin and Arabic during the Middle Ages: Searching for the Classical Tradition', *Speculum*, 90 (2015), 28–59 (52–53)).

63 Berschin, *Greek Letters*, pp.30–33.

64 Jerome, *In Sophoniam*, ed. by Marcus Adriaen, *CCSL* 76A (Turnhout: Brepols, 1969), pp.655–711 (III.14/18.541–542).

65 Gilbert Dahan (ed.), 'Une introduction à la philosophie au XIIe siècle. Le *Tractatus quidam de philosophia et partibus eius*', *Archives d'histoire doctrinale et littéraire du Moyen Âge*, 49 (1982), 155–193 (189).

66 Fyler, *Language and the Declining World*, p.39.

67 For other examples, see Gilbert Dahan, *Les intellectuels chrétiens et les juifs au Moyen Âge* (Paris: Éditions du Cerf, 1990), p.240.

68 Frank Barlow, 'Goscelin (b. c. 1035, d. in or after 1107)', www.oxforddnb.com/view/article/11105. 'The *Liber confortatorius* of Goscelin of Saint Bertin', ed. by C. H. Talbot, *Studia Anselmiana*, 37 (1955), 1–117 (41).

69 '*Liber confortatorius* of Goscelin', p.41.

70 Ibid., p.115; 'Goscelin's *Liber confortatorius*', trans. by W. R. Barnes and Rebecca Hayward, in *Writing the Wilton Women*, ed. by Stephanie Hollis et al. (Turnhout: Brepols, 2004), pp.95–212 (205).

71 Dante, *De vulgari eloquentia*, ed. and trans. by Steven Botterill (Cambridge: Cambridge University Press, 1996), p.20.

72 On the uses of archaism amongst Latin writers of the second century, see Leofranc Holford-Strevens, *Aulus Gellius: An Antonine Scholar and His Achievement*, rev. edn (Oxford: Oxford University Press, 2003), pp.4–8, 49–64, 354–363.

73 Varro, *On the Latin Language*, trans. by Roland G. Kent, 2 vols (Cambridge, MA: Harvard University Press, 1967), I.vii–xi. L. D. Reynolds, 'Varro', in *Texts*

and Transmission: A Survey of the Latin Classics, ed. by L. D. Reynolds (Oxford: Clarendon, 1983), pp.430–431.

74 Horace, *Satires, Epistles and Ars Poetica*, trans. by H. Rushton Fairclough (Cambridge, MA: Harvard University Press, 1978), *Ars Poetica*, vv.58–62.

75 Horace, *Ars Poetica*, vv.70–71.

76 *Seneca ad Lucilium: Epistulae morales*, trans. by Richard M. Gummere, 3 vols (London: Heinemann, 1962–1967), 114.13–14; Quintilian, *The Orator's Education, Books 1–2*, ed. and trans. by Donald A. Russell (Cambridge, MA: Harvard University Press, 2001), 1.6.39. On the availability of these texts in the Middle Ages, see M. Winterbottom, 'Quintilian', in Reynolds, *Texts and Transmission*, pp.332–334, and L. D. Reynolds, 'The Younger Seneca: *Letters*', ibid., pp.369–375.

77 Mark Amsler, 'History of Linguistics, "Standard Latin", and Pedagogy', in *History of Linguistic Thought in the Early Middle Ages*, ed. by Vivien Law (Amsterdam: Benjamins, 1993), pp.49–66 (59).

78 E.g. Louis Holtz (ed.), *Donat et la tradition de l'enseignement grammatical: étude sur l'Ars Donati et sa diffusion (IVe-IXe siècle) et édition critique* (Paris: Centre National de la Recherche Scientifique, 1981), p.651.9–10; Priscian, *Grammaire: Livre XVII – Syntaxe, 1*, ed. by the Ars Grammatica Group (Paris: Vrin, 2010), 122.14–16.

79 Note also the example of an archaism justified via Priscian in Ralph Hexter, '*Latinitas* in the Middle Ages: Horizons and Perspectives', *Helios*, 14 (1987), 69–92 (73).

80 J. N. Adams, Michael Lapidge and Tobias Reinhardt, 'Introduction', in *Aspects of the Language of Latin Prose*, ed. by Tobias Reinhardt, Michael Lapidge and J. N. Adams (Oxford: Oxford University Press, 2005), pp.1–36 (33–34).

81 Although note the comparisons made between ancient and contemporary usage in some of the unusually full glosses recorded in A. C. Dionisotti, 'On the Nature and Transmission of Latin Glossaries', in *Les manuscrits des lexiques et glossaires de l'Antiquité tardive à la fin du Moyen Âge*, ed. by Jacqueline Hamesse (Louvain-la-Neuve: Fédération Internationale des Instituts d'Études Médiévales, 1996), pp.205–252 (229–230: *fruges, marmor*).

82 E.g. 'tutarier', 'to be made safe' (*Bedas metrische Vita sancti Cuthberti*, ed. by Werner Jaager (Leipzig: Mayer and Müller, 1935), v.147). Michael Lapidge, 'Poeticism in Pre-Conquest Anglo-Latin Prose', in Reinhardt et al., *Aspects of the Language of Latin Prose*, pp.321–337 (323).

83 Mark Amsler, *Etymology and Grammatical Discourse in Late Antiquity and the Early Middle Ages* (Amsterdam: Benjamins, 1989), p.17.

84 Ibid., pp.20–22.

85 Aristotle, *De interpretatione uel Periermenias*, trans. by Boethius, ed. by Lorenzo Minio-Paluello, *Aristoteles Latinus*, II.1 (Bruges-Paris: de Brouwer, 1965), pp.5–38 (6).

86 Suzanne Reynolds, *Medieval Reading: Grammar, Rhetoric, and the Classical Text* (Cambridge: Cambridge University Press, 1996), p.87.

87 For the resources available to them, see Helmut Gneuss, 'The Study of Language in Anglo-Saxon England', *Bulletin of the John Rylands University Library of Manchester*, 72 (1990), 3–32.

88 Joyce Hill, 'Ælfric: His Life and Works', in *A Companion to Ælfric*, ed. by Hugh Magennis and Mary Swan (Leiden: Brill, 2009), pp.35–65 (57, 60).

89 *Ælfric's Prefaces*, ed. by Jonathan Wilcox (Durham, NC: Jasprint, 1994), 3a.2, 3a.12–14: 'nos contenti sumus, sicut didicimus in scola Aðelwoldi venerabilis presulis'; 'I am happy [to translate], just as I learned it in the school of the venerable bishop Æthelwold'.

90 Ælfric's source was a compilation based primarily on Priscian, but also including some material from Donatus and Isidore of Seville: David W. Porter (ed.), *Excerptiones de Prisciano: The Source for Ælfric's Latin-Old English Grammar* (Cambridge: Brewer, 2002).

91 For a list of Ælfric's Old English grammatical terminology, see T. Pàroli, 'Indice della terminologia grammaticale di Ælfric', *Istituto Orientale di Napoli: Annali, Sezione Linguistica*, 8 (1968), 113–138.

92 Mechthild Gretsch, 'Ælfric, Language and Winchester', in Magennis and Swan, *A Companion to Ælfric*, pp.109–138 (120–121 (citation and translation at 120)).

93 Elizabeth Closs Traugott, 'Syntax', in *The Cambridge History of the English Language, Volume 1: The Beginnings to 1066*, ed. by Richard M. Hogg (Cambridge: Cambridge University Press, 1992), pp.168–289 (181–182).

94 *Ælfric's Prefaces*, 3b.23–5.

95 Described in N. R. Ker, *Catalogue of Manuscripts Containing Anglo-Saxon*, reissued with supplement (Oxford: Clarendon, 1990), items 17, 71, 107B, 154A, 158, 227, 239 art.5, 242, 265, 269, 362 art.1, 363, 384, 398, 406.

96 Tony Hunt, *Teaching and Learning Latin in Thirteenth-Century England*, 3 vols (Cambridge: Brewer, 1991), I.100. They are London, British Library, MS Cotton Faustina A.x, and Cambridge, University Library, Hh.1.10.

97 The glosses are edited in Hunt, *Teaching and Learning*, I.101–113. Cotton Faustina A.x., f.44r: '*amabo*: I will love/*amabis*: you will love'.

98 *Byrhtferth's Enchiridion*, ed. by Peter S. Baker and Michael Lapidge (Oxford: Early English Text Society, 1995), pp.xxvi–xxviii.

99 See *Byrhtferth's Enchiridion*, II.iii.248–253. On Byrhtferth's pedagogical interest in translation, see René Derolez, 'Those Things Are Difficult to Express in English ...', *English Studies*, 70 (1989), 469–476.

100 *Byrhtferth's Enchiridion*, II.i.504. For a comparison of the grammatical terminology of Byrhtferth and Ælfric, see Gneuss, 'Study of Language', 16–17.

101 *Byrhtferth's Enchiridion*, II.i.450–454.

102 Other potential sources for this passage are discussed in Rosa Bianca Finazzi, 'In margine all'*Enchiridion* di Byrhtferth', in *Per una storia della grammatica in Europa*, ed. by Celestina Milani and Rosa Bianca Finazzi (Milan: I.S.U. Università Cattolica, 2004), pp.95–108.

103 Short, 'Faus Franceis', p.42.

104 René Derolez, 'Language Problems in Anglo-Saxon England: *Barbara loquella* and *barbarismus*', in *Words, Texts, and Manuscripts: Studies in Anglo-Saxon Culture Presented to Helmut Gneuss*, ed. by Michael Korhammer et al. (Cambridge: Brewer, 1992), pp.285–292 (290–291).

105 Byrhtferth glosses the title: 'We gesetton on þissum enchiridion (þæt ys manualis on Lyden and handboc on Englisc) manega þing' ('We have written in this *enchiridion* (*manualis* in Latin and handbook in English) many things' (*Enchiridion*, II.3.248–249)). On his Latin lexis: Michael Lapidge (ed.), Byrhtferth of Ramsey, *The Lives of St Oswald and St Ecgwine* (Oxford: Clarendon, 2009), pp.xliv–lxv. On the innovative nature of his English lexis: Mechthild Gretsch, *The Intellectual Foundations of the English Benedictine Reform* (Cambridge: Cambridge University Press, 1999), p.399; on his French, pp.407–410, 419–420.

106 Bede, *EH*, pp.18 (*Dalreudini*), 216 (*Hefenfeld*). The alphabets covered in the tract are Hebrew, Greek, Latin, that of Aethicus Ister, and one composed of a mixture of Norse and English runes; it also includes a cipher whose origin is ascribed to St Boniface. The tract is attributed to Hrabanus Maurus and printed under the name *De inventione linguarum* in *PL* 112, cols 1579–1583. On its composition and sources: R. Derolez, *Runica Manuscripta: The English Tradition* (Bruges: De Tempel, 1954), pp.279–383.

107 For a stimulating introduction to these issues: Yasemin Yildiz, *Beyond the Mother Tongue: The Postmonolingual Condition* (New York: Fordham University Press, 2012), pp.1–29.

108 Whilst Augustine and Jerome used *populus* with some nuance to reflect ideas of God's chosen people, a *gens* could either be the same as a *populus* or reflect a group of people defined by common biological descent or language (Jeremy Duquesnay Adams, *The* Populus *of Augustine and Jerome: A Study in the Patristic Sense of Community* (New Haven, CT: Yale University Press, 1971), pp.109–112). In contrast, Isidore used *gens*, *populus* and *natio* near-synonymously to denote linguistic groups (Jeremy D. Adams, 'The Political Grammar of Isidore of Seville', *Arts libéraux et philosophie au Moyen Âge* (Montreal: Vrin, 1969), pp.763–775). In view of the lack of correspondence between medieval and modern terminology, I have followed Susan Reynolds in translating *gens* as 'people' rather than as 'race' or 'nation' (*Kingdoms and Communities in Western Europe, 900–1300*, 2nd edn (Oxford: Clarendon, 1997), pp.253–256).

109 Augustine, *De civitate Dei*, XVI.6.

110 Heber and his son Peleg shared Hebrew, thought by Augustine to have been the common tongue spoken before Babel. As Peleg's name means 'division' in Hebrew, Augustine assumed that he was born after Babel and hence did not found a nation: *De civitate Dei*, XVI.11; XVI.6.

111 Augustine, *De civitate Dei*, XVI.6.

112 Arnobius Junior, *Commentarii in Psalmos*, ed. by Klaus-D. Daur, *CCSL* XXV (Turnhout: Brepols, 1990), p.159, cited by Bede, *De temporum ratione*, ed. by Th. Mommsen and C. W. Jones, *CCSL* CXXIII B.2 (Turnhout: Brepols, 1977), lxvi.26.

113 *Bede: The Reckoning of Time*, trans. by Faith Wallis (Liverpool: Liverpool University Press, 1999, repr. 2004), p.164.

114 Henry of Huntingdon, *Historia Anglorum*, p.504. Gervase of Tilbury, *Otia Imperialia: Recreation for an Emperor*, ed. and trans. by S. E. Banks and J. W. Binns (Oxford: Clarendon, 2002), pp.538–539.

115 Gerald of Wales, *De invectionibus*, ed. by W. S. Davies, *Y Cymmrodor*, 30 (1920), 1–248 (142), cited in Robert Bartlett, 'Medieval and Modern Concepts of Race and Ethnicity', *Journal of Medieval and Early Modern Studies*, 31 (2001), 39–56 (47).

116 Bede, *EH*, p.16.

117 E.g. Henry of Huntingdon, *Historia Anglorum*, p.24.

118 E.g. Geoffrey of Monmouth, *HRB*, p.7.

119 For discussion of some twelfth-century responses to this tradition, see Amanda Jane Hingst, *The Written World: Past and Place in the Work of Orderic Vitalis* (Notre Dame, IN: University of Notre Dame Press, 2009), pp.20–24.

120 However, many modern commentators have seen an awareness of geographical distinctiveness as an important factor in building medieval perceptions of nationhood: e.g. Kathy Lavezzo, *Angels on the Edge of the World: Geography, Literature, and English Community, 1000–1534* (Ithaca, NY: Cornell University Press, 2006), p.14.

121 Nennius, *British History and the Welsh Annals*, ed. and trans. by John Morris (London: Phillimore, 1980), p.64.23. On the work's date (first recension written in 829/30) and sources, see David N. Dumville, 'The Historical Value of the *Historia Brittonum*', *Arthurian Literature*, VI (1986), 1–26.

122 Gildas, *The Ruin of Britain and Other Works*, ed. and trans. by Michael Winterbottom (London: Phillimore, 1978), 23.3.

123 On the view that this passage may be a later Anglo-Saxon interpolation, see Alex Woolf, 'An Interpolation in the Text of Gildas's *De Excidio Britanniae*', *Peritia*, 16 (2002), 161–167, but also the response of Barbara Yorke, 'Anglo-Saxon Origin Legends', in *Myth, Rulership, Church and Charters: Essays in Honour of Nicholas Brooks*, ed. by Julia Barrow and Andrew Wareham (Aldershot: Ashgate, 2008), pp.15–29 (20–21).

124 Bede, *EH*, p.16.

125 James Campbell, 'The United Kingdom of England: The Anglo-Saxon Achievement', in *Uniting the Kingdom? The Making of British History*, ed. by Alexander Grant and Keith J. Stringer (New York: Routledge, 1995), pp.31–47 (43).

126 Sarah Foot, 'The Making of *Angelcynn*: English Identity before the Norman Conquest', *TRHS*, Sixth Series, 6 (1996), 25–49 (28–29).

127 Patrick Wormald, '*Engla Lond*: The Making of an Allegiance', *Journal of Historical Sociology*, 7 (1994), 1–24 (10).

128 *Itinerarium Kambriae*, in *Giraldi Cambrensis Opera*, ed. by J. S. Brewer, James F. Dimock and George F. Warner, 8 vols, *RS* 21 (London: H.M. Stationery Office, 1861–1891), VI.3–152; *Descriptio Kambriae*, in *Giraldi Cambrensis Opera*, VI.154–227. On the dating of the works, see Lewis Thorpe (trans.), Gerald of Wales, *The Journey through Wales* and *The Description of Wales*

(London: Penguin, 1978, repr. 2004), pp.36–39, 49–50: both exist in three versions (the *Itinerarium* was composed in 1191, revised *c*.1197, and in 1214; the *Descriptio* was composed in 1193 or 1194, revised in 1215, and again after 1215). All subsequent translations are taken from this edition. On the originality of Gerald's ethnography, see Robert Bartlett, *Gerald of Wales, 1146–1223* (Oxford: Clarendon, 1982), pp.178–210.

129 Gerald of Wales, *Itinerarium*, I.8.

130 Julia Crick, 'The British Past and the Welsh Future: Gerald of Wales, Geoffrey of Monmouth and Arthur of Britain', *Celtica*, 23 (1999), 60–75 (74).

131 Gerald of Wales, *Descriptio*, II.10.

132 Gerald of Wales, *Descriptio*, II.10.

133 *Gesta Stephani*, ed. and trans. by K. R. Potter, with R. H. C. Davis (Oxford: Clarendon, 1976), pp.14–15.

134 Bartlett, 'Concepts of Race and Ethnicity', 46.

135 *Radulfi de Diceto Decani Lundoniensis Opera Historica*, ed. by William Stubbs, 2 vols, *RS* 68 (London: H.M. Stationery Office, 1876), I.10–15 (14–15). Authorship discussed p.10 n2.

136 E.g. Willene B. Clark (ed.), *A Medieval Book of Beasts: The Second-Family Bestiary* (Woodbridge: Boydell, 2006), pp.169–170.

137 Dudo of Saint-Quentin, *De moribus et actis primorum Normanniae ducum*, ed. by Jules Lair (Caen: Le Blanc-Hardel, 1865), pp.146–147. For an interpretation of this episode, see Cassandra Potts, '"Atque unum ex diversis gentibus populum effecit": Historical Tradition and the Norman Identity', *ANS*, 18 (1995), 139–152; responses to her argument are found in Ewan Johnson, 'Normandy and Norman Identity in the Southern Italian Chronicles', *ANS*, 27 (2004), 85–100 (88–89); and Nick Webber, *The Evolution of Norman Identity, 911–1154* (Woodbridge: Boydell, 2005), pp.21–22, 25–26.

138 Dudo of Saint-Quentin, *De Moribus et Actis primorum Normanniae ducum*, p.221.

139 For other early medieval examples of ethnic identity marked by bilingualism, see Reinhard Wenskus, 'Die deutschen Stämme im Reiche Karls des Großen', *Karl der Große. Lebenswerk und Nachleben I* (Düsseldorf: Schwann, 1965), pp.178–219 (209–211). On Dudo's portrayals of bilingualism, see Webber, *Evolution of Norman Identity*, pp.32–33.

140 On the relationship of *patria* and the Norman *gens*, see Hingst, *Past and Place in the Work of Orderic Vitalis*, pp.29–30.

141 *Ecclesiastical History of Orderic Vitalis*, V.24–25.

142 The earliest citation is found in a resolution of the Council of Tours in 813, which recommended that preaching to the laity should take place through the medium of the 'rustica romana lingua' (Ti Alkire and Carol Rosen, *Romance Languages: A Historical Introduction* (Cambridge: Cambridge University Press, 2010), p.322).

143 *DMLBS*, s.v. *Romanus*, 3b, c; *Francigena, -us, -is*, 1d and 2c; *Gallicus*, 2 (<Classical Latin *Gallic, of Gaul*).

144 E.g. Geffrei Gaimar, *Estoire des Engleis: History of the English*, ed. and trans. by Ian Short (Oxford: Oxford University Press, 2009), v.6443; *Wace's Roman de Brut: A History of the British*, ed. and trans. by Judith Weiss, rev. edn (Exeter: Exeter University Press, 2002), v.6921.

145 Philippe de Thaon, *Comput*, ed. by Ian Short (London: Anglo-Norman Text Society, 1984), v.1702, cf. v.361; Wace, *Brut*, v.13649.

146 Gill Page, *Being Byzantine: Greek Identity before the Ottomans* (Cambridge: Cambridge University Press, 2008), p.11. In England, however, the Normans were happy to call themselves and their speech 'French': Webber, *Norman Identity*, pp.131–133.

147 For the surviving pre-eleventh-century French literature, see Wendy Ayres-Bennett, *A History of the French Language through Texts* (London: Routledge, 1996), pp.15–57.

148 *The* Carmen de Hastingae proelio *of Guy, Bishop of Amiens*, ed. and trans. by Frank Barlow (Oxford: Clarendon, 1999), vv.812, 818.

149 *The Gesta Guillelmi of William of Poitiers*, ed. and trans. by R. H. C. Davis and Marjorie Chibnall (Oxford: Clarendon, 1998), p.xx.

150 *Gesta Guillelmi of William of Poitiers*, pp.150–151.

151 *Ecclesiastical History of Orderic Vitalis*, II.xv. On Orderic's English relatives, and his 'lifelong sympathy' for the English after his emigration to the Norman abbey of St Évroul as a ten-year-old oblate, see Marjorie Chibnall, *The World of Orderic Vitalis* (Oxford: Clarendon, 1984), pp. 3–16 (11).

152 *Ecclesiastical History of Orderic Vitalis*, II.184–185.

153 Hugh M. Thomas, *The English and the Normans: Ethnic Hostility, Assimilation, and Identity, 1066–c.1220* (Oxford: Oxford University Press, 2003), p.379.

154 Aulus Gellius, *Attic Nights*, 17.17.1, cited in Andrew Wallace-Hadrill, *Rome's Cultural Revolution* (Cambridge: Cambridge University Press, 2008), p.3.

155 Wallace-Hadrill, *Rome's Cultural Revolution*, pp.13, 27–28.

156 Walter Pohl, 'Telling the Difference: Signs of Ethnic Identity', in *From Roman Provinces to Medieval Kingdoms*, ed. by Thomas F. X. Noble (London: Routledge, 2006), pp.120–167.

1 METHODS AND MOTIVATIONS FOR STUDYING THE VERNACULAR LINGUISTIC PAST

1 Ann Williams, *The English and the Norman Conquest* (Woodbridge: Boydell, 1995), pp.126, 142–145.

2 Francesca Tinti, *Sustaining Belief: The Church of Worcester from c.870 to c.1100* (Farnham: Ashgate, 2010), p.3.

3 M. T. Clanchy, *From Memory to Written Record*, pp.323–324. Alfred Hiatt, *The Making of Medieval Forgeries: False Documents in Fifteenth-Century England* (London: British Library, 2004), pp.7–9. Note e.g. the penalties for falsifying a charter under Henry II (*The Treatise on the Laws and Customs of the Realm of England Commonly Called Glanvill*, ed. by G. D. G. Hall (Oxford: Clarendon, 1965, repr. 1993), pp.176–177); and Hugh, Archbishop of Rouen's claim that

Guerno, a forger of documents from Saint-Ouen and St Augustine's, Canterbury, had confessed and repented on his deathbed (Robert F. Berkhofer III, 'Guerno the Forger and His Confession', *ANS*, 36 (2013), 53–68).

4 Bates, *Regesta*, pp.48–50. However, it seems that English remained a habitual medium for some types of documents into the twelfth century: see further Kathryn A. Lowe, 'Post-Conquest Bilingual Composition in Memoranda from Bury St Edmunds', *Review of English Studies*, 59 (2007), 52–66.

5 Susan Kelly, 'Anglo-Saxon Lay Society and the Written Word', in *The Uses of Literacy in Early Mediaeval Europe*, ed. by Rosamond McKitterick (Cambridge: Cambridge University Press, 1990), pp.36–62 (46–47).

6 Kelly, 'Anglo-Saxon Lay Society', p.56.

7 Kathryn A. Lowe, 'The Development of the Anglo-Saxon Boundary Clause', *Nomina*, 21 (1998), 63–100 (68).

8 For an argument that these clauses reflect the demands of reading aloud to a lay audience, and a summary of previous scholarship, see Mark Rabuck, 'The Imagined Boundary: Borders and Frontiers in Anglo-Saxon England' (unpublished doctoral thesis, Yale University, 1996), pp.149–165 (150–151); on their role in the ritualised, memorial enactment of the agreement recorded by the charter, see Patrick J. Geary, 'Land, Language, and Memory in Europe, 700–1100', *Transactions of the Royal Historical Society*, Sixth Series, 9 (1999), 169–184 (177).

9 Lowe, 'Development of the Anglo-Saxon Boundary Clause', p.74.

10 Post-Conquest approaches to boundary clauses varied, perhaps influenced by scribal linguistic competence. Anglo-Saxon practices of altering charter boundaries survived beyond the Conquest, as with the modifications made to the survey of a central St Albans estate, Cassio (*Charters of St Albans*, ed. by Julia Crick (Oxford: Oxford University Press for the British Academy, 2007), p.118, cf. Nicholas Brooks, 'Anglo-Saxon Charters: The Work of the Last Twenty Years', *Anglo-Saxon England*, 3 (1974), 211–231 (223–224)). However, many cartulary scribes seem to have found the Old English beyond their capabilities and omitted the boundary clauses altogether (Lowe, 'Development of the Anglo-Saxon Boundary Clause', pp.71–72).

11 Motives for creating charters are summarised by Sarah Foot, 'Internal and External Audiences: Reflections on the Anglo-Saxon Archive of Bury St Edmunds Abbey in Suffolk', *Haskins Society Journal*, 24 (2012), 163–193 (172–173, 186); on the relationship between charter and narrative, see Marjorie Chibnall, 'Charter and Chronicle: The Use of Archive Sources by Norman Historians', in *Church and Government in the Middle Ages: Essays Presented to C. R. Cheney*, ed. by C. N. L. Brooke, D. E. Luscombe, G. H. Martin and Dorothy Owen (Cambridge: Cambridge University Press, 1976), 1–17 (1).

12 *Chronicon abbatiae Rameseiensis*, ed. by W. Dunn Macray, *RS* 83 (London: Longman, 1886), p.xxii. On some motives behind the creation of the *Liber benefactorum*, see Jennifer Ann Paxton, 'Charter and Chronicle in Twelfth-Century England: The House-Histories of the Fenland Abbeys' (unpublished doctoral thesis, Harvard University, 1999), pp.6–7, 106; for the intended effect

of recording benefactions on the laity, see her 'Textual Communities in the English Fenlands: A Lay Audience for Monastic Chronicles?', *ANS*, 26 (2003), 123–137 (129–131).

13 *Chronicon abbatiae Rameseiensis*, p.4.

14 Ibid., c.108, p.176: 'universis itaque cartis et cyrographis quae in archivis nostris Anglica barbarie exarata invenimus non sine difficultate et taedio in Latinos apices transmutatis'.

15 Ibid., c.96, p.161.

16 Ibid., c.39, p.65.

17 The *Chronicon* claims that 'we found nearly all [of the documents] written in English' ('universa fere Anglice scripta invenimus', c.39, p.65): this itself seems contrary to standard Anglo-Saxon royal practice. Views of the authenticity of Edgar's charter are listed under S 798 in *The Electronic Sawyer: Online Catalogue of Anglo-Saxon Charters*, Peter Sawyer, rev. Simon Keynes et al. (London: Royal Historical Society, 1968, rev. 1991–present), www.esawyer.org.uk/charter/798.html.

18 *Chronicon abbatiae Rameseiensis*, c.25, p.49.

19 S 980, *Electronic Sawyer*, www.esawyer.org.uk/charter/980.html.

20 K. A. Lowe, 'Bury St Edmunds and Its Liberty: A Charter-Text and Its Afterlife', *English Manuscript Studies, 1100–1700*, 17 (2012), 155–172 (155ff.).

21 Foot, 'Anglo-Saxon Archive of Bury St Edmunds', 172–173.

22 Lowe, 'Bury St Edmunds and Its Liberty', 159–160.

23 This perception is not matched by the surviving evidence. See *Anglo-Saxon Charters*, ed. and trans. by A. J. Robertson, 2nd edn (Cambridge: Cambridge University Press, 1956), pp.xxi–ii: 'The scarcity of royal grants in the vernacular shows that documents of [this] kind were usually drawn up in Latin and that only in exceptional cases were they accompanied by an English version'.

24 Richard Sharpe, 'The Use of Writs in the Eleventh Century', *Anglo-Saxon England*, 32 (2003), 247–291 (268, 248).

25 On potential reasons for this, see Sarah Foot, 'The Abbey's Armoury of Charters', in *Bury St Edmunds and the Norman Conquest*, ed. by Tom Licence (Woodbridge: Boydell, 2014), pp.31–52 (36–43).

26 Crick, *Charters of St Albans*, pp.30–31.

27 In the twelfth century and beyond, the community preserved the memory of pre-Conquest benefactions which its existing charters did not record: although some claims were probably spurious, others seem more credible (ibid., pp.38–39, 229–231, 237–240). Ann Williams notes that 'one of the challenges facing post-Conquest cartularists was that in pre-Conquest England ownership of land was conveyed orally by means of a formal ceremony before witnesses; even royal diplomas were merely written records of that oral ceremony' ('Thegnly Piety and Ecclesiastical Patronage in the Late Old English Kingdom', *ANS*, 24 (2001), 1–24 (4)).

28 Crick, *Charters of St Albans*, p.38.

29 Julia Crick, 'St Albans, Westminster, and Some Twelfth-Century Views of the Anglo-Saxon Past', *ANS*, 25 (2002), 65–83 (79).

30 Julia Crick, 'Liberty and Fraternity: Creating and Defending the Liberty of St Albans', in *Expectations of the Law in the Middle Ages*, ed. by Anthony Musson (Woodbridge: Boydell, 2001), pp.91–103 (92). On the campaign's place within other contemporary attempts to restore reputedly Anglo-Saxon privileges and liberties, see Julia Crick, '*Pristina libertas*: Liberty and the Anglo-Saxons Revisited', *TRHS, Sixth Series*, 14 (2004), 47–71.

31 Crick, *Charters of St Albans*, p.32.

32 Ibid., p.39.

33 Simon Keynes, 'A Lost Cartulary of St Albans Abbey', *Anglo-Saxon England*, 22 (1993), 253–279; Crick, *Charters of St Albans*, p.39.

34 In its surviving form, this diploma forms part of a related set of documents which bear traces of eighth-century material, but the set was rewritten after the monastery's refoundation (? *c*.970) and underwent a series of further modifications stretching beyond the Conquest. Ibid., pp.66–68, 109–131.

35 Ibid., pp.40–41. Only one Old English document in the lost cartulary is certain to have been intentionally fabricated, itself recasting a Latin forgery (document 2); document 1A offers a vernacular translation of the forged Latin diploma, document 1.

36 This is preserved in London, British Library, MS Cotton Nero D.i. A copy was made as part of a longer chronicle of St Albans compiled by Thomas Walsingham in the fourteenth century (London, British Library, MS Cotton Claudius E.iv). A more condensed version is now lost, but was owned by Sir Henry Spelman in the seventeenth century and used by William Wats in his 1640 and 1684 edition of the *Vitae Abbatum* (discussed by Henry Thomas Riley (ed.), Thomas of Walsingham, *Gesta Abbatum Monasterii Sancti Albani*, vol. I, *RS* 28.4 (London: H.M. Stationery Office, 1867), pp.xvii–xix). On the status of the charters and papal privileges within the manuscript, see Crick, *Charters of St Albans*, pp.49–51.

37 London, British Library, MS Cotton Nero D.i, fol. 30r: marginal note.

38 Richard Vaughan, *Matthew Paris* (Cambridge: Cambridge University Press, 1958), p.183.

39 Mark Hagger, 'The *Gesta Abbatum Monasterii Sancti Albani*: Litigation and History at St Albans', *Historical Research*, 81 (2008), 373–398 (375).

40 Printed in Crick, *Charters of St Albans*, pp.233–235.

41 Riley, *Gesta Abbatum*, I.73–75.

42 Keynes, 'Lost Cartulary', p.269. The charters from the lost cartulary were later copied into Cotton Nero D.i in an abbreviated Latin form by Matthew Paris, omitting the Old English (see further Crick, *Charters of St Albans*, pp.49–51).

43 Discussed in Hagger, '*Gesta Abbatum*', pp.373ff.

44 Antonia Gransden, *Historical Writing in England, c.550–c.1307* (London: Routledge, 1974), p.375.

45 Crick, *Charters of St Albans*, pp.19–20.

46 *Gesta Abbatum*, p.26.

47 Ibid., p.27.

48 Ibid.

49 The development of this tradition is charted in Friedrich Wilhelm, 'Antike und Mittelalter. Studien zur Literaturgeschichte. I. Ueber fabulistische Quellenangaben', *Beiträge zur Geschichte der deutschen Sprache und Literatur*, 33 (1908), 286–339.

50 *The Anglo-Saxon Chronicle: A Collaborative Edition, Volume 7, MS E*, ed. by Susan Irvine (Cambridge: Brewer, 2004), p.57.

51 *The Anglo-Saxon Chronicles*, trans. by M. J. Swanton (London: J. M. Dent, 1996, rev. 2000), pp.115–116 (slightly modified here).

52 Discussed in Irvine, *Anglo-Saxon Chronicle, MS E*, pp.xc–xcviii. This can be compared with the bilingual F manuscript of the *Anglo-Saxon Chronicle*, produced at Canterbury in the first decade of the twelfth century, which incorporates several forged charters from the eleventh and twelfth centuries (N. P. Brooks and S. E. Kelly (eds), *Charters of Christ Church, Canterbury, Part I* (Oxford: Oxford University Press for the British Academy, 2013), p.66).

53 *Charters of Peterborough Abbey*, ed. by S. E. Kelly (Oxford: Oxford University Press for the British Academy, 2009), p.86.

54 Ibid., p.7; Jennifer Paxton, 'Forging Communities: Memory and Identity in Post-Conquest England', *Haskins Society Journal*, 10 (2001), 97–109 (107–109).

55 The text is edited in Kelly, *Charters of Peterborough Abbey*, pp.359–360; for the privileges, see pp.131–174, 258–275, and Paxton, 'Forging Communities', 101–103 (102).

56 Avril Morris, 'Forging Links with the Past: The Twelfth-Century Reconstruction of Anglo-Saxon Peterborough' (unpublished doctoral thesis, Leicester University, 2006), p.10.

57 Bede, *EH*, p.28.

58 *Liber Eliensis*, ed. by E. O. Blake (London: Royal Historical Society, 1962), pp.176–177. For further discussion, see Vaughan, *Matthew Paris*, pp.198–204.

59 *Gesta Abbatum*, pp.34–38.

60 Geoffrey of Monmouth, *HRB*, pp.4–5.

61 The cult is discussed in Florence McCulloch, 'Saints Alban and Amphibalus in the Works of Matthew Paris: Dublin, Trinity College MS 177', *Speculum*, 56 (1981), 761–785 (767–769).

62 Geoffrey of Monmouth, *HRB*, pp.95, 119, 255. J. S. P. Tatlock, 'St Amphibalus', *University of California Publications in English*, 4 (1934), 249–257, 268–270.

63 Henry George Liddell and Robert Scott, *A Greek-English Lexicon*, rev. by Henry Stuart Jones with Roderick McKenzie (Oxford: Clarendon, 1940), s.v. ἀμφίβολ-ος, III.

64 The first descriptions of Alban as *Anglorum protomartyr* appeared at the end of the tenth century, but only became widespread in the post-Conquest era. See Paul Antony Hayward, 'The Cult of St. Alban, *Anglorum Protomartyr*, in Anglo-Saxon and Anglo-Norman England', in *More Than a Memory: The Discourse of Martyrdom and the Construction of Christian Identity in the History of Christianity*, ed. by Johan Leemans (Leuven: Peeters, 2005), pp.169–199 (181–185); Crick, *Charters of St Albans*, p.12.

65 See Chapter 3.

66 Crick, *Charters of St Albans*, pp.111, 125, 128, 133, 138.

67 See R. D. Fulk, 'Unferth and His Name', *Modern Philology*, 85 (1987), 113–127 (120–121 n28); cf. the discussion in Donald A. Bullough, 'What Has Ingeld to Do with Lindisfarne?', *Anglo-Saxon England*, 22 (1993), 93–125 (114–115).

68 Discussed in Vaughan, *Matthew Paris*, pp.189ff.

69 Michael Swanton (ed. and trans.), *The Lives of Two Offas: Vitae Offarum Duorum* (Crediton: Medieval Press, 2010), pp.81, 103.

70 *GPC*, s.v. *un*, 1a.

71 *MED*, s.v. *unwon(e* (adj.) (first attested in the late-thirteenth-century *Cursor Mundi*, but c.f. Old English *ungewuna* (adj.)).

72 Otter, *Inventiones*, p.57.

73 *Gesta Abbatum*, pp.26–27. Material in square brackets is included as a marginal gloss by Matthew Paris in British Library MS Cotton Nero D.i, fol. 31v.

74 On medieval awareness of regionally distinctive language, see Mark Faulkner, 'Gerald of Wales and Standard Old English', *Notes and Queries*, 58:1 (2011), 19–24 (and response of Harris, '*Tam Anglis*', 140–142).

75 Bede, *EH*, pp.34–35.

76 *Gesta Abbatum*, p.27.

77 William of St Albans, *Interpretatio*, *Acta Sanctorum*, 22 June, Junii Tomus Quartus (Antwerp: Jacobs, 1707), cols 149–159. Dating discussed by Thomas O'Donnell and Margaret Lamont (trans.), in *The Life of Saint Alban by Matthew Paris, with the Passion of Saint Alban by William of St. Albans*, trans. by Jocelyn Wogan-Browne et al. (Tempe, AZ: ACMRS, 2010), pp.133–165 (133).

78 William of St Albans, *Interpretatio*, col.149A; O'Donnell and Lamont (trans.), *Passion of St Alban by William of St Albans*, p.139.

79 William of St Albans, *Interpretatio*, col.149C-D.

80 William of St Albans, *Interpretatio*, col.149C; corrected with reference to O'Donnell and Lamont (trans.), *Passion of St Alban by William of St Albans*, p.139 n6.

81 O'Donnell and Lamont (trans.), *Passion of St Alban by William of St Albans*, p.139.

82 Scott Thompson Smith, *Land and Book: Literature and Land Tenure in Anglo-Saxon England* (Toronto: University of Toronto Press, 2012), p.29.

83 For early examples of this trope, see Patrick Wormald, *Bede and the Conversion of England: The Charter Evidence*, Jarrow Lecture 1984 (Jarrow: St Paul's Church, 1985), pp.10–11.

84 S 888, www.esawyer.org.uk/charter/888.html; printed and discussed in Crick, *Charters of St Albans*, pp.167–174 (168); cf. Simon Keynes, *The Diplomas of King Æthelred 'the Unready', 978–1016: A Study in Their Use as Historical Evidence* (Cambridge: Cambridge University Press, 1980), pp.122–123.

85 S 687; cf. the treatment of similar subject matter in a second charter of Edgar, S 696.

86 See Crick, *Charters of St Albans*, p.173.

87 Edited and discussed ibid., pp.109–119.

88 *Gesta Abbatum*, p.25.

89 William of St Albans, *Interpretatio*, col.153E.

90 Bede, *EH*, pp.32–33.

91 *Gesta Abbatum*, p.25. Cf. Bosworth and Toller, s.v. *ostre*, *AND*, *oistre*, *MED*, *oistre*; *MED*, *hil(le*; Bosworth and Toller, *scealu*, *MED*, *shel(le*; *MED*, *ford*; Toronto A-G, *ancor*, *ancra*, *MED*, *anker*, *ancre*, *AND*, *ancre* (n.1); *MED*, *pol(e* (n.3). Whilst the surviving forms of these names hence reflect thirteenth-century scribal practice, they could also be based on earlier English.

92 London, British Library MS Cotton Nero D.i, fol. 31v.

93 Elisabeth van Houts, *Memory and Gender in Medieval Europe, 900–1200* (Toronto: University of Toronto Press, 1999), p.38.

94 Richard H. Britnell, *The Commercialisation of English Society, 1000–1500*, 2nd edn (Manchester: Manchester University Press, 1996), p.66–67.

95 Boundary clauses at St Albans were omitted by all medieval copyists after the twelfth century (Crick, *Charters of St Albans*, pp.40–41).

96 Amsler, *Etymology and Grammatical Discourse*, p.170.

97 For an overview of Anglo-Saxon etymological activity, see Gneuss, 'Study of Language', pp.92–95.

98 Geoffrey of Burton, *Life and Miracles of St Modwenna*, pp.2–3; on the date of the text (probably 1118 × 1135, possibly 1118 × 1150), see p.xi, note 1.

99 Mario Esposito, 'Conchubrani Vita Sancti Monennae', *Proceedings of the Royal Irish Academy*, xxviii C (1910), 202–251 (222–223). Conchubranus was perhaps writing in the eleventh century but was working from earlier models that dated from the seventh and tenth centuries. For discussion, see further Mario Esposito, 'The Sources of Conchubranus' Life of St Monenna', *English Historical Review*, xxxv (1920), 71–78.

100 Geoffrey, *Life of Modwenna*, pp.90–91.

101 The text was relatively popular: it now survives in full in two manuscripts and as a fragment in a third, in three independent abbreviated versions, and in an Anglo-Norman verse translation (see further ibid., pp.xxxvii–xliii).

102 Petrus Helias, *Summa super Priscianum*, ed. by Leo Reilly, 2 vols (Toronto: Pontifical Institute of Mediaeval Studies, 1993), I.70.

103 Cited and translated in Reynolds, *Medieval Reading*, p.83.

104 Petrus Helias, *Summa super Priscianum*, I.70; trans. Reynolds, *Medieval Reading*, p.83.

105 Olga Weijers, 'Lexicography in the Middle Ages', *Viator*, 20 (1989), 139–153 (141).

106 Osbern, *Derivazioni*, ed. by Paola Busdraghi et al., 2 vols (Spoleto: Centro italiano di studi sull'alto medioevo, 1996), II.599.

107 Ibid., I.1.

108 On the extent of medieval authors' sense of temporal particularity, cf. Hans-Werner Goetz, 'The Concept of Time in the Historiography of the Eleventh and Twelfth Centuries', in *Medieval Concepts of the Past: Ritual, Memory,*

Historiography, ed. by Gerd Althoff, Johannes Fried and Patrick J. Geary (Cambridge: Cambridge University Press, 2002), pp.139–165 (162).
109 *Gesta Abbatum*, p.25.
110 Isidore, I.xxix.3.
111 Rachel Koopmans, *Wonderful to Relate: Miracle Stories and Miracle Collecting in High Medieval England* (Philadelphia: University of Pennsylvania Press, 2011), p.97.
112 Bernhard W. Scholz (ed.), 'Eadmer's Life of Bregwine, Archbishop of Canterbury, 761–764', *Traditio*, 22 (1966), 127–148 (144–145); the *Vita* is dated by Scholz to 1123 (p.131), the same year that Canterbury's forged replacement bulls were presented before the papal curia, where they met with an incredulous reception (for references, see Robert F. Berkhofer, 'The Canterbury Forgeries Revisited', *Haskins Society Journal*, 18 (2006), 36–50).
113 Brooks and Kelly, *Charters of Christ Church, Canterbury*, p.58.
114 *Eadmeri Historia novorum in Anglia*, ed. by Martin Rule, *RS* 81 (London: Longman, 1884), pp.261ff.

2 PERCEPTIONS OF ENGLISH LINGUISTIC AND LITERARY CONTINUITY

1 The most influential portrayal of post-Conquest English culture as characterised by 'nostalgia' has been R. W. Southern, 'Aspects of the European Tradition of Historical Writing: 4. The Sense of the Past', *TRHS*, Fifth Series, 23 (1973), 243–263 (246–248). E.g. Elaine Treharne, 'Reading from the Margins: The Uses of Old English Homiletic Manuscripts in the Post-Conquest Period', in *Beatus Vir: Studies in Early English and Norse Manuscripts in Memory of Phillip Pulsiano*, ed. by A. N. Doane and Kirsten Wolf (Tempe, AZ: ACMRS, 2006), pp.329–358 (331–332).
2 A case for this approach has recently been made in Mark Faulkner's study of twelfth-century annotations to a tenth-century copy of Ælfric's *Catholic Homilies*, 'Archaism, Belatedness and Modernisation: "Old" English in the Twelfth Century', *Review of English Studies*, n.s. 63 (2012), 179–203 (202).
3 These are catalogued in *The Production and Use of English Manuscripts 1060 to 1220*, ed. by Orietta Da Rold et al. (Leicester: University of Leicester, 2010), www.le.ac.uk/ee/em1060to1220.
4 Mark Faulkner, 'The Uses of Anglo-Saxon Manuscripts, *c.*1066–1200' (unpublished doctoral thesis, Oxford University, 2008), p.48.
5 Ibid., p.14. See further Christine Franzen, 'Late Copies of Anglo-Saxon Charters', in *Studies in English Language and Literature: 'Doubt Wisely': Papers in Honour of E. G. Stanley*, ed. by M. J. Toswell and E. M. Tyler (London: Routledge, 1996), pp.42–70; Kathryn A. Lowe, 'Two Thirteenth-Century Cartularies from Bury St Edmunds: A Study in Textual Transmission', *Neuphilologische Mitteilungen*, 93 (1992), 293–301; Kathryn A. Lowe, '"As Fre as Thowt?" Some Medieval Copies and Translations of Old English Wills', *English Manuscript Studies, 1100–1700*, 4 (1993), 1–23.

6 See the descriptions of making a final judgement in John Hudson, *The Oxford History of the Laws of England, Volume II: 871–1216* (Oxford: Oxford University Press, 2012), pp.87–91, 329–331. However, the manuscripts were not exclusively of historical interest: much of the legislation has been adapted by twelfth-century scribes to reflect subsequent legal developments, making contemporary law appear closer to the *laga Edwardi* (Mary P. Richards, 'The Manuscript Contexts of the Old English Laws: Tradition and Innovation', in *Studies in Earlier Old English Prose*, ed. by Paul E. Szarmach (Albany: State University of New York Press, 1986), pp.171–192 (181–186); Bruce O'Brien, 'The Becket Conflict and the Invention of the Myth of *Lex Non Scripta*', in *Learning the Law: Teaching and the Transmission of Law in England, 1150–1900*, ed. by Jonathan A. Bush and Alain Wijffels (London: Hambledon Press, 1999), pp.1–16).

7 The legal implications of this oath are discussed in George Garnett, *Conquered England: Kingship, Succession and Tenure, 1066–1166* (Oxford: Oxford University Press, 2007), pp.12ff. Patrick Wormald, *The Making of English Law: King Alfred to the Twelfth Century, Volume I: Legislation and Its Limits* (Oxford: Blackwell, 1999), p.224.

8 Thomson, *William of Malmesbury*, p.46. William's Old English sources included the *Anglo-Saxon Chronicle*, Coleman's life of St Wulfstan, Æthelwold's translation of the Benedictine Rule, a life of St Dunstan, and potentially a life of St Indract (his hagiographical sources are discussed in William of Malmesbury, *Saints' Lives: Lives of SS. Wulfstan, Dunstan, Patrick, Benignus and Indract*, ed. by M. Winterbottom and R. M. Thomson (Oxford: Clarendon, 2002), pp.xv–xxv, 310–313).

9 For William's comments on his ancestry, see his *Gesta regum Anglorum: The History of the English Kings*, ed. and trans. by R. A. B. Mynors et al., 2 vols (Oxford: Clarendon, 1998–1999), I.424–425. On his English translations, see his *Saints' Lives*, pp.xv–xxv, 310–313.

10 In his Latin translation of Coleman's *Life of Wulfstan*, William stated that he had removed the 'barbarous names' so that they should not 'wound the sensibilities of the fastidious reader' ('ne uocabulorum barbaries delicati lectoris sautiaret aures' (William of Malmesbury, *Vita Wulfstani*, in *Saints' Lives*, pp.7–155 (58–59), cf. his *Gesta Pontificum Anglorum: The History of the English Bishops*, ed. and trans. by Michael Winterbottom, with R. M. Thomson, 2 vols (Oxford: Clarendon, 2007), I.494). He often preferred to record Anglo-Saxon names in a 'Normanised' form: R. M. Thomson, *Books and Learning in Twelfth-Century England: The Ending of 'alter orbis'* (Walkern: Red Gull, 2006), p.14 and n.77.

11 William of Malmesbury, *Gesta regum*, I.98–99.

12 Gildas, *Ruin of Britain*, 23.3.

13 William of Malmesbury, *Gesta regum*, I.90, 192–194. William was less impressed by the *Anglo-Saxon Chronicle* (I.14).

14 *Anglo-Saxon Chronicle, MS E*, pp.xxxii–xxxvi. Other authors who made extensive use of the *Chronicle* include William of Malmesbury (see *Gesta regum*,

II.12–13) and, potentially, Symeon of Durham (*Libellus de exordio atque procursu istius, hoc est Dunhelmensis, ecclesie: Tract on the Origins and Progress of this the Church of Durham*, ed. and trans. by David Rollason (Oxford: Clarendon, 2000), p.lxxi). MS F of the *Anglo-Saxon Chronicle*, compiled at Christ Church, Canterbury in the first decade of the twelfth century, provides English and Latin versions of the *Chronicle*, augmented with a range of other sources (*The Anglo-Saxon Chronicle: A Collaborative Edition: Volume 8, MS F*, ed. by Peter S. Baker (Cambridge: Brewer, 2000)).

15 Alexander R. Rumble, '*Interpretationes in latinum*: Some Twelfth-Century Translations of Anglo-Saxon Charters', in *Early Medieval English Texts and Interpretations: Studies Presented to Donald G. Scragg*, ed. by Elaine Treharne and Susan Rosser (Tempe, AZ: ACMRS, 2002), pp.101–117 (116).

16 Kemp Malone, 'When Did Middle English Begin?', *Language*, 6 (1930), 110–117.

17 Gneuss, 'Origin of Standard Old English and Æthelwold's School at Winchester', 63–83; Walter Hofstetter, 'Winchester and the Standardization of Old English Vocabulary', *ASE*, 17 (1988), 139–161; Gretsch, 'Winchester Vocabulary and Standard Old English'.

18 See above, Chapter 1, note 4.

19 Peter R. Kitson, 'When Did Middle English Begin? Later Than You Think!', in *Studies in Middle English Linguistics*, ed. by Jacek Fisiak (Berlin: De Gruyter, 1997), pp.221–269.

20 For a summary, see Roger Lass, 'Phonology and Morphology', in Blake, *The Cambridge History of the English Language: Volume II, 1066–1476*, pp.23–155. Olga Fischer, 'Syntax', ibid., pp.207–408 (370–83).

21 David Burnley, 'Lexis and Semantics', in *Cambridge History of the English Language: Volume II*, pp.409–499 (423–432, 414–423).

22 For an introduction to the 'Tremulous Hand', see Christine Franzen, *The Tremulous Hand of Worcester: A Study of Old English in the Thirteenth Century* (Oxford: Clarendon, 1991). On comprehension of Old English in the post-Conquest period, see Angus F. Cameron, 'Middle English in Old English Manuscripts', in *Chaucer and Middle English Studies in Honour of Rossell Hope Robbins*, ed. by Beryl Rowland (London: Allen and Unwin, 1974), pp.218–229; Hans Sauer, 'Knowledge of Old English in the Middle English Period?', in *Language History and Linguistic Modelling: A Festschrift for Jacek Fisiak on His Sixtieth Birthday*, ed. by Raymond Hickey and Stanisław Puppel, 2 vols (Berlin: de Gruyter, 1997), I.791–814. George Younge argues that not only linguistic but social and economic factors may explain why Old English texts gradually ceased to be copied in the later twelfth century ('Monks, Money, and the End of Old English', *New Medieval Literatures*, 16 (2016), 39–82).

23 See further the introduction to this volume.

24 Henry, *Historia*, pp.24–25.

25 On the chronology of the *Historia*'s composition, see Henry of Huntingdon, *Historia Anglorum*, pp.lxvi–lxxvii. All references and translations in the text are taken from this edition. The text was copied in full in more than forty

manuscripts (described ibid., pp.cxvii–cxliv; a provisional list of nineteen further manuscripts which preserve fragments of the *Historia Anglorum* is given on pp.839–842).

26 Bede, *EH*, p.16. 'Anglorum uidelicet Brettonum Scottorum Pictorum et Latinorum'.

27 Ibid., pp.16–17.

28 J. M. Wallace-Hadrill, *Bede's Ecclesiastical History of the English People: A Historical Commentary* (Oxford: Clarendon, 1988), pp.7–8.

29 Geoffrey of Monmouth, *HRB*, p.7. 'Normannis uidelicet atque Britannis, Saxonibus, Pictis, et Scotis'. Unlike Bede, Geoffrey means by 'Scotis', the Scots (*DMLBS*, s.v. *Scotus*, 1 and 2).

30 Katherine Forsyth, 'Literacy in Pictland', in *Literacy in Medieval Celtic Societies*, ed. by Huw Pryce (Cambridge: Cambridge University Press, 1998), pp.39–61 (39).

31 Augustine, *De doctrina Christiana*, ed. and trans. by R. P. H. Green (Oxford: Clarendon, 1995), I.85: 'Hoc ergo ut nossemus atque possemus facta est tota pro nostra salute per divinam providentiam dispensatio temporalis'. ('To enlighten us and enable us, the whole temporal dispensation was set up by divine providence for our salvation'.)

32 Shortly after (pp.26–27), Henry quotes a passage of Bede without alteration which portrays the Picts as continuing to exist in the 'present day' ('hodie'): this anachronism may stem from the mechanical copying of an amanuensis. (On errors in Henry's citations from Bede, see Greenway, *Historia Anglorum*, pp.lxxxvii–lxxxviii.)

33 Arnobius Junior, *Commentarii in Psalmos*, p.159, cited by Bede, *De temporum ratione*, lxvi.26. Cited in Henry's *Historia Anglorum*, p.504.

34 Genesis 11:9. 'There the language of the whole earth was confounded'.

35 On Henry's family, see Greenway, *Historia Anglorum*, pp.xxiii–xxviii.

36 Henry, *Historia*, pp.348–349. See also his correct gloss of 'Irenside' as 'latus ferreum', p.356.

37 His *Chronicle* text also contained elements of version C, as well as material that is found in no surviving version. Greenway, *Historia Anglorum*, pp.xci–xcviii. See also Irvine, *Anglo-Saxon Chronicle, MS E*, pp.l–lv.

38 Greenway, *Historia Anglorum*, p.xcvii. For several examples, see the genealogy on p.246, as well as p.282 n38.

39 Henry, *Historia*, p.240; cf. pp.108, 234, 304, 356, 412.

40 Ibid., pp.114, 120, 184, 188, 194, 262.

41 Greenway, *Historia Anglorum*, p.cii. See further A. G. Rigg, 'Henry of Huntingdon's Metrical Experiments', *Journal of Medieval Latin*, 1 (1991), 60–72 (64–65).

42 The five manuscripts are discussed in *The Battle of Brunanburh*, ed. by Alistair Campbell (London: Heinemann, 1938), pp.1–15.

43 Rigg, 'Metrical Experiments', pp.65–69.

44 Cf. *Brunanburh*, ed. Campbell, p.93.2: 'beorna beahgifa'. All quotations from the Old English are taken from this edition.

45 Rigg, 'Metrical Experiments', pp.60–64. Further elaborately structured poems have since been discovered: see A. G. Rigg, 'Henry of Huntingdon's Herbal', *Mediaeval Studies*, 65 (2003), 213–292; Winston Black, 'Henry of Huntingdon's Lapidary Rediscovered and His *Anglicanus ortus* Reassembled', *Mediaeval Studies*, 68 (2006), 43–88.

46 This title was first used by Bartlett Jere Whiting, 'The Rime of King William', in *Philologica: The Malone Anniversary Studies*, ed. by Thomas A. Kirby and Henry Bosley Woolf (Baltimore: Johns Hopkins University Press, 1949), pp.89–96 (89). Estimates of the number of poems in the *Chronicle* differ: I follow the table included in Thomas A. Bredehoft, *Textual Histories: Readings in the* Anglo-Saxon Chronicle (Toronto: University of Toronto Press, 2001), p.79.

47 Irvine, *Anglo-Saxon Chronicle, MS E*, p.97.

48 Swanton, *Anglo-Saxon Chronicles*, pp.220–221. The meaning of *deorfrið* (translated here as 'game-preserves') is uncertain: Stefan Jurasinski, 'The *Rime of King William* and Its Analogues', *Neophilologus*, 88 (2004), 131–144 (134–136).

49 Seth Lerer, 'Old English and Its Afterlife', in *The Cambridge History of Medieval English Literature* (Cambridge: Cambridge University Press, 1999), pp.7–34 (18); 'The Genre of the Grave and the Origins of the Middle English Lyric', *Modern Language Quarterly*, 58 (1997), 127–161 (134).

50 Bredehoft, *Textual Histories*, p.203 n94.

51 Jurasinski, '*Rime of King William* and Its Analogues', 131–144. However, Thomas Bredehoft has also pointed out the author's employment of diction shared with Ælfric's alliterative works (*Authors, Audiences, and Old English Verse* (Toronto: University of Toronto Press, 2009), p.190).

52 The *Historia Anglorum* includes elegies on Alfred (p.298); Æthelflæd (p.308); Edgar (p.322); Henry's father, Nicholas (p.458); Edith/Matilda (p.462); Robert Bloet, Bishop of Lincoln (p.470); Henry I (p.492).

53 All translations of the Old English text of 'Brunanburh' are taken from Swanton, *Anglo-Saxon Chronicles*, pp.106, 108–110.

54 Janet Coleman, *Ancient and Medieval Memories: Studies in the Reconstruction of the Past* (Cambridge: Cambridge University Press, 1992), p.320.

55 The relevant manuscripts are: Hereford, Cathedral Library, MS P.v.I + Bodleian, E Mus. 93 (3632); Oxford, Bodleian Library, MS Bodley 163; Oxford, Bodleian Library, MS Hatton 43; Oxford, Bodleian Library, MS Laud Misc. 243; Oxford, Lincoln College, MS Lat. 31; Oxford, Magdalen College, MS Lat. 105; Tournai, Bibliothèque Municipale MS 134.

56 They are: Cambridge, Trinity College, MS R.7.28; Clitheroe, Stonyhurst College, MS 69; Dublin, Trinity College, MS 492 (E.2.23); Durham, University Library, MS Cosin V.ii.6; London, British Library, MS Cotton Faustina A.v + Dublin, Trinity College, MS 114 (A.5.2); London, British Library, MS Stow 104; Oxford, Bodleian Library, MS Bodley 297; Oxford, Bodleian Library, MS Digby 211. A ninth witness occurs as a marginal gloss to the mid-twelfth-century copy of Bede's *Historia Ecclesiastica* in Oxford, Lincoln College, MS Lat. 31, fol. 112v.

57 H.S. Offler, 'The date of Durham (Carmen de situ Dunelmi)', *Journal of English and Germanic Philology*, 61 (1962), 591–594. An English poem entitled 'De situ Dunelmi' was on fol. 20v of London, British Library, MS Cotton Vitellius D.xx + Miscellaneous Burnt Cotton Fragments, Bundle I (16), before it was destroyed by fire. For the second witness, see n.61 below.

58 The surviving copy of the dossier is now divided between Cambridge, Corpus Christi College, MS 66, and Cambridge, University Library, MS Ff.1.27: for this view of its origins, see Christopher Norton, 'History, Wisdom and Illumination', in *Symeon of Durham: Historian of Durham and the North*, ed. by David Rollason (Stamford: Shaun Tyas, 1998), pp.61–105 (99–100).

59 'Cuius de Beda sententie concordat etiam illud Anglico sermone compositum carmen, ubi cum de statu huius loci et de sanctorum reliquiis que in eo continentur agitur, etiam reliquiarum Bede una cum ceteris ibidem mentio habetur' ('[Cuthbert's] account of Beda agrees also with that poem in the English language which, when it speaks of the condition of this church and the relics of saints which are contained in it, mentions the relics of Bede there together with those of other saints', Symeon of Durham, *Libellus de exordio*, ed. Rollason, pp.166–167).

60 Bede, *EH*, pp.416–417.

61 Jerome, Epistola 57.5, *PL* 22, col.571.

62 Although, like Henry, many other writers preferred to quote Jerome rather than to follow his advice: Rita Copeland, 'The Fortunes of 'non verbum pro verbo': or, Why Jerome is not a Ciceronian', in *The Medieval Translator: The Theory and Practice of Translation in the Middle Ages*, ed. by Roger Ellis et al. (Cambridge: Brewer, 1989), pp.15–35.

63 The poem's language is discussed by Campbell, *Brunanburh*, pp.8–13.

64 *MED*, s.v. *hamer*, 1; *hōm*, 1; Bosworth and Toller, s.v. *hām*.

65 E.g. 'sweorda ecgum', 'with the edges of swords' (p.93.4, my translation), is rendered as the singular 'acie gladii', and 'wiþ laþra gehwæne', 'against every foe' [*lit.* 'each of the hostile ones'] (p.93.9), is translated as 'ab infestis nationibus', 'from hostile nations' (pp.310–311). Cf. correct translations like 'Norðmanna', 'of the men of the North' (p.94.33) as 'Normannorum' (pp.312–313).

66 Campbell, *Brunanburh*, pp.98–102 n12b–13a.

67 Ibid., p.95.68–69.

68 Kenneth Tiller, 'Anglo-Norman Historiography and Henry of Huntingdon's Translation of *The Battle of Brunanburh*', *Studies in Philology*, 109 (2012), 173–191 (179–180).

69 For an example of this negative view of Henry's translation, see Edith Rickert, 'The Old English Offa Saga I', *Modern Philology*, 2 (1904), 29–76 (65–66).

70 Symeon of Durham, *Libellus de exordio*, p.72. The poem has been edited by Elliott van Kirk Dobbie, in *The Anglo-Saxon Minor Poems* (London: Routledge, 1942), pp.c–cvii, 107–108, 199.

71 *Liber Eliensis: A History of the Isle of Ely*, trans. by Janet Fairweather (Woodbridge: Boydell, 2005), p.xxii–xxiii.

72 *Liber Eliensis*, p.63.

73 Ibid., pp.164–165.

74 Ibid., pp.153–154.

75 W. W. Skeat's comments on the language of the song are included in C. W. Stubbs, *Historical Memorials of Ely Cathedral* (London: Dent, 1897), pp.49–52.

76 *Liber Eliensis*, p.154; trans. Fairweather, p.182.

77 Henry, *Historia*, p.558. Nothing is known of Warin's identity (p.559 n2).

78 This survives as Paris, Bibliothèque Nationale, MS lat. 6042: Greenway, *Historia*, pp.cxxii–cxxiii.

79 Henry, *Historia*, p.584. On the case for Walter as archdeacon of Leicester, see p.584 n2.

80 Henry, *Historia*, p.14.

81 On the importance of the Old English poem as an indication of the battle's impact on English identity, see Sarah Foot, 'Where English Becomes British: Rethinking Contexts for *Brunanburh*', in *Myth, Rulership, Church and Charters: Essays in Honour of Nicholas Brooks*, ed. by Julia Barrow and Andrew Wareham (Aldershot: Ashgate, 2008), pp.127–144.

82 Tiller, 'Anglo-Norman Historiography', p.188.

83 Ibid., p.189.

84 Ibid., pp.190–191.

85 George Younge, 'The *Canterbury Anthology*: An Old English Manuscript in its Anglo-Norman Context' (unpublished doctoral thesis, Cambridge University, 2012), pp.31–39.

86 R. W. Pfaff, 'Some Anglo-Saxon Sources for the "Theological Windows" at Canterbury Cathedral', *Mediaevalia*, 10 (1984), 49–62 (52–57).

87 Younge, '*Canterbury Anthology*', p.90.

88 Ibid., pp.121–131; Elaine Treharne, 'The Life of English in the Mid-Twelfth Century: Ralph D'Escures' Homily on the Virgin Mary', in *Writers of the Reign of Henry II*, ed. by Ruth Kennedy and Simon Meecham-Jones (London: Palgrave, 2006), pp.169–186.

89 Younge, '*Canterbury Anthology*', pp.189–215. Different views are expressed in Malcolm Godden, 'The Old English Life of St Neot and the Legends of King Alfred', *ASE*, 39 (2010), 193–225; Elaine Treharne, 'Categorization, Periodization: The Silence of (the) English in the Twelfth Century', *New Medieval Literatures*, 8 (2006), 247–273 (265–268).

90 Younge, '*Canterbury Anthology*', p.213. On the text's diction, see Godden, 'St Neot', p.202; Younge, *Canterbury Anthology*, pp.193–195.

91 Margaret Gibson, 'Conclusions: The Eadwine Psalter in Context', in *The Eadwine Psalter: Text, Image and Monastic Culture in Twelfth-Century Canterbury*, ed. by Margaret Gibson, T. A. Heslop, and Richard W. Pfaff (London: Modern Humanities Research Association, 1992), pp.209–213 (209).

92 The most recent description is by Elaine Treharne, 'Cambridge, Trinity College, R.17.1', in The Production and Use of English Manuscripts 1060 to 1220, www.le.ac.uk/english/em1060to1220/mss/EM.CTC.R.17.1.htm. M. R. James, *The Ancient Libraries of Canterbury and Dover* (Cambridge: Cambridge University Press, 1903), p.51 n323: *tripartitum psalterium Eadwini*.

93 Some possible candidates are discussed by Gibson, 'Conclusions', in *Eadwine*, pp.211–212.
94 See the relevant essays in Gibson et al., *Eadwine*.
95 E. F. Sutcliffe, 'Jerome', in *The Cambridge History of the Bible*, ed. by G. W. H. Lampe, 3 vols (Cambridge: Cambridge University Press, 1963–1970), II.80–101 (84–85, 88).
96 Celia and Kenneth Sisam (eds), *The Salisbury Psalter, edited from Salisbury Cathedral MS 150* (London: Early English Text Society, 1959), p.57.
97 Patrick P. O'Neill, 'The English Version', in *Eadwine Psalter*, pp.123–138. For an overview of the three distinct traditions of Anglo-Saxon psalter glossing, which follow the Vespasian Psalter (A-type), the Regius Psalter (D-type) and the Lambeth Psalter (I-type), see C. and K. Sisam, *Salisbury Psalter*, pp.52–75.
98 O'Neill, 'The English Version', p.134. Only the first eighteen of the Psalter's thirty-six quires have been corrected.
99 The information displayed here is indebted to O'Neill, 'The English Version'; a misprint there regarding the Metrical Psalms has been corrected with reference to Patrick P. O'Neill, 'Another Fragment of the Metrical Psalms in the Eadwine Psalter', *Notes and Queries*, n.s. 35 (1988), 434–436. Compare Philip Pulsiano, 'The Old English Gloss of the *Eadwine Psalter*', in Swan and Treharne, *Rewriting Old English in the Twelfth Century*, pp.166–194.
100 O'Neill, 'Old English Gloss', p.133.
101 Ibid., pp.134–135: 'The Stages of Copying in the Old English Gloss'.
102 Dominique Markey, 'The Anglo-Norman Version', in *Eadwine Psalter*, pp.139–156 (147).
103 Dominique Markey, 'Le Psautier d'Eadwine: Édition critique de la version *Iuxta Hebraeos* et de sa traduction interlinéaire anglo-normande' (unpublished doctoral thesis, University of Ghent, 1989), p.159.
104 For detailed analysis of the Eadwine Psalter's illustrations in comparison to the Utrecht Psalter, see William Noel, 'The Utrecht Psalter in England: Continuity and Experiment', in *The Utrecht Psalter in Medieval Art: Picturing the Psalms of David*, ed. by Koert van der Horst et al. (Tuurdijk: HES, 1996), pp.121–165 (153–155).
105 Margaret Gibson, 'The Latin Apparatus', in *Eadwine Psalter*, pp.108–122 (109).
106 Elaine Treharne, *Living through Conquest: The Politics of Early English, 1020–1220* (Oxford: Oxford University Press, 2012), p.172.
107 Teresa Webber identifies five different scribes involved in writing the Old English gloss ('The Script', in *Eadwine Psalter*, pp.13–24 (18–21)). For different interpretations, see Philip Pulsiano, *Old English Glossed Psalters: Psalms 1–50* (Toronto: University of Toronto Press, 2001), pp.xxxiii–iv, and Frank-Günter Berghaus, *Die Verwandtschaftsverhältnisse der altenglischen Interlinearversionen des Psalters und der Cantica* (Göttingen: Vandenhoeck and Ruprecht, 1979), pp.19–21.

108 O'Neill, 'Another Fragment of the Metrical Psalms in the Eadwine Psalter', p.436.
109 Peter S. Baker, 'A Little-Known Variant Text of the Old English Metrical Psalms', *Speculum*, 59:2 (1984), 263–281 (265). The translation's mistakes, including several visual errors such as *hefre* for *nefre* (Psalm 93.12.1) as well as those less easily corrected, are discussed on p.270.
110 O'Neill, 'English Version', p.133.
111 The manuscript, Paris, Bibliothèque nationale MS lat. 8846, currently features only some isolated words from an Old English gloss to the *Romanum*, which were included in the process of copying out other texts. However, Toswell points out that from Psalm 25, the pages were lined in plummet for the insertion of a continuous English translation (M. J. Toswell, *The Anglo-Saxon Psalter* (Turnhout: Brepols, 2014), p.281). The book also features an insular French gloss to Psalms 1–97 of the *Hebraicum*, which is related to, but not directly copied from the Eadwine Psalter; Eadwine, however, did provide a model for the Paris mise-en-page and other elements (Markey, 'Anglo-Norman Version', pp.151–154; Patricia Stirnemann, 'Paris, B.N., MS lat. 8846 and the Eadwine Psalter', in *Eadwine Psalter*, pp.186–192).
112 Mechthild Gretsch, 'The Roman Psalter, Its Old English Glosses and the English Benedictine Reform', in *The Liturgy of the Late Anglo-Saxon Church*, ed. by Helen Gittos and M. Bradford Bedingfield (Woodbridge: Boydell, 2005), pp.13–28 (esp. p.22).
113 Listed in Gretsch, 'Roman Psalter', pp.14–15.
114 Brooks, *Anglo-Saxon Myths*, pp.139–140.
115 Abbot Gasquet and Edmund Bishop, *The Bosworth Psalter* (London: Bell, 1908), pp.24–27, 34–39 (assessed in David N. Dumville, *Liturgy and the Ecclesiastical History of Late Anglo-Saxon England: Four Studies* (Woodbridge: Boydell, 1992), pp.39–51 (48–49)); but cf. Nicholas Orchard's arguments for St Augustine's Abbey, Canterbury ('The Bosworth Psalter and the St Augustine's Missal', in *Canterbury and the Norman Conquest: Churches, Saints, and Scholars, 1066–1109*, ed. by Richard Eales and Richard Sharpe (Rio Grande: Hambledon, 1995), pp.87–94.
116 Gretsch, 'Roman Psalter', pp.15ff. See also Mechthild Gretsch, 'The Junius Psalter Gloss: Its Historical and Cultural Context', *ASE*, 29 (2000), 85–122; and Patrick P. O'Neill, 'Latin Learning at Winchester in the Eleventh Century: The Evidence of the Lambeth Psalter', *ASE*, 20 (1991), 143–166.
117 Psalm 134.11, in Cambridge, Trinity College, MS R.17.1, fol. 243r. Psalms 1–50 of the Eadwine Psalter are edited by Pulsiano in *Old English Glossed Psalters*, partially replacing the transcription of the complete Psalter by Fred Harsley, *Eadwine's Canterbury Psalter: Part 2, Text and Notes* (London: Trübner, 1889). I will quote from Pulsiano for Psalms 1–50, and Harsley for the remainder, supplemented with references to the manuscript where necessary.
118 O'Neill, 'English Version', p.132. On the construction of the Regius Psalter gloss, see Mechthild Gretsch, *Intellectual Foundations of the English Benedictine Reform*, *passim*, esp. pp.261–331.

119 For this now discredited view, see Karl Wildhagen, *Der Psalter des Eadwine von Canterbury: die Sprache der altenglischen Glosse: ein frühchristliches Psalterium die Grundlage* (Halle: Niemeyer, 1905), esp. §§115–23.

120 Paul Saenger, *Space between Words: The Origins of Silent Reading in the West* (Stanford, CA: Stanford University Press, 1997), p.41.

121 Eadwine Psalter, fol. 104r.

122 Lewis and Short, s.v. *galea* I, *maneo* Ia and b.1, *fero* I.

123 Eadwine Psalter, fol. 104v. Jerome, *Liber interpretationis Hebraicum nominum*, ed. by Paul de Lagarde, in *S. Hieronymi presbyteri Opera Pars I, Opera Exegetica 1, CCSL* 72 (Turnhout: Brepols, 1959), pp.57–161 (139).

124 *The Vespasian Psalter*, ed. by Sherman M. Kuhn (Ann Arbor: University of Michigan Press, 1965), pp.146–147.

125 They are the Vitellius Psalter (London, British Library MS Cotton Vitellius E.xviii), the Bosworth Psalter (London, British Library MS Additional 37517), the Salisbury Psalter (Salisbury Cathedral Library MS 150) and the Lambeth Psalter (London, Lambeth Palace Library MS 427).

126 *Eadwine Psalter*, fol. 281r.

127 However, the main gloss may have been planned in advance: there are potential transcription errors such as 'imog' for 'imong' and 'heodan' for 'heondan' (O'Neill, 'English Version', p.131).

128 Like OE4, he also made corrections to the gloss, although OE2's were more limited in their scope and tended to incline more to the modern than the old-fashioned: it is noticeable that he was responsible for the only other occurrence of 'heauod' rather than 'heafod', at Psalm 7.17.

129 Richard Jordan, *Handbuch der mittel-englischen Grammatik, Teil 1: Lautlehre*, rev. edn by H. C. Matthes (Heidelberg: Winter, 1934), §17, who, however, notes that *Beowulf* already contains *hliuade* ('it towered').

130 Markey, 'Anglo-Norman Version', in *Eadwine Psalter*, pp.146–147.

131 Ian Short, Maria Careri and Christine Ruby, 'Les Psautiers d'Oxford et de Saint Albans: liens de parenté', *Romania*, 128 (2010), 29–45. The St Albans Psalter also incorporates a pre-existing quire which contains a copy of an eleventh-century continental verse life of St Alexis, one of the first surviving works of Old French. Maria Careri, Christine Ruby and Ian Short, *Livres et écritures en français et en occitan au XIIe siècle* (Rome: Viella, 2011), cat. 60, 27/1. For a recent assessment of the date of the St Albans Psalter, see Kristen Collins, 'Pictures and the Devotional Imagination in the St Albans Psalter', in *The St Albans Psalter: Painting and Prayer in Medieval England*, by Kristen Collins, Peter Kidd, and Nancy K. Turner (Los Angeles: J. Paul Getty Trust, 2013), pp.9–63 (13).

132 T. A. Heslop, 'The Visual Sources of the Picture Leaves', in *Eadwine Psalter*, pp.29–34 (31). As one of the most popular French works of the twelfth century, the Douce 320 *Gallicanum* translation now survives in seven further manuscripts and fragments from the period: of these, three may originate from Christ Church, Canterbury. (See Careri et al., *Livres et écritures*, cat. 19, 31, 34, 36, 49, 76, 88.)

3 EXPLORATIONS AND APPROPRIATIONS OF BRITISH LINGUISTIC HISTORY

1 Geoffrey of Monmouth, *HRB*, pp.4–5. In this chapter, all further translations and page references for this text are taken from this edition.

2 Brooks and Kelly, *Charters of Christ Church, Canterbury, Part I*, pp.64–66.

3 *Anglo-Saxon Chronicle, MS F*, ed. Baker, p.1. The passage may reflect other attempts in late eleventh- and early-twelfth-century Canterbury to portray their archbishops as exercising authority over the whole of Britain (Brooks and Kelly, *Charters of Christ Church, Canterbury, Part I*, pp.64–66).

4 J. R. Davies, '*Liber Landavensis*: Its Date and the Identity of Its Editor', *Cambrian Medieval Celtic Studies*, 35 (1998), 1–11 (11).

5 The contents of the manuscript have been transcribed in *The Text of the Book of Llan Dav*, ed. by J. Gwenogvryn Evans, with John Rhys (Oxford, 1893).

6 Wendy Davies, *An Early Welsh Microcosm: Studies in the Llandaff Charters* (London: Royal Historical Society, 1978); *The Llandaff Charters* (Aberystwyth: National Library of Wales, 1979).

7 John Reuben Davies, *The Book of Llandaf and the Norman Church in Wales* (Woodbridge: Boydell, 2003), p.142.

8 Gwenogvryn Evans suggests that Caradoc may have been the author of parts of the *Historia* (*Text of the Book of Llan Dav*, pp.xviii–xxvii). This now seems unlikely. Michael J. Curley points out discrepancies between the portrayal of Dubricius as the first Bishop of Llandaff in the *Liber Landavensis* and the depiction of him as Bishop of Caerleon in Geoffrey's *Historia* (*Geoffrey of Monmouth* (New York: Twayne, 1994), p.6, based on the rebuttal of E. D. Jones, 'The Book of Llandaff', *National Library of Wales Journal*, 4 (1945–1946), 123–157 (154–155)).

9 His acquaintance with these languages was not very extensive, however: see *EH*, pp.18–19 and note 1, where Irish *dal*, 'meadow or valley', is confused with Old English *dæl*, 'part'.

10 Bede, *EH*, p.16.

11 *Felix's Life of Saint Guthlac*, ed. and trans. by Bertram Colgrave (Cambridge: Cambridge University Press, 1956), p.110 and note 16. Alaric Hall, 'Interlinguistic Communication in Bede's *Historia Ecclesiastica Gentis Anglorum*', in Hall et al., *Interfaces between Language and Culture in Medieval England*, pp.37–80 (65).

12 Gillingham, *English in the Twelfth Century*, pp.31–33, 27–29.

13 R. William Leckie Jr., *The Passage of Dominion: Geoffrey of Monmouth and the Periodization of Insular History in the Twelfth Century* (Toronto: University of Toronto Press, 1981), p.19.

14 Elizabeth Tyler, 'Trojans in Anglo-Saxon England: Precedent without Descent', *Review of English Studies*, n.s. 64 (2013), 1–20.

15 Geraldine Heng, *Empire of Magic: Medieval Romance and the Politics of Cultural Fantasy* (New York: Columbia University Press, 2003), p.3.

16 Geoffrey, *HRB*, e.g. pp.37 and 181. *GPC*, s.v. 'caer', 1a; 'pen', 1a.

17 Curley, *Geoffrey of Monmouth*, pp.11–12. See also the explanation given by Stefan Zimmer, who posits that the medieval etymologist began in Latin with 'Trojan Greek' (*troiana graeca*), and then connected *troiana* to Welsh *troi* ('twist/distort'). From this 'distorted Greek', he was hence able to derive Welsh (*Cymraeg*) from 'crooked Greek' (**camroeg*) ('A Medieval Linguist: Gerald de Barri', *Études celtiques*, 35 (2003), 313–349 (343–344)).

18 T. D. Crawford, 'On the Linguistic Competence of Geoffrey of Monmouth', *Medium Ævum*, 51 (1982), 152–162 (155–156).

19 Stuart Piggott, 'The Sources of Geoffrey of Monmouth: I. The "Pre-Roman" King List', *Antiquity*, 15 (1941), 269–286. See also Brynley F. Roberts, 'Geoffrey of Monmouth, *Historia Regum Britanniae* and *Brut y Brenhinedd*', in *The Arthur of the Welsh: The Arthurian Legend in Medieval Welsh Literature*, ed. by Rachel Bromwich et al. (Cardiff: University of Wales Press, 1991), pp. 97–116 (101).

20 Gaimar, *Estoire*, vv.6436–6482. Different arguments for the dating of the *Estoire* are discussed in Paul Dalton, 'The Date of Gaimar's *Estoire des Engleis*, the Connections of his Patrons, and the Politics of Stephen's Reign', *Chaucer Review*, 42.1 (2007), 23–47.

21 Ian Short, 'Gaimar's Epilogue and Geoffrey of Monmouth's Liber vetustissimus', *Speculum*, 69 (1994), 323–343 (341).

22 A useful survey of terminology is given in T. M. Charles-Edwards, *Wales and the Britons, 350–1064* (Oxford: Oxford University Press, 2013), pp.1–2.

23 J. S. P. Tatlock, *The Legendary History of Britain: Geoffrey of Monmouth's Historia Regum Britanniae and Its Early Vernacular Versions* (Berkeley: University of California Press, 1950), p.423. Piggott, 'Sources', p. 286. Huw Pryce, 'British or Welsh? National Identity in Twelfth-Century Wales', *English Historical Review*, 116 (2001), 775–801 (780–781).

24 See Crawford, 'Linguistic Competence', who points out that 'some of Geoffrey's Celtic is definitely Welsh and not Breton' (p.157).

25 Julia Crick, 'Monmouth, Geoffrey of (d.1154/5)', *ODNB*, www.oxforddnb .com/view/article/10530.

26 Curley, *Geoffrey*, p.12.

27 H. E. Salter, 'Geoffrey of Monmouth and Oxford', *English Historical Review*, 34 (1919), 382–385.

28 William of Newburgh, *The History of English Affairs*, Book I, ed. and trans. by P. G. Walsh and M. J. Kennedy (Warminster: Aris and Phillips, 1988), pp.28–29. All further page numbers given in this chapter refer to this edition.

29 Ernst Robert Curtius, *European Literature and the Latin Middle Ages*, trans. by Willard R. Trask (London: Routledge, 1953), pp.83–85.

30 Louis Faivre D'Arcier, *Histoire et géographie d'un mythe: la circulation des manuscrits du* De excidio Troiae *de Darès le Phrygien (VIIIe-XVe siècles)* (Paris: École des chartes, 2006), pp.151–153.

31 A full account of the text's medieval reception is given by Frederic N. Clark, 'Reading the "First Pagan Historiographer": Dares Phrygius and Medieval Genealogy', *Viator*, 41:2 (2010), 203–226.

32 Stefan Merkle, 'The Truth and Nothing but the Truth: Dictys and Dares', in *The Novel in the Ancient World*, ed. by Gareth Schmeling (Leiden: Brill, 1996), pp.563–580.

33 Dares Phrygius, *De excidio Troiae historia*, ed. by Ferdinand Meister (Leipzig: Teubner, 1873), p.1.

34 See the comments by Meister, Dares Phrygius, *De excidio*, pp.xvii–xviii.

35 Gildas, *Ruin of Britain*, 4.1.

36 Bede, *EH*, pp.50–51.

37 Henry of Huntingdon, *Historia Anglorum*, pp.4–5.

38 Gillingham, *English in the Twelfth Century*, p.30.

39 Kirsten A. Fenton notes that William's 'sense of Englishness' was constructed by 'bringing together ideas of Englishness and Normanness in relation to a perceived inferior "other"' (*Gender, Nation and Conquest in the Works of William of Malmesbury* (Woodbridge: Boydell, 2008), p.92).

40 Bede, *EH*, pp.220–221.

41 William of Malmesbury, *Gesta regum Anglorum*, I.70–3. Cf. his perceptions of English (discussed above, Chapter 1, note 10).

42 Isidore, I.xxix.2.

43 *GPC*, s.v. 'caer', 1a. A list of cities beginning with 'cair' is included in *Nennius: British History and Welsh Annals*, p.66a.

44 Crawford, 'Linguistic Competence', p.154. Crawford concludes that Geoffrey derived this name from the English himself rather than having knowledge of a now-lost Welsh name for the town.

45 On perceptions of French's derivation from Latin, see below.

46 Note Gerald of Wales's historical explanation for the similarities between Greek and Trojan, suggesting that he thought Geoffrey's portrayal of the links between the two languages required further explanation (discussed below).

47 Other examples of this trope are given by Wilhelm, 'Ueber fabulistiche Quellenangaben', pp.286–339.

48 Gerald of Wales solved the chronological discrepancies in Geoffrey's presentation of Merlin by stating that there were two Merlins: Merlin Ambrosius and Merlin Silvester (or Celeidon) (*Itinerarium Kambriae*, II.8). For discussion, see Ad Putter, 'Gerald of Wales and the Prophet Merlin', *ANS*, 31 (2008), 90–103 (92–93).

49 *Ecclesiastical History of Orderic Vitalis*, VI.380–88, p.xviii.

50 David M. Smith, 'Alexander (*d.* 1148)', *ODNB*, www.oxforddnb.com/view/article/324.

51 Michael J. Curley, 'Animal Symbolism in the *Prophecies of Merlin*', in *Beasts and Birds of the Middle Ages: The Bestiary and Its Legacy*, ed. by Willene B. Clark and Meradith T. McMunn (Philadelphia: University of Pennsylvania Press, 1989), pp.151–163 (154–156).

52 A. O. H. Jarman, 'The Merlin Legend and the Welsh Tradition of Prophecy', in Bromwich et al., *The Arthur of the Welsh*, pp.117–145, esp.132–136.

53 Geoffrey of Monmouth, *Life of Merlin: Vita Merlini*, ed. and trans. by Basil Clarke (Cardiff: University of Wales Press, 1973), v.1

54 See Julia Crick, *The* Historia regum Britannie *of Geoffrey of Monmouth, III: A Summary Catalogue of the Manuscripts* (Cambridge: Brewer, 1989), and further, Geoffrey, *HRB*, p.vii n.5, Jaakko Tahkokallio, 'An Update to the List of Manuscripts of Geoffrey of Monmouth's *Historia regum Britanniae*', *Arthurian Literature*, 32 (2015), 187–203; Caroline D. Eckhardt, 'The *Prophetia Merlini* of Geoffrey of Monmouth: Latin Manuscript Copies', *Manuscripta*, 26 (1982), 167–176.

55 *Oeuvres complètes de Suger*, ed. by A. Lecoy de la Marche (Paris: Renouard, 1867), p.54. *Materials for the history of Thomas Becket, Archbishop of Canterbury, Volume V*, ed. by James Craigie Robertson, *RS* 67.5 (London: H.M. Stationery Office, 1881), pp.291–292. *The Letters of John of Salisbury, Volume Two: The Later Letters (1163–1180)*, ed. by W. J. Millor and C. N. L. Brooke (Oxford: Clarendon, 1979), pp.668–669, 134–136.

56 *Wace's Roman de Brut*, vv.7535–7542.

57 For this view, see Jean Blacker, '"Ne vuil sun livre translater": Wace's Omission of Merlin's Prophecies from the *Roman de Brut*', in *Anglo-Norman Anniversary Essays*, ed. by Ian Short (London: Anglo-Norman Text Society, 1993), pp.49–59.

58 *Ecclesiastical History of Orderic Vitalis*, VI.388–389.

59 Alan Cooper, '"The Feet of Those That Bark Shall Be Cut Off": Timorous Historians and the Personality of Henry I', *ANS*, 23 (2000), 47–67 (56).

60 William of Newburgh, *History*, I.28–30. *DMLBS*, s.v. 'nenia', 'naenia', 2, 3: the sense of the word also encompasses 'untruthful account' (4) and 'trifle' (5).

61 Gildas, *Ruin of Britain*, 21.3.

62 Julia Crick provides an overview of their reception in 'Geoffrey and the Prophetic Tradition', in *The Arthur of Medieval Latin Literature: The Development and Dissemination of the Arthurian Legend in Medieval Latin*, ed. by Siân Echard (Cardiff: University of Wales Press, 2011), pp.67–82. Opinion is divided over whether the marginal and interlinear commentaries found in London, British Library MS Cotton Claudius B.vii and Paris, Bibliothèque Nationale, MS fonds lat. 6233 represent two different works, or are part of the same work; the marginal commentary is additionally represented in Paris, Bibl. Nat. MS fonds lat. 4126. For bibliography, see Jean Blacker, 'Where Wace Feared to Tread: Latin Commentaries on Merlin's Prophecies in the Reign of Henry II', *Arthuriana*, 6:1 (1996), 36–52 (46–47 n6).

63 *Ecclesiastical History of Orderic Vitalis*, VI.384–385.

64 Lesley A. Coote, *Prophecy and Public Affairs in Later Medieval England* (York: York Medieval Press, 2000), p.36.

65 *Ecclesiastical History of Orderic Vitalis*, VI.386–387.

66 Julia Crick, 'Geoffrey of Monmouth, Prophecy and History', *Journal of Medieval History*, 18 (1992), 357–371 (368–370).

67 Alanus, *Prophetia anglicana Merlini Ambrosii Britanni* (Frankfurt: Brathering, 1603), p.2.

68 Lewis and Short, s.v. 'peregrinus'.

69 Rita Copeland, *Rhetoric, Hermeneutics and Translation in the Middle Ages* (Cambridge: Cambridge University Press, 1991), p.83.

70 Christopher Baswell, *Virgil in Medieval England: Figuring the* Aeneid *from the Twelfth Century to Chaucer* (Cambridge: Cambridge University Press, 1995), pp.63–68.

71 Anna A. Grotans, *Reading in Medieval St Gall* (Cambridge: Cambridge University Press, 2006), p.101: 'It is clear that the Old High German translation was not just a mere lexical gloss to be referred to in extremely difficult passages, but that it played an integral part of the *lectio* process, which was usually reserved for Latin. In this case the Old High German is placed on an equal level with the Latin and becomes the object of the rhetorical commentary usually reserved for the Latin'.

72 Bede, *EH*, p.416. *Byrhtferth's Enchiridion*, ed. Baker and Lapidge.

73 Michael J. Curley, 'A New Edition of John of Cornwall's *Prophetia Merlini*', *Speculum* 57:2 (1982), 217–249 (240 n2). There are other candidates: Warelwast's short-lived successor was another 'R.', the unpopular Robert of Chichester (1155–1160/1). He was a man with Welsh connections, addressed as kinsman by David fitzGerald, Bishop of St David's and uncle of Gerald of Wales, although they are likely to have been related through the Norman side of the family (Frank Barlow, 'Chichester, Robert of (*d.* 1160?)', *ODNB*, www.oxforddnb.com/view/article/5279). Julia Crick has even suggested that the dedicatee may be the following bishop, Bartholomew (d.1184), a member of the circle of John of Salisbury ('Prophecy and History', 366).

74 Curley, 'John of Cornwall', 222–223. This may potentially make John the earliest surviving commentator on Merlin's prophecies, although there is also an anonymous interlinear commentary which Caroline D. Eckhart dates from 1147 (or 1149) to 1154 ('The Date of the "Prophetia Merlini" Commentary in MSS. Cotton Claudius B VII and Bibliothèque Nationale fonds latin 6233', *Notes and Queries*, n.s.23 (1976), 146–147).

75 Curley, 'John of Cornwall', 229.

76 Teresa Webber has kindly confirmed this point for me in a private communication.

77 For speculation concerning the content of some of these legends, see O. J. Padel, 'Evidence for Oral Tales in Medieval Cornwall', *Studia Celtica*, 40 (2006), 127–153.

78 O. J. Padel, 'Geoffrey of Monmouth and Cornwall', *Cambridge Medieval Celtic Studies*, 8 (1984), 1–28 (8–9).

79 Hermann of Laon, *De miracula S. Mariae Laudunensis: De gestis venerabilis Bartholomaei Episcopi et S. Nortberti*, *PL* 156, cols 961–1017 (983).

80 On the dating of the work, see J. S. P. Tatlock, 'The English Journey of the Laon Canons', *Speculum*, 8 (1933), 454–465. William of Malmesbury, *Gesta regum Anglorum*, I.520: 'Sed Arturis sepulchrum nusquam uisitur, unde antiquitas neniarum adhuc eum uenturum fabulatur'.

81 Johannes de Hauvilla, *Architrenius*, ed. by Winthrop Wetherbee (Cambridge: Cambridge University Press, 1994), pp.10–11. Gerald of Wales, *Vita S. Remigii*,

ed. by James F. Dimock, in *Opera*, ed. Brewer, VII.1–80 (38): 'Walterus, de Constanciis dictus sed revera de Corinei domo Cornubiaque natus, et nobili Britonum gente de Trojana stirpe originaliter propagatus'.

82 Eleanor Rathbone, 'John of Cornwall: A Brief Biography', *Recherches de théologie ancienne et médiévale*, 17 (1950), 46–60.

83 C. F. R. de Hamel, *Glossed Books of the Bible and the Origins of the Paris Booktrade* (Cambridge: Brewer, 1984), p.15.

84 E. K. Chambers, *Arthur of Britain* (London: Sidgwick and Jackson, 1927), p.29. Curley, 'John of Cornwall', 224–225.

85 Curley, 'John of Cornwall', vv.215–216 (discussed further below). All line references in the text are taken from this edition.

86 Padel, 'Evidence for Oral Tales', p.149. Michael A. Faletra has recently argued that John was primarily 'drawing from, if not directly translating, an Old Cornish original that most likely dates from the early twelfth century' ('Merlin in Cornwall: The Source and Contexts of John of Cornwall's *Prophetia Merlini*', *Journal of English and Germanic Philology*, 111 (2012), 304–338 (306)). Whilst the text is certainly informed by earlier Cornish traditions and perhaps writings, the confused copying of the Brittonic glosses and the mix of Welsh, Cornish, and Galfridian materials does not permit us to make firm conclusions about John's main source.

87 Frank Barlow (ed.), *English Episcopal Acta XI: Exeter, 1046–1184* (Oxford: Oxford University Press, 1996), p.xxix.

88 On Welsh interest in links with other Brittonic territories as an explanation for the lukewarm reception of the Trojan origin legend in Wales, see Pryce, 'British or Welsh?', 789.

89 Michael Curley, 'Gerallt Gymro a Siôn o Gernyw fel Cyfieithwyr Proffwydoliaethau Myrddin', *Llên Cymru*, 15 (1984), 23–33 (28).

90 All translations of the Brittonic glosses are based on the relevant notes in Curley (ed.), 'John of Cornwall' and L. Fleuriot, 'Les fragments du texte brittonique de la "Prophetia Merlini"', *Études celtiques*, 14 (1974), 43–56. Cf. Faletra, 'Merlin in Cornwall', 315–324.

91 Discussed in Curley, 'John of Cornwall', pp.230–231.

92 Fleuriot, 'Fragments', pp.49–50; cf. Curley, 'John of Cornwall', pp.230–231.

93 Michael Curley speculates that 'mal igasuet' may originally have been a form of the Welsh 'mabwysiadu', 'adopting', although he finds no attested instances of this word as early as the twelfth century (Curley, 'John of Cornwall', 230–231).

94 Gerald of Wales, *De invectionibus*, 189.

95 Gerald of Wales, *Gemma Ecclesiastica*, ed. by J. S. Brewer, in *Opera*, II.343.

96 Similarly, Alderik H. Blom has recently posited that the glossator(s) of the mid-twelfth-century *Vocabularium Cornicum* perceived Cornish and Welsh as 'varieties of essentially the same language' ('Multilingualism and the *Vocabularium Cornicum*', in *Multilingualism in Medieval Britain (c.1066–1520): Sources and Analysis*, ed. by Judith A. Jefferson et al. (Turnhout: Brepols, 2013), pp.59–71 (68)).

97 The glosses exhibit final -*nt* (*guent*), as well as its later development, -*ns* (*ugens*). This may indicate that one of John's sources was composed in a language that pre-dated this sound change in the second half of the eleventh century, or that both -*nt* and -*ns* were still in current use at the time he wrote (Fleuriot, 'Fragments', 48, 45–46; Faletra, 'Merlin in Cornwall', 316–317. Jackson, *Language and History in Early Britain*, §110).

98 Gerald of Wales, *Descriptio*, I.6.

99 Fleuriot, 'Fragments', 51–52.

100 Padel, 'Geoffrey of Monmouth and Cornwall', 20–27.

101 Cf. Geoffrey, *HRB*, p.28.

102 Gerald of Wales, *Expugnatio Hibernica: The Conquest of Ireland*, ed. and trans. by A. B. Scott and F. X. Martin (Dublin: Royal Irish Academy, 1978), pp.256–257.

103 Ibid.

104 Blacker, 'Where Wace Feared to Tread', p.43.

105 Gerald of Wales, *Expugnatio*, pp.256–257.

106 Crick, 'British Past and the Welsh Future', 71–74.

107 Putter, 'Gerald of Wales and Merlin', pp.98–101.

108 *Rhetorica ad Herennium*, trans. by Harry Caplan (London: Heinemann, 1954), 4.20.28; *Rhetorica ad Herennium*, 4.23.32 (I have slightly modified Caplan's translation). Potentially, John also may have known the satirist Lucilius's attack on *homoeoteleuta* as 'silly, useless and puerile' ('insubida et inertia et puerilia') (*The Attic Nights of Aulus Gellius*, trans. by John C. Rolfe (Cambridge, MA: Harvard University Press, 1927, repr. 1961–1968), 18.8.1. A summary of Gellius's circulation in the Middle Ages is given in P. K. Marshall, 'Aulus Gellius', in Reynolds, *Texts and Transmission*, pp.176–180).

109 Gerald of Wales, *Expugnatio*, pp.256–257.

110 Heng, *Empire of Magic*, p.3.

111 See Zimmer, 'Gerald de Barri'.

112 E.g. Gerald, *Itinerarium* I.4, I.7, I.11.

113 E.g. Gerald, *De rebus a se gestis*, ed. by J. S. Brewer, in *Giraldi Cambrensis Opera*, I.1–122 (21).

114 Gerald's two accounts of this are collected and translated in Gerald, *Journey*, pp.280–288 (taken from his *De principis instructione*, I.20 and *Speculum Ecclesiae*, II.8–10).

115 Gerald, *Itinerarium*, I.5.

116 In the *Itinerarium*, notable instances include Gerald's etymology of Arthur's chair (I.2); his description of Caerleon (I.5); his etymology of Carmarthen as 'urbs Merlini' ('town of Merlin', I.10); and his depiction of St David's as heir to the metropolitan see of Caerleon (II. preface and 1).

117 Assessed in Yoko Wada, 'Gerald on Gerald: Self-Presentation by Giraldus Cambrensis', *ANS*, 20 (1997), 223–246 (237–241), and Zimmer, 'Gerald de Barri', pp.347–348. Ben Guy demonstrates that Gerald consulted vernacular Welsh genealogies ('Gerald and Welsh Genealogical Learning', in *Gerald of Wales*, ed. by Georgia Henley and A. Joseph McMullen (Cardiff: University of Wales Press, forthcoming)).

118 Gerald, *Descriptio*, II.10.
119 Gerald, *Itinerarium*, I.8.
120 Ibid.
121 On the dating of the *Descriptio*, see Thorpe, *Journey through Wales and Description of Wales*, pp.49–50.
122 Gerald of Wales, *Descriptio*, I.7.
123 Ibid.
124 *OED*, s.v. 'Welsh'.
125 This is in fact a Dutch word, probably picked up from the Flemish colony in South Wales in the early twelfth century, who included Gerald's uncle by marriage (Zimmer, 'Gerald de Barri', p.341). (Cf. the *Encomium Emmae Reginae*, ed. by Alistair Campbell with Simon Keynes (Cambridge: Cambridge University Press, 1998), datable to 1041/2; here, *theutonice* seems to refer to Norse as Germanic (II,18.9).)
126 Gerald of Wales, *Itinerarium*, I.8.
127 Zimmer, 'Gerald de Barri', p.341, notes that 'the Greek word for salt is quoted without the nominative ending'; 'Welsh *halein*, standing for *halen* [...] means "salt, saltwater" (salt as substance or spice is *hallt*)'; and that 'the Irish word given is purely fictitious'. On this passage, see also Cornelia C. Coulter and F.P. Magoun, Jr., 'Giraldus Cambrensis on Indo-Germanic Philology', *Speculum*, 1 (1926), 104–109; Putter, 'Multilingualism in England and Wales', pp.104–105.
128 Gerald of Wales, *Descriptio*, I.15.
129 Crick, 'British Past', p.75.

4 THE VERNACULARS OF ANCESTRAL LAW

1 Richard fitz Nigel, *Dialogus de scaccario*, ed. and trans. by Emilie Amt, with the *Constitutio domis regis*, ed. and trans. by S. D. Church (Oxford: Clarendon, 2007), p.xx. All subsequent page numbers given in the text refer to this edition; its translations have occasionally been adapted slightly.
2 Dudo of Saint-Quentin, *De moribus et actis primorum Normanniae ducum*, p.221. Bruce O'Brien, *Reversing Babel: Translation among the English during an Age of Conquests, c.800 to c.1200* (Newark: University of Delaware Press, 2011), p.215. David Bates assesses Dudo's portrayal of Norse, arguing that it is somewhat understated: he points out that a Norwegian skald was still welcome in Rouen in c.1025 (*Normandy before 1066* (London: Longman, 1982), pp.20–21).
3 The earliest surviving Old Norse manuscript sources date from the twelfth century, although they may be modelled on eleventh-century precedents: none originates from England or Normandy. (Guðvarður Már Gunnlaugsson, 'Manuscripts and Palaeography', in *A Companion to Old Norse–Icelandic Literature and Culture*, ed. by Rory McTurk (Oxford: Blackwell, 2005), pp.245–264 (249, 246).) Very little was written in Romance orthography before the late eleventh century: see the four works collected in Ayres-Bennett, *History of the French Language through Texts*, pp.15–57.

4 Frederick Pollock and Frederic William Maitland, *The History of English Law before the Time of Edward I*, 2nd edn, with S. F. C. Milsom, 2 vols (Cambridge: Cambridge University Press, 1968; first published 1895), I.136–138.

5 E.g. Wormald, *Making of English Law*, pp.142, 474.

6 For an edition and vocabulary study, see Yorio Otaka, 'Sur la langue des *Leis Willelme*', in *Anglo-Norman Anniversary Essays*, ed. by Ian Short (London: Anglo-Norman Text Society, 1993), pp.293–308; a new edition of both French redactions and the later Latin translation of the text is soon to appear as part of the *Early English Laws Online* project by Paul Brand, Ian Short, Bruce O'Brien, and Yorio Otaka, www.earlyenglishlaws.ac.uk/laws/texts/leis-wl1.

7 Webber, *Evolution of Norman Identity*, pp.172–174, 177–179.

8 Gillingham, *The English in the Twelfth Century*, p.140; Thomas, *English and the Normans*, p.42.

9 Thomas, *English and the Normans*, p.41.

10 See further Leah Shopkow, *History and Community: Norman Historical Writing in the Eleventh and Twelfth Centuries* (Washington, DC: Catholic University of America Press, 1997), and Emily Albu, *The Normans in Their Histories: Propaganda, Myth, and Subversion* (Woodbridge: Boydell, 2001).

11 Albu, *Normans in Their Histories*, p.221.

12 E.g. Ian Short, '*Tam Angli quam Franci*: Self-Definition in Anglo-Norman England', *ANS*, 18 (1995), 153–175 (172–173).

13 Bruce O'Brien, *God's Peace and King's Peace: The Laws of Edward the Confessor* (Philadelphia: University of Pennsylvania Press, 1999), pp.19–21.

14 The earliest is the code of Æthelberht of Kent (d.616?): see Wormald, *Making of English Law*, pp.93–101.

15 Thomas, *English and the Normans*, p.278.

16 Williams, *The English and the Norman Conquest*, p.162.

17 Even William's ostensible commitment to maintaining tenurial rights as they were on the day that Edward the Confessor died led to radical changes in post-Conquest law: see George Garnett, *Conquered England*, pp.31–32.

18 Thomas, *English and the Normans*, p.278.

19 O'Brien, *God's Peace*, p.45–46, 158–159.

20 *Ecclesiastical History of Orderic Vitalis*, II.256.

21 O'Brien, *God's Peace*, p.137; Wormald, *Making of English Law*, p.409.

22 O'Brien, *God's Peace*, pp.29–30. Felix Liebermann suggests one or two possible resemblances to writs of William the Conqueror and the source material of Chapter 17 of the *Leis Willelme*, another text which attempts to record the laws of Edward as enforced by William; the author also seems to have had access to a work of continental law, from which the depiction of the opening council is borrowed (Felix Liebermann, *Die Gesetze der Angelsachsen*, 3 vols (Halle: Niemeyer, 1903–1916), I:629 n.b; I.634 n.a. For bibliography on the *Leis Willelme*, see Wormald, *Making of English Law*, pp.407–409. On possible continental sources, see O'Brien, *God's Peace*, pp.32–33.)

23 Wormald, *Making of English Law*, p.410.

24 See e.g. O'Brien, *God's Peace*, 'toll' ('tax', pp.180–181); 'team' (right to the fines arising from warranty procedure in sales, pp.180–181); 'emcristen' ('brother', pp.198–199); 'flesmangres' ('butchers', pp.200–203). Note also the two English proverbs included at pp.170, 182.

25 Ibid., pp.188–189.

26 Ibid., pp.190–191.

27 Ibid.; cf. Bosworth and Toller, s.v. Old English *māra*, 'more', and Toronto A-G, s.v. *ealdordōm*, I, 'authority'.

28 This might be contrasted with Henry of Huntingdon's view of post-Conquest reeves: 'more frightful than thieves and robbers, and more savage than the most savage' ('furibus et raptoribus atrociores erant, et omnibus seuissimis seuiores', Greenway, *Historia Anglorum*, pp.402–403).

29 See the two words labelled as Norse in the *Institutes of Cnut* (*Instituta Cnuti*, ed. Liebermann, *Gesetze der Angelsachsen*, I.278–372: II, 37; II, 46), and the three words labelled as Norse in a perhaps late-twelfth-century treatise which purports to record the forest law of Cnut (*Constitutiones de foresta*, ed. by Felix Liebermann, *Gesetze*, I.620–626: 2, 3.1, 14, 21). Discussed in Harris, '*Tam Anglis quam Danis*', 131–148.

30 Judith A. Green, *Henry I: King of England and Duke of Normandy* (Cambridge: Cambridge University Press, 2006), p.116.

31 See Patrick Wormald, 'Quadripartitus', in *Law and Government in Medieval England and Normandy: Essays in Honour of Sir James Holt*, ed. by George Garnett and John Hudson (Cambridge: Cambridge University Press, 1994), pp.111–147. For further discussion of the internal organisation of the *Leges Henrici*, see Nicholas Karn, 'Rethinking the *Leges Henrici Primi*', in *English Law before Magna Carta: Felix Liebermann and* Die Gesetze der Angelsachsen, ed. by Stefan Jurasinski et al. (Leiden: Brill, 2010), pp.199–220.

32 On the author's Anglo-Saxon sources, see the *Leges Henrici Primi*, ed. and trans. by L. J. Downer (Oxford: Clarendon, 1972), pp.28–30.

33 See Patrick Wormald, '*Laga Eadwardi:* The *Textus Roffensis* and Its Context', *ANS*, 17 (1994), 243–266.

34 Mary P. Richards, *Texts and Their Traditions in the Medieval Library of Rochester Cathedral Priory* (Philadelphia: American Philosophical Society, 1988), p.45.

35 Although providing influential guidance, precedent was not legally binding at this date: see further Anthony Musson, *Medieval Law in Context: The Growth of Legal Consciousness from Magna Carta to the Peasants' Revolt* (Manchester: Manchester University Press, 2001), pp.42–44.

36 O'Brien, *God's Peace*, p.114.

37 For the changing meanings of *seisin* over the twelfth century, see Hudson, *Oxford History*, pp.337, 670–676. Paul Brand, '"Time out of Mind": The Knowledge and Use of the Eleventh- and Twelfth-Century Past in Thirteenth-Century Litigation', *ANS*, 16 (1993), 37–54 (37).

38 Hall, *The Treatise on the Laws and Customs of the Realm of England Commonly Called Glanvill*, p.xxxi. For an assessment of the potential authors of the text,

see R. V. Turner, 'Who Was the Author of *Glanvill*? Reflections on the Education of Henry II's Common Lawyers', *Law and History Review*, 8 (1990), 97–127.

39 See John Hudson, 'From the *Leges* to *Glanvill*: Legal Expertise and Legal Reasoning', in Jurasinski et al., *English Law before Magna Carta*, pp.221–249.

40 *Glanvill*, p.2.

41 Ibid., p.3.

42 R. C. van Caenegem, *The Birth of the English Common Law*, 2nd edn (Cambridge: Cambridge University Press, 1988), pp.2–3.

43 O'Brien, *God's Peace*, pp.116–117.

44 Frank Barlow, *Thomas Becket* (London: Weidenfeld and Nicholson, 1986), p.94.

45 *Councils and Synods with Other Documents Relating to the English Church, I, A.D. 871–1204: Pt. II, 1066–1204*, ed. by D. Whitelock, M. Brett and C. N. L. Brooke (Oxford: Clarendon, 1981), no.159, p.878.

46 Whitelock et al., *Councils and Synods*, pp.870–871 (870).

47 Barlow, *Thomas Becket*, p.94.

48 Anne J. Duggan, 'Henry II, the English Church and the Papacy, 1154–76', in *Henry II: New Interpretations*, ed. by Christopher Harper-Bill and Nicholas Vincent (Woodbridge: Boydell, 2007), pp.154–183 (183).

49 *Glanvill*, p.2.

50 On the dating of these works, see Elisabeth van Houts, 'Hereward and Flanders', *ASE*, 28 (1999), 201–223 (202); *History of William Marshal*, ed. A. J. Holden, with S. Gregory and D. Crouch, 3 vols (London: Anglo-Norman Text Society, 2002–2006), III.25; Judith Weiss, 'Thomas and the Earl: Literary and Historical Contexts for the *Romance of Horn*', in *Tradition and Transformation in Medieval Romance*, ed. by Rosalind Field (Cambridge: Brewer, 1999), pp.1–14.

51 Godfried Croenen, 'Princely and Noble Genealogies, Twelfth to Fourteenth Century: Form and Function', in *The Medieval Chronicle*, ed. by Erik Kooper (Amsterdam: Rodopi, 1999), pp.84–95 (84–85). Adrian Ailes, 'The Knight, Heraldry and Armour: The Role of Recognition and the Origins of Heraldry', in *Medieval Knighthood IV: Papers from the fifth Strawberry Hill Conference, 1990*, ed. by Christopher Harper-Bill and Ruth Harvey (Woodbridge: Boydell, 1992), pp.1–21 (10). Maurice Keen, *Chivalry* (New Haven, CT: Yale University Press, 1984), p.126–127.

52 See e.g. R. I. Moore, *The First European Revolution, c.970–1215* (Oxford: Blackwell, 2000), p.144; W. L. Warren, *Henry II* (London: Methuen, 1973), p.267.

53 John Hudson, 'Administration, Family and Perceptions of the Past in Late Twelfth-Century England: Richard FitzNigel and the Dialogue of the Exchequer', in *The Perception of the Past in Twelfth-Century Europe*, ed. by Paul Magdalino (London: Hambledon Press, 1992), pp.75–98.

54 Amt, Richard fitz Nigel, *Dialogus*, pp.xviii–xx.

55 *The Red Book of the Exchequer*, ed. by Hubert Hall, *RS* 99 (London: H.M. Stationery Office, 1896), I.4.

56 Amt, Richard fitz Nigel, *Dialogus*, pp.xv–xvi.
57 John Hudson, 'Richard fitz Nigel (*c.*1130–1198)', *ODNB*, www.oxforddnb .com/view/article/9619.
58 Robert of Torigni claimed that Sigebert of Gembloux (d.1112) compiled an eight-column history (*Chronique de Robert de Torigni*, ed. by Léopold Delisle, 2 vols (Rouen: Le Brument, 1872–1873), I.94, cited in Hudson, 'Administration, Family and Perceptions of the Past', 80).
59 *Glanvill*, p.3.
60 S. D. Church, in Richard fitzNigel, *Dialogus de scaccario: The Dialogue of the Exchequer*, ed. and trans. by Emilie Amt, with the *Constitutio domus regis*, ed. and trans. by S. D. Church (Oxford: Clarendon, 2007), p.lxvi.
61 Church, in Richard fitzNigel, *Dialogus de scaccario* with the *Constitutio domus regis*, pp.lix–lxv (manuscripts), xxxviii–xxxix (date), lxvi (language).
62 Stephen Baxter, 'The Making of the Domesday Book and the Languages of Lordship in Conquered England', in *Conceptualizing Multilingualism in Medieval England, c. 800–c.1250*, ed. by Elizabeth M. Tyler (Turnhout: Brepols, 2011), pp.271–308 (306–307). Baxter explains that 'lords with soke rights were entitled to collect certain customary renders and dues and any judicial fines incurred in public courts from those who owed them soke' (p.306).
63 See e.g. *Quadripartitus*, Cnut II.37, in Liebermann, *Gesetze der Angelsachsen*, 3 vols, I.339. On *healsfang*, see Hudson, *Oxford History*, p.179.
64 *Consiliatio Cnuti*, II.37, in Liebermann, *Gesetze*, I.339. These translation strategies (amongst others) are discussed more fully in Bruce O'Brien, 'Translating Technical Terms in Law-Codes from Alfred to the Angevins', in Tyler, *Conceptualizing Multilingualism*, pp.57–76.
65 Paul Hyams, 'The Common Law and the French Connection', *ANS*, 4 (1981), 77–92 (92).
66 For further discussion, see A. C. Dyson, 'The Career, Family and Influence of Alexander le Poer, Bishop of Lincoln, 1123–1148' (unpublished BLitt thesis, University of Oxford, 1972), pp.19–21.
67 Laura Wright, *Sources of London English: Medieval Thames Vocabulary* (Oxford: Clarendon, 1996), p.12.
68 The relevant manuscripts are London, the National Archives, PRO E164/2 (Red Book of the Exchequer); London, the National Archives, PRO E36/266 (Black Book of the Exchequer); London, British Library, MS Cotton Cleopatra, A.xvi; London, British Library, Hargrave 313. See further Amt, *Dialogus*, pp.xxvii–xxx.
69 The 1902 edition of the *Dialogus* notes that some of these may have been culled from a *florilegium* (Arthur Hughes, C. G. Crump and C. Johnson (eds), Richard fitzNigel, *De necessariis observantiis scaccarii dialogus, Commonly called Dialogus de scaccario* (Oxford: Clarendon, 1902), pp.10–11). Richard may have also read literature in Anglo-Norman: his description of Viking raids is potentially indebted to Gaimar's *Estoire des Engleis* (p.84).
70 Curtius, *European Literature and the Latin Middle Ages*, pp.83–85.
71 Lewis and Short, s.v. 'agrestis', I and II; s.v. 'rusticanus'.

72 See the entries for all these words in the *DMLBS*.

73 *DMLBS*, s.v. *censēre*, 5a.

74 Blanching a farm refers to a specific exchequer procedure where a set weight of the coin collected as tax revenue would be melted down to remove its impurities and weighed again to find out how much silver was proportionally lacking from the overall payment. Amt, Richard fitz Nigel, *Dialogus*, p.xxv.

75 *DMLBS*, s.v. *dealbare*, 2b; *blancus*.

76 *DMLBS*, s.v. *essaium*. This also describes the procedure where the purity of the sheriff's silver was tested at the exchequer (see note 78).

77 See the entries for all these words in the *DMLBS*.

78 In part I of the *Dialogus* alone, examples include: 'scaccarium' ('exchequer', p.8); 'recepta' ('receipt', p.10); 'miles argentarius' ('knight silverer', p.12); 'camerarius' ('chamberlain', p.12); 'constabularius' ('constable', p.24); 'talea' ('tally, p.34); 'memoranda' ('memoranda tally', p.34); 'libra' ('pound', p.34); 'firma' ('farm', p.46); 'census' ('cess', p.46); 'summonitiones' ('summonses', p.50); 'essaium' ('assayed', p.56); 'esnecca' ('the ship 'Snake', p.60); 'communes assise' ('common assizes', p.72); 'deambulatorios uel perlustrantes iudices' ('itinerant or travelling justices', p.72); 'scutagium' ('scutage', p.78); 'murdrum' ('murder', p.80); 'uillani' ('villains', p.80); 'danegeldum' ('Danegeld', p.84); 'dominia' ('demesnes', p.86); 'foresta' ('forest', p.92); 'uastum' ('waste', p.92); 'thesaurus' ('treasure, treasury', p.94); 'rotulus exactorius' ('roll of exactions', p.94); 'breue de firmis' ('writ of farms', p.94); 'Domesdei' ('Domesday', p.96); 'librum iudiciarium' ('Domesday Book', p.98); 'centuriata' ('century', p.98); 'comitatus' ('county', p.98); 'comes' ('earl, count', p.98); 'uicecomes' ('sheriff', p.98).

79 They are 'essaium' ('assay', p.16); 'marescallus' ('marshal', p.24); 'contrabreue' ('counter-writ', p.48); 'perdonata' ('pardons', p.74); 'reguarda' ('regard', p.88); 'essarta' ('assart', p.92); 'ligius' ('liege-lord', p.124); 'proprestura' ('purpresture', p.138–40); 'escaeta' ('esceat', p.138, 140); 'utlagatus' ('outlaw', p.152); 'senescallus' ('seneschal', p.174); 'releuium' ('relief fine', p.180).

80 Isidore, I.xxix.2.

81 See Mary Carruthers, 'Inventional Mnemonics and the Ornaments of Style: The Case of Etymology', *Connotations*, 2 (1992), 103–14.

82 John of Salisbury, *Metalogicon*, ed. by J.B. Hall with K.S.B. Keats-Rohan, *CCCM* 98 (Turnhout: Brepols, 1991), I.14.5–7; *The Metalogicon: A Twelfth-Century Defense of the Verbal and Logical Arts of the Trivium*, trans. by Daniel D. McGarry (Berkeley: University of California Press, 1955), p.39.

83 On the possible administrative meanings of 'waste' as 'land unable to produce its accustomed revenue', see Emilie Amt, *The Accession of Henry II in England: Royal Government Restored, 1149–1159* (Woodbridge: Boydell, 1993), pp.133–141.

84 This is unlikely to be a correct etymology: 'forest' is usually derived from Latin 'foris', 'outside', although other possibilities have been suggested. See further Charles Higounet, 'Les forêts de l'Europe occidentale du Ve au XIe siècle', in *Paysages et villages neufs du Moyen Âge* (Bordeaux: Fédération historique

du Sud-Ouest, 1975, repr. from *Settimane di studio del Centro italiano di studi sull'alto medioevo*. XIII, (1966), 343–98), p.51.

85 Both 'uastum' and 'foresta' fit into the grammatical category of barbarism and its poetic equivalent, metaplasm. Barbarisms are defined by Donatus as a 'faulty' or 'defective' aspect of speech ('una pars orationis uitiosa') which can be formed in four ways: by adding an extra letter or letters to a word (*adiectio*), by taking one away (*detractio*), by changing one letter for another (*inmutatio*), or by changing the order of the letters (*transmutatio*). Donatus lists 'syncope', 'the removal of something from the middle of a word' ('ablatio de media dictione') as one of the ways of producing a metaplasm. (Holtz, *Donat et la tradition de l'enseignement grammatical*, pp.653, 661.)

86 Serge Lusignan, *Parler vulgairement: les intellectuels et la langue française aux XIIIe et XIVe siècles* (Paris: Vrin, 1986), pp.23–24, and note the late-twelfth-century comments of Gerald of Wales, discussed below.

87 E.g. Alcuin's shock at finding that at the abbey of Centula (Saint-Riquier), around 800, the monks saw nothing wrong in their preference for reading aloud from texts written in 'simple and less polished diction' ('simplex et minus polita locutio') than from texts closer to classical Latin (*Vita Richarii confessoris Centulensis*, ed. by B. Krusch, in *Passiones vitaeque sanctorum aevi Merovingici, Monumenta Germaniae Historica, Scriptores rerum Merovingicarum*, 5 vols (Hanover: Hahn, 1902), IV.381–401 (389)). The chronology of the transition from Latin to Romance remains disputed: for bibliography, see Adam Ledgeway, *From Latin to Romance: Morphosyntactic Typology and Change* (Oxford: Oxford University Press, 2012), and Roger Wright, *A Sociophilological Study of Late Latin* (Turnhout: Brepols, 2002).

88 Dudo of Saint-Quentin, *De moribus et actis primorum Normanniae ducum*, p.221; *History of the Normans*, p.97.

89 The earliest surviving text written in the vernacular is the Strasbourg Oaths of 842, but 'very few French vernacular texts for the period up to about AD 1100 are extant' (Ayres-Bennett, *History of the French Language through Texts*, p.15).

90 *The First French Version of Marbode's Lapidary*, in *Anglo-Norman Lapidaries*, ed. by Paul Studer and Joan Evans (Paris: Champion, 1924), pp.19–69 (61–62).

91 Adelard of Bath, 'De avibus tractatus', in *Conversations with His Nephew: On the Same and the Different, Questions on Natural Science, and on Birds*, ed. and trans. by Charles Burnett, with Italo Ronca, Pedro Mantas España and Baudouin van den Abeele (Cambridge: Cambridge University Press, 1998), pp.237–274 (242).

92 Richard similarly made punning connections between the 'firma' ('firm') revenue provided by a 'firma' ('a farm, fixed payment, rent', pp.46–47. *DMLBS*, s.v. *firma*, 2 < OF *ferme*).

93 *Le Bestiaire de Philippe de Thaün*, ed. by E. Walberg (Lund and Paris: Möller and Welter, 1900), pp.xviii, 18.465, 1.15–18. Discussed by M. Dominica Legge, *Anglo-Norman Literature and its Background* (Oxford: Clarendon, 1963), pp.24–25.

94 Gerald of Wales, *Itinerarium*, I.8. On the dating, see Thorpe, *Journey*, p.38. The significance of this clause in relation to French is not noted in Zimmer, 'Gerald de Barri', pp.313–349.

95 Amsler, *Etymology and Grammatical Discourse*, p.150.

96 Isidore, XVI.xviii.6.

97 M. T. Clanchy, '*Moderni* in Education and Government in England', *Speculum*, 50 (1975), 671–688 (678).

98 Judith Green, 'Unity and Disunity in the Anglo-Norman State', *Historical Research*, 62 (1989), 115–134 (117).

99 Green, 'Unity and Disunity', p.121.

100 *The Great Roll of the Pipe for the Twenty-First Year of the Reign of King Henry the Second* (London: Love and Wyman, 1897), pp.187–188; Green, 'Unity and Disunity', p.122 and n.42.

101 Richard's uncle and father were also arrested, and on two occasions, Richard was used as a child hostage to guarantee the compliance of his father (Amt, Richard fitz Nigel, *Dialogus*, p.xiv).

102 Graeme J. White, *Restoration and Reform, 1153–1165: Recovery from Civil War in England* (Cambridge: Cambridge University Press, 2000), p.137. However, Kenji Yoshitake notes that Richard could be referring here to the procedure of blanch farm, which seems to have been discontinued in Stephen's reign ('The Exchequer in the Reign of Stephen', *English Historical Review*, 103 (1988), 950–959 (952)).

103 Nicholas Karn, 'Nigel, Bishop of Ely, and the Restoration of the Exchequer after the "Anarchy" of King Stephen's Reign', *Historical Research*, 80 (2007), 299–314 (313–314).

104 R. L. Poole, *The Exchequer in the Twelfth Century* (Oxford: Clarendon, 1912), pp.9–10, 61–62.

105 Whilst Richard's assertion about the Domesday Book is likely to reflect a desire to maximise the extent of Roger's innovation, his claim here is probably correct: Kenji Yoshitake points out that Roger may well have been the first person to establish payment of the county farms in blanch at the exchequer ('Exchequer in the Reign of Stephen', pp.954–955).

106 Hudson, 'Administration, Family and Perceptions', p.85.

107 E.g. ibid., p.90, and Arthur Hughes, C. G. Crump and C. Johnson (eds), Richard fitzNigel, *De Necessariis Observantiis Scaccarii Dialogus*, pp.67, 171.

108 Amt, Richard fitz Nigel, *Dialogus*, pp.xxxi–xxxiv.

109 Hudson, 'Administration, Family and Perceptions', p.93.

110 Ralph V. Turner, 'Changing Perceptions of the New Administrative Class in Anglo-Norman and Angevin England: The *Curiales* and Their Conservative Critics', *Journal of British Studies*, 29 (1990), 93–117 (93–94, 107).

111 Richard's approach to the history of the exchequer is thus consonant with the broader transmission of kin-centred memories discussed in van Houts, *Memory and Gender in Medieval Europe*, p.143.

112 This allowed litigants to bring actions to recover an inheritance wrongfully claimed by another following the death of an ancestor (Hudson, *Oxford History*, pp.604–606).

113 John Hudson, *Land, Law, and Lordship in Anglo-Norman England* (Oxford: Clarendon, 1994), p.101; J. C. Holt, 'Feudal Society and the Family in Early Medieval England, II: Notions of Patrimony', *TRHS*, Fifth Series, 33 (1983), 193–220.

114 Bruce O'Brien, 'From *Morðor* to *Murdrum*: The Preconquest Origin and Norman Revival of the Murder Fine', *Speculum*, 71:2 (1996), 321–357 (351–352).

115 The evidence for the attribution of the murder fine to Cnut is discussed in O'Brien, '*Morðor*', but George Garnett defends Richard's view ('*Franci et Angli*: The Legal Distinctions between Peoples after the Conquest', *ANS*, 8 (1985), 109–137 (117)).

116 Hudson, *Land, Law and Lordship*, p.275. The assize of *novel disseisin* allowed litigants to bring actions to recover their seisin (justified enjoyment of possession) of a holding following their dispossession from it by another (Hudson, *Oxford History*, pp.609–614; for 'seisin', see above, note 38; for *mort d'ancestor*, see above, note 116).

117 Rosalind Faith, *The English Peasantry and the Growth of Lordship* (London: Leicester University Press, 1997, repr. 1999), p.220.

118 Aelred of Rievaulx, *Vita S. Edwardi regis et confessoris*, PL 195, cols 737–790 (773); *The Life of Saint Edward, King and Confessor*, in *Aelred of Rievaulx: The Historical Works*, ed. by Marsha L. Dutton, trans. by Jane Patricia Freeland (Kalamazoo: Cistercian Publications, 2005), pp.123–243 (206).

119 Aelred, 'Vita S. Edwardi', cols 738–739, cf. col.774; *Life of Saint Edward*, p.127.

120 Discussed in Hudson, 'Administration, Family and Perceptions of the Past', p.87.

121 R. Howard Bloch, *Etymologies and Genealogies: A Literary Anthropology of the French Middle Ages* (Chicago: University of Chicago Press, 1983), p.93.

122 Zrinka Stahuljak, *Bloodless Genealogies of the French Middle Ages: Translatio, Kinship, and Metaphor* (Gainesville: University Press of Florida, 2005), p.68.

5 PLACING FRENCH IN MULTILINGUAL BRITAIN

1 Laura Ashe, *Fiction and History in England, 1066–1200* (Cambridge: Cambridge University Press, 2007), p.59; see also Thomas, *English and Normans*, p.273.

2 For a list and discussion, see Williams, *English and the Norman Conquest*, pp.98ff.

3 David Crouch, 'Normans and Anglo-Normans: A Divided Aristocracy?', in *England and Normandy in the Middle Ages*, ed. by David Bates and Anne Curry (London: Hambledon Press, 1994), pp.51–68 (61, 62).

4 Judith A. Green, *The Aristocracy of Norman England* (Cambridge: Cambridge University Press, 1997), p.335.

5 C. P. Lewis, 'The Domesday Jurors', *Haskins Society Journal*, 5 (1993), 17–44 (23–24); Green, *Aristocracy*, pp.342–344.

6 For a summary of the critical discussion of the term (used only within this work), see *The Warenne (Hyde) Chronicle*, ed. by Elisabeth van Houts and Rosalind Love (Oxford: Clarendon, 2013), pp.lxiii–lxviii.

7 On such curiosity, and its potential effect on identity, see Thomas, *English and the Normans*, pp.360–361.

8 For John Gillingham, the works of William and Henry in particular are markers of the development of a Norman sense of Englishness, complete by the 1150s (*English in the Twelfth Century*, p.140).

9 Elisabeth van Houts, 'Intermarriage in Eleventh-Century England', in *Normandy and Its Neighbours, 900–1250: Essays for David Bates*, ed. by David Crouch and Kathleen Thompson (Turnhout: Brepols, 2011), pp.237–270. William of Malmesbury famously described himself as having 'the blood of both nations in my veins' ('utriusque gentis sanguinem traho', *Gesta regum Anglorum*, I.424–425). On Henry of Huntingdon's probable English mother, see Greenway, *Historia Anglorum*, p.xxvi. Geoffrey of Monmouth's patronymic of Arthur may indicate potential Breton connections: for discussion and bibliography, see Curley, *Geoffrey of Monmouth*, p.2.

10 The fullest discussion of these works remains Damian-Grint, *New Historians of the Twelfth-Century Renaissance*; on patronage, see Diana Tyson, 'Patronage of French Vernacular History Writers in the Twelfth and Thirteenth Centuries', *Romania*, 100 (1979), 180–222.

11 Possible parameters for the composition of the *Estoire* (1135 × 1180) are discussed in Dalton, 'Date of Gaimar's *Estoire des Engleis*', 23–47.

12 Crucially, Gaimar stated that he then augmented this translation with reference to the British book of Archdeacon Walter of Oxford (vv.6462–6466): this may be the same text as Geoffrey's *liber uetustissimus*. On his sources, see Short, 'Gaimar's Epilogue and Geoffrey of Monmouth's Liber vetustissimus', 323–343.

13 For a list and bibliography of the anonymous *Brut* manuscripts, see Damian-Grint, *New Historians*, pp.61–65; also Ian Short, 'Un *Roman de Brut* anglo-normand inédit', *Romania*, 126 (2008), 273–295.

14 Jane Zatta, 'Translating the *Historia*: The Ideological Transformation of the *Historia regum Britannie* in Twelfth-Century Vernacular Chronicles', *Arthuriana*, 8:4 (1998), 148–161.

15 Damian-Grint, *New Historians*, p.194. On Richard of Devizes's late-twelfth-century fusion of Galfridian and Anglo-Saxon material, see John Gillingham, 'Richard of Devizes and "a rising tide of nonsense": How Cerdic met King Arthur', in *The Long Twelfth-Century View of the Anglo-Saxon Past*, ed. by Martin Brett and David A. Woodman (Aldershot: Ashgate, 2015), pp.141–156.

16 Philippe de Thaon, *Comput*, vv.101–102.

17 Cited and translated in Ian Short, '*Verbatim et literatim*: oral and written French in twelfth-century Britain', *Vox Romanica*, 68 (2009), 156–168 (160).

18 On Anglo-Norman's fluidity, see Trotter, '*Deinz certeins boundes*'. Thomas of Kent, *The Anglo-Norman* Alexander *(Le Roman de Toute Chevalerie)*, ed. by Brian Foster, with Ian Short, 2 vols (London: Anglo-Norman Text Society, 1976–1977), II.76.

19 Thomas of Kent, *The Anglo-Norman* Alexander, I, vv.4673–4676.

20 *OED*, s.v. *Charles' Wain*. If *Carleswæn* was originally intended to signify 'the man's wagon', the ascription to 'Charles' recorded here may possibly have arisen through confusion with Old English *ceorl* > Middle English *chĕrl*, 'man'; or Old Norse *karl* > Middle English *carl*, 'man' (*MED* s.v. *chĕrl*, *carl*).

21 In the first century B.C., the Latin author Hyginus already noted that the Greeks called this constellation Hamaxa, 'Chariot' (*L'Astronomie*, ed. and trans. André le Bœuffle (Paris: Les Belles Lettres, 1983), II.2.2. *AND*, s.v. *char*, 2.

22 Short, '*Tam Angli quam Franci*', 156.

23 *AND*, s.v. 'wain', 1.

24 Ardis Butterfield, *The Familiar Enemy: Chaucer, Language, and Nation in the Hundred Years War* (Oxford: Oxford University Press, 2009), p.265.

25 Lusignan, *Parler vulgairement*, pp.23–24.

26 Geoffrey of Monmouth, *HRB*, pp.66–67.

27 A list of the relevant manuscripts is included in the appendix to Jean Blacker's 'Courtly Revision of Wace's *Roman de Brut* in British Library Egerton MS 3028', in *Courtly Arts and the Art of Courtliness*, ed. by Keith Busby and Christopher Kleinhenz (Cambridge: Brewer, 2006), pp.237–258 (251–254). Note also the existence of a further fragment on the verso side of London, College of Arms, MS 12/45A (Short, 'Un *Roman de Brut* anglo-normand inédit', 274).

28 Wace, *The Roman de Rou*, ed. by Anthony J. Holden, trans. by Glyn S. Burgess (St Helier: Société Jersiaise, 2002), III.5305–5318; discussed in F. H. M. Le Saux, *A Companion to Wace* (Cambridge: Brewer, 2005), pp.1–10. On the evidence for a visit to south-west England before the completion of the *Brut*: Margaret Houck, *Sources of the* Roman de Brut *of Wace* (Berkeley: University of California Press, 1938), pp.220–228.

29 Laȝamon, *Brut*, ed. by G. L. Brook and R. F. Leslie, 2 vols (London: Early English Text Society, 1963–1978), Prologue, vv.22–23.

30 Neil Wright (ed.), *The Historia regum Britannie of Geoffrey of Monmouth II: The First Variant Version: A Critical Edition* (Cambridge: Brewer, 1988), pp.liv–lxii, lxxi, lxvi–lxx.

31 On his scrupulous treatment of sources, see Elisabeth van Houts, 'Wace as Historian', in *Family Trees and the Roots of Politics: The Prosopography of Britain and France from the Tenth to the Twelfth Century*, ed. by K. S. B. Keats-Rohan (Woodbridge: Boydell, 1997), pp.103–132.

32 Wright, *First Variant*, p.lxxvii.

33 As with the thirteenth-century copy in London, British Library, MS Harley 6358 (Wright, *First Variant*, pp.lxxxvi–lxxxvii).

34 Cardiff, South Glamorgan Central Library, MS 2.611 (late thirteenth or early fourteenth century); cf. Aberystwyth, National Library of Wales, MS 13210 (second half of the thirteenth century), which offers a conflation of the First and Second Variant texts of the *Historia* (Wright, *First Variant*, pp.lxxviii–lxxx).

35 Writing at Rouen (*c.*1184), Johannes made use of both redactions in his *Architrenius* (Wright, *First Variant*, pp.lxxv–vi). On Gervase, see below.
36 Geoffrey, *HRB*, p.279.
37 Ibid., pp.257–259.
38 Wright, *First Variant*, pp.176–177.
39 Geoffrey, *HRB*, p.281. Wright, *First Variant*, p.190.
40 Wright, *First Variant*, pp.189–190, lxvi–lxx.
41 On Wace's adaptation of the First Variant: Leckie, *Passage of Dominion*, pp.109–116.
42 *Wace's* Roman de Brut, vv.14757–14774. All subsequent line numbers refer to this edition.
43 Leckie, *Passage of Dominion*, p.110.
44 This tradition is discussed in Lesley Johnson, 'The Anglo-Norman *Description of England*: An Introduction', in *Anglo-Norman Anniversary Essays*, ed. by Ian Short (London: Anglo-Norman Text Society, 1993), pp.11–30 (17–20). See also A. Bell in the same volume, 'The Anglo-Norman *Description of England*: An Edition', pp.31–47.
45 For recent bibliography, see Sally Harvey, *Domesday: Book of Judgement* (Oxford: Oxford University Press, 2014).
46 On Wace's awareness of Latin linguistic theory, see Gioia Paradisi, '"Par muement de languages": Il tempo, la memoria e il volgare in Wace', *Francofonia*, 45 (2003), 27–45 (Augustine's concept of 'consuetudo' discussed pp.37–38).
47 See Weiss, *Brut*, p.370 n6.
48 Wace dated the beginning of the process of composition in *Roman de Rou*, ed. Holden, trans. Burgess, *Chronique Ascendante*, 1–4. The *Rou* also referred to the Siege of Rouen in 1174 (*Chronique Ascendante*, 62–66), although this is generally accepted to have been added later. See further, Wace, *Roman de Rou*, ed. by A. J. Holden, 3 vols (Paris: Picard, 1970–1973), III.13–14.
49 Wace, *Rou*, III.141.
50 Ibid., III.81–84.
51 For Gervase's career, see Gransden, *Historical Writing in England, c.550–c.1307*, pp.253–260.
52 Although the *Gesta regum* extends to 1210, it is unclear whether Gervase or another hand wrote the section after 1199 (for discussion, see William Stubbs (ed.), *Gervasii Cantuariensis Opera Historica*, 2 vols, RS 73 (London: H.M. Stationery Office, 1879–1880), I.xxx–xxxii, II.xiii).
53 Both the *Gesta regum* and the *Mappa mundi* are found in a single manuscript, Cambridge, Corpus Christi College, MS 438; the *Mappa mundi* and the portions of the *Gesta regum* discussed here are both written in the same hand from the second half of the thirteenth century.
54 David Knowles, 'The *Mappa Mundi* of Gervase of Canterbury', *Downside Review*, 48 (1930), 237–247 (241).
55 Gervase of Canterbury, *Gesta regum*, in *Gervasii Cantuariensis Opera Historica*, II.3–106 (21), *Mappa mundi*, in *Gervasii Cantuarensis Opera Historica*,

II.414–449 (416); *Gesta regum*, p.20. Wright, *First Variant*, pp.177, 178; cf. Geoffrey, *HRB*, p.259.

56 Gervase of Canterbury, *Mappa mundi*, pp.414–415.

57 Gervase of Canterbury, *Gesta regum*, p.21; *Mappa mundi*, p.416; *Gesta regum*, p.20.

58 Gervase, *Gesta regum*, p.5.

59 Pryce, 'British or Welsh', p.797.

60 Gervase, *Gesta regum*, pp.7, 9, 10, 13.

61 Ibid., p.11.

62 Gervase, *Mappa mundi*, p.416.

63 Gervase, *Gesta regum*, p.60.

64 Gervase, *Mappa mundi*, p.416; cf. Henry of Huntingdon, *Historia Anglorum*, p.14.

65 Gervase, *Mappa mundi*, p.416.

66 *DMLBS*, s.v. *Normannicus*, 3b.

67 William of Malmesbury, *Gesta regum*, I.538–539.

68 Antonia Gransden, 'Realistic Observation in Twelfth-Century England', in *Legends, Traditions and History in Medieval England* (London: Hambledon Press, 1992), pp.175–197 (185–186). Gervase has previously been suggested as the possible creator of two unique maps of the cathedral's plumbing found in the final folios of the Eadwine Psalter (Francis Woodman, 'The Waterworks Drawings of the Eadwine Psalter', in *Eadwine Psalter*, pp.168–177 (177)); but new assessments of the drawings' date consider this unlikely (Peter Fergusson, *Canterbury Cathedral Priory in the Age of Becket* (New Haven, CT: Yale University Press, 2011), pp.30–31).

69 Cited in Reynolds, *Kingdoms and Communities*, p.257. An ability to speak several languages was itself a symbol of royal wisdom in the twelfth century: the biography of Gruffudd ap Cynan, king of Gwynedd (d.1137), noted that he excelled at foreign languages ('externarum linguarum excellens', *Vita Griffini filii Conani: The Medieval Latin Life of Gruffudd ap Cynan*, ed. and trans. by Paul Russell (Cardiff: University of Wales Press, 2005), §20). Walter Map stated that Henry II of England 'had a knowledge of all the tongues used from the French sea to the Jordan, but used only Latin and French' ('linguarum omnium que sunt a mari Gallico usque ad Iordanem habens scienciam, Latina tantum utens et Gallica', Walter Map, *De nugis curialium*, pp.476–477).

70 *Le Roman de Waldef*, ed. by A. J. Holden (Cologny-Genève: Fondation Martin Bodmer, 1984), pp.17–18; Rosalind Field, '*Waldef* and the Matter of/with England', in *Medieval Insular Romance: Translation and Innovation*, ed. by Judith Weiss et al. (Cambridge: Brewer, 2000), pp.25–39 (37 n26). For an assessment of the influence of Wace's *Brut* on *Waldef*, see Holden, *Waldef*, pp.27–28.

71 Thomas, *English and the Normans*, pp.356–357, 387, 389–390.

72 Ralph V. Turner, 'England in 1215: An Authoritarian Angevin Dynasty Facing Multiple Threats', in *Magna Carta and the England of King John*, ed. by Janet S. Loengard (Woodbridge: Boydell, 2010), pp.10–26 (10–11, 13, 19).

73 Rosalind Field, '"Pur les franc homes amender": Clerical Authors and the Thirteenth-Century Context of Historical Romance', in *Medieval Romance, Medieval Contexts*, ed. by Rhiannon Purdie and Michael Cichon (Cambridge: Brewer, 2011), pp.175–188 (187). O'Brien, *God's Peace*, p.158.

74 Susan Crane, *Insular Romance: Politics, Faith, and Culture in Anglo-Norman and Middle English Literature* (Berkeley: University of California Press, 1986), p.14.

75 Robert Allen Rouse, *The Idea of Anglo-Saxon England in Middle English Romance* (Cambridge: Brewer, 2005), p.4.

76 Holden, *Waldef*, p.7; the manuscript contains two other romances, *Gui de Warewic* and *Otinel*, and has an insular provenance.

77 A full synopsis can be found in Holden, *Waldef*, pp.7–16.

78 Ibid., v.75, 87–92. All line references found in the text are taken from this edition.

79 On the cult of Waltheof, see Brian J. Levy, 'Waltheof "Earl" de Huntingdon et de Northampton: la naissance d'un héros anglo-normand', *Cahiers de civilisation médiévale*, 18 (1975), pp.183–196; Emma Mason, 'Invoking Earl Waltheof', in *The English and Their Legacy, 900–1200: Essays in Honour of Ann Williams*, ed. by David Roffe (Woodbridge: Boydell, 2012), pp.185–204.

80 Rosalind Field, 'What's in a Name? Arthurian Name-Dropping in the *Roman de Waldef*', in *Arthurian Studies in Honour of P. J. C. Field*, ed. by Bonnie Wheeler (Woodbridge: Brewer, 2004), pp.63–64.

81 This strategy of retrospective feudalism is not limited to *Waldef*: see John Hudson, 'Imposing Feudalism on Anglo-Saxon England: Norman and Angevin Presentation of Pre-Conquest Lordship and Landholding', in *Feudalism: New Landscapes of Debate*, ed. by Sverre Bagge, Michael H. Gelting and Thomas Lindkvist (Turnhout: Brepols, 2011), pp.115–134.

82 For further medieval examples of the strategic 'Anglicisation' of Britain, see Ilya Afanasyev, '"In gente Britanniarum, sicut quaedam nostratum testatur historia . . .": National Identity and Perceptions of the Past in John of Salisbury's *Policraticus*', *Journal of Medieval History*, 38 (2012), 278–294 (286–288).

83 See discussion in Holden, *Waldef*, pp.27–28.

84 However, after the Romans leave, Atle bestows his name on Attleborough: see vv.347–351. The author may have been reading Latin hagiography or may be recording a wider tradition: cf. Geoffrey of Wells's etymology for Attleborough ('*De infantia sancti Edmundi* (BHL 2393)', ed. by R. M. Thomson, *Analecta Bollandiana*, 95 (1977), 25–42 (40)) (composed *c.*1148 × 1156). Cf. Holden, *Waldef*, vv.248–252.

85 *Johannes Bramis' Historia regis Waldei*, ed. by Rudolf Imelmann (Bonn: Hanstein, 1912), pp.3, 254–257. Note the scepticism of Judith Weiss and Rosalind Field concerning the accuracy of Johannes's summary (Weiss, '"History" in Anglo-Norman Romance: The Presentation of the Pre-Conquest Past', in *The Long Twelfth-Century View of the Anglo-Saxon Past*, ed. Brett and Woodman, pp.275–287 (287); cf. Field, '*Waldef* and the Matter of/with England', p.39 n30).

86 Wace, *Brut*, vv.13013–13015.

87 Holden, *Waldef*, vv.39–50, 53–54, trans. by Rosalind Field in '*Waldef* and the Matter of/with England', p.33.

88 Thomas, *The Romance of Horn*, ed. by Mildred K. Pope, with T. B. W. Reid, 2 vols (Oxford: Blackwell, 1955–64), I, vv.1–2.

89 Weiss, 'Thomas and the Earl', 1–14. Laura Ashe sees ideas of the 'good old law' and the 'exile-and-return' theme in romance plots (both of which feature in *Waldef*) as derived from pre-Conquest events and texts ('"Exile-and-Return" and English Law: The Anglo-Saxon Inheritance of Insular Romance', *Literature Compass*, 3 (2006), 300–317).

90 See further Rachel Bromwich, 'Some Remarks on the Celtic Sources of "Tristan"', *Transactions of the Honourable Society of Cymmrodorion* (1953), 32–60; O. J. Padel, 'The Cornish Background of the Tristan Stories', *Cambridge Medieval Celtic Studies*, 1 (1981), 53–81.

91 Jehan Bodel, *La Chanson des Saisnes*, ed. by Annette Brasseur, 2 vols (Geneva: Droz, 1989), I, vv.6–11.

92 See Rosalind Field, 'The Curious History of the Matter of England', in *Boundaries in Medieval Romance*, ed. by Neil Cartlidge (Cambridge: Brewer, 2008), 29–42.

93 See R. R. Davies, *Conquest, Coexistence, and Change: Wales, 1063–1415* (Oxford: Clarendon, 1987), pp.292–297, esp. p.294.

94 Ifor W. Rowlands, 'King John and Wales', in *King John: New Interpretations*, ed. by S. D. Church (Woodbridge: Boydell, 1999), pp.273–287 (279).

95 On translators' prologues as a genre, see Elizabeth Dearnley, 'French-English Translation 1189–*c*.1450, with Special Reference to Translators and Their Prologues' (unpublished doctoral thesis, University of Cambridge, 2011), p.3. For a survey of their Latin roots, see Minnis, *Medieval Theory of Authorship*, pp.9–72.

96 Map, *De nugis curialium*, pp.312–313, cited in Minnis, *Medieval Theory*, p.12.

97 On the differing themes of French prologues, see Damian-Grint, *New Historians*, pp.87–142.

98 For a summary of these potential sources, see Joan Tasker Grimbert, '*Cligés* and the Chansons: A Slave to Love', in *A Companion to Chrétien de Troyes*, ed. by Norris J. Lacy and Joan Tasker Grimbert (Cambridge: Brewer, 2005), pp.120–136 (123–127 (123)).

99 Chrétien de Troyes, *Cligés*, ed. by Stewart Gregory and Claude Luttrell (Cambridge: Brewer, 1993), vv.24–26.

100 Ibid., vv.30–35.

101 See Curtius, *European Literature and the Latin Middle Ages*, pp.27–29.

102 Horace, *Satires, Epistles, and Ars Poetica*, trans. Fairclough, *Epistles*, 2.1.156–157.

103 Both romances of Hue de Rotelande (fl. c.1175–1185 × 90) notably claim spurious Latin sources (*Ipomedon*, ed. by A. J. Holden (Paris: Klincksieck, 1979), vv.25–32; *Protheselaus*, ed. by A. J. Holden, 3 vols (London: Anglo-Norman Text Society, 1991–1993), II.12706–12710). Writing in 1188, Aimon de Varennes

stated (probably falsely) that his romance *Florimont* was based on a Latin translation of a Greek original (*Florimont: Ein altfranzösischer Abenteuerroman*, ed. by Alfons Hilka (Halle: Niemeyer, 1932), vv.7–36). He went to some lengths to create verisimilitude, including nine quotations from medieval Greek acquired in the course of travels in the Byzantine world (see discussion and bibliography in Laurence Harf-Lancner, 'Le *Florimont* d'Aimon de Varennes: un prologue du *Roman d'Alexandre*', *Cahiers de civilisation médiévale*, 37 (1994), 241–253 (242)). The author of the *Lai d'Haveloc* emphasised its Breton connections, despite the romance's probable Scandinavian roots: see discussion in Weiss, *Birth of Romance in England*, pp.155–169 (155).

104 For this corpus of material, see Rouse, *Idea of Anglo-Saxon England*, pp.11–51.
105 Gaimar, *Estoire des Engleis*, v.1682, 828.
106 Ibid., vv.2314–2338, 3449–3454.
107 *Fables of Marie de France*, ed. and trans. by Mary Lou Martin (Birmingham, AL: Summa, 1984), p.252. Marie's phrasing implies that she thought of Aesop as a translator ('Esope apelë um cest livre, kil translata e fist escrivre, de Griu en Latin le turna', p.252). For Marie's sources, see discussion in Martin, *Fables of Marie*, pp.20–24.
108 Martin, *Fables of Marie*, pp.22–24.
109 Ibid., p.252.
110 Melissa Furrow, *Expectations of Romance: The Reception of a Genre in Medieval England* (Cambridge: Brewer, 2009), pp.2, 115.
111 See e.g. Rosalind Field, 'Romance as History, History as Romance', in *Romance in Medieval England*, ed. by Maldwyn Mills et al. (Cambridge: Brewer, 1991), pp.163–173 (167).
112 David Wallace, *Premodern Places: Calais to Surinam, Chaucer to Aphra Behn* (Oxford: Blackwell, 2004), p.16.

CONCLUSION

1 The foundational work of secondary criticism remains Franzen, *Tremulous Hand*.
2 This was first discussed by E. G. Stanley, 'Laȝamon's Antiquarian Sentiments', *Medium Ævum*, 38 (1969), 23–37.
3 *Seinte Margarete*, in *Medieval English Prose for Women: Selections from the Katherine Group and Ancrene Wisse*, ed. by Bella Millett and Jocelyn Wogan-Browne (Oxford: Clarendon, 1990), pp.44–85 (82–83).
4 Horace, *Ars Poetica*, vv.70–71.
5 On Wace's vocabulary, see Brian Woledge, 'Notes on Wace's Vocabulary', *Modern Language Review*, 46 (1951), 16–30; Hans-Erich Keller, *Étude descriptive sur le vocabulaire de Wace* (Berlin: Akademie-Verlag, 1953); and the review of Keller by Félix Lecoy, *Romania*, 76 (1955), 534–538.
6 David Trotter, 'Language Labels, Language Change, and Lexis', in *Medieval Multilingualism: The Francophone World and Its Neighbours*, ed. by Christopher Kleinhenz and Keith Busby (Turnhout: Brepols, 2010), pp.43–61 (51).

7 On some of the creative possibilities afforded by this inter-lingualism in the late Middle Ages, see e.g. Christopher Baswell, 'Multilingualism on the Page', in *Middle English*, ed. by Paul Strohm (Oxford: Oxford University Press, 2009), pp.38–50; Jonathan Hsy, *Trading Tongues: Merchants, Multilingualism and Medieval Literature* (Columbus: Ohio State University Press, 2013), pp.6–7.

Bibliography

PRIMARY SOURCES

Adelard of Bath, 'De avibus tractatus', in *Conversations with his Nephew: On the Same and the Different, Questions on Natural Science, and On Birds*, ed. and trans. by Charles Burnett with Italo Ronca, Pedro Mantas España and Baudouin van den Abeele (Cambridge: Cambridge University Press, 1998), pp.237–274

Ælfric, *Ælfrics Grammatik und Glossar: Text und Varianten*, ed. by Julius Zupitza, with a new introduction by Helmut Gneuss (Hildesheim: Weidmann, 2001)

Ælfric's Prefaces, ed. by Jonathan Wilcox (Durham: Jasprint, 1994)

Aelred of Rievaulx, *The Life of Saint Edward, King and Confessor*, in *Aelred of Rievaulx: The Historical Works*, ed. by Marsha L. Dutton, trans. by Jane Patricia Freeland (Kalamazoo: Cistercian, 2005), pp.123–243

Vita S. Edwardi regis et confessoris, PL 195, cols 737–790

Æthelweard, *The Chronicle of Æthelweard*, ed. by A. Campbell (London: Nelson, 1962)

Aimon de Varennes, *Florimont: Ein altfranzösischer Abenteuerroman*, ed. by Alfons Hilka (Halle: Niemeyer, 1932)

Alanus, *Prophetia anglicana Merlini Ambrosii Britanni* (Frankfurt: Brathering, 1603)

Aristotle, *De interpretatione uel Periermenias*, trans. by Boethius, ed. by Lorenzo Minio-Paluello, *Aristoteles Latinus*, II.1 (Bruges-Paris: de Brouwer, 1965), pp.5–38

Arnobius Junior, *Commentarii in Psalmos*, ed. by Klaus-D. Daur, *CCSL* 25 (Turnhout: Brepols, 1990)

Augustine, *Confessionum libri XIII*, ed. by Martin Skutella and Lucas Verheijen, *CCSL* 27 (Turnhout: Brepols, 1981)

De civitate Dei, ed. by Bernard Dombart and Alphonse Kalb, *CCSL* 47–48 (Turnhout: Brepols, 1955)

De doctrina Christiana, ed. and trans. by R. P. H. Green (Oxford: Clarendon, 1995)

De Genesi ad litteratim, PL 34, cols 245–486

De Genesi contra Manichaeos, ed. by Dorothea Weber (Vienna: Verlag der österreichischen Akademie der Wissenschaften, 1998)

De Trinitate, CCSL 50–50A, ed. by W. J. Mountain with Fr. Glorie (Turnhout: Brepols, 1968)

Aulus Gellius, *The Attic Nights of Aulus Gellius*, trans. by John C. Rolfe (Cambridge, MA: Harvard University Press, 1927, repr. 1961–1968)

Baker, Peter S. (ed.), *The Anglo-Saxon Chronicle: A Collaborative Edition: Volume 8, MS F* (Cambridge: Brewer, 2000)

Barlow, Frank (ed.), *English Episcopal Acta XI: Exeter, 1046–1184* (Oxford: Oxford University Press, 1996)

Bates, David (ed.), *Regesta regum Anglo-Normannorum: The Acta of William I (1066–1087)* (Oxford: Clarendon, 1998)

Bede, *Bedas metrische Vita sancti Cuthberti*, ed. by Werner Jaager (Leipzig: Mayer and Müller, 1935)

Bede's Ecclesiastical History of the English People, ed. by Bertram Colgrave and R. A. B. Mynors (Oxford: Clarendon, 1969, repr. 1991)

De temporum ratione, ed. by Th. Mommsen and C. W. Jones, *CCSL* CXXIII B.2 (Turnhout: Brepols, 1977)

The Reckoning of Time, trans. by Faith Wallis (Liverpool: Liverpool University Press, 1999, repr. 2004)

Bell, Alexander (ed.), 'The Anglo-Norman Description of England: An Edition', in *Anglo-Norman Anniversary Essays*, ed. by Ian Short (London: Anglo-Norman Text Society, 1993), pp.31–47

(ed.), *Le Lai d'Haveloc* (Manchester: Manchester University Press, 1925)

Benoît de Sainte-Maure, *Chronique des Ducs de Normandie*, ed. by Carin Fahlinand Sven Sandqvist, 4 vols. (Uppsala: Almqvist and Wiksells, 1951–1979)

Berger, Roger, and Annette Brasseur (eds), *Les Séquences de Sainte Eulalie* (Geneva: Droz, 2004)

Blacker, Jean (ed. and trans.), 'Anglo-Norman Verse Prophecies of Merlin', *Arthuriana*, 15:1 (2005), 1–125

Blake, E. O. (ed.), *Liber Eliensis* (London: Royal Historical Society, 1962)

Brooks, N. P., and S. E. Kelly (eds), *Charters of Christ Church, Canterbury*, 2 vols (Oxford: Oxford University Press for the British Academy, 2013)

Byrhtferth of Ramsey, *Byrhtferth's Enchiridion*, ed. by Peter S. Baker and Michael Lapidge (Oxford: Early English Text Society, 1995)

The Lives of St Oswald and St Ecgwine, ed. by Michael Lapidge (Oxford: Clarendon, 2009)

Calder, George (ed.), *Auraicept na n-Éces: The Scholars' Primer* (Edinburgh: Grant, 1917)

Campbell, Alistair (ed.), *The Battle of Brunanburh* (London: Heinemann, 1938)

Campbell, Alistair, with Simon Keynes, *Encomium Emmae Reginae* (Cambridge: Cambridge University Press, 1998)

Caplan, Harry (trans.), *Rhetorica ad Herennium* (London: Heinemann, 1954)

Chrétien de Troyes, *Cligés*, ed. by Stewart Gregory and Claude Luttrell (Cambridge: Brewer, 1993)

Church, S. D. (ed. and trans.), *Constitutio domis regis*, in Richard fitz Nigel, *Dialogus de scaccario*, ed. and trans. by Emilie Amt, with the *Constitutio domis regis* (Oxford: Clarendon, 2007)

Clark, Willene B. (ed.), *A Medieval Book of Beasts: The Second-Family Bestiary* (Woodbridge: Boydell, 2006)

Conchubranus, 'Conchubrani Vita Sancti Monennae', ed. by Mario Esposito, *Proceedings of the Royal Irish Academy*, xxviii C (1910), 202–251

Crick, Julia (ed.), *Charters of St Albans* (Oxford: Oxford University Press for the British Academy, 2007)

Dahan, Gilbert (ed.), 'Une introduction à la philosophie au XIIe siècle. Le *Tractatus quidam de philosophia et partibus eius*', *Archives d'histoire doctrinale et littéraire du Moyen Âge*, 49 (1982), 155–193

Dante, *De vulgari eloquentia*, ed. and trans. by Steven Botterill (Cambridge: Cambridge University Press, 1996)

Dares Phrygius, *De excidio Troiae historia*, ed. by Ferdinand Meister (Leipzig: Teubner, 1873)

Dickins, Bruce, and R. M. Wilson (eds), 'A Worcester Fragment', in *Early Middle English Texts* (London: Bowes & Bowes, 1951), pp.1–2

Dobbie, Elliott van Kirk (ed.), *The Anglo-Saxon Minor Poems* (London: Routledge, 1942)

Donatus, *Donat et la tradition de l'enseignement grammatical: étude sur l'Ars Donati et sa diffusion (IVe–IXe siècle) et édition critique*, ed. by Louis Holtz (Paris: Centre National de la Recherche Scientifique, 1981)

Downer, L. J. (ed. and trans.), *Leges Henrici Primi* (Oxford: Clarendon, 1972)

Dudo of Saint-Quentin, *De moribus et actis primorum Normanniae ducum*, ed. by Jules Lair (Caen: Le Blanc-Hardel, 1865)

Eadmeri historia novorum in Anglia, ed. by Martin Rule, *RS* 81 (London: Longman, 1884)

'Eadmer's Life of Bregwine, Archbishop of Canterbury, 761–764', ed. by Bernhard W. Scholz, *Traditio*, 22 (1966), 127–148

Evans, J. Gwenogvryn, with John Rhys (eds), *The Text of the Book of Llan Dav* (Oxford, 1893)

Fairweather, Janet (trans.), *Liber Eliensis: A History of the Isle of Ely* (Woodbridge: Boydell, 2005)

Felix, *Felix's Life of Saint Guthlac*, ed. and trans. by Bertram Colgrave (Cambridge: Cambridge University Press, 1956)

Gaimar, Geffrei, *Estoire des Engleis: History of the English*, ed. and trans. by Ian Short (Oxford: Oxford University Press, 2009)

Geoffrey of Burton, *Life and Miracles of St Modwenna*, ed. and trans. by Robert Bartlett (Oxford: Clarendon, 2002)

Geoffrey of Monmouth, *The History of the Kings of Britain: An Edition and Translation of the De gestis Britonum [Historia Regum Britanniae]*, ed. by Michael D. Reeve, trans. by Neil Wright (Woodbridge: Boydell, 2007)

Life of Merlin: Vita Merlini, ed. and trans. by Basil Clarke (Cardiff: University of Wales Press, 1973)

Geoffrey of Wells, 'De infantia sancti Edmundi (BHL 2393)', ed. by R. M. Thomson, *Analecta Bollandiana*, 95 (1977), 25–42

Gerald of Wales, *De invectionibus*, ed. by W. S. Davies, *Y Cymmrodor*, 30 (1920), 1–248

Expugnatio Hibernica: The Conquest of Ireland, ed. and trans. by A. B. Scott and F. X. Martin (Dublin: Royal Irish Academy, 1978)

Giraldi Cambrensis Opera, ed. by J. S. Brewer, James F. Dimock, and George F. Warner, 8 vols (London: H.M. Stationery Office, 1861–1891)

The Journey through Wales and The Description of Wales, trans. by Lewis Thorpe (London: Penguin, 1978, repr. 2004)

Gervase of Canterbury, *Gervasii Cantuariensis Opera Historica*, ed. by William Stubbs, 2 vols, *RS* 73 (London: H.M. Stationery Office, 1879)

Gervase of Tilbury, *Otia Imperialia: Recreation for an Emperor*, ed. and trans. by S. E. Banks and J. W. Binns (Oxford: Clarendon, 2002)

Gilbertus Universalis, et al., *Glossa ordinaria in Genesim*, PL 113, cols 67–182

Gildas, *The Ruin of Britain and Other Works*, ed. and trans. by Michael Winterbottom (London: Phillimore, 1978)

Goscelin of Saint Bertin, 'Goscelin's Liber confortatorius', trans. by W. R. Barnes and Rebecca Hayward, in *Writing the Wilton Women*, ed. by Stephanie Hollis et al. (Turnhout: Brepols, 2004), pp.95–212

'The *Liber confortatorius* of Goscelin of Saint Bertin', ed. by C. H. Talbot, *Studia Anselmiana*, 37 (1955), 1–117

The Great Roll of the Pipe for the Twenty-First Year of the Reign of King Henry the Second, Publications of the Pipe Roll Society, 22 (London: Love and Wyman, 1897)

Guy, Bishop of Amiens, *The Carmen de Hastingae proelio of Guy, Bishop of Amiens*, ed. and trans. by Frank Barlow (Oxford: Clarendon, 1999)

Hall, G. D. G. (ed.), *The Treatise on the Laws and Customs of the Realm of England Commonly Called Glanvill* (Oxford: Clarendon, 1965, repr. 1993)

Hall, Hubert (ed.), *The Red Book of the Exchequer, RS 99* (London: H.M. Stationery Office, 1896)

Harsley, Fred (ed.), *Eadwine's Canterbury Psalter: Part 2, Text and Notes* (London: Trübner, 1889)

Haugen, Einar (ed.), *The First Grammatical Treatise: The Earliest Germanic Phonology*, 2nd edn (London: Longman, 1972)

Henry of Huntingdon, *Historia Anglorum*, ed. and trans. by Diana Greenway (Oxford: Clarendon, 1996)

Hermann of Laon, *De miracula S. Mariae Laudunensis: De gestis venerabilis Bartholomaei Episcopi et S. Nortberti*, PL 156, cols 961–1018

Holden, A. J. (ed.), *Le Roman de Waldef* (Cologny-Genève: Fondation Martin Bodmer, 1984)

Holden, A. J., with S. Gregory and D. Crouch, *History of William Marshal*, 3 vols (London: Anglo-Norman Text Society, 2002–2006)

Horace, *Satires, Epistles and Ars Poetica*, trans. by H. Rushton Fairclough (Cambridge, MA: Harvard University Press, 1978)

Houts, Elisabeth van, and Rosalind Love (eds), *The Warenne (Hyde) Chronicle* (Oxford: Clarendon, 2013)

[Hrabanus Maurus], *De inventione linguarum*, PL 122, cols 1579–1583

Hue de Rotelande, *Ipomedon*, ed. by A. J. Holden (Paris: Klincksieck, 1979)

    Protheselaus, ed. by A. J. Holden, 3 vols (London: Anglo-Norman Text Society, 1991–1993)

Hyginus, *L'Astronomie*, ed. and trans. André le Bœuffle (Paris: Les Belles Lettres, 1983)

Irvine, Susan (ed.), *The Anglo-Saxon Chronicle: A Collaborative Edition*, vol. 7, *MS E* (Cambridge: Brewer, 2004)

    (ed.), *Old English Homilies from MS Bodley 343* (Oxford: Early English Text Society, 1993)

Isidore of Seville, *Etymologiarum sive originum*, ed. by W. M. Lindsay, 2 vols (Oxford: Clarendon, 1911)

    The Etymologies of Isidore of Seville, trans. by Stephen Barney et al. (Cambridge: Cambridge University Press, 2006, corrected printing 2008)

Jehan Bodel, *La Chanson des Saisnes*, ed. by Annette Brasseur, 2 vols (Geneva: Droz, 1989)

Jerome, *Epistolae*, PL 22, cols 325–1224

    In Sophoniam, ed. by Marcus Adriaen, CCSL 76A (Turnhout: Brepols, 1969)

    Liber interpretationis Hebraicum nominum, ed. by Paul de Lagarde, in *S. Hieronymi presbyteri Opera Pars I, Opera Exegetica 1*, CCSL 72 (Turnhout: Brepols, 1959), pp.57–161

Johannes Bramis, *Johannes Bramis' Historia regis Waldei*, ed. by Rudolf Imelmann (Bonn: Hanstein, 1912)

Johannes de Hauvilla, *Architrenius*, ed. by Winthrop Wetherbee (Cambridge: Cambridge University Press, 1994)

John of Cornwall, 'A New Edition of John of Cornwall's *Prophetia Merlini*', ed. by Michael J. Curley, *Speculum*, 57:2 (1982), 217–249

John of Salisbury, *The Letters of John of Salisbury, Volume Two: The Later Letters (1163–1180)*, ed. by W. J. Millor and C. N. L. Brooke (Oxford: Clarendon, 1979)

    Metalogicon, ed. by J. B. Hall, with K. S. B. Keats-Rohan, CCCM 98 (Turnhout: Brepols, 1991)

    The Metalogicon: A Twelfth-Century Defense of the Verbal and Logical Arts of the Trivium, trans. by Daniel D. McGarry (Berkeley: University of California Press, 1955)

    Policraticus, ed. by C. C. J. Webb (Oxford: Clarendon, 1909)

Kelly, S. E. (ed.), *Charters of Peterborough Abbey* (Oxford: Oxford University Press for the British Academy, 2009)

Koble, Nathalie, and Mireille Séguy (ed. and trans.), *Lais bretons (XIIe-XIIIe siècles): Marie de France et ses contemporains* (Paris: Champion, 2011)

Krusch, B. (ed.), *Vita Richarii confessoris Centulensis*, in *Passiones vitaeque sanctorum aevi Merovingici, Monumenta Germaniae Historica, Scriptores rerum Merovingicarum*, 5 vols (Hanover: Hahn, 1902), IV.381–401

Kuhn, Sherman M. (ed.), *The Vespasian Psalter* (Ann Arbor: University of Michigan Press, 1965)

Laȝamon, *Brut*, ed. by G. L. Brook and R. F. Leslie, 2 vols (London: Early English Text Society, 1963–1978)

Liebermann, Felix (ed.), *Die Gesetze der Angelsachsen*, 3 vols (Halle: Niemeyer, 1903–1916)

Lucian, *Extracts from the MS. Liber Luciani: De laude Cestrie, written about the year 1195 and now in the Bodleian Library, Oxford*, ed. by M. V. Taylor (Edinburgh: Printed for the Record Society of Lancashire and Cheshire, 1912)

Macray, W. Dunn (ed.), *Chronicon abbatiae Rameseiensis*, RS 83 (London: Longman, 1886)

Marie de France, *Fables of Marie de France*, ed. and trans. by Mary Lou Martin (Birmingham, AL: Summa, 1984)

Millett, Bella, and Jocelyn Wogan-Browne (eds), *Seinte Margarete*, in *Medieval English Prose for Women: Selections from the Katherine Group and Ancrene Wisse* (Oxford: Clarendon, 1990), pp.44–85

Monaco, Francesco Lo, and Claudia Villa (eds), *I Giuramenti di Strasburgo: Testi e Tradizione, The Strasbourg Oaths: Texts and Transmission* (Florence: Galluzzo, 2009)

Nennius, *British History and the Welsh Annals*, ed. and trans. by John Morris (London: Phillimore, 1980)

O'Brien, Bruce (ed.), *God's Peace and King's Peace: The Laws of Edward the Confessor* (Philadelphia: University of Pennsylvania Press, 1999)

Orderic Vitalis, *The Ecclesiastical History of Orderic Vitalis*, ed. by Marjorie Chibnall, 6 vols (Oxford: Clarendon, 1969–1980)

Orrm, *The Ormulum*, ed. by Robert Holt, with R. M. White, 2 vols (Oxford: Clarendon, 1878)

Osbern, *Derivazioni*, ed. by Paola Busdraghi et al., 2 vols (Spoleto: Centro italiano di studi sull'alto medioevo, 1996)

Pelteret, David A. E. (ed.), *Catalogue of English Post-Conquest Vernacular Documents* (Woodbridge: Boydell, 1990)

Petrus Abaelardus, *Expositio in Hexameron*, ed. by Mary Romig with David Luscombe, CCCM 15 (Turnhout: Brepols, 2004)

Petrus Helias, *Summa super Priscianum*, ed. by Leo Reilly, 2 vols (Toronto: Pontifical Institute of Mediaeval Studies, 1993)

Philippe de Thaon, *Le Bestiaire de Philippe de Thaün*, ed. by E. Walberg (Lund: Möller and Welter, 1900)

Comput, ed. by Ian Short (London: Anglo-Norman Text Society, 1984)

Priscian, *Grammaire: Livre XVII – Syntaxe, 1*, ed. by the Ars Grammatica Group (Paris: Vrin, 2010)

Porter, David W. (ed.), *Excerptiones de Prisciano: The Source for Ælfric's Latin-Old English Grammar* (Cambridge: Brewer, 2002)

Potter, K. R. (ed. and trans.), with R. H. C. Davis, *Gesta Stephani* (Oxford: Clarendon, 1976)

Pulsiano, Philip (ed.), *Old English Glossed Psalters: Psalms 1–50* (Toronto: University of Toronto Press, 2001)

Quintilian, *The Orator's Education, Books 1–2*, ed. and trans. by Donald A. Russell (Cambridge, MA: Harvard University Press, 2001)

Richard fitz Nigel, *De necessariis observantiis scaccarii dialogus, Commonly called Dialogus de scaccario*, ed. by Arthur Hughes, C. G. Crump, and C. Johnson (Oxford: Clarendon, 1902)

    Dialogus de scaccario, ed. and trans. by Emilie Amt, with the *Constitutio domis regis*, ed. and trans. by S. D. Church (Oxford: Clarendon, 2007)

Robertson, A. J. (ed. and trans.), *Anglo-Saxon Charters*, 2nd edn (Cambridge: Cambridge University Press, 1956)

Robertson, James Craigie (ed.), *Materials for the History of Thomas Becket, Archbishop of Canterbury (canonized by Pope Alexander III, A.D. 1173)*, Vol. V, *RS* 67.5 (London: H.M. Stationery Office, 1881)

Russell, Paul (ed. and trans.), *Vita Griffini filii Conani: The Medieval Latin Life of Gruffudd ap Cynan* (Cardiff: University of Wales Press, 2005)

Seneca ad Lucilium: Epistulae morales, trans. by Richard M. Gummere, 3 vols (London: Heinemann, 1962–1967)

Sisam, Celia, and Kenneth Sisam (eds), *The Salisbury Psalter, edited from Salisbury Cathedral MS 150* (London: Early English Text Society, 1959)

Stubbs, William (ed.), *Radulfi de Diceto decani Lundoniensis opera historica*, 2 vols, *RS* 68 (London: H.M. Stationery Office, 1876)

Studer, Paul, and Joan Evans (eds), *Anglo-Norman Lapidaries* (Paris: Champion, 1924)

Suger, Abbot of Saint Denis, *Oeuvres complètes de Suger*, ed. by A. Lecoy de la Marche (Paris: Renouard, 1867)

Swanton, Michael (trans.), *The Anglo-Saxon Chronicles*, rev. edn (London: Phoenix, 2000)

Symeon of Durham, *Libellus de exordio atque procursu istius, hoc est Dunhelmensis, ecclesie: Tract on the Origins and Progress of this the Church of Durham*, ed. and trans. by David Rollason (Oxford: Clarendon, 2000)

Thomas, *The Romance of Horn*, ed. by Mildred K. Pope, with T. B. W. Reid, 2 vols (Oxford: Blackwell, 1955–1964)

Thomas of Kent, *The Anglo-Norman Alexander (Le Roman de Toute Chevalerie)*, ed. by Brian Foster, with Ian Short, 2 vols (London: Anglo-Norman Text Society, 1976–1977)

Thomas of Walsingham, *Gesta Abbatum Monasterii Sancti Albani*, ed. by Henry Thomas Riley, *RS* 28.4 (London: H.M. Stationery Office, 1867)

Varro, *On the Latin Language*, trans. by Roland G. Kent, 2 vols (Cambridge, MA: Harvard University Press, 1967)

Wace, *Roman de Rou*, ed. by A. J. Holden, 3 vols (Paris: Picard 1970–1973)

    The Roman de Rou, ed. by Anthony J. Holden, trans. by Glyn S. Burgess (St Helier: Société Jersiaise, 2002)

    Wace's Roman de Brut: A History of the British, ed. and trans. by Judith Weiss, rev. edn (Exeter: Exeter University Press, 2002)

Walter Map, *De nugis curialium: Courtiers' Trifles*, ed. and trans. by M. R. James, rev. by C. N. L. Brooke and R. A. B. Mynors (Oxford: Clarendon, 1983, repr. 2002)

Weiss, Judith (trans.), *The Lai of Haveloc*, in *The Birth of Romance in England: Four Twelfth-Century Romances in the French of England* (Tempe, AZ: ACMRS, 2009), pp.155–169

Whitelock, D., M. Brett, and C. N. L. Brooke (eds), *Councils and Synods with Other Documents Relating to the English Church, I,* A.D. *871–1204: Pt. II, 1066–1204* (Oxford: Clarendon, 1981)

William of Malmesbury, *Gesta Pontificum Anglorum: The History of the English Bishops*, ed. and trans. by Michael Winterbottom, with R. M. Thomson, 2 vols (Oxford: Clarendon, 2007)

Gesta regum Anglorum: The History of the English Kings, ed. and trans. by R. A. B. Mynors, R. M. Thomson and M. Winterbottom, 2 vols (Oxford: Clarendon, 1998–1999)

Saints' Lives: Lives of SS. Wulfstan, Dunstan, Patrick, Benignus and Indract, ed. by M. Winterbottom and R. M. Thomson (Oxford: Clarendon, 2002)

William of Newburgh, *Historia rerum anglicarum*, in *Chronicles of the Reigns of Stephen, Henry II, and Richard I*, ed. by Richard Howlett, RS 82.1–2 (London: H.M. Stationery Office, 1884)

The History of English Affairs, Book I, ed. and trans. by P. G. Walsh and M. J. Kennedy (Warminster: Aris and Phillips, 1988)

William of Poitiers, *The Gesta Guillelmi of William of Poitiers*, ed. and trans. by R. H. C. Davis and Marjorie Chibnall (Oxford: Clarendon, 1998)

William of St Albans, *Interpretatio, Acta Sanctorum*, 22 June, Junii Tomus Quartus (Antwerp: Jacobs, 1707), cols 149–159

The Life of Saint Alban by Matthew Paris, with the Passion of Saint Alban by William of St. Albans, ed. by Jocelyn Wogan-Browne et al. (Tempe, AZ: ACMRS, 2010)

Wright, Neil (ed.), *The Historia regum Britannie of Geoffrey of Monmouth II: The First Variant Version: A Critical Edition* (Cambridge: Brewer, 1988)

SECONDARY SOURCES

Adams, Jeremy Duquesnay, 'The Political Grammar of Isidore of Seville', in *Arts libéraux et philosophie au Moyen Âge* (Montreal: Vrin, 1969), pp.763–775.

The Populus of Augustine and Jerome: A Study in the Patristic Sense of Community (New Haven, CT: Yale University Press, 1971)

Adams, J. N., *Bilingualism and the Latin Language* (Cambridge: Cambridge University Press, 2003)

Adams, J. N., Michael Lapidge, and Tobias Reinhardt (eds), 'Introduction', in *Aspects of the Language of Latin Prose* (Oxford: Oxford University Press, 2005), pp.1–36

Afanasyev, Ilya, '"In gente Britanniarum, sicut quaedam nostratum testatur historia …"': National Identity and Perceptions of the Past in John of Salisbury's *Policraticus*', *Journal of Medieval History*, 38 (2012), 278–294

Ailes, Adrian, 'The Knight, Heraldry and Armour: The Role of Recognition and the Origins of Heraldry', in *Medieval Knighthood IV: Papers from the Fifth*

Strawberry Hill Conference, 1990, ed. by Christopher Harper-Bill and Ruth Harvey (Woodbridge: Boydell, 1992), pp.1–21

Albu, Emily, *The Normans in Their Histories: Propaganda, Myth, and Subversion* (Woodbridge: Boydell, 2001)

Alkire, Ti, and Carol Rosen, *Romance Languages: A Historical Introduction* (Cambridge: Cambridge University Press, 2010)

Amsler, Mark, *Etymology and Grammatical Discourse in Late Antiquity and the Early Middle Ages* (Amsterdam: Benjamins, 1989)

'History of Linguistics, "Standard Latin", and Pedagogy', in *History of Linguistic Thought in the Early Middle Ages*, ed. by Vivien Law (Amsterdam: Benjamins, 1993), pp.49–66

Amt, Emilie, *The Accession of Henry II in England: Royal Government Restored, 1149–1159* (Woodbridge: Boydell, 1993)

Anderson, Benedict, *Imagined Communities: Reflections on the Origin and Spread of Nationalism*, rev. edn (London: Verso, 1991)

Anderson, Carolyn, 'Wace's *Roman de Rou* and Henry II's Court: Character and Power', *Romance Quarterly*, 47 (2000), 67–82

Ashe, Geoffrey, '"A Certain Very Ancient Book": Traces of an Arthurian Source in Geoffrey of Monmouth's *History*', *Speculum*, 56 (1981), 301–323

Ashe, Laura, '"Exile-and-Return" and English Law: The Anglo-Saxon Inheritance of Insular Romance', *Literature Compass*, 3 (2006), 300–317

Fiction and History in England, 1066–1200 (Cambridge: Cambridge University Press, 2007)

Aurell, Martin, 'Geoffrey of Monmouth's *History of the Kings of Britain* and the Twelfth-Century Renaissance', *Haskins Society Journal*, 18 (2006), 1–18

Ayres-Bennett, Wendy, *A History of the French Language through Texts* (London: Routledge, 1996)

Bainton, Henry, 'Literate Sociability and Historical Writing in Later Twelfth-Century England', *ANS*, 34 (2011), 23–39

Baker, Peter S., 'A Little-Known Variant Text of the Old English Metrical Psalms', *Speculum*, 59:2 (1984), 263–281

Banniard, Michel, *Viva voce: communication écrite et communication orale du IVe au IXe siècle en Occident latin* (Paris: Institut des études augustiniennes, 1992)

Barlow, Frank, *Thomas Becket* (London: Weidenfeld and Nicholson, 1986)

Barnes, Michael, 'Norse in the British Isles', in *Viking Revaluations: Viking Society Centenary Symposium, 14–15 May 1992*, ed. by Anthony Faulkes and Richard Perkins (London: Viking Society for Northern Research, 1993), pp.65–84

Barrow, Julia, 'How the Twelfth-Century Monks of Worcester Perceived Their Past', in *The Perception of the Past in Twelfth-Century Europe*, ed. by Paul Magdalino (London: Hambledon, 1992), pp.53–74

Bartlett, Robert, *Gerald of Wales, 1146–1223* (Oxford: Clarendon, 1982)

'Medieval and Modern Concepts of Race and Ethnicity', *Journal of Medieval and Early Modern Studies*, 31 (2001), 39–56

Baswell, Christopher, 'Multilingualism on the Page', in *Middle English*, ed. by Paul Strohm (Oxford: Oxford University Press, 2009), pp.38–50

Virgil in Medieval England: Figuring the Aeneid from the Twelfth Century to Chaucer (Cambridge: Cambridge University Press, 1995)

Baswell, Christopher, Christopher Cannon, Jocelyn Wogan-Browne, and Kathryn Kerby-Fulton, 'Competing Archives, Competing Histories: French and its Cultural Location in Late-Medieval England', *Speculum*, 90 (2015), 635–700

Bates, David, *Normandy before 1066* (London: Longman, 1982)

Baxter, Stephen, 'The Making of the Domesday Book and the Languages of Lordship in Conquered England', in *Conceptualizing Multilingualism in Medieval England, c.800–c.1250*, ed. by Elizabeth M. Tyler (Turnhout: Brepols, 2011), pp.271–308

Bennett, Matthew, 'The Normans in the Mediterranean', in *A Companion to the Anglo-Norman World*, ed. by Christopher Harper-Bill and Elisabeth van Houts (Woodbridge: Boydell, 2002), pp.87–102

'Poetry as History? The 'Roman de Rou' of Wace as a Source for the Norman Conquest', *ANS*, 5 (1982), 21–39

Berghaus, Frank-Günter, *Die Verwandtschaftsverhältnisse der altenglischen Interlinearversionen des Psalters und der Cantica* (Göttingen: Vandenhoeck and Ruprecht, 1979)

Bergs, Alexander, and Janne Skaffari (eds), *The Language of the Peterborough Chronicle* (Frankfurt-am-Main: Peter Lang, 2007)

Berkhofer, Robert F., III, 'The Canterbury Forgeries Revisited', *Haskins Society Journal*, 18 (2006), 36–50

'Guerno the Forger and His Confession', *ANS*, 36 (2013), 53–68

Berschin, Walter, *Greek Letters and the Latin Middle Ages: From Jerome to Nicholas of Cusa*, rev. edn, trans. by Jerold C. Frakes (Washington, DC: Catholic University of America Press, 1988)

Black, Winston, 'Henry of Huntingdon's Lapidary Rediscovered and His *Anglicanus ortus* Reassembled', *Mediaeval Studies*, 68 (2006), 43–88

Blacker, Jean, 'Courtly Revision of Wace's Roman de Brut in British Library Egerton MS 3028', in *Courtly Arts and the Art of Courtliness*, ed. by Keith Busby and Christopher Kleinhenz (Cambridge: Brewer, 2006), pp.237–258

The Faces of Time: Portrayal of the Past in Old French and Latin Historical Narrative of the Anglo-Norman Regnum (Austin: University of Texas Press, 1994)

'"La geste est grande, longue e grieve a translater": History for Henry II', *Romance Quarterly*, 37 (1990), 387–396

'"Ne vuil sun livre translater": Wace's Omission of Merlin's Prophecies from the Roman de Brut', in *Anglo-Norman Anniversary Essays*, ed. by Ian Short (London: Anglo-Norman Text Society, 1993), pp.49–59

'Where Wace Feared to Tread: Latin Commentaries on Merlin's Prophecies in the Reign of Henry II', *Arthuriana*, 6:1 (1996), 36–52

Blacker-Knight, Jean, 'Wace's Craft and His Audience: Historical Truth, Bias and Patronage in the *Roman de Rou*', *Kentucky Romance Quarterly* 31 (1984), 355–362

Blake, Norman (ed.), *The Cambridge History of the English Language: Volume II, 1066–1476* (Cambridge: Cambridge University Press, 1992)

Blatt, Franz, 'L'évolution du latin médiéval', *Archivum Latinitatis Medii Aevi*, 28 (1958), 201–219

Bloch, R. Howard, *Etymologies and Genealogies: A Literary Anthropology of the French Middle Ages* (Chicago: University of Chicago Press, 1983)

Blom, Alderik H., 'Multilingualism and the Vocabularium Cornicum', in *Multilingualism in Medieval Britain (c.1066–1520): Sources and Analysis*, ed. by Judith A. Jefferson et al. (Turnhout: Brepols, 2013), pp.59–71

Bodden, Mary Catherine, 'Anglo-Saxon Self-Consciousness in Language', *English Studies*, 68 (1987), 24–39

Borst, Arno, *Der Turmbau von Babel: Geschichte der Meinungen über Ursprung und Vielfalt der Sprachen und Völker*, 6 vols (Stuttgart: Hiersemann, 1957–1963)

Bourgain, Pascale, 'Réflexions médiévales sur les langues de savoir', in *Tous vos gens à latin: le latin, langue savante, langue mondaine (XIVe-XVIIe siècles)*, ed. by Emmanuel Bury (Geneva: Droz, 2005), pp.23–46

Brand, Paul, '"Multis Vigiliis Excogitatam et Inventam": Henry II and the Creation of the English Common Law', *Haskins Society Journal*, 2 (1990), 197–222

—— '"Time Out of Mind": The Knowledge and Use of the Eleventh- and Twelfth-Century Past in Thirteenth-Century Litigation', *ANS*, 16 (1993), 37–54

Bredehoft, Thomas A., *Authors, Audiences, and Old English Verse* (Toronto: University of Toronto Press, 2009)

—— *Textual Histories: Readings in the Anglo-Saxon Chronicle* (Toronto: University of Toronto Press, 2001)

Breen, Katharine, *Imagining an English Reading Public, 1150–1400* (Cambridge: Cambridge University Press, 2010)

Britnell, Richard H., *The Commercialisation of English Society, 1000–1500*, 2nd edn (Manchester: Manchester University Press, 1996)

Brooke, Christopher, *Medieval Church and Society: Collected Essays* (London: Sidgwick and Jackson, 1971)

Brooks, Nicholas, 'Anglo-Saxon Charters: The Work of the Last Twenty Years', *ASE*, 3 (1974), 211–231

—— *Anglo-Saxon Myths: State and Church, 400–1066* (London: Hambledon Press, 2000)

Bromwich, Rachel, 'Some Remarks on the Celtic Sources of "Tristan"', *Transactions of the Honourable Society of Cymmrodorion* (1953), 32–60

Brosnahan, Leger, 'Wace's Use of Proverbs', *Speculum*, 39 (1964), 444–473

Brown, Elizabeth A. R., 'Falsitas pia sive reprehensibilis: Medieval Forgers and their Intentions', in *Fälschungen im Mittelalter*, 6 vols (Hannover: Hahn, 1988–1990), pp.I:101–119

Brown, George H., 'The Psalms as the Foundation of Anglo-Saxon learning', in *The Place of the Psalms in the Intellectual Culture of the Middle Ages*, ed. by Nancy van Deusen (Albany: State University of New York Press, 1999), pp.1–24

Bullough, Donald A., 'What Has Ingeld to Do with Lindisfarne?', *ASE*, 22 (1993), 93–125

Burchfield, R. W., 'The Language and Orthography of the Ormulum MS', *Transactions of the Philological Society*, 55 (1956), 56–87

Burnley, David, 'Lexis and Semantics', in *The Cambridge History of the English Language: Volume II, 1066–1476*, ed. by Norman Blake (Cambridge: Cambridge University Press, 1992), pp.409–499

Butterfield, Ardis, *The Familiar Enemy: Chaucer, Language, and Nation in the Hundred Years War* (Oxford: Oxford University Press, 2009)

Caenegem, R. C., van, *The Birth of the English Common Law*, 2nd edn (Cambridge: Cambridge University Press, 1988)

Calin, William, *The French Tradition and the Literature of Medieval England* (Toronto: University of Toronto Press, 1994)

Cameron, Angus F., 'Middle English in Old English Manuscripts', in *Chaucer and Middle English Studies in Honour of Rossell Hope Robbins*, ed. by Beryl Rowland (London: Allen and Unwin, 1974), pp.218–229

Campbell, James, 'Some Twelfth-Century Views of the Anglo-Saxon Past', *Peritia*, 3 (1984), 131–150

'The United Kingdom of England: The Anglo-Saxon Achievement', in *Uniting the Kingdom? The Making of British History*, ed. by Alexander Grant and Keith J. Stringer (London: Routledge, 1995), pp.31–47

Cannon, Christopher, *The Grounds of English Literature* (Oxford: Oxford University Press, 2007)

Careri, Maria, Christine Ruby, and Ian Short, *Livres et écritures en français et en occitan au XIIe siècle* (Rome: Viella, 2011)

Carruthers, Mary, *The Book of Memory: A Study of Memory in Medieval Culture*, 2nd edn (Cambridge: Cambridge University Press, 2008)

The Craft of Thought: Meditation, Rhetoric, and the Making of Images, 400–1200 (Cambridge: Cambridge University Press, 1998)

The Experience of Beauty in the Middle Ages (Oxford: Oxford University Press, 2013)

'Inventional Mnemonics and the Ornaments of Style: The Case of Etymology', *Connotations*, 2 (1992), 103–114

Chambers, E. K., *Arthur of Britain* (London: Sidgwick and Jackson, 1927)

Charles-Edwards, T. M., *Wales and the Britons, 350–1064* (Oxford: Oxford University Press, 2013)

Chibnall, Marjorie, 'Charter and Chronicle: The Use of Archive Sources by Norman Historians', in *Church and Government in the Middle Ages: Essays Presented to C. R. Cheney*, ed. by C. N. L. Brooke, D. E. Luscombe, G. H. Martin, and Dorothy Owen (Cambridge: Cambridge University Press, 1976), pp.1–17

The World of Orderic Vitalis (Oxford: Clarendon, 1984)

Clanchy, M. T., *From Memory to Written Record: England, 1066–1307*, 3rd edn (London: Wiley-Blackwell, 2013)

'*Moderni* in Education and Government in England', *Speculum*, 50 (1975), 671–688

Clark, Cecily, *Words, Names and History: Selected Writings*, ed. by Peter Jackson (Cambridge: Brewer, 1995)

Clark, Frederic N., 'Reading the "First Pagan Historiographer": Dares Phrygius and Medieval Genealogy', *Viator*, 41:2 (2010), 203–226

Coleman, Janet, *Ancient and Medieval Memories: Studies in the Reconstruction of the Past* (Cambridge: Cambridge University Press, 1992)

Colish, Marcia L., *The Mirror of Language: A Study in the Medieval Theory of Knowledge*, rev. edn (London: University of Nebraska Press, 1983)

Collins, Kristen, 'Pictures and the Devotional Imagination in the St Albans Psalter', in *The St Albans Psalter: Painting and Prayer in Medieval England*, by Kirsten Collins, Peter Kidd, and Nancy K. Turner (Los Angeles: J. Paul Getty Trust, 2013), pp.9–63

Constable, Giles, 'Forgery and Plagiarism in the Middle Ages', *Archiv für Diplomatik*, 29 (1983), 1–41

Cooper, Alan, '"The Feet of those that Bark shall be Cut Off": Timorous Historians and the Personality of Henry I', *ANS*, 23 (2000), 47–67

Coote, Lesley A., *Prophecy and Public Affairs in Later Medieval England* (York: York Medieval Press, 2000)

Copeland, Rita, 'The Fortunes of "Non Verbum pro Verbo": or, Why Jerome Is Not a Ciceronian', in *The Medieval Translator: The Theory and Practice of Translation in the Middle Ages*, ed. by Roger Ellis et al. (Cambridge: Brewer, 1989), pp.15–35

Rhetoric, Hermeneutics and Translation in the Middle Ages (Cambridge: Cambridge University Press, 1991)

Coulter, Cornelia C., and F. P. Magoun Jr., 'Giraldus Cambrensis on Indo-Germanic Philology', *Speculum*, 1 (1926), 104–109

Crane, Susan, *Insular Romance: Politics, Faith, and Culture in Anglo-Norman and Middle English Literature* (Berkeley: University of California Press, 1986)

Crawford, T. D., 'On the Linguistic Competence of Geoffrey of Monmouth', *Medium Ævum*, 51 (1982), 152–162

Crépin, André, 'Le "Psautier d'Eadwine": L'Angleterre Pluriculturelle', in *Journée d'études anglo-normandes. Organisée par l'Académie des inscriptions et belles-lettres, Palais de l'Institut, 20 juin 2008*, ed. by André Crépin and Jean Leclant (Paris: Académie des inscriptions et belles-lettres, 2009), pp.139–170

Crick, Julia, 'The British Past and the Welsh Future: Gerald of Wales, Geoffrey of Monmouth and Arthur of Britain', *Celtica*, 23 (1999), 60–75

'Geoffrey and the Prophetic Tradition', in *The Arthur of Medieval Latin Literature: The Development and Dissemination of the Arthurian Legend in Medieval Latin*, ed. by Siân Echard (Cardiff: University of Wales Press, 2011), pp.67–82

'Geoffrey of Monmouth, Prophecy and History', *Journal of Medieval History*, 18 (1992), 357–371

The Historia regum Britannie of Geoffrey of Monmouth, III: A Summary Catalogue of the Manuscripts (Cambridge: Brewer, 1989)

The Historia regum Britannie of Geoffrey of Monmouth, IV: Dissemination and Reception in the Later Middle Ages (Cambridge: Brewer, 1991)

'Liberty and Fraternity: Creating and Defending the Liberty of St Albans', in *Expectations of the Law in the Middle Ages*, ed. by Anthony Musson (Woodbridge: Boydell, 2001), pp.91–103

'*Pristina libertas*: Liberty and the Anglo-Saxons Revisited', *TRHS*, Sixth Series, 14 (2004), 47–71

'St Albans, Westminster, and Some Twelfth-Century Views of the Anglo-Saxon Past', *ANS*, 25 (2002), 65–84

Croenen, Godfried, 'Princely and Noble Genealogies, Twelfth to Fourteenth Century: Form and Function', in *The Medieval Chronicle*, ed. by Erik Kooper (Amsterdam: Rodopi, 1999), pp.84–95

Crouch, David, *The Image of Aristocracy in Britain, 1000–1300* (London: Routledge, 1992)

'Normans and Anglo-Normans: A Divided Aristocracy?', in *England and Normandy in the Middle Ages*, ed. by David Bates and Anne Curry (London: Hambledon Press, 1994), pp.51–68

Crowley, Joseph, 'Anglicized Word Order in Old English Continuous Interlinear Glosses in British Library, Royal 2.A.XX', *ASE*, 29 (2000), 123–151

Curley, Michael J., 'Animal Symbolism in the *Prophecies of Merlin*', in *Beasts and Birds of the Middle Ages: The Bestiary and Its Legacy*, ed. by Willene B. Clark and Meradith T. McMunn (Philadelphia: University of Pennsylvania Press, 1989), pp.151–163

Geoffrey of Monmouth (New York: Twayne, 1994)

'Gerallt Gymro a Siôn o Gernyw fel Cyfieithwyr Proffwydoliaethau Myrddin', *Llên Cymru*, 15 (1984), 23–33

Curtius, Ernst Robert, *European Literature and the Latin Middle Ages*, trans. Willard R. Trask (London: Routledge, 1953)

Dahan, Gilbert, *Les intellectuels chrétiens et les juifs au Moyen Âge* (Paris: Éditions du Cerf, 1990)

Dalton, Paul, 'The Date of Gaimar's *Estoire des Engleis*, the Connections of His Patrons, and the Politics of Stephen's Reign', *Chaucer Review*, 42.1 (2007), 23–47

Damian-Grint, Peter, *The New Historians of the Twelfth-Century Renaissance: Inventing Vernacular Authority* (Woodbridge: Boydell, 1999)

Dance, Richard, *Words Derived from Old Norse in Early Middle English: Studies in the Vocabulary of the South-West Midland Texts* (Tempe, AZ: ACMRS, 2003)

D'Arcier, Louis Faivre, *Histoire et géographie d'un mythe: la circulation des manuscrits du De excidio Troiae de Darès le Phrygien (VIIIe-XVe siècles)* (Paris: École des chartes, 2006)

Davies, J. R., *The Book of Llandaf and the Norman Church in Wales* (Woodbridge: Boydell, 2003)

'*Liber Landavensis*: Its Date and the Identity of Its Editor', *Cambrian Medieval Celtic Studies*, 35 (1998), 1–11

Davies, R. R., *Conquest, Coexistence, and Change: Wales, 1063–1415* (Oxford: Clarendon, 1987)
The First English Empire: Power and Identities in the British Isles 1093–1343 (Oxford: Oxford University Press, 2000)
'The Peoples of Britain and Ireland 1100–1400', *TRHS*, Sixth Series, 4–7 (1994–1997)
Davies, Wendy, *An Early Welsh Microcosm: Studies in the Llandaff Charters* (London: Royal Historical Society, 1978)
'Liber Landavensis: Its Construction and Credibility', *English Historical Review*, 88 (1973), 335–351
The Llandaff Charters (Aberystwyth: National Library of Wales, 1979)
Davis, R. H. C., *The Normans and Their Myth* (London: Thames and Hudson, 1976)
Dean, Ruth J., with Maureen B. M. Boulton, *Anglo-Norman Literature: A Guide to Texts and Manuscripts* (London: Anglo-Norman Text Society, 1999)
Dearnley, Elizabeth, 'French-English Translation 1189–c.1450, with Special Reference to Translators and Their Prologues' (unpublished doctoral thesis, University of Cambridge, 2011)
Derolez, R., 'Language Problems in Anglo-Saxon England: Barbara Loquella and Barbarismus', in *Words, Texts, and Manuscripts: Studies in Anglo-Saxon Culture Presented to Helmut Gneuss*, ed. by Michael Korhammer et al. (Cambridge: Brewer, 1992), pp.285–292
Runica Manuscripta: The English Tradition (Bruges: De Tempel, 1954)
'Those Things Are Difficult to Express in English ...', *English Studies*, 70:6 (1989), 469–476
Dionisotti, A. C., 'On the Nature and Transmission of Latin Glossaries', in *Les manuscrits des lexiques et glossaires de l'Antiquité tardive à la fin du Moyen Âge*, ed. by Jacqueline Hamesse (Louvain-la-Neuve: Fédération Internationale des Instituts d'Études Médiévales, 1996), pp.205–252
Douglas, David C., *William the Conqueror: The Norman Impact upon England* (London: Eyre and Spottiswoode, 1964)
Duggan, Anne J., 'Henry II, the English Church and the Papacy, 1154–76', in *Henry II: New Interpretations*, ed. by Christopher Harper-Bill and Nicholas Vincent (Woodbridge: Boydell, 2007), pp.154–183
Thomas Becket (London: Arnold, 2004)
Dumville, David N., 'The Historical Value of the *Historia Brittonum*', *Arthurian Literature*, VI (1986), 1–26
Liturgy and the Ecclesiastical History of Late Anglo-Saxon England: Four Studies (Woodbridge: Boydell, 1992)
Dunbabin, Jean, 'Discovering a Past for the French Aristocracy', in *The Perception of the Past in Twelfth-Century Europe*, ed. by Paul Magdalino (London and Rio Grande: Hambledon Press, 1992), pp.1–14
Dyson, A. C., 'The Career, Family and Influence of Alexander le Poer, Bishop of Lincoln, 1123–1148' (unpublished BLitt thesis, University of Oxford, 1972)
Echard, Siân, *Arthurian Narrative in the Latin Tradition* (Cambridge: Cambridge University Press, 1998)

Eckhardt, Caroline D., 'Another Manuscript of the Commentary on the *Prophetia Merlini* Attributed to Alain de Lille', *Manuscripta*, 29 (1985), 143–147

'The Date of the "Prophetia Merlini" Commentary in MSS. Cotton Claudius B VII and Bibliothèque Nationale fonds latin 6233', *Notes and Queries*, n.s. 23 (1976), 146–147

'Geoffrey of Monmouth's *Prophetia Merlini* and the Construction of Liège University MS 369C', *Manuscripta*, 32 (1988), 176–184

(ed.), *The Prophetia Merlini of Geoffrey of Monmouth: A Fifteenth-Century English Commentary* (Cambridge, MA: Medieval Academy of America, 1982)

'The *Prophetia Merlini* of Geoffrey of Monmouth: Latin Manuscript Copies', *Manuscripta*, 26 (1982), 167–176

Esposito, Mario, 'The Sources of Conchubranus' Life of St Monenna', *English Historical Review*, xxxv (1920), 71–78

Faith, Rosalind, *The English Peasantry and the Growth of Lordship* (London: Leicester University Press, 1997, repr. 1999)

Faletra, Michael A., 'Merlin in Cornwall: The Source and Contexts of John of Cornwall's *Prophetia Merlini*', *Journal of English and Germanic Philology*, iii (2012), 304–338

Faulkner, Mark, 'Archaism, Belatedness and Modernisation: "Old" English in the Twelfth Century', *Review of English Studies*, n.s. 63 (2012), 179–203

'Gerald of Wales and Standard Old English', *Notes and Queries*, 58:1 (2011), 19–24

'Rewriting English Literary History, 1042–1215', *Literature Compass*, 9 (2012), 275–291

'The Uses of Anglo-Saxon Manuscripts, c.1066–1200' (unpublished doctoral thesis, Oxford University, 2008)

Fenton, Kirsten A., *Gender, Nation and Conquest in the Works of William of Malmesbury* (Woodbridge: Boydell, 2008)

Ferguson, C. A., 'Diglossia', *Word*, 15 (1959), 325–340

Fergusson, Peter, *Canterbury Cathedral Priory in the Age of Becket* (New Haven, CT: Yale University Press, 2011)

Field, Rosalind, 'The Curious History of the Matter of England', in *Boundaries in Medieval Romance*, ed. by Neil Cartlidge (Cambridge: Brewer, 2008), pp.29–42

'"Pur les franc homes amender": Clerical Authors and the Thirteenth-Century Context of Historical Romance', in *Medieval Romance, Medieval Contexts*, ed. by Rhiannon Purdie and Michael Cichon (Cambridge: Brewer, 2011), pp.175–188

'Romance as History, History as Romance', in *Romance in Medieval England*, ed. by Maldwyn Mills, Jennifer Fellows and Carol M. Meale (Cambridge: Brewer, 1991), pp.163–173

'Waldef and the Matter of/with England', in *Medieval Insular Romance: Translation and Innovation*, ed. by Judith Weiss et al. (Cambridge: Brewer, 2000), pp.25–39

'What's in a Name? Arthurian Name-Dropping in the *Roman de Waldef*', in *Arthurian Studies in Honour of P. J. C. Field*, ed. by Bonnie Wheeler (Woodbridge: Brewer, 2004), pp.63–64

Finazzi, Rosa Bianca, 'In margine all'Enchiridion di Byrhtferth', in *Per una storia della grammatica in Europa*, ed. by Celestina Milani and Rosa Bianca Finazzi (Milan: I.S.U. Università Cattolica, 2004), pp.95–108

Finke, Laurie A., and Martin B. Shichtman, *King Arthur and the Myth of History* (Gainesville: University Press of Florida, 2004)

Fischer, Andreas, 'The Hatton MS of the West Saxon Gospels: The Preservation and Transmission of Old English', in *The Preservation and Transmission of Anglo-Saxon Culture*, ed. by Paul E. Szarmach and Joel T. Rosenthal (Kalamazoo, MI: Medieval Institute Publications, 1997), pp.353–367

Fischer, Olga, 'Syntax', in *The Cambridge History of the English Language: Volume II, 1066–1476*, ed. by Norman Blake (Cambridge: Cambridge University Press, 1992), pp.207–408

Fishman, Joshua A., 'Bilingualism with and without Diglossia; Diglossia with and without Bilingualism', *Journal of Social Issues*, 23:2 (1967), 29–38

Fleuriot, L., 'Les fragments du texte brittonique de la "Prophetia Merlini"', *Études celtiques*, 14 (1974), 43–56

Flint, Valerie I. J., 'The *Historia regum Britanniae* of Geoffrey of Monmouth: Parody and Its Purpose. A Suggestion', *Speculum*, 54 (1979), 447–468

Foot, Sarah, 'The Abbey's Armoury of Charters', in *Bury St Edmunds and the Norman Conquest*, ed. by Tom Licence (Woodbridge: Boydell, 2014), pp.31–52

'Internal and External Audiences: Reflections on the Anglo-Saxon Archive of Bury St Edmunds Abbey in Suffolk', *Haskins Society Journal*, 24 (2012), 163–193

'The Making of *Angelcynn*: English Identity before the Norman Conquest', *TRHS*, Sixth Series, 6 (1996), 25–49

'Where English Becomes British: Rethinking Contexts for Brunanburh', in *Myth, Rulership, Church and Charters: Essays in Honour of Nicholas Brooks*, ed. by Julia Barrow and Andrew Wareham (Aldershot: Ashgate, 2008), pp.127–144

Forsyth, Katherine, 'Literacy in Pictland', in *Literacy in Medieval Celtic Societies*, ed. by Huw Pryce (Cambridge: Cambridge University Press, 1998), pp.39–61

Frank, Roberta, 'King Cnut in the Verse of His Skalds', in *The Reign of Cnut: King of England, Denmark, and Norway*, ed. by Alexander R. Rumble (London: Leicester University Press, 1994), pp.106–124

Franzen, Christine, 'Late Copies of Anglo-Saxon Charters', in *Studies in English Language and Literature: "Doubt Wisely": Papers in Honour of E. G. Stanley*, ed. by M. J. Toswell and E. M. Tyler (London: Routledge, 1996), pp.42–70

The Tremulous Hand of Worcester: A Study of Old English in the Thirteenth Century (Oxford: Clarendon, 1991)

Fredborg, Karin Margareta, 'Universal Grammar According to Some Twelfth-Century Grammarians', *Historiographica Linguistica*, 7 (1980), 69–84

Fulk, Robert D., 'Unferth and His Name', *Modern Philology*, 85 (1987), 113–127

Furrow, Melissa, *Expectations of Romance: The Reception of a Genre in Medieval England* (Cambridge: Brewer, 2009)

Fyler, John M., *Language and the Declining World in Chaucer, Dante, and Jean de Meun* (Cambridge: Cambridge University Press, 2007)

Galbraith, V. H., 'Nationality and Language in Medieval England', *TRHS*, Fourth Series, 23 (1941), 113–128

Garnett, George, *Conquered England: Kingship, Succession and Tenure, 1066–1166* (Oxford: Oxford University Press, 2007)

'*Franci et Angli*: The Legal Distinctions between Peoples after the Conquest', *ANS*, 8 (1985), 109–137

Gasquet, Abbot F. A., and Edmund Bishop, *The Bosworth Psalter* (London: Bell, 1908)

Geary, Patrick, 'Ethnic Identity as a Situational Construct in the Early Middle Ages', *Mitteilungen der Anthropologischen Gesellschaft in Wien*, 113 (1983), 15–26

'Land, Language, and Memory in Europe, 700–1100', *TRHS*, Sixth Series, 9 (1999), 169–184

The Myth of Nations: The Medieval Origins of Europe (Princeton, NJ: Princeton University Press, 2002)

Gibson, Margaret, 'Conclusions: The Eadwine Psalter in Context', in *The Eadwine Psalter: Text, Image and Monastic Culture in Twelfth-Century Canterbury*, ed. by Margaret Gibson, T. A. Heslop, and Richard W. Pfaff (London: Modern Humanities Research Association, 1992), pp.209–213

'The Latin Apparatus', in *The Eadwine Psalter: Text, Image and Monastic Culture in Twelfth-Century Canterbury*, ed. by Margaret Gibson, T. A. Heslop, and Richard W. Pfaff (London: Modern Humanities Research Association, 1992), pp.108–122

Gibson, Margaret, T. A. Heslop, and Richard W. Pfaff (eds), *The Eadwine Psalter: Text, Image and Monastic Culture in Twelfth-Century Canterbury* (London: Modern Humanities Research Association, 1992)

Gilbert, Jane, and Sara Harris, 'The Written Word: Literacy across Languages', in *The Cambridge Companion to Medieval British Manuscripts*, ed. by Orietta da Rold and Elaine Treharne (Cambridge: Cambridge University Press, forthcoming)

Gillingham, John, *The English in the Twelfth Century: Imperialism, National Identity and Political Values* (Woodbridge: Boydell, 2000)

'Richard of Devizes and "a Rising Tide of Nonsense": How Cerdic met King Arthur', in *The Long Twelfth-Century View of the Anglo-Saxon Past*, ed. by Martin Brett and David A. Woodman (Aldershot: Ashgate, 2015), pp.141–156

'"Slaves of the Normans"? Gerald de Barri and Regnal Solidarity in Early Thirteenth-Century England', in *Law, Laity and Solidarities: Essays in Honour of Susan Reynolds*, ed. by Pauline Stafford, Janet L. Nelson, and Jane Martindale (Manchester: Manchester University Press, 2001), pp.160–171

Gneuss, Helmut, '*Anglicae linguae interpretatio*: Language Contact, Lexical Borrowing and Glossing in Anglo-Saxon England', *Proceedings of the British Academy*, 82 (1992), 107–148

'Giraldus Cambrensis und die Geschichte der englischen Sprachwissenschaft im Mittelalter', in *Language and Civilization: A Concerted Profusion of Essays and Studies in Honour of Otto Hietsch*, ed. by Claudia Blank et al. (Frankfurt-am-Main: Peter Lang, 1992), pp.164–172

'The Origin of Standard Old English and Æthelwold's School at Winchester', *ASE*, 1 (1972), 63–83

'The Study of Language in Anglo-Saxon England', *Bulletin of the John Rylands University Library of Manchester*, 72 (1990), 3–32

Gobbitt, Thomas John, 'The Production and Use of MS Cambridge, Corpus Christi College 383 in the Late Eleventh and First Half of the Twelfth Centuries' (unpublished doctoral thesis, University of Leeds, 2010)

Godden, Malcolm, 'The Old English Life of St Neot and the Legends of King Alfred', *ASE*, 39 (2010), 193–225

Goetz, Hans-Werner, 'The Concept of Time in the Historiography of the Eleventh and Twelfth Centuries', in *Medieval Concepts of the Past: Ritual, Memory, Historiography*, ed. by Gerd Althoff, Johannes Fried, and Patrick J. Geary (Cambridge: Cambridge University Press, 2002), pp.139–166

Golding, Brian, 'Trans-border Transactions: Patterns of Patronage in Anglo-Norman Wales', *Haskins Society Journal*, 16 (2005), 27–46

Gouttebroze, Jean-Guy, 'Pourquoi congédier un historiographe, Henri II Plantagenêt et Wace (1155–1174)', *Romania*, 112 (1991), 289–311

Gransden, Antonia, *Historical Writing in England, c.550–c.1307* (London: Routledge, 1974)

Legends, Traditions and History in Medieval England (London: Hambledon Press, 1992)

Green, Judith, *The Aristocracy of Norman England* (Cambridge: Cambridge University Press, 1997)

Henry I: King of England and Duke of Normandy (Cambridge: Cambridge University Press, 2006)

'Unity and Disunity in the Anglo-Norman State', *Historical Research*, 62 (1989), 115–134

Green, Richard Firth, *A Crisis of Truth: Literature and Law in Ricardian England* (Philadelphia: University of Pennsylvania Press, 1999)

Greenway, Diana, 'Authority, Convention and Observation in Henry of Huntingdon's *Historia Anglorum*', *ANS*, 18 (1995), 105–121

'Henry of Huntingdon and Bede', in *L'historiographie médiévale en Europe*, ed. by Jean-Philippe Genet (Paris: Éditions du CNRS, 1991), pp.43–50

'Henry of Huntingdon and the Manuscripts of His *Historia Anglorum*', *ANS*, 11 (1986), 103–126

Gretsch, Mechthild, 'Ælfric, Language and Winchester', in *A Companion to Ælfric*, ed. by Hugh Magennis and Mary Swan (Leiden: Brill, 2009), pp.109–138

The Intellectual Foundations of the English Benedictine Reform (Cambridge: Cambridge University Press, 1999)

'The Junius Psalter Gloss: Its Historical and Cultural Context', *ASE*, 29 (2000), 85–122

'The Roman Psalter, Its Old English Glosses and the English Benedictine Reform', in *The Liturgy of the Late Anglo-Saxon Church*, ed. by Helen Gittos and M. Bradford Bedingfield (Woodbridge: Boydell, 2005), pp.13–28

'Winchester Vocabulary and Standard Old English: The Vernacular in Late Anglo-Saxon England', *Bulletin of the John Rylands Library*, 83 (2001), 41–87

Griffiths, Margaret Enid, *Early Vaticination in Welsh with English Parallels*, ed. by T. Gwynn Jones (Cardiff: Oxford University Press, 1937)

Grondeux, Anne, 'Le latin et les autres langues au Moyen Âge: contacts avec des locuteurs étrangers, bilinguisme, interprétation et traduction (800–1200)', in *Tous vos gens à latin: Le latin, langue savante, langue mondaine (XIVe-XVIIe siècles)*, ed. by Emmanuel Bury (Geneva: Droz, 2005), pp.47–67

Grotans, Anna A., *Reading in Medieval St Gall* (Cambridge: Cambridge University Press, 2006)

Gunnlaugsson, Guðvarður Már, 'Manuscripts and Palaeography', in *A Companion to Old Norse–Icelandic Literature and Culture*, ed. by Rory McTurk (Oxford: Blackwell, 2005), pp.245–264

Guy, Ben, 'Gerald and Welsh Genealogical Learning', in *Gerald of Wales*, ed. by Georgia Henley and A. Joseph McMullen (Cardiff: University of Wales Press, forthcoming)

Hagger, Mark, 'The *Gesta Abbatum Monasterii Sancti Albani*: Litigation and History at St Albans', *Historical Research*, 81 (2008), 373–398

Hall, Alaric, 'Interlinguistic Communication in Bede's Historia Ecclesiastica Gentis Anglorum', in *Interfaces between Language and Culture in Medieval England: A Festschrift for Matti Kilpiö*, ed. by Alaric Hall et al. (Leiden: Brill, 2010), pp.37–80

Hamel, C. F. R., de, *Glossed Books of the Bible and the Origins of the Paris Booktrade* (Cambridge: Brewer, 1984)

Hammer, Jacob, 'Bref commentaire de la Prophetia Merlini du ms 3514 de la bibliothèque de la cathédrale d'Exeter', in *Hommages à Joseph Bidez et à Franz Cumont* (Brussels, 1948), pp.111–119

'A Commentary on the *Prophetia Merlini* (Geoffrey of Monmouth's *Historia regum Britanniae*, Book VII)', *Speculum*, 10 (1935), 3–30

'A Commentary on the *Prophetia Merlini* (Geoffrey of Monmouth's *Historia regum Britanniae*, Book VII) (Continuation)', *Speculum*, 15 (1940), 409–431

Hanning, Robert W., *The Vision of History in Early Britain: From Gildas to Geoffrey of Monmouth* (New York: Columbia University Press, 1966)

Harf-Lancner, Laurence, 'Le *Florimont* d'Aimon de Varennes: un prologue du *Roman d'Alexandre*', *Cahiers de civilisation médiévale*, 37 (1994), 241–253

Haring, N. M., 'The *Eulogium ad Alexandrum Papam tertium* of John of Cornwall', *Medieval Studies*, 13 (1951), 253–300

Harris, Sara, '*Tam Anglis quam Danis*: "Old Norse" Terminology in the *Constitutiones de foresta*', *ANS*, 37 (2014), 131–148

Harvey, Sally, *Domesday: Book of Judgement* (Oxford: Oxford University Press, 2014)

Hay, Denys, *Europe: The Emergence of an Idea*, rev. edn (Edinburgh: Edinburgh University Press, 1968)

Hayward, Paul Antony, 'The Cult of St. Alban, Anglorum Protomartyr, in Anglo-Saxon and Anglo-Norman England', in *More Than a Memory: The Discourse of Martyrdom and the Construction of Christian Identity in the History of Christianity*, ed. by Johan Leemans (Leuven: Peeters, 2005), 169–199

Henderson, George, and T. A. Heslop, 'Decoration and Illustration', in *The Eadwine Psalter: Text, Image and Monastic Culture in Twelfth-Century Canterbury*, ed. by Margaret Gibson, T. A. Heslop, and Richard W. Pfaff (London: Modern Humanities Research Association, 1992), pp.25–61

Heng, Geraldine, *Empire of Magic: Medieval Romance and the Politics of Cultural Fantasy* (New York: Columbia University Press, 2003)

Herren, Michael W., 'Latin and the Vernacular Languages', in *Medieval Latin: An Introduction and Bibliographical Guide*, ed. by F. A. C. Mantello and A. G. Rigg (USA: Catholic University of America Press, 1996), pp.127–128

Heslop, T. A., 'The Visual Sources of the Picture Leaves', in *The Eadwine Psalter: Text, Image and Monastic Culture in Twelfth-Century Canterbury*, ed. by Margaret Gibson, T. A. Heslop, and Richard W. Pfaff (London: Modern Humanities Research Association, 1992), pp.29–34

Hexter, Ralph, '*Latinitas* in the Middle Ages: Horizons and Perspectives', *Helios*, 14 (1987), 69–92

Hiatt, Alfred, *The Making of Medieval Forgeries: False Documents in Fifteenth-Century England* (London: British Library, 2004)

Higounet, Charles, 'Les forêts de l'Europe occidentale du Ve au XIe siècle', *Paysages et villages neufs du Moyen Âge* (Bordeaux: Fédération historique du Sud-Ouest, 1975), repr. from *Settimane di studio del Centro italiano di studi sull'alto medioevo*, XIII (1966), 343–398

Hill, Joyce, 'Ælfric: His Life and Works', in *A Companion to Ælfric*, ed. by Hugh Magennis and Mary Swan (Leiden: Brill, 2009), pp.35–65

Hingst, Amanda Jane, *The Written World: Past and Place in the Work of Orderic Vitalis* (Notre Dame, IN: University of Notre Dame Press, 2009)

Hofstetter, Walter, 'Winchester and the Standardization of Old English Vocabulary', *ASE*, 17 (1988), 139–161

Hogg, Richard M. (ed.), *The Cambridge History of the English Language, Volume 1: The Beginnings to 1066* (Cambridge: Cambridge University Press, 1992)
A Grammar of Old English, 2 vols (Oxford: Wiley-Blackwell, 1992–2011)

Holford-Strevens, Leofranc, *Aulus Gellius: An Antonine Scholar and His Achievement*, rev. edn (Oxford: Oxford University Press, 2003)

Holt, J. C., 'Feudal Society and the Family in Early Medieval England, II: Notions of Patrimony', *TRHS*, Fifth Series, 33 (1983), 193–220

Houck, Margaret, *Sources of the Roman de Brut of Wace* (Berkeley: University of California Press, 1938)

Houts, Elisabeth M. C., van, 'The Adaptation of the Gesta Normannorum Ducum by Wace and Benoît', in *Non nova, sed nove: Mélanges de civilisation médiévale dédiés à Willem Noomen*, ed. by Martin Gosman and Jaap van Os (Groningen: Bouma, 1984), pp.115–124

'Genre Aspects of the Use of Oral Information in Medieval Historiography', in *Gattungen mittelalterlicher Schriftlichkeit*, ed. by Barbara Frank, Thomas Haye, and Doris Tophinke (Tübingen: Gunter Narr, 1997), pp.297–312

'Hereward and Flanders', *ASE*, 28 (1999), 201–223

'Intermarriage in Eleventh-Century England', in *Normandy and Its Neighbours, 900–1250: Essays for David Bates*, ed. by David Crouch and Kathleen Thompson (Turnhout: Brepols, 2011), pp.237–270

Memory and Gender in Medieval Europe, 900–1200 (Toronto: University of Toronto Press, 1999)

'Wace as Historian', in *Family Trees and the Roots of Politics: The Prosopography of Britain and France from the Tenth to the Twelfth Century*, ed. by K. S. B. Keats-Rohan (Woodbridge: Boydell, 1997), pp.103–132

Howlett, D. R., *The English Origins of Old French Literature* (Dublin: Four Courts, 1996)

'The Literary Context of Geoffrey of Monmouth: An Essay on the Fabrication of Sources', *Arthuriana*, 5 (1995), 25–69

Hsy, Jonathan, *Trading Tongues: Merchants, Multilingualism and Medieval Literature* (Columbus: Ohio State University Press, 2013)

Hudson, John, 'Administration, Family and Perceptions of the Past in Late Twelfth-Century England: Richard FitzNigel and the Dialogue of the Exchequer', in *The Perception of the Past in Twelfth-Century Europe*, ed. by Paul Magdalino (London: Hambledon Press, 1992), pp.75–98

The Formation of the English Common Law: Law and Society in England from the Norman Conquest to Magna Carta (London: Longman, 1996)

'From the Leges to Glanvill: Legal Expertise and Legal Reasoning', in *English Law before Magna Carta: Felix Liebermann and Die Gesetze der Angelsachsen*, ed. by Stefan Jurasinski et al. (Leiden: Brill, 2010), pp.221–249

'Imposing Feudalism on Anglo-Saxon England: Norman and Angevin Presentation of Pre-Conquest Lordship and Landholding', in *Feudalism: New Landscapes of Debate*, ed. by Sverre Bagge, Michael H. Gelting, and Thomas Lindkvist (Turnhout: Brepols, 2011), pp.115–134

Land, Law, and Lordship in Anglo-Norman England (Oxford: Clarendon, 1994)

'The Making of English Law and the Varieties of Legal History', in *Early Medieval Studies in Memory of Patrick Wormald*, ed. by Stephen Baxter et al. (Farnham: Ashgate, 2009), pp.421–432

The Oxford History of the Laws of England, Volume II: 871–1216 (Oxford: Oxford University Press, 2012)

Hunt, R. W., *The History of Grammar in the Middle Ages: Collected Papers*, ed. by G. L. Bursill-Hall (Amsterdam: Benjamins, 1980)

Hunt, Tony, *Teaching and Learning Latin in Thirteenth-Century England*, 3 vols (Cambridge: Brewer, 1991)

Hyams, Paul, 'The Common Law and the French Connection', *ANS*, 4 (1981), 77–92

Ingham, Patricia Clare, *Sovereign Fantasies: Arthurian Romance and the Making of Britain* (Philadelphia: University of Pennsylvania Press, 2001)

Ingham, Richard (ed.), *The Anglo-Norman Language and Its Contexts* (Woodbridge: York Medieval Press, 2010)

'Mixing Languages on the Manor', *Medium Aevum*, 78:1 (2009), 80–97

'The Persistence of Anglo-Norman 1230–1362: A Linguistic Perspective', in *Language and Culture in Medieval Britain: The French of England c.1100–c.1500*, ed. by Jocelyn Wogan-Browne et al. (York: York Medieval Press, 2009), pp.44–54

The Transmission of Anglo-Norman: Language History and Language Acquisition (Amsterdam: Benjamins, 2012)

Ingledew, Francis, 'The Book of Troy and the Genealogical Construction of History: The Case of Geoffrey of Monmouth's *Historia regum Britanniae*', *Speculum*, 69 (1994), 665–704

Irvine, Martin, *The Making of Textual Culture: 'Grammatica' and Literary Theory, 350–1100* (Cambridge: Cambridge University Press, 1994)

Jackson, Kenneth, *Language and History in Early Britain: A Chronological Survey of the Brittonic Languages, First to Twelfth Century* A.D. (Edinburgh: Edinburgh University Press, 1953)

Jager, Eric, *The Tempter's Voice: Language and the Fall in Medieval Literature* (Ithaca, NY: Cornell University Press, 1993)

James, M. R., *The Ancient Libraries of Canterbury and Dover* (Cambridge: Cambridge University Press, 1903)

Jarman, A. O. H., 'The Merlin Legend and the Welsh Tradition of Prophecy', in *The Arthur of the Welsh: The Arthurian Legend in Medieval Welsh Literature*, ed. by Rachel Bromwich et al. (Cardiff: University of Wales Press, 1991), pp.117–145

Jeauneau, Édouard, '"Nani gigantum humeris insidentes": Essai d'interprétation de Bernard de Chartres', *Vivarium*, 5 (1967), 79–99

Jefferson, Judith A., and Ad Putter (eds), with Amanda Hopkins, *Multilingualism in Medieval Britain (c.1066–1520): Sources and Analysis* (Turnhout: Brepols, 2013)

Johnson, Ewan, 'Normandy and Norman Identity in the Southern Italian Chronicles', *ANS*, 27 (2004), 85–100

Johnson, Lesley, 'The Anglo-Norman Description of England: An Introduction', in *Anglo-Norman Anniversary Essays*, ed. by Ian Short (London: Anglo-Norman Text Society, 1993), pp.11–30

Jones, E. D., 'The Book of Llandaff', *National Library of Wales Journal*, 4 (1945–1946), 123–157

Jordan, Richard, *Handbuch der mittel-englischen Grammatik, Teil 1: Lautlehre*, rev. edn, ed. by H. C. Matthes (Heidelberg: Winter, 1934)

Jurasinski, Stefan, 'The *Rime of King William* and Its Analogues', *Neophilologus*, 88 (2004), 131–144

Karn, Nicholas, 'Nigel, Bishop of Ely, and the Restoration of the Exchequer after the "Anarchy" of King Stephen's Reign', *Historical Research*, 80 (2007), 299–314

'Rethinking the Leges Henrici Primi', in *English Law before Magna Carta: Felix Liebermann and Die Gesetze der Angelsachsen*, ed. by Stefan Jurasinski et al. (Leiden: Brill, 2010), pp.199–220

Keen, Maurice, *Chivalry* (New Haven, CT: Yale University Press, 1984)

Keller, Hans-Erich, *Étude descriptive sur le vocabulaire de Wace* (Berlin: Akademie, 1953)

Kelly, Susan, 'Anglo-Saxon Lay Society and the Written Word', in *The Uses of Literacy in Early Mediaeval Europe*, ed. by Rosamond McKitterick (Cambridge: Cambridge University Press, 1990), pp.36–62

Kennedy, Ruth, and Simon Meecham-Jones (eds), *Writers of the Reign of Henry II: Twelve Essays* (New York: Palgrave Macmillan, 2006)

Ker, N. R., *Catalogue of Manuscripts Containing Anglo-Saxon*, reissued with supplement (Oxford: Clarendon, 1990)

Keynes, Simon, *The Diplomas of King Æthelred 'the Unready', 978–1016: A Study in Their Use as Historical Evidence* (Cambridge: Cambridge University Press, 1980)

'A Lost Cartulary of St Albans Abbey', *ASE*, 22 (1993), 253–279

Kibbee, Douglas A., *For to Speke Frenche Trewely: The French Language in England, 1000–1600: Its Status, Description and Instruction* (Amsterdam: Benjamins, 1991)

Kitson, Peter R., 'When Did Middle English Begin? Later Than You Think!', in *Studies in Middle English Linguistics*, ed. by Jacek Fisiak (Berlin: De Gruyter, 1997), pp.221–269

Kleinhenz, Christopher, and Keith Busby (eds), *Medieval Multilingualism: The Francophone World and Its Neighbours* (Turnhout: Brepols, 2010)

Klinck, Roswitha, *Die Lateinische Etymologie des Mittelalters* (Munich: Fink, 1970)

Knowles, David, 'The *Mappa Mundi* of Gervase of Canterbury', *Downside Review*, 48 (1930), 237–247

Koopmans, Rachel, *Wonderful to Relate: Miracle Stories and Miracle Collecting in High Medieval England* (Philadelphia: University of Pennsylvania Press, 2011)

Lapidge, Michael, 'Poeticism in Pre-Conquest Anglo-Latin Prose', in *Aspects of the Language of Latin Prose*, ed. by Tobias Reinhardt, Michael Lapidge, and J. N. Adams (Oxford: Oxford University Press, 2005), pp.321–337

Lass, Roger, 'Phonology and Morphology', in *The Cambridge History of the English Language: Volume II, 1066–1476*, ed. by Norman Blake (Cambridge: Cambridge University Press, 1992), pp.23–155

Old English: A Historical Linguistic Companion (Cambridge: Cambridge University Press, 1994)

Lavezzo, Kathy, *Angels on the Edge of the World: Geography, Literature, and English Community, 1000–1534* (Ithaca, NY: Cornell University Press, 2006)

'Introduction', in *Imagining a Medieval English Nation*, ed. by Kathy Lavezzo (Minneapolis: University of Minnesota Press, 2004), pp.vii–xxxiv

Leckie, R. William, Jr., *The Passage of Dominion: Geoffrey of Monmouth and the Periodization of Insular History in the Twelfth Century* (Toronto: University of Toronto Press, 1981)

Lecoy, Félix, 'Review of Hans-Erich Keller, *Étude descriptive sur le vocabulaire de Wace*', *Romania*, 76 (1955), 534–538

Ledgeway, Adam, *From Latin to Romance: Morphosyntactic Typology and Change* (Oxford: Oxford University Press, 2012)

Lees, Clare A., 'Analytical Survey 7: Actually Existing Anglo-Saxon Studies', *New Medieval Literatures*, 7 (2005), 223–252

Legge, M. Dominica, *Anglo-Norman Literature and Its Background* (Oxford: Clarendon, 1963)

Léglu, Catherine E., *Multilingualism and Mother Tongue in Medieval French, Occitan and Catalan Narratives* (University Park: Pennsylvania State University Press, 2010)

Lejeune, Rita, 'Le role littéraire de la famille d'Aliénor d'Aquitaine', *Cahiers de civilisation médiévale*, 1 (1958), 319–337

Lerer, Seth, 'The Genre of the Grave and the Origins of the Middle English Lyric', *Modern Language Quarterly*, 58 (1997), 127–161

'Old English and Its Afterlife', in *The Cambridge History of Medieval English Literature*, ed. by David Wallace (Cambridge: Cambridge University Press, 1999), pp.7–34

Le Saux, Françoise H. M., *A Companion to Wace* (Cambridge: Brewer, 2005)

'Du temps historique au temps mythique dans le "Roman de Brut" de Wace', in *Temps et histoire dans le roman arthurien*, ed. by Jean-Claude Faucon (Toulouse: Éditions universitaires du Sud, 1999), pp.137–143

'The Languages of England: Multilingualism in the Work of Wace', in *Language and Culture in Medieval Britain: The French of England c.1100–c.1500*, ed. by Jocelyn Wogan-Browne et al. (York: York Medieval Press, 2009), pp.188–197

Levy, Brian J., 'Waltheof "Earl" de Huntingdon et de Northampton: la naissance d'un héros anglo-normand', *Cahiers de civilisation médiévale*, 18 (1975), 183–196

Lewis, C. P., 'The Domesday Jurors', *Haskins Society Journal*, 5 (1993), 17–44

'The French in England before the Norman Conquest', *ANS*, 17 (1994), 123–144

Liuzza, Roy Michael, 'Scribal Habit: The Evidence of the Old English Gospels', in *Rewriting Old English in the Twelfth Century*, ed. by Mary Swan and Elaine M. Treharne (Cambridge: Cambridge University Press, 2000), pp.143–165

Lodge, R. Anthony, *French: From Dialect to Standard* (London: Routledge, 1993)

Löfstedt, Einar, *Late Latin* (Cambridge, MA: Harvard University Press, 1959)

Loth, J., 'S. Amphibalus', *Révue celtique*, xi (1890), 348–349

Loud, G. A., 'The "Gens Normannorum" – Myth or Reality?', *ANS*, 4 (1982), 104–116

Lowe, Kathryn A., '"As Fre as Thowt?" Some Medieval Copies and Translations of Old English Wills', *English Manuscript Studies, 1100–1700*, 4 (1993), 1–23

'Bury St Edmunds and Its Liberty: A Charter-Text and Its Afterlife', *English Manuscript Studies, 1100–1700*, 17 (2012), 155–172

'The Development of the Anglo-Saxon Boundary Clause', *Nomina*, 21 (1998), 63–100

'Post-Conquest Bilingual Composition in Memoranda from Bury St Edmunds', *Review of English Studies*, 59 (2007), 52–66

'Two Thirteenth-Century Cartularies from Bury St Edmunds: A Study in Textual Transmission', *Neuphilologische Mitteilungen*, 93 (1992), 293–301

Lusignan, Serge, *Parler vulgairement: les intellectuels et la langue française aux XIIIe et XIVe siècles* (Paris: Vrin, 1986)

MacColl, Alan, 'The Meaning of "Britain" in Medieval and Early Modern England', *Journal of British Studies*, 45 (2006), 248–269

Machan, Tim William, 'Language and Society in Twelfth-Century England', in *Placing Middle English in Context*, ed. by Irma Taavitsainen et al. (Berlin: Mouton de Gruyter, 2000), pp.43–65

Malone, Kemp, 'When Did Middle English Begin?', *Language*, 6 (1930), 110–117

Markey, Dominique, 'The Anglo-Norman Version', in *The Eadwine Psalter: Text, Image and Monastic Culture in Twelfth-Century Canterbury*, ed. by Margaret Gibson, T. A. Heslop, and Richard W. Pfaff (London: Modern Humanities Research Association, 1992), pp.139–156

'Le Psautier d'Eadwine: Édition critique de la version *Iuxta Hebraeos* et de sa traduction interlinéaire anglo-normande' (unpublished doctoral thesis, University of Ghent, 1989)

Marsden, Richard, 'Latin in the Ascendant: The Interlinear Gloss of Oxford, Bodleian Library, Laud Misc. 509', in *Latin Learning and English Lore: Studies in Anglo-Saxon Literature for Michael Lapidge*, ed. by Katherine O'Brien O'Keeffe and Andy Orchard, 2 vols (Toronto: University of Toronto Press, 2005), II:132–152

Mason, Emma, 'Invoking Earl Waltheof', in *The English and Their Legacy, 900–1200: Essays in Honour of Ann Williams*, ed. by David Roffe (Woodbridge: Boydell, 2012), pp.185–204

Mathey-Maille, Laurence, *Écritures du passé: Histoires de ducs de Normandie* (Paris: Champion, 2007)

'L'étymologie dans le Roman de Rou de Wace', in *'De sens rassis': Essays in Honour of Rupert T. Pickens*, ed. by Keith Busby, Bernard Guidot, and Logan E. Whalen (Amsterdam: Rodopi, 2005), pp.403–414

'Traduction et création: de l'Historia Regum Britanniae de Geoffroy de Monmouth au Roman de Brut de Wace', in *Écriture et modes de pensée au Moyen Âge (VIIIe-XVe siècles)*, ed. by Dominique Boutet and Laurence Harf-Lancner (Paris: Presses de l'ÉNS, 1993), pp.187–193

Mavroudi, Maria, 'Translations from Greek into Latin and Arabic during the Middle Ages: Searching for the Classical Tradition', *Speculum*, 90 (2015), 28–59

McCulloch, Florence, 'Saints Alban and Amphibalus in the Works of Matthew Paris: Dublin, Trinity College MS 177', *Speculum*, 56 (1981), 761–785

Meehan, Bernard, 'Geoffrey of Monmouth, *Prophecies of Merlin*: New Manuscript Evidence', *Bulletin of the Board of Celtic Studies*, 28 (1978), 37–46

Merkle, Stefan, 'The Truth and Nothing but the Truth: Dictys and Dares', in *The Novel in the Ancient World*, ed. by Gareth Schmeling (Leiden: Brill, 1996), pp.563–580

Minnis, A. J., *Medieval Theory of Authorship: Scholastic Literary Attitudes in the Later Middle Ages* (London: Scolar Press, 1984)

Moore, R. I., *The First European Revolution, c.970–1215* (Oxford: Blackwell, 2000)

Morris, Avril, 'Forging Links with the Past: The Twelfth-Century Reconstruction of Anglo-Saxon Peterborough' (unpublished doctoral thesis, Leicester University, 2006)

Morse, Ruth, *Truth and Convention in the Middle Ages: Rhetoric, Representation, and Reality* (Cambridge: Cambridge University Press, 1991)

Mullen, Alex, 'Introduction: Multiple Languages, Multiple Identities', in *Multilingualism in the Graeco-Roman Worlds*, ed. by Alex Mullen and Patrick James (Cambridge: Cambridge University Press, 2012), pp.1–35

Musson, Anthony, *Medieval Law in Context: The Growth of Legal Consciousness from Magna Carta to the Peasants' Revolt* (Manchester: Manchester University Press, 2001)

Nilgen, Ursula, 'Psalter für Gelehrte und Ungelehrte im hohen Mittelalter', in *The Illuminated Psalter*, ed. by F. O. Büttner (Turnhout: Brepols, 2004), pp.239–247, 518–520

Noel, William, 'The Utrecht Psalter in England: Continuity and Experiment', in *The Utrecht Psalter in Medieval Art: Picturing the Psalms of David*, ed. by Koert van der Horst, William Noel, and Wilhelmina C. M. Wüstefeld (Tuurdijk: HES, 1996), pp.121–165

Norton, Christopher, 'History, Wisdom and Illumination', in *Symeon of Durham: Historian of Durham and the North*, ed. by David Rollason (Stamford: Shaun Tyas, 1998), pp.61–105

O'Brien, Bruce, 'An English Book of Laws from the Time of Glanvill', in *Laws, Lawyers and Texts: Studies in Medieval Legal History in Honour of Paul Brand*, ed. by S. Jenks, J. Rose and C. Whittick (Leiden: Brill, 2012), pp.51–67

'The Becket Conflict and the Invention of the Myth of Lex Non Scripta', in *Learning the Law: Teaching and the Transmission of Law in England, 1150–1900*, ed. by Jonathan A. Bush and Alain Wijffels (London: Hambledon Press, 1999), pp.1–16

'Forgery and the Literacy of the Early Common Law', *Albion*, 27 (1995), 1–18

'From *Morðor* to *Murdrum*: The Preconquest Origin and Norman Revival of the Murder Fine', *Speculum*, 71:2 (1996), 321–357

'The *Instituta Cnuti* and the Translation of English Law', *ANS*, 25 (2002), 177–197

'Legal Treatises as Perceptions of Law in Stephen's Reign', in *King Stephen's Reign (1135–1154)*, ed. by Paul Dalton and Graeme J. White (Woodbridge: Boydell, 2008), pp.182–195

'Pre-Conquest Laws and Legislators in the Twelfth Century', in *The Long Twelfth-Century View of the Anglo-Saxon Past*, ed. by Martin Brett and David A. Woodman (Farnham: Ashgate, 2015), pp.229–274

Reversing Babel: Translation among the English during an Age of Conquests, c.800 to c.1200 (Newark: University of Delaware Press, 2011)

'Translating Technical Terms in Law-Codes from Alfred to the Angevins', in *Conceptualizing Multilingualism in Medieval England, c.800–c.1250*, ed. by Elizabeth M. Tyler (Turnhout: Brepols, 2011), pp.57–76

O'Donnell, Daniel P., 'Bede's Strategy in Paraphrasing *Cædmon's Hymn'*, *Journal of English and Germanic Philology*, 103 (2004), 417–432

O'Donnell, Thomas, Matthew Townend and Elizabeth M. Tyler, 'European Literature and Eleventh-Century England', in *The Cambridge History of Early Medieval English Literature*, ed. by Clare A. Lees (Cambridge: Cambridge University Press, 2013), pp.607–636

Offler, H. S., 'The Date of Durham (Carmen de situ Dunelmi)', *Journal of English and Germanic Philology*, 61 (1962), 591–594

Olszowy-Schlanger, Judith, *Les manuscrits hébreux dans l'Angleterre médiévale* (Paris: Peeters, 2003)

O'Neill, Patrick P., 'Another Fragment of the Metrical Psalms in the Eadwine Psalter', *Notes and Queries*, n.s. 35 (1988), 434–436

'The English Version', in *The Eadwine Psalter: Text, Image and Monastic Culture in Twelfth-Century Canterbury*, ed. by Margaret Gibson, T. A. Heslop, and Richard W. Pfaff (London: Modern Humanities Research Association, 1992), pp.123–138

'Latin Learning at Winchester in the Eleventh Century: The Evidence of the Lambeth Psalter', *ASE*, 20 (1991), 143–166

Orchard, Nicholas, 'The Bosworth Psalter and the St Augustine's Missal', in *Canterbury and the Norman Conquest: Churches, Saints, and Scholars, 1066–1109*, ed. by Richard Eales and Richard Sharpe (Rio Grande: Hambledon, 1995), pp.87–94

Otaka, Yorio, 'Sur la langue des *Leis Willelme'*, in *Anglo-Norman Anniversary Essays*, ed. by Ian Short (London: Anglo-Norman Text Society, 1993), pp.293–308

Otter, Monika, *Inventiones: Fiction and Referentiality in Twelfth-Century Historical Writing* (Chapel Hill: University of North Carolina Press, 1996)

'1066: The Moment of Transition in Two Narratives of the Norman Conquest', *Speculum*, 74 (1999), 565–586

Padel, O. J., 'The Cornish Background of the Tristan Stories', *Cambridge Medieval Celtic Studies*, 1 (1981), 53–81

'Evidence for Oral Tales in Medieval Cornwall', *Studia Celtica*, 40 (2006), 127–153

'Geoffrey of Monmouth and Cornwall', *Cambridge Medieval Celtic Studies*, 8 (1984), 1–28

Page, Gill, *Being Byzantine: Greek Identity before the Ottomans* (Cambridge: Cambridge University Press, 2008)

Page, R. I., 'The Study of Latin Texts in late Anglo-Saxon England: The Evidence of English Glosses', in *Latin and the Vernacular Languages in Early Medieval Britain*, ed. by Nicholas Brooks (Leicester: Leicester University Press, 1982), pp.141–165

Paradisi, Gioia, *Le passioni della storia: Scrittura e memoria nell'opera di Wace* (Rome: Bagatto Libri, 2002)

'"Par muement de languages": Il tempo, la memoria e il volgare in Wace', *Francofonia*, 45 (2003), 27–45

'Remarques sur l'exégèse onomastique et étymologique chez Wace (expositio, ratio nominis)', in *Maistre Wace: A Celebration: Proceedings of the International Colloquium held in Jersey, 10–12 September 2004*, ed. by Glyn S. Burgess and Judith Weiss (St Helier: Société Jersiaise, 2006), pp.149–165

Parkes, M. B., '*Rædan, areccan, smeagan*: How the Anglo-Saxons Read', *ASE*, 26 (1997), 1–22

Pàroli, T., 'Indice della terminologia grammaticale di Ælfric', *Istituto Orientale di Napoli: Annali, Sezione Linguistica*, 8 (1968), 113–138

Parsons, David N., 'How Long Did the Scandinavian Language Survive in England? Again', in *Vikings and the Danelaw: Select Papers from the Proceedings of the Thirteenth Viking Congress, Nottingham and York, 21–30 August 1997*, ed. by James Graham-Campbell, Richard Hall, Judith Jesch, and David N. Parsons (Oxford: Oxbow Books, 2001), pp.299–312

Partner, Nancy F., *Serious Entertainments: The Writing of History in Twelfth-Century England* (Chicago: University of Chicago Press, 1977)

Paxton, Jennifer Ann, 'Charter and Chronicle in Twelfth-Century England: The House-Histories of the Fenland Abbeys' (unpublished doctoral thesis, Harvard University, 1999)

'Forging Communities: Memory and Identity in Post-Conquest England', *Haskins Society Journal*, 10 (2001), 95–109

'Monks and Bishops: The Purpose of the *Liber Eliensis*', *Haskins Society Journal*, 11 (1998), 17–30

'Textual Communities in the English Fenlands: A Lay Audience for Monastic Chronicles?', *ANS*, 26 (2003), 123–137

Pearsall, Derek, 'The Idea of Englishness in the Fifteenth Century', in *Nation, Court and Culture: New Essays on Fifteenth-Century English Poetry*, ed. by Helen Cooney (Dublin: Four Courts Press, 2001), pp.15–27

Pfaff, R. W., 'Some Anglo-Saxon Sources for the "Theological Windows" at Canterbury Cathedral', *Mediaevalia*, 10 (1984), 49–62

Piggott, Stuart, 'The Sources of Geoffrey of Monmouth', *Antiquity*, 15 (1941), 269–286, 305–319

Pohl, Walter, 'Telling the Difference: Signs of Ethnic Identity', in *From Roman Provinces to Medieval Kingdoms*, ed. by Thomas F. X. Noble (London: Routledge, 2006), pp.120–167

Pollock, Frederick, and Frederic William Maitland, with S. F. C. Milsom, *The History of English Law before the Time of Edward I*, 2nd edn, 2 vols (Cambridge: Cambridge University Press, 1968; first published 1895)

Poole, R. L., *The Exchequer in the Twelfth Century* (Oxford: Clarendon, 1912)

Potts, Cassandra, '"Atque unum ex diversis gentibus populum effecit": Historical Tradition and the Norman Identity', *ANS*, 18 (1995), 139–152

Pryce, Huw, 'British or Welsh? National Identity in Twelfth-Century Wales', *English Historical Review*, 116 (2001), 775–801

Pulsiano, Philip, 'The Old English Gloss of the Eadwine Psalter', in *Rewriting Old English in the Twelfth Century*, ed. by Mary Swan and Elaine M. Treharne (Cambridge: Cambridge University Press, 2000), pp.166–194

Putter, Ad, 'Gerald of Wales and the Prophet Merlin', *ANS*, 31 (2008), 90–103
  'Multilingualism in England and Wales, c.1200: The Testimony of Gerald of Wales', in *Medieval Multilingualism: The Francophone World and Its Neighbours*, ed. by Christopher Kleinhenz and Keith Busby (Turnhout: Brepols, 2010), pp.83–105

Rabuck, Mark, 'The Imagined Boundary: Borders and Frontiers in Anglo-Saxon England' (unpublished doctoral thesis, Yale University, 1996)

Rathbone, Eleanor, 'John of Cornwall: A Brief Biography', *Recherches de théologie ancienne et médiévale*, 17 (1950), 46–60

Resnick, Irven M., 'Lingua Dei, Lingua Hominis: Sacred Language and Medieval Texts', *Viator*, 21 (1990), 51–74

Reuter, Timothy, 'Whose Race, Whose Ethnicity? Recent Medievalists' Discussions of Identity', in *Medieval Polities and Modern Mentalities*, ed. by Janet L. Nelson (Cambridge: Cambridge University Press, 2006), pp.100–108

Reynolds, L. D. (ed.), *Texts and Transmission: A Survey of the Latin Classics* (Oxford: Clarendon, 1983)

Reynolds, Susan, *Kingdoms and Communities in Western Europe, 900–1300*, 2nd edn (Oxford: Clarendon, 1997)
  'Medieval *Origines Gentium* and the Community of the Realm', *History*, 68 (1983), 375–390

Reynolds, Suzanne, *Medieval Reading: Grammar, Rhetoric, and the Classical Text* (Cambridge: Cambridge University Press, 1996)

Richards, Mary P., 'The Manuscript Contexts of the Old English Laws: Tradition and Innovation', in *Studies in Earlier Old English Prose*, ed. by Paul E. Szarmach (Albany: State University of New York Press, 1986), pp.171–192
  Texts and Their Traditions in the Medieval Library of Rochester Cathedral Priory (Philadelphia: American Philosophical Society, 1988)

Richardson, H. G., 'Richard fitz Neal and the *Dialogus de Scaccario*', *English Historical Review*, 43 (1928), 161–171, 321–340

Richter, Michael, *Giraldus Cambrensis: The Growth of the Welsh Nation* (Aberystwyth: National Library of Wales, 1972)
  Sprache und Gesellschaft im Mittelalter: Untersuchungen zur mündlichen Kommunikation in England von der Mitte des elften bis zum Beginn des vierzehnten Jahrhunderts (Stuttgart: Hiersemann, 1979)

Rickert, Edith, 'The Old English Offa Saga I', *Modern Philology*, 2 (1904), 29–76

Rigg, A. G., 'Henry of Huntingdon's Herbal', *Mediaeval Studies*, 65 (2003), 213–292
  'Henry of Huntingdon's Metrical Experiments', *Journal of Medieval Latin*, 1 (1991), 60–72

Roberts, Brynley F., 'Geoffrey of Monmouth, Historia Regum Britanniae and Brut y Brenhinedd', in *The Arthur of the Welsh: The Arthurian Legend in Medieval*

Welsh Literature, ed. by Rachel Bromwich et al. (Cardiff: University of Wales Press, 1991), pp.97–116

Robinson, Fred C., 'The Significance of Names in Old English Literature', *Anglia*, 86 (1968), 14–58

'Syntactical Glosses in Latin Manuscripts of Anglo-Saxon Provenance', *Speculum*, 48 (1973), 443–475

Rold, Orietta da, Takako Kato, Mary Swan, and Elaine Treharne (eds), *The Production and Use of English Manuscripts 1060 to 1220* (Leicester: University of Leicester, 2010), www.le.ac.uk/ee/em1060to1220.

Rouse, Robert Allen, *The Idea of Anglo-Saxon England in Middle English Romance* (Cambridge: Brewer, 2005)

Rowlands, Ifor W., 'King John and Wales', in *King John: New Interpretations*, ed. by S. D. Church (Woodbridge: Boydell, 1999), pp.273–287

Rudolf, Winfried, 'The Old English Translations of the Verba Seniorum in Late Eleventh-Century Worcester', in *Lost in Translation? The Medieval Translator/Traduire au Moyen Age, Volume 12*, ed. by Denis Renevey and Christiania Whitehead (Turnhout: Brepols, 2009), pp.33–43

Rumble, Alexander R., 'Interpretationes in Latinum: Some Twelfth-Century Translations of Anglo-Saxon Charters', in *Early Medieval English Texts and Interpretations: Studies Presented to Donald G. Scragg*, ed. by Elaine Treharne and Susan Rosser (Tempe, AZ: ACMRS, 2002), pp.101–117

Russell, Paul, 'Brittonic Words in Irish Glossaries', in *Hispano-Gallo-Brittonica: Essays in Honour of Professor D. Ellis Evans* (Cardiff: University of Wales Press, 1995), pp.166–182

Saenger, Paul, *Space between Words: The Origins of Silent Reading* (Stanford, CA: Stanford University Press, 1997)

Salter, H. E., 'Geoffrey of Monmouth and Oxford', *English Historical Review*, 34 (1919), 382–385

Sauer, Hans, 'Knowledge of Old English in the Middle English Period?', in *Language History and Linguistic Modelling: A Festschrift for Jacek Fisiak on His Sixtieth Birthday*, ed. by Raymond Hickey and Stanisław Puppel, 2 vols (Berlin: de Gruyter, 1997), I:791–814

Sayers, William, 'Norse Nautical Terminology in Twelfth-Century Anglo-Norman Verse', *Romanische Forschungen*, 109 (1997), 383–426

Sharpe, Richard, 'Peoples and Languages in Eleventh- and Twelfth-Century Britain and Ireland: Reading the Charter Evidence', in *The Reality behind Charter Diplomatic in Anglo-Norman Britain*, ed. by Dauvit Broun (Glasgow: University of Glasgow, 2011), pp.1–119

'The Use of Writs in the Eleventh Century', *ASE*, 32 (2003), 247–291

Shopkow, Leah, *History and Community: Norman Historical Writing in the Eleventh and Twelfth Centuries* (Washington, DC: Catholic University of America Press, 1997)

Short, Ian, '*Anglice loqui nesciunt*: Monoglots in Anglo-Norman England', *Cultura Neolatina*, 69 (2009), 245–262

'Another Look at "Le Faus Franceis"', *Nottingham Medieval Studies*, 54 (2010), 35–55

'Gaimar's Epilogue and Geoffrey of Monmouth's Liber vetustissimus', *Speculum*, 69 (1994), 323–343

Manual of Anglo-Norman, 2nd edn (London: Anglo-Norman Text Society, 2013)

'Patrons and Polyglots: French Literature in Twelfth-Century England', *ANS*, 14 (1991), 229–249

'*Tam Angli quam Franci*: Self-Definition in Anglo-Norman England', *ANS*, 18 (1995), 153–175

'Un *Roman de Brut* anglo-normand inédit', *Romania*, 126 (2008), 273–295

'*Verbatim et literatim*: Oral and Written French in Twelfth-Century Britain', *Vox Romanica*, 68 (2009), 156–168

Short, Ian, Maria Careri, and Christine Ruby, 'Les Psautiers d'Oxford et de St Albans: liens de parenté', *Romania*, 128 (2010), 29–45

Sims-Williams, Patrick, 'The Emergence of Old Welsh, Cornish and Breton Orthography, 600–800: The Evidence of Archaic Old Welsh', *The Bulletin of the Board of Celtic Studies*, 38 (1991), 20–86

'Review of Wendy Davies, The Llandaff Charters and An Early Welsh Microcosm: Studies in the Llandaff Charters', *Journal of Ecclesiastical History*, 33 (1982), 124–129

'The Settlement of England in Bede and the *Chronicle*', *ASE*, 12 (1983), 1–41

'The Uses of Writing in Early Medieval Wales', in *Literacy in Medieval Celtic Societies*, ed. by Huw Pryce (Cambridge: Cambridge University Press, 1998), pp.15–38

Sisam, Kenneth, 'MSS. Bodley 340 and 342: Ælfric's Catholic Homilies', *Review of English Studies*, 9 (1933), 1–12

Smalley, Beryl, 'Gilbertus Universalis, Bishop of London (1128–34) and the Problem of the *Glossa ordinaria*', *Recherches de théologie ancienne et médiévale*, 7 (1935), 235–262

Smith, Scott Thompson, *Land and Book: Literature and Land Tenure in Anglo-Saxon England* (Toronto: University of Toronto Press, 2012)

Smyth, Alfred P., 'The Emergence of English Identity, 700–1000', in *Medieval Europeans: Studies in Ethnic Identity and National Perspectives in Medieval Europe*, ed. by Alfred P. Smyth (Basingstoke: Macmillan, 1998), pp.24–52

Southern, R. W., 'Aspects of the European Tradition of Historical Writing: 1. The Classical Tradition from Einhard to Geoffrey of Monmouth', *TRHS*, Fifth Series, 20 (1970), 173–196

'Aspects of the European Tradition of Historical Writing: 3. History as Prophecy', *TRHS*, Fifth Series, 22 (1972), 159–180

'Aspects of the European Tradition of Historical Writing: 4. The Sense of the Past', *TRHS*, Fifth Series, 23 (1973), 243–263

Spiegel, Gabrielle M., *Romancing the Past: The Rise of Vernacular Prose Historiography in Thirteenth-Century France* (Berkeley: University of California Press, 1993)

Stahuljak, Zrinka, *Bloodless Genealogies of the French Middle Ages: Translation, Kinship, and Metaphor* (Gainesville: University Press of Florida, 2005)

Stanley, E. G., 'La3amon's Antiquarian Sentiments', *Medium Ævum*, 38 (1969), 23–37

Stanton, Robert, *The Culture of Translation in Anglo-Saxon England* (Cambridge: Brewer, 2002)

Stirnemann, Patricia, 'Paris, B.N., MS lat. 8846 and the Eadwine Psalter', in *The Eadwine Psalter: Text, Image and Monastic Culture in Twelfth-Century Canterbury*, ed. by Margaret Gibson, T. A. Heslop, and Richard W. Pfaff (London: Modern Humanities Research Association, 1992), pp.186–192

Stock, Brian, *The Implications of Literacy: Written Language and Models of Interpretation in the Eleventh and Twelfth Centuries* (Princeton, NJ: Princeton University Press, 1983)

Stubbs, C. W., *Historical Memorials of Ely Cathedral* (London: Dent, 1897)

Sutcliffe, E. F., 'Jerome', in *The Cambridge History of the Bible*, ed. by G. W. H. Lampe, 3 vols (Cambridge: Cambridge University Press, 1963–1970), II:80–101

Swan, Mary, and Elaine Treharne (eds), *Rewriting Old English in the Twelfth Century* (Cambridge: Cambridge University Press, 2000)

Tahkokallio, Jaakko, 'French Chroniclers and the Credibility of Geoffrey of Monmouth's History of the Kings of Britain, c.1150–1225', in *L'Historia regum Britannie et les 'Bruts' en Europe*, vol. I, ed. by Hélène Tétrel and Géraldine Veysseyre (Paris: Classiques Garnier, 2015), pp.53–67

'Monks, Clerks, and King Arthur: Reading Geoffrey of Monmouth in the Twelfth and Thirteenth Centuries' (unpublished doctoral thesis, University of Helsinki, 2012)

'Update to the List of Manuscripts of Geoffrey of Monmouth's *Historia regum Britanniae*', *Arthurian Literature*, 32 (2015), 187–203

Tasker Grimbert, Joan, 'Cligés and the Chansons: A Slave to Love', in *A Companion to Chrétien de Troyes*, ed. by Norris J. Lacy and Joan Tasker Grimbert (Cambridge: Brewer, 2005), pp.120–136

Tatlock, J. S. P., 'The English Journey of the Laon Canons', *Speculum*, 8 (1933), 454–465

The Legendary History of Britain: Geoffrey of Monmouth's Historia Regum Britanniae and Its Early Vernacular Versions (Berkeley: University of California Press, 1950)

'St Amphibalus', *University of California Publications in English*, 4 (1934), 249–257, 268–270

Taylor, Rupert, *The Political Prophecy in England* (New York: Columbia University Press, 1911)

Thiel, M., 'Grundlagen und Gestalt der Hebräischkenntnisse des frühen Mittelalters', *Studi medievali*, 10.3 (1969), 3–212

Thomas, Hugh M., *The English and the Normans: Ethnic Hostility, Assimilation, and Identity, 1066–c.1220* (Oxford: Oxford University Press, 2003)

Thomson, R. M., *Books and Learning in Twelfth-Century England: The Ending of 'alter orbis'* (Walkern: Red Gull, 2006)

'The Use of the Vernacular in Manuscripts from Worcester Cathedral Priory', *Transactions of the Worcestershire Archaeological Society*, Third Series, 20 (2006), 113–119

William of Malmesbury (Woodbridge: Boydell, 1987, rev. edn 2003)

Tiller, Kenneth, 'Anglo-Norman Historiography and Henry of Huntingdon's Translation of *The Battle of Brunanburh*', *Studies in Philology*, 109 (2012), 173–191

Timofeeva, Olga, 'Anglo-Latin Bilingualism before 1066: Prospects and Limitations', in *Interfaces between Language and Culture in Medieval England: A Festschrift for Matti Kilpiö*, ed. by Alaric Hall et al. (Leiden: Brill, 2010), pp.1–36

Tinti, Francesca, *Sustaining Belief: The Church of Worcester from c.870 to c.1100* (Farnham: Ashgate, 2010)

Toswell, M. J., *The Anglo-Saxon Psalter* (Turnhout: Brepols, 2014)

'The Late Anglo-Saxon Psalter: Ancestor of the Book of Hours?', *Florilegium*, 14 (1995–1996), 1–24

Townend, Matthew, 'Contacts and Conflicts: Latin, Norse, and French', in *The Oxford History of English*, ed. by Lynda Mugglestone (Oxford: Oxford University Press, 2006), pp.61–85

Language and History in Viking Age England: Linguistic Relations between Speakers of Old Norse and Old English (Turnhout: Brepols, 2002)

Townsend, David, and Andrew Taylor (eds), *The Tongue of the Fathers: Gender and Ideology in Twelfth-Century Latin* (Philadelphia: University of Pennsylvania Press, 1998)

Traugott, Elizabeth Closs, 'Syntax', in *The Cambridge History of the English Language, Volume 1: The Beginnings to 1066*, ed. by Richard M. Hogg (Cambridge: Cambridge University Press, 1992), pp.168–289

Treharne, Elaine, 'Categorization, Periodization: The Silence of (the) English in the Twelfth Century', *New Medieval Literatures*, 8 (2006), 247–273

'The Life of English in the Mid-Twelfth Century: Ralph D'Escures' Homily on the Virgin Mary', in *Writers of the Reign of Henry II*, ed. by Ruth Kennedy and Simon Meecham-Jones (London: Palgrave, 2006), pp.169–186

'Reading from the Margins: The Uses of Old English Homiletic Manuscripts in the Post-Conquest Period', in *Beatus Vir: Studies in Early English and Norse Manuscripts in Memory of Phillip Pulsiano*, ed. by A. N. Doane and Kirsten Wolf (Tempe, AZ: ACMRS, 2006), pp.329–358

Treharne, Elaine, Orietta Da Rold, and Mary Swan (eds), *Living through Conquest: The Politics of Early English, 1020–1220* (Oxford: Oxford University Press, 2012)

(eds), *Producing and Using English Manuscripts in the Post-Conquest Period*, Special Edition of *New Medieval Literatures*, 13 (2011)

Trilling, Renée R., *The Aesthetics of Nostalgia: Historical Representation in Old English Verse* (Toronto: University of Toronto Press, 2009)

Trotter, David, '*Deinz certeins boundes*: Where Does Anglo-Norman Begin and End?', *Romance Philology*, 67 (2013), 139–177

'Language Labels, Language Change, and Lexis', in *Medieval Multilingualism: The Francophone World and Its Neighbours*, ed. by Christopher Kleinhenz and Keith Busby (Turnhout: Brepols, 2010), pp.43–61

'(Socio)linguistic Realities of Cross-Channel Communication in the Thirteenth Century', *Thirteenth-Century England*, 13 (2009), 117–131

Turner, R. V., 'Changing Perceptions of the New Administrative Class in Anglo-Norman and Angevin England: The *Curiales* and Their Conservative Critics', *Journal of British Studies*, 29 (1990), 93–117

'England in 1215: An Authoritarian Angevin Dynasty Facing Multiple Threats', in *Magna Carta and the England of King John*, ed. by Janet S. Loengard (Woodbridge: Boydell, 2010), pp.10–26

'Who Was the Author of *Glanvill*? Reflections on the Education of Henry II's Common Lawyers', *Law and History Review*, 8 (1990), 97–127

Turville-Petre, Thorlac, *England the Nation: Language, Literature, and National Identity, 1290–1340* (Oxford: Oxford University Press, 1996)

Tyler, Elizabeth M. (ed.), *Conceptualizing Multilingualism in Medieval England, c.800–c.1250* (Turnhout: Brepols, 2011)

'From Old English to Old French', in *Language and Culture in Medieval Britain: The French of England c.1100–c.1500*, ed. by Jocelyn Wogan-Browne et al. (York: York Medieval Press, 2009), pp.164–178

'Trojans in Anglo-Saxon England: Precedent without Descent', *Review of English Studies*, n.s. 64 (2013), 1–20

Tyson, Diana, 'Patronage of French Vernacular History Writers in the Twelfth and Thirteenth Centuries', *Romania*, 100 (1979), 180–222

Ullmann, Walter, 'On the Influence of Geoffrey of Monmouth in English History', in *Speculum Historiale: Geschichte im Spiegel von Geschichtsschreibung und Geschichtsdeutung*, ed. by Clemens Bauer, Laetitia Boehm, and Max Müller (Freiburg: Karl Alber, 1965), pp.257–276

Vaughan, Richard, *Matthew Paris* (Cambridge: Cambridge University Press, 1958)

Vitali, D., 'Les rouages de l'emprunt vernaculaire', *Bulletin du Cange*, 63 (2005), 197–206

Wada, Yoko, 'Gerald on Gerald: Self-Presentation by Giraldus Cambrensis', *ANS*, 20 (1997), 223–246

Wallace, David, *Premodern Places: Calais to Surinam, Chaucer to Aphra Behn* (Oxford: Blackwell, 2004)

Wallace-Hadrill, Andrew, *Rome's Cultural Revolution* (Cambridge: Cambridge University Press, 2008)

Wallace-Hadrill, J. M., *Bede's Ecclesiastical History of the English People: A Historical Commentary* (Oxford: Clarendon, 1988)

Warren, Michelle, *History on the Edge: Excalibur and the Borders of Britain, 1100–1300* (Minneapolis: University of Minnesota Press, 2000)

'Memory out of Line: Hebrew Etymology in the *Roman de Brut* and Merlin', *Modern Language Notes*, 118 (2003), 989–1014

Warren, W. L., *Henry II* (London: Methuen, 1973)

Watkins, C. S., *History and the Supernatural in Medieval England* (Cambridge: Cambridge University Press, 2007)

Webber, Nick, *The Evolution of Norman Identity, 911–1154* (Woodbridge: Boydell, 2005)

Webber, Teresa, 'The Script', in *The Eadwine Psalter: Text, Image and Monastic Culture in Twelfth-Century Canterbury*, ed. by Margaret Gibson, T. A. Heslop, and Richard W. Pfaff (London: Modern Humanities Research Association, 1992), pp.13–24

'Script and Manuscript Production at Christ Church, Canterbury, after the Norman Conquest', in *Canterbury and the Norman Conquest: Churches, Saints, and Scholars, 1066–1109*, ed. by Richard Eales and Richard Sharpe (London: Hambledon Press, 1995), pp.145–158

Weijers, Olga, 'Lexicography in the Middle Ages', *Viator*, 20 (1989), 139–153

Weiss, Judith, '"History" in Anglo-Norman Romance: The Presentation of the Pre-Conquest Past', in *The Long Twelfth-Century View of the Anglo-Saxon Past*, ed. by Martin Brett and David A. Woodman (Aldershot: Ashgate, 2015), pp.275–287

'Thomas and the Earl: Literary and Historical Contexts for the Romance of Horn', in *Tradition and Transformation in Medieval Romance*, ed. by Rosalind Field (Cambridge: Brewer, 1999), pp.1–14

Wenskus, Reinhard, 'Die deutschen Stämme im Reiche Karls des Großen', in *Karl der Große. Lebenswerk und Nachleben I* (Düsseldorf: Schwann, 1965), pp.178–219

White, Graeme J., *Restoration and Reform, 1153–1165: Recovery from Civil War in England* (Cambridge: Cambridge University Press, 2000)

Whiting, Bartlett Jere, 'The Rime of King William', in *Philologica: The Malone Anniversary Studies*, ed. by Thomas A. Kirby and Henry Bosley Woolf (Baltimore: Johns Hopkins University Press, 1949), pp.89–96

Wiesenekker, Evert, *Word be worde, andgit of andgite: Translation Performance in the Old English Interlinear Glosses of the Vespasian, Regius and Lambeth Psalters* (Huizen: Bout, 1991)

Wildhagen, Karl, *Der Psalter des Eadwine von Canterbury: die Sprache der altenglischen Glosse: ein frühchristliches Psalterium die Grundlage* (Halle: Niemeyer, 1905)

Wilhelm, Friedrich, 'Antike und Mittelalter. Studien zur Literaturgeschichte. I. Ueber fabulistische Quellenangaben', *Beiträge zur Geschichte der deutschen Sprache und Literatur*, 33 (1908), 286–339

Wille, Claire, 'Le dossier des commentaires latins des Prophetie Merlini', in *Moult obscures paroles: études sur la prophétie médiévale*, ed. by Richard Trachsler, with Julien Abed and David Expert (Paris: Presses de l'Université Paris-Sorbonne, 2007), pp.167–184

Williams, Ann, *The English and the Norman Conquest* (Woodbridge: Boydell, 1995)

'Thegnly Piety and Ecclesiastical Patronage in the Late Old English Kingdom', *ANS*, 24 (2001), 1–24

Wilson, R. M., *The Lost Literature of Medieval England* (London: Methuen, 1952)

Wiseman, T. P., *Clio's Cosmetics: Three Studies in Greco-Roman Literature* (Woking: Leicester University Press, 1979)

Wogan-Browne, Jocelyn, 'General Introduction: What's in a Name: The "French" of "England"', in *Language and Culture in Medieval Britain: The French of England c.1100–c.1500*, ed. by Jocelyn Wogan-Browne et al. (York: York Medieval Press, 2009), pp.1–16

Wogan-Browne, Jocelyn, Carolyn Collette, Maryanne Kowaleski, Linne Mooney, Ad Putter, and David Trotter (eds), *Language and Culture in Medieval Britain: The French of England c.1100–c.1500* (York: York Medieval Press, 2009)

Woledge, Brian, 'Notes on Wace's Vocabulary', *Modern Language Review*, 46 (1951), 16–30

Woodman, Francis, 'The Waterworks Drawings of the Eadwine Psalter', in *The Eadwine Psalter: Text, Image and Monastic Culture in Twelfth-Century Canterbury*, ed. by Margaret Gibson, T. A. Heslop, and Richard W. Pfaff (London: Modern Humanities Research Association, 1992), pp.168–177

Woolf, Alex, 'An Interpolation in the Text of Gildas's *De Excidio Britanniae*', *Peritia*, 16 (2002), 161–167

Wormald, Patrick, *Bede and the Conversion of England: The Charter Evidence*, Jarrow Lecture 1984 (Jarrow: St Paul's Church, 1985)

'*Engla Lond*: The Making of an Allegiance', *Journal of Historical Sociology*, 7 (1994), 1–24

'*Laga Eadwardi*: The *Textus Roffensis* and Its Context', *ANS*, 17 (1994), 243–266

'Lordship and Justice in the Early English Kingdom: Oswaldslow Revisited', in *Property and Power in the Early Middle Ages*, ed. by Wendy Davies and Paul Fouracre (Cambridge: Cambridge University Press, 1995), pp.114–136

The Making of English Law: King Alfred to the Twelfth Century, Volume I: Legislation and Its Limits (Oxford: Blackwell, 1999)

'Quadripartitus', in *Law and Government in Medieval England and Normandy: Essays in Honour of Sir James Holt*, ed. by George Garnett and John Hudson (Cambridge: Cambridge University Press, 1994), pp.111–147

Wright, Laura, *Sources of London English: Medieval Thames Vocabulary* (Oxford: Clarendon, 1996)

Wright, Roger, *A Sociophilological Study of Late Latin* (Turnhout: Brepols, 2002)

Yildiz, Yasemin, *Beyond the Mother Tongue: The Postmonolingual Condition* (New York: Fordham University Press, 2012)

Yorke, Barbara, 'Anglo-Saxon Origin Legends', in *Myth, Rulership, Church and Charters: Essays in Honour of Nicholas Brooks*, ed. by Julia Barrow and Andrew Wareham (Aldershot: Ashgate, 2008), pp.15–29

Yoshitake, Kenji, 'The Exchequer in the Reign of Stephen', *English Historical Review*, 103 (1988), 950–959

Younge, George, 'An Old English Compiler and His Audience: London, British Library MS Cotton Vespasian D.xiv, fols 4–169', *English Manuscript Studies, 1100–1700*, 17 (2012), 1–26

'The *Canterbury Anthology*: An Old English Manuscript in Its Anglo-Norman Context' (unpublished doctoral thesis, Cambridge University, 2012)

'Monks, Money, and the End of Old English', *New Medieval Literatures*, 16 (2016), 39–82

'"Those Were Good Days": Representations of the Anglo-Saxon Past in the Old English Homily on Saint Neot', *Review of English Studies*, 63 (2012), 349–369

Zatta, Jane, 'Translating the *Historia*: The Ideological Transformation of the *Historia regum Britannie* in Twelfth-Century Vernacular Chronicles', *Arthuriana*, 8:4 (1998), 148–161

Zimmer, Stefan, 'A Medieval Linguist: Gerald de Barri', *Études Celtiques*, 35 (2003), 313–349

Zumthor, Paul, *Merlin le prophète: un thème de la littérature polémique de l'historiographie et des romans* (Lausanne: Imprimeries Réunies, 1943)

WORKS OF REFERENCE

Anglo-Norman Dictionary, ed. by William Rothwell et al., online edn (Aberystwyth: Aberystwyth University, 2012), www.anglo-norman.net.

Bosworth, Joseph, and T. Northcote Toller, *An Anglo-Saxon Dictionary* (London: Oxford University Press, 1898, repr. 1954)

Dictionary of Medieval Latin from British Sources, prepared by R. E. Latham et al. (London: Oxford University Press, 1975–2012)

Dictionary of Old English, A–G (Toronto: University of Toronto, 2009), www.doe.utoronto.ca.

The Electronic Sawyer: Online Catalogue of Anglo-Saxon Charters, ed. by Peter Sawyer, rev. by Simon Keynes et al. (London: Royal Historical Society, 1968, rev. 1991–present), www.esawyer.org.uk.

Geiriadur Prifysgol Cymru: A Dictionary of the Welsh Language, ed. by R. J. Thomas, Gareth A. Bevan, and P. J. Donovan, 1st edn (Cardiff: Gwasg Prifysgol Cymru, 1967–2002); 2nd edn (currently to *brig*) at http://welsh-dictionary.ac.uk/gpc/gpc.html.

Latham, R. E., *Revised Medieval Latin Word-List* (London: British Academy, 1965)

Lewis, Charlton T., and Charles Short, *A Latin Dictionary* (Oxford: Clarendon, 1879)

Liddell, Henry George, and Robert Scott, *A Greek-English Lexicon*, rev. by Henry Stuart Jones, with Roderick McKenzie (Oxford: Clarendon, 1940)

Middle English Dictionary, ed. by Hans Kurath et al. (Ann Arbor: University of Michigan Press, *c*.1952–*c*.2001), http://quod.lib.umich.edu/m/med.

Oxford Dictionary of National Biography (Oxford: Oxford University Press, 2004; online edn 2007), www.oxforddnb.com.

Oxford English Dictionary, 3rd edn (Oxford: Oxford University Press, 2011; online edn 2012), www.oed.com.

Tobler, Adolf, and Erhard Lommatzsch, *Altfranzösisches Wörterbuch* (Stuttgart: Steiner, 1915–2002)

Index